D1278944

RUSSIAN MUSIC AND NATIONALISM

RUSSIAN MUSIC AND NATIONALISM
FROM GLINKA TO STALIN

MARINA FROLOVA-WALKER

YALE UNIVERSITY PRESS
NEW HAVEN AND LONDON

For information about this and other Yale University Press publications please contact:

U.S. Office:	sales.press@yale.edu	yalebooks.com
Europe Office:	sales@yaleup.co.uk	www.yalebooks.co.uk

Set in Minion by J&L Composition, Filey, North Yorkshire
Printed in Great Britain by St Edmundsbury Press Ltd, Bury St Edmunds

Library of Congress Cataloging-in-Publication Data

Frolova-Walker, Marina.
  Russian music and nationalism from Glinka to Stalin/Marina Frolova-Walker.
    p. cm.
  Includes bibliographical references and index.
  ISBN 978–0–300–11273–3
  1. Music—Russia—History and criticism.   2. Nationalism in music. I. Title.
  ML300.F76 2007
  780.947'09034—dc22   2007033565

A catalogue record for this book is available from the British Library

10 9 8 7 6 5 4 3 2 1

CONTENTS

Preface   vii

1   Constructing the Russian national character: literature and music   1

2   The Pushkin and Glinka mythologies   52

3   Glinka's three attempts at Russianness   74

4   The beginning and the end of the Russian style   140

5   Nationalism after the Kuchka   226

6   Musical nationalism in Stalin's Soviet Union   301

Notes   356

Glossary of names   380

Index   396

To the memory of my father

PREFACE

Every Russian, listening to this or that piece of music, has more than once had a chance to say: "Ah, this is something Russian!"

Vladimir Odoyevsky

Over the past century and a half, Western audiences, like Odoyevsky, have more than once had the opportunity to say "Ah, this is something Russian!" Russian classical music is now a ubiquitous presence in the world's concert halls, and with increasing frequency in the opera houses. The mystique of the music's "Russianness" is a powerful selling point, now as much as ever. For more than ten years, as a Russian in the West, I have attempted to speak and write about Russian music without taking advantage of this mystique; indeed, on the contrary, I have frequently discussed the process of mystification in the open, in order to undermine its hold on the musical public, and even on surprisingly many musicologists. This book is a summation of these efforts.

But although this mystification takes its own shape in the West, it is not simply a Western invention. As a music student in Russia, from school, through music college to conservatoire, I found one aspect of the musical education system increasingly frustrating: Russian classical music was taught as if it had arisen and flourished quite independently of Western music. The categories under which Western music was commonly discussed, such as counterpoint or sonata form, were considered only tangentially relevant to Russian music, which was discussed in relation to folksong and *narodnost'* (nationality). Russian music was regarded as a separate tree, with its roots firmly planted in Russian soil. It had its own, internal network of references and its own value system. I sometimes idly wondered what Western music education had made of Glinka, the great "father of Russian music". Was he regarded as a Beethoven, or a Liszt, or merely a Spohr? But it was considered unwholesome to raise such questions, and the Western and Russian music departments continued along their separate paths, meeting only in the conservatoire canteen for lunch.

When I chose to pursue my career in the West, I was soon able to find the answer to such questions: for university students in the United Kingdom, where I was now based, or in the USA, I found that Glinka was a non-entity. And not only Glinka, but every other Russian composer until Stravinsky, who was regarded as a special case. When Musorgsky or Shostakovich made an appearance on rare occasions, they were relegated to specialist options for final-year students, an eccentric dessert rather than a solid, nutritious main course. The mystique that worked prodigiously well for concert promoters from Diaghilev onwards, was clearly poison in the more rarefied atmosphere inhabited by students and academics.

Against this bizarre dichotomy in the West, the only alternative seemed to be the bloated and complacent nationalism of the Russian approach. I found both distasteful and ultimately wrong-headed, and I set myself the task of helping to construct a more considered discourse on Russian music, avoiding both mystification and its twin, disdain, in order to bring Russian music within the proper remit of musicology or the broader field of cultural studies. It would be ungracious, of course, for me to give the impression that I was alone in such endeavours. Musicology in the English-speaking world was undergoing radical changes at the time when I left Russia. While some of these changes turned out to be no more than passing fads, there have been substantial and lasting consequences of this upheaval, not least an openness to the questioning of former prejudices. Foremost among those musicologists who promoted this new openness and questioning was Richard Taruskin, whose inspiring volume *Defining Russia Musically* made musicologists in the West take Russian music much more seriously, and is currently exerting its influence even among Russian musicologists. But the task of dispelling both mystique and hostile prejudice – two sides of the same coin – is nowhere near accomplished. Historians of nationalism from Eric Hobsbawm nearly half a century ago to Benedict Anderson in recent years have been busy exposing the fraudulent origins of nationalist and imperialist myths. But these myths are not simply honest conceptual errors, to be abandoned once they are intellectually defeated. Politicians and the media, both in the West and in Russia, have been rebuilding them over the past decade-and-a-half. Yet for many years such myths were widely considered alien or repugnant after decolonization and defeat in Vietnam, while in the East, for a briefer period, Russians had to come to terms with defeat in Afghanistan and the loss of Russia's Soviet empire. But now official rhetoric once again tells us of "new-caught sullen peoples, Half devil and half child" as Kipling's "white man's burden" re-enters not merely conservative but also liberal discourse. The purpose of this volume is to a large extent to demonstrate how such myths are born and perpetuated, how they flourish and reach the stage of self-defeating absurdity, how they can die off only to be resurrected in an instant.

Thus the story of Russian musical nationalism should begin from its central myth, that of the Russian national character, or "Russian soul" as it is usually called. Chapter 1 serves, in part, as a foundation for the later chapters, since it examines the evolution of the national-character myth in Russia. The idea that nations, like individuals, have varied and distinctive characters, was first developed and incorporated into an elaborate ideology by Herder, inaugurating what we now call Romantic nationalism. The national-character myth has dominated the reception and historiography of Russian music for the past two centuries, beginning from the premières of Glinka's Russian operas, through to the commercial success of Russian concert music in the West during the twentieth century.

For those who cling to a belief in the Russian soul (sometimes beneath a rational veneer), it will come as a surprise that as late as the 1830s the Russian intelligentsia could not describe any such entity, although they certainly sought after it. By this time, Herderian ideas had been already become quite widespread in Europe, and the European elites thought they knew what "a true Frenchman" or "a true German" was. It was only over the next four decades that a stereotype was slowly constructed, largely through the works of literary figures in the two generations following Pushkin. Russians came to define themselves in opposition to "Europe" or "the West", and they saw themselves endowed with melancholy or even tragic soul that searched, however vainly, after ultimate truth, as against a supposed Western focus on whatever was commercially expedient. But in rational terms, this can be seen as the self-portrait of a declining class filtered through European Romanticism; that class was the Russian gentry, which was no longer able to sustain its old ways after centuries of dividing up estates among successive generations of sons.

But this principal version of the Russian national character, generated through literature, is not necessarily reflected in Russian nationalist music. At first, among Glinka's contemporaries, there was a certain reciprocation between musicians and writers in constructing the melancholy aspect of the stereotype, but after Glinka, and indeed because of him, the two arts diverged sharply. In the works of The Five (or the "Kuchka", to use their Russian sobriquet) a very different image of the Russian soul was constructed, not on the inward gaze of the nineteenth-century intelligentsia, but rather on the intelligentsia's idealizations of "the people" (consisting of peasants, rather than urban workers). This image was accordingly much more sanguine and robust and, for lack of inspiration in contemporary reality, it was firmly rooted in an epic past.

Both these national stereotypes became successful Russian exports: the first came to the West through translations of Chekhov and Dostoyevsky, and the second through the Diaghilev enterprise. Both continue to fascinate Western consumers of Russian artistic produce, even if they often fail to remark that the musical stereotype differs from the literary.

Chapter 2 is devoted to another myth which has assumed great importance for Russian cultural consciousness: the myth of Pushkin, to whom Russians habitually refer to as "our everything". The chapter shows how the construction of the "founding father" myth was driven by political expediency (whether in the times of Tsar Alexander III or of Stalin), and how the Pushkin cult served as a useful model for creating a smaller cult for Glinka, whose exalted status in Russia contrasts starkly with his obscurity in the West. The cult of Glinka has led to exaggerated and essentializing claims for this composer's "Russianness", damaging much Glinka literature in Russia and the West alike.

Nevertheless, Glinka's output is of considerable weight by any standards and deserved more attention in the West regardless of the mythology. That he never entered the Western canon was due largely to mischance: by the time Diaghilev popularized Russian music in the West, Glinka was rather passé, his harmonies and orchestration rather plain by the standards of the Kuchka. Chapter 3 attempts a fresh look at Glinka's "Russianness" and its perceptions. He was the first major composer to reflect the mature, conscious cultural nationalism of the Russian liberal intelligentsia (although the Russian state's official nationalism also left its mark). Glinka deliberately and painstakingly attempted to create a Russian national music, and his various approaches to the task left three main paths which his successors could follow. The first is represented by *A Life for the Tsar*: the assimilation of popular styles that already carried national associations led to the construction of Russianness through public consensus. *Ruslan and Lyudmila*, on the contrary, was considered much less Russian by its first audiences, but decades later came to be heard as the epitome of Russianness thanks to the Kuchka, who turned its novel and original idioms into the main component of their house style (and they added personal idioms of their own to the mix). The third path arose from the project of Glinka's final years, the creation of a Russian national church music through a hybridization of Russian folksong and Palestrina. This was taken up by Russian musicians late in the century as a kind of mystified archaeology.

Chapter 4 is the centrepiece of this book, since it is devoted to the creation of the "Russian style" by the composers of the Kuchka. Within the given space, a detailed discussion of all five composers' contributions would not have been possible, and Rimsky-Korsakov has been chosen to represent the group. The choice is by no means arbitrary: exceptionally for the Kuchka, Rimsky-Korsakov

left behind an immense oeuvre, which played the major role in consolidating
the Russian public's perception of the style. Of equal importance for present
purposes, he also left behind an expansive and often very candid record of his
thoughts on the Kuchka and the Russian style (contained in his memoirs and
the diaries of his disciple Yastrebtsev). The three sections of the chapter deal
with different aspects of the Russian style. The first traces the progress of a single
item in the Kuchka's musical vocabulary, which can be viewed as their trademark and which the Western musical public would readily identify as carrying
Russian or Oriental associations. This kernel of "Russianness" was no age-old
feature of Russian music, but stemmed from Balakirev, the mentor of the others,
who encouraged its use by his disciples and let them carry it forward. The
second essay seeks to disentangle the various strands of the Russian style at the
moment of its emergence: it looks at the refashioned use of folksong, the adoption of Orthodox church idioms, and the Kuchka's own "progressive" harmony.
A comparison of the original version and the much later revision of Rimsky-
Korsakov's first opera, *The Maid of Pskov*, allows us to see how the boldness of
the early Kuchka manner was later tempered into something more polished
but perhaps less striking (a tendency by no means peculiar to Rimsky-
Korsakov). The final section examines the disenchantment with the Russian
style that marked Rimsky-Korsakov's last years; in his writings, he demytholo-
gizes the Kuchka enterprise quite ruthlessly, in spite of the work he had invested
in the cause. This disenchantment takes two forms in his late operas: the
Russian style is either set aside, as in his operas *Servilia* or *Pan Voyevoda*, or it is
applied in a self-conscious and knowing manner, as in the high parody of his
last opera, *The Golden Cockerel*.

Chapter 5 moves beyond the Kuchka to the next generation of musical
nationalists, who concluded that their predecessors had set out in the wrong
direction; to find true Russianness in music, they believed it was necessary to
start afresh. Their progress is charted along two courses, independent but often
running in parallel: the first half of the chapter examines the search for authenticity in Russian folksong, and the second the search for authenticity in Russian
church music. To justify their efforts, the new generation of nationalists devised
an historical narrative which was entirely consonant with the Slavophile
scheme: the original pristine Russianness of folksong/chant is contaminated by
the importation of Western ideas and practices from the seventeenth century
onwards, but since assimilation to the West is not Russia's destiny, history
produces men who can serve the nation by restoring Russian music to its original purity, building the foundations of a cultural rebirth. Today, most of the
actors in this drama remain obscure; the composers were outnumbered by
scholars, and even the composers generally failed to translate this "authenticity"
into anything musically appealing (quite the opposite of the Kuchka). Many of

the theories produced by these nationalists left mundane facts far behind, as their speculations took them ever further afield; in attempting to support the unsupportable, they generated a staggering quantity of obfuscation and fraud. For many, this was a quest for a musical "philosopher's stone", which they hoped to find in the rules of harmonizing folksong and/or chant melodies, and which would supposedly help them to grow a new tree of Russian music, this time genuinely independent from the West.

In time, the nationalist projects based around folksong were abandoned: on the scholarly side, much more rigorous and empirical ethnomusicologists emerged, and on the compositional side, the trend was away from nationalism altogether, and towards Scriabin and various Western developments. There was, of course, the example of Stravinsky, who was undoubtedly influenced by the post-Kuchka generation of folksong scholars, but since he worked outside Russia, was largely ignored or spurned by nationalist musicians within Russia, and could scarcely be mentioned during the Stalin period, he is outside the scope of this book (In recent years, Richard Taruskin has produced landmark studies of this and other aspects of Stravinsky's multifarious career.) The projects based around church music proved rather more fruitful within Russia, giving rise to the flourishing "New Trend" school of liturgical music, whose music is still performed in larger Orthodox churches on a daily basis, and frequently aired abroad by Russian choirs on tour. The greatest artistic product of the New Trend is undoubtedly Rakhmaninov's All-Night Vigil, and indeed the influence of the liturgical style can be discerned in the composer's secular works, both before and after his emigration. The chapter also considers the colourful figure of Alexander Kastalsky. Before the Revolution, Kastalsky was a nationalist music theorist and a leading composer of church music in the New Trend manner. After the Revolution, he enthusiastically declared himself a Red long before this could be regarded as mere opportunism, and he now worked as a composer, administrator and theorist in the service of the proletariat during the last years of his life (prior to Stalin's rule).

If there was any creative force left in Russian musical nationalism at the beginning of the twentieth century, this soon vanished: the Russian army was decisively defeated by Japan, and this was swiftly followed by Revolution in 1905. Although the *status quo ante* was fully re-established by the end of 1907 (with a little liberal window dressing), the intelligentsia was polarized. Most of the intelligentsia swung to the left, and the remnants of musical nationalism were now aligned with the most reactionary circles of the Russian empire. After the Revolution of 1917 and the ensuing civil war, it seemed for a time that Russian nationalism had been abolished in the new Soviet Union, and Soviet musicologists of the 1920s coolly dissected the work of their nationalist predecessors. But once Stalin had concentrated power in his hands and re-shaped the state during the first Five Year Plan, there was a marked tendency away from revolutionary rhetoric, and towards nationalist rhetoric (which suited Stalin's purposes much better). In the early 1930s this was directed towards the fostering of (purely) cultural nationalism in the various non-Russian republics of the Soviet Union. This seemed merely to extend the policies of the 1920s, in compensating for the effects of Russian nationalism under the Tsars, but Stalin's next move repudiated any such notion: he began to revive Russian nationalism. This appeared first in the cultural sphere, with lavish celebrations of the Pushkin centenary, and of other artists such as Glinka. Following this, Russian nationalist rhetoric was deepened as the prospect of war loomed, while underneath the rhetoric there was a return to the imperial scheme within the Soviet Union. After the "Great Patriotic War" had been fought and won at enormous cost, Russian nationalism was used in cultural policy to eradicate the residue of modernism, and in the final years of Stalin's rule, it was used to support the anti-cosmopolitanism campaign (which was very thinly veiled anti-Semitism). Even before the War, Russian composers were increasingly required to return to the Russian style of the Kuchka and its followers, while the composers of the various other national-ities were to look towards the Kuchka's Orientalist manner (leavened with some more accurate local colouring). Shostakovich and Prokofiev were unofficially made exempt from these requirements, but after 1948 even they had to conform. The close of the Stalin period saw nationalist rhetoric taken to absurd and cynical extremes as both the creators of the ideology and those who embodied it in musical works struggled to maintain the pretence. Stalin's death was soon followed by the abandonment of the anti-cosmopolitan campaign, and nationalism in the arts was also on the wane. The Khruschev thaw confirmed the retreat from the extremes of Russian nationalism, and although many composers showed a new interest in Russian folksong, this was inspired by Stravinsky and ethnomusicological research, and not by the Kuchka – such music never became a mainstay of official Russian nationalism.

Much of the material in the book was originally presented in the form of conference and seminar papers at various institutions, and benefited from the many exchanges that followed my presentations. The earliest incarnation of a section from Chapter 1 appeared in the 1997 proceedings of the IMS, a section from Chapter 2 overlaps with my recent article "Ivan Dzerzhinsky vs *Ivan Susanin*" (*Cambridge Opera Journal*, 2006), a section from Chapter 3 appeared as "Ruslan and Russianness" (*Cambridge Opera Journal*, 1997), and a large part of Chapter 6 appeared in an earlier version as "National in Form, Socialist in Content" (*JAMS*, 1998). I am grateful to everyone who took part in preparing these pieces for publication, among them Arthur Groos, Roger Parker, and Richard Taruskin. Great thanks are due to my teachers at the

Moscow Conservatoire: my doctoral supervisor Yekaterina Tsaryova, Yevgeniy Levashev, Aleksandr Mikhailov, Oleg Semyonov, whose work remains a great inspiration. At various points I received enlightening pieces of advice from Kevin Bartig, David Fanning, Nataliya Firsova, Simon Franklin, Hubertus Jahn, Nicholas Marston, Martin Stokes, and Olga Velitchkina-Kane. My heartfelt thanks to the staff of various archives and libraries, in particular of RGALI and the music section of the Russian State Library ("Leninka").

I owe a very special debt to Richard Taruskin, whose article "Some thoughts on the history and historiography of Russian music" (*Journal of Musicology*, 1984) clarified the vague ideas I was beginning to form around this project, and whose later writings proved to be an inexhaustible source of inspiration. He generously agreed to subject a late draft of the book to a thorough reading, and I am grateful for the invaluable contribution that resulted from this.

This book owes a great debt to Malcolm Gerratt from Yale University Press who initiated its commission; I am extremely grateful to him for his unwavering support and trust in this project over the years. My archival research in Russia was also assisted in the early years of the project by two travel grants awarded by the British Academy.

Finally, this book would not have existed without the selfless help of my husband, Jonathan Walker, who devoted a large part of his life to it. Not only were most of the arguments shaped in conversation with him, but every sentence of my non-native English was patiently discussed, polished, and more often than not, re-written. I thank all of my extended family for their immeasurable help and support.

Note on transliteration

The system of transliteration I have adopted is based on the system used in the *New Grove Dictionary of Music and Musicians* (London, 1980, vol. 1, xvi–xvii), and has been widely used by Anglophone music scholars. The sole exception is the use of the standard English-language rendering of familiar names (e.g. Tchaikovsky, Glière, Asafyev) within the main text of the book. In the endnotes, however, where Russian sources are cited, the same names are spelled in accordance with the transliteration system used in *Grove* (e.g. Chaykovskiy, Gliyer, Asaf'yev).

Note on dates

Dates are given in accordance with the Russian convention in operation at the time; thus dates before 1 February 1918 follow the "old style" (Julian calendar), while dates after this point follow the "new style" (Gregorian calendar).

CHAPTER 1

CONSTRUCTING THE RUSSIAN NATIONAL CHARACTER
LITERATURE AND MUSIC

By 1900 Europeans thought they had discerned the essential characteristics of Russian literature, largely on the basis of readings in Tolstoy, Dostoyevsky and Chekhov. Their assumptions were concisely stated by Edmund Wilson, namely that the Russians (i.e. the writers, or their novels and characters) are (1) formless and unkempt; (2) gloomy; (3) crudely realistic; (4) morbid and hysterical; and (5) mystical. This stereotype is still, to some extent, current today. However, the new prominence of Russian music in the West, owing largely to Diaghilev's efforts from 1907 onwards, presented a very different face of Russia, with equally strong features: it was exotic, brilliant, more often fantastic than realistic, and largely festive rather than gloomy. This musical image of the nation was based on the works of the Kuchka, their predecessor Glinka and their various pupils, and defined the "Russian style" for Western audiences. Tchaikovsky, by contrast, was almost absent from Diaghilev's programmes until 1921, and even then his music met with little success. Yet Russians, from the mid-nineteenth century to the present day, have undoubtedly elected for the literary image of their nation and not the musical; the "tragic soul", ubiquitous in Russian discourse, is, after all, a creature of literature if it is anything, yet it is altogether absent from the music that characterizes the "Russian style". In this chapter we shall investigate how nineteenth-century Russian composers arrived at such a different image of Russianness, even though they were no less determined to create an artistic representation of the national character than their literary counterparts.

Before we examine the reasons for this divergence, let us look at some of the landmarks in the construction of the Russian national character.[1] This work of construction began, with no such end in mind, during the reign of Peter the Great, who brought Russia to an uneasy awareness of early modern Western developments; in so doing, he created the prerequisites for the emergence of national consciousness, and a sense of distinctness from Europe. Russia's naval successes, new governmental institutions, the foundation of the first

Russian university, the reform of the Russian language, progress made in the arts and sciences – all these were events which certainly boosted Russia's pride in itself, but, we must note, without any of the trappings of nationalism. The late eighteenth century, with its interest in folk life and lore, converted this burgeoning national consciousness into a more specifically nationalistic consciousness: even Catherine the Great proudly adopted Russian-style dress, unthinkable in the Petrine court. At the outset of the nineteenth century, we find the first significant revolt against the dominance of foreign culture. Reforms initiated by Alexander I, to some extent under the influence of French republicanism, found much resistance among those who feared a similar revolution in Russia. Such fears gave rise to ideas of building Russian culture from its own native foundations, which are manifest, for example, in Alexander Shishkov's *Dissertation on the Old and New Styles in the Russian Language*.[2] This work is considered the precursor of the Russian Slavophilism, for it sought to establish the special value of ancient literature to be found in Church-Slavonic texts and orally transmitted in the oldest stratum of folksong.

At this stage, the foundation of Russian national identity was almost exclusively sought in Russian language and literature. Only in the 1830s, in the later years of Pushkin's career, was it generally believed that a Russian literary language was fully formed and ready for any literary purpose (Pushkin will receive special attention in Chapter 2). While Shishkov attempted to Slavonicize Russian, Karamzin did not see anything amiss in modelling his neologisms on French words by translating them morpheme for morpheme. Imitations of folk sources also widened the urban vocabulary. The high goals of national literature were now set forth: under the influence of Herder, Russian men of letters found new inspiration in Homer, whose epics were now seen as the ultimate expression of the spirit of the ancient Greeks. Ossian, the alleged bard of the Scots, supplied nationalists with another model for the manifestation of national spirit. In 1800, *Slovo o polku Igoreve* (A Tale of Igor's Army), a supposedly ancient Russian epic, was published, and in 1805 Shishkov supplied a translation into modern Russian together with an influential commentary, in which he drew a direct parallel between *Slovo* and the epics of Homer and Ossian. In 1804 Kirsha Danilov's texts of epic songs (*bïlinï*) were brought out; in 1807 the poet Gnedich started translating the *Iliad* (published in 1829) in a new, purpose-made Russian hexameter, seeking his linguistic inspiration in the sacred texts of Church Slavonic.

But the intellectuals' interest in Russia's heritage and folklore could hardly help to lessen the yawning gap between the French-speaking, European-educated nobility and the largely illiterate peasantry; they were, indeed, two distinct nations.[3] In the course of the nineteenth century the most adventurous nationalists tried to acquaint themselves with and emulate the "simple people": they wore peasant dress, lived in the villages, and dined with the peasants. The peasants, for their part, greeted these noble outsiders with at worst open hostility, or at best feigned acceptance of them, but they ultimately remained aloof, showing no desire to embrace these gentlemen in a new-found community as the Russian Nation. Dostoyevsky is a useful witness to this stubborn non-acceptance of outsiders who tried to ingratiate themselves with the peasantry, for he himself was forced to spend his long years of exile at the bottom of the social order:

> A "simple man" [*prostolyudin*] would talk to you, tell you about himself, laugh together with you; he might even weep before you (though not with you), but would never consider you one of his own kind. He would never seriously count you as his relative, his brother, his true [*poskonnïy*] fellow-countryman.[4]

But educated gentlemen fired by nationalist ideals largely ignored this attitude, preferring to fantasize abstractly on the organic *russkiy narod* (Russian nation), constantly developing and refining the content of the national character this entity was supposed to possess. In the following section we shall trace the main stages of this development.

1812 and the Rostopchin posters

It is usually said that the crucial moment in the emergence of the Russian nation was the Patriotic War of 1812, when two distinct cultures coexisting within the Russian borders were united by a common purpose and came to identify themselves as a single *russkiy narod*. One might imagine that these extraordinary circumstances somehow overcame rigid class divisions within Russia, as described very plausibly by Tolstoy in *War and Peace*. But Tolstoy notwithstanding, the peasantry was little affected by the commotion. It was only the intelligentsia that imagined it had discovered and unified "the people", and that Russianness resided in this entity.

The document we shall examine played a significant role in the nation-building of 1812: it is the first of the so-called Rostopchin posters celebrated by Tolstoy.[5] Count Rostopchin had been appointed Chief Commander of the Moscow forces in May 1812; as the likelihood of Napoleon's reaching Moscow threatened, Rostopchin felt the need to act outside the normal confines of his military duties, and sought to "influence the spirit of the people, arouse it and prepare it for every sacrifice needed to save the fatherland".[6] He appealed to all Russians, in town and country, and among lords and serfs alike; the appeals were printed in the newspaper *Moskovskiye vedomosti* in Moscow and flysheets were distributed to Muscovites' homes, while in the surrounding towns and villages he had the appeal broadcast aloud to the inhabitants. Only church texts – prayers and the lives of the saints – had previously become known universally to the populace.

Among the posters there are many simple summaries of operations, although even these bear an imprint of Rostopchin's personal style and are quite startling in their directness and passion. But the first, which appeared on 1 July 1812, differed from its successors: it took the form of a parable, in the manner of those told in marionette theatre at Moscow Sunday fairs. It is replete with colourful metaphors, rhymes, and coarse jokes – every characteristic of the puppet-show rhetoric is present. The text collects together those symbols of nationhood which, according to Rostopchin, were recognized by all the social strata in 1812. Here is the beginning of this unique document:

> Karnyushka Chirikhin,[7] a Moscow *meshchanin*[8] who'd been in the army, had a few glasses too many at Tichok,[9] then heard about Buonaparte wanting to attack Moscow. In a rage he cursed the French, and on his way out of the public house, had this to say under the eagle:[10]
>
> "What? You're going to come and see us? You're welcome, at Christmastide or Shrovetide, no matter when; but our girls will cover you with strokes of the whip like a horse-cloth, so your back will swell like a mountain. We've had enough of you acting like a devil: we'll say a prayer, and you'll vanish before the cock crows. You'd better stay at home and play tag or blind man's buff. We've had enough of your playing about: your soldiers are dwarfs and little fops – they don't want to spoil their appearance with sheepskin, mittens, *malakhai*,[11] or *onuchi*.[12] How will they endure Russian life? They'll get bloated on cabbage, they'll burst with *kasha*, choke on *shchi*,[13] and any who survive till winter will be killed by the Epiphany frost.[14] They'll freeze outside the gates, die in the yard, suffer in the *seni*,[15] suffocate in the *izba*, and burn on the stove."[16]

Rostopchin took care to construct an image of a Russian fit to withstand the Napoleonic forces. He does this gradually and consistently, first only hinting at the size of his figure (obviously no dwarf), and then adding more and more telling details: his clothes, food, and the size of his dwelling. Further on in the poster Rostopchin enlarges his backdrop by bringing in the landmarks of "mother Moscow" (the Kremlin bell-tower, Ivan the Great, and the Poklonnaya Hill), and finally adds an epic, historical dimension by reminding us of past triumphs over the Poles, Tatars and Swedes. Then religion enters the picture: the icons, and golden cupolas of Holy Russia, completing the image of Russia and its saviour. Chirikhin finishes his speech and walks away cheerily, singing "Vo pole beryoza stoyala" (In the field stood a birch-tree, the same tune that Tchaikovsky used in the finale of his Fourth Symphony). At the end of the speech, Chirikhin's audience ask themselves "Where did such a man spring from? But he was certainly talking sense!"

One might perhaps see Rostopchin's appeal as a tasteless flirtation with the simple people, a condescending attempt to speak their language. How the peasants reacted to the appeal we have no way of knowing, but we do know how effective they proved in rousing a wave of patriotism throughout the Moscow high society. The upper classes suddenly realized with shock that they shared a culture with the invaders, rather than with the wearers of *onuchi* and *malakhai* – and they felt ashamed. As Pushkin witnessed:

> [O]ne fellow emptied out all the French snuff from his snuff-box, and began taking the Russian variety instead; another consigned a dozen French pamphlets to the fire; another stopped drinking Château Lafitte and turned to sour cabbage soup. Everyone forswore the French language; everyone shouted about Pozharsky and Minin and started preaching the people's war, intending to lope off on their old nags to some forsaken village near Saratov.[17]

In other words, it was the culture of the Russian peasant with which the high classes now wanted to identify. Returning to the text of Rostopchin's appeal, one might well ask whether it provides any evidence for the emergence at this time of the Russian national character, as this notion was later understood. But behind all the details of peasant life, we find remarkably little in this respect: no mention of any special Russian courage, or ingenuity, or industry – none of the things which one could have expected from any similar appeal later in the century. The only characteristic that emerges from the description of Russian peasant life is endurance: this is a people which can withstand severe frost, the oppressive heat of the stove and meagre rations, and even the womenfolk take willing recourse to physical violence in the task of beating back the invader. In the eyes of Russian gentlemen, French refinement was losing out for the first time to the Russian coarseness.

In short, Rostopchin's posters demonstrate that a fully formed conception of the Russian national character had not yet developed, and that Russianness was conveyed merely through the external features of peasant life. But the very cornerstone of future developments was already in place, namely, opposition to the West together with a paradoxical reinterpretation of this opposition, so that the apparent inferiority of Russians is transformed into something more praiseworthy than the many advantages of Westerners.

Admittance of failure: Chaadayev's Letter

Pyotr Yakovlevich Chaadayev (1794–1856) was one of the many Russian thinkers whose views became widely known through a network of literary coteries rather than through published work. Born a gentleman, he received the best possible education and embarked on a military career. He fought in the 1812 war and entered Paris a victor. Like many other Russian gentlemen, he retired from service early, spent some years in Western Europe, and flirted with freemasonry. His political views and contacts with the Decembrists brought him to the attention of the authorities, but his absence from the country during the uprising removed him from suspicion. Leading the life of a near hermit, he wrote his eight philosophical letters addressed "to a lady", who happened to be a certain Mme Panova, although the letters were clearly intended for a wider readership. His many efforts to publish the letters met with partial success in 1836, when the journal *Telescope* published the first letter; unfortunately for Chaadayev, the proofs were not inspected properly by the censor, and the outspoken nature of the unaltered original brought the wrath of the authorities down upon him. The editor of *Telescope* was exiled to Siberia, and all copies of the offending issue were confiscated; Chaadayev escaped severer punishment by signing an agreement to refrain from all further publication: he was officially declared insane, and initially placed under house arrest. This accounts for the title of Chaadayev's other celebrated essay, "The Apologia of a Madman", which he wrote without any hope of publication. Although political and medical surveillance was soon lifted, the ban on publication was not, and Chaadayev spent the rest of his life as a peripatetic savant, winning influence again through his frequent appearances before literary coteries.

The "First Philosophical Letter", written in 1829, is particularly germane in the present context. It was written in a tone of remarkable frankness and bitterness, in such a way that no Russian reader could scan its pages with indifference; as Russians, they felt insulted, albeit by one of their own, but its force owed much to the truths it contained, truths that many Russians would sooner have left unsaid; it retains this power for Russian readers even to the present day, since many of the questions it raises about Russia's relationship to the West remain no less relevant today than they were in Chaadayev's time.

Chaadayev's argument was that all the peoples of Europe shared essential aspects of their history and tradition, holding in common the same conceptions of duty, justice, law and order. But, his argument continued, Russia had never been a participant in this European history and it therefore lacks these underlying principles. Due to this peculiar position of the

Russian people, "its participation in the general movement of the human spirit was confined to the blind, superficial, even awkward imitation of other nations".[18] Russians were only able to imitate arbitrary features of European culture; the imitation could never advance beyond the most superficial level, because, as Chaadayev insisted, no Russian was able to grasp European culture in its organic integrity. Even the finest Russian thinkers, he said, have no grounding in the logic of the West and so their ideas lack coherence, clarity and confidence.

Moreover, even those perceived national characteristics which *were* undoubtedly positive actually arose from Russia's deficiencies, according to Chaadayev:

> Some foreigners have credited us with a kind of careless temerity which is especially noticeable among the lower classes in the nation; but, only able to observe certain isolated effects of the national character, they were not able to assess the whole. They did not realize that the same principle which makes us so bold sometimes also makes us always incapable of profundity and perseverance; they failed to see that what renders us so indifferent to the hazards of life also renders us equally indifferent to good and evil, to truth and falsehood, and that this very characteristic deprives us of all the incentives which urge men along the paths of improvement . . .[19]

Even the sheer size of the Russian empire, the perennial source of national pride, received a scathing treatment:

> If the barbarian hordes which convulsed the world had not passed through the country in which we live before precipitating themselves upon the West, we would scarcely have furnished a chapter in world history. In order to call attention to ourselves, we had to expand from the Bering Straits to the Oder.[20]

Chaadayev looks as far back as the tenth century in order to explain why Russia has failed to participate in European history: the crucial event was Prince Vladimir's decision to submit Russia to the Eastern church:

> What were we doing as the edifice of modern civilization was arising out of the struggle between the northern peoples' energetic barbarism and the lofty religious thought? Forced by a fatal destiny, we proceeded to seek the moral code which was to constitute our education in miserable Byzantium, an object held in profound contempt by these peoples.[21]

Himself a devout Christian, Chaadayev believed in the power of Christianity to establish a perfect society on earth, generally favouring any variety of Western Christianity to the Eastern church; indeed he reserved only contempt for the Russian version of Eastern Orthodoxy:

> When Christianity was advancing majestically along the road which had been traced for it by its divine founder and was sweeping generations along with it, in spite of the fact that we called ourselves Christians, we did not budge. While the world was being completely rebuilt, nothing was being built on our land: we remained squatting in our hovels made of small joists and thatch. In a word, the new destinies of the human race were not accomplished in our land. Though we were Christians, the fruit of Christianity did not mature for us.[22]

In support of his ideas, Chaadayev provided a history of England couched purely in terms of its religious development. Like many other Russian thinkers, Chaadayev was an Anglophile and considered England to be "the nation whose features are most strongly delineated, whose institutions are the most permeated by the modern spirit".[23]

It should be admitted that it was not Chaadayev's prognoses for a better Russia that made his Letter so notorious: they were rather weak, too general and obviously utopian. Its notoriety was earned, rather, by his description of Russia as a country without a history, with no identity and no influence on the world – this was what scandalized the Letter's readers. The Letter quickly polarized the intelligentsia: those who were largely sympathetic to Chaadayev's arguments are customarily known as the Westernizers, while those who largely repudiated him are the Slavophiles (while the latter were quite prepared to concede that Russia was backward by Western standards, they denied that Russia should ultimately be judged on this basis). While such tendencies had already been manifest before the Letter, Chaadayev effectively forced a choice upon members of the intelligentsia. The Letter brought Chaadayev official censure, to the extent that he was socially marginalized, and driven underground as a polemicist; his later pamphlet, "The Apologia of a Madman", accordingly had to be circulated illegally – to reduce the number of incriminating copies in circulation, his supporters often preferred to read it out at meetings. Partly in reaction to the new flourishing of the Official Nationalism in the 1830s ("Orthodoxy, Autocracy and Nationality"),[24] he vigorously defended his earlier views on the virtual absence of any culture in Russia before Peter the Great:

In his land, Peter the Great found only a blank sheet of paper, and he wrote on it: "Europe and the West"; since then we have belonged to Europe and the West. [25]

Here he did not seem to consider Peter's imitation of the West blind or clumsy, but rather saw it as a radical (and beneficial) change of course which nothing in Russia could now reverse; this, of course, was the basis of the Westernizers' position. Chaadayev dismissed any attempt to consider Russia's special geographical position a catch-all excuse. He was quick to puncture the current notion that the country's proximity to the Orient somehow made its adherence to non-Western values natural:

We are situated in eastern Europe, that is positive, but we were never part of the East because of that. . . . We are simply just a northern country, and on the basis of our ideas as much as that of our climates, far removed from the perfumed valley of Kashmir and the sacred shores of the Ganges. True, some of our provinces border on the eastern empires, but our centres are not there, our life is not there and will never be there . . .[26]

Chaadayev's conviction that Russia's Westernization was inevitable allowed him to rebut accusations that he lacked any sense of patriotism. He launched a counter-attack, on what he called "sanctimonious" and "lazy" patriotism:

There are different ways of loving one's country. For example, the Samoyed, who loves the native snows which have rendered him near-sighted, the smoky hut in which he remains cowering for half of his life, the rancid grease of his reindeer which surrounds him with a nauseous atmosphere, assuredly does not love his country in the same way as the Englishman, proud of his institutions and of the high civilization in his fortunate island, and it would undoubtedly be quite unfortunate if we were still at the state of cherishing the localities which saw us born in the way that the Samoyeds do.[27]

But the "Apologia" nevertheless demonstrates that Chaadayev's position was not purely that of a Westernizer; the Slavophiles would have found some faint comfort in various passages. For example, here Chaadayev clearly expresses a belief that Russia had a special destiny, that it had been elected to play out its own role in the world:

The history of this people will begin only from the day on which it will be seized by an idea entrusted to it, one which it is called upon to realize, and the day on which it will begin to pursue this idea with this persevering, though obscure, instinct which leads people to their destinies. That is the moment which I evoke for my country with all the powers of my heart; that is the task which I would like to see us undertake . . .[28]

While Chaadayev shares such an idea with the Slavophiles, unlike them he does not find the content of that destiny in Russia's past. The most he is prepared to grant is that Russia's earlier ignorance and lassitude would allow the nation to learn from the mistakes made by those in the West which had reached maturity more quickly – in this sense, Russia was in a privileged position. While this conclusion was hardly designed to please the Slavophiles, they were eager, nevertheless, to adopt the image of a young Russia opposed to an old Europe, and accepted such Chaadayev metaphors as that of Russia being "a genuine jury for countless trials being handled before the great tribunals of the world". This opposition signalled an important turning point in the debate on the destiny of Russia: from being the most wretched of nations it suddenly becomes the most favoured, to be spared all the calamities which the others had undergone (how far, alas, from the truth!). In general, the "Apologia" presents a more optimistic Chaadayev than the Letter:

The past is no longer within our powers, but the future belongs to us.[29]

In spite of the vigorous debates between Slavophiles and Westernizers in the wake of Chaadayev's Letter, the passing of a century and a half allows us to see that the two factions were not entirely at odds. The Slavophiles, as we have seen, were prepared to accept Chaadayev's central contention, that Russia was indeed lagging far behind the West (according to Western standards), while Westernizers such as Herzen or Turgenev, came to believe that only some ineffable force, leading Russia to an unknown destiny, could fully explain the failure of enlightened and civilized values in Russia. Both factions consisted of patriots who loved their country, and yet all of them hated it for refusing to conform to their ideals. Loving and hating their motherland simultaneously became the favourite pastime of the Russian intelligentsia to the point that what once seemed offensive and paradoxical became quite fashionable. In Turgenev's *Smoke* one finds the following exchange:

"What about Russia, Sozont Ivanïch, do you love your motherland?"
Potugin wiped his face with his hand.
"I love her passionately and I hate her passionately."
Litvinov shrugged his shoulders.
"This is banal, Sozont Ivanïch, it is a commonplace."[30]

Creating oppositions

The construction of the Russian national character only took off in earnest around 1840. A little later, we shall see that the issue was discussed by a few writers from the late eighteenth century onwards, but this was a mere ethnographical and literary amusement, based entirely around the "evidence" provided by a single genre of folksong. By contrast, the main wave of national-character building that we shall discuss now drew from diverse sources and involved most Russian men of letters (whether in support or reaction). But most crucially, this main wave was motivated by economic and political factors, and in turn had its own political consequences.

Earlier, limited discussions of a Russian national character therefore had little wider impact. Not only were they largely ignored by the wider world of Russian letters up to about 1840, but the very notion that there might be a Russian national character was unknown in the West before this time. By way of illustration, here is Pavel Annenkov recalling his time in Berlin during the 1830s:

Every Russian newcomer was wryly asked by his fellow-countrymen (those who had already lived several years in this centre of German learning) whether he wished to stay in it, and if so, what exactly he intended to become: a true, noble German (*der treue, edle Deutsche*) or a vain, eccentric Frenchman (*der eitle alberne Französe*). There could be no question of his wanting to remain a Russian, because Russians as such did not exist: there were registrars, assessors, advisors of all possible kinds, then landowners, officers, students who spoke Russian, but a positively Russian type, an independent and active personality who would not crack under the strain had not yet been born.[31]

In the first part of *Dead Souls* (1842), Gogol had promised his readers that he would provide some positive Russian types in the sequel, since the first part had contained only characters set up for satirical purposes. He would provide a "man endowed with divine valour", depict "the virtue of a wonderful Russian maiden"; these would make "virtuous people of other nations . . . look lifeless".[32] The promise remained unfulfilled, for the second part continued in satirical vein until madness eventually prevented Gogol from completing the work. Gogol's mysterious image of Russia as the troika flying into the unknown was alluded to by everyone, but it does not further the construction of a national character (although we shall return to examine its significance at the end of this chapter).

The credit for fleshing out the details of the Russian national character should be given to a nationalist grouping known as the "Slavophiles". Here we shall consistently follow the narrow definition. The founding documents of Slavophilism appeared in 1845, in the journal *Moskvityanin* (The Muscovite). Ivan Kireyevsky (1806–56) and Alexei Khomyakov (1804–60) were the two main figures; the former dealt mainly with Russia's identity and her place in world history, while the latter covered the theology of Eastern Christianity. They were joined by three younger writers: the Aksakov brothers and Yuri Samarin. In this text, the scope of the term "Slavophile" will be restricted to these chief propagators of the doctrine (the more vague and generalized usage often to be found elsewhere would not be helpful here). We should also note that in the West, Slavophilism is often erroneously equated with Pan-Slavism, while in fact pan-Slavic ideas occupy a relatively insignificant place in Slavophile teaching. The Slavophiles directed most of their intellectual energies in two directions: negatively, they protested against the progressive absorption of Western culture; positively, they sought to formulate an identity and peculiar role for Russia. They had little time for any political project calling for an international brotherhood of all the Slavs.

Admittedly, these figures are virtually unknown outside Russia, and hardly to be found within any belles-lettristic pantheon within Russia either, so Russians and foreigners alike consider Dostoyevsky, Tolstoy and Chekhov to be responsible for shaping the established characteristics of Russianness; these more celebrated writers were, nevertheless, only helping to fix the Slavophiles' creation in the imagination of Russians and outsiders. Their fictions worked powerfully to this effect, but they did not initiate the project.

The Slavophiles formed an image of Russia drawn from their rejection of European values; this was their answer to the hundred-and-fifty years that had elapsed since Peter the Great set Russia on a Westernizing course, a hundred and fifty years during which failure led to envy and distrust. If Russians were not to languish, embittered, in their humiliation, the Petrine project had to be abandoned, and the Slavophiles sought an alternative which would rescue Russia's self-image. The scheme was simple: whatever Russians previously took to be the virtues of European civilization were now portrayed as vices; and conversely, Russian failings were now portrayed as virtuous negations of these European characteristics.[33] Of course, such a scheme was never stated explicitly, but it was the pattern followed in Russian discourse for generations. Western rationality, creative energy and industriousness were so grossly misshapen in the distorting mirrors of caricature that they began to appear pathological, while the proposed Russian negations – intuition, contemplation and underachievement – were offered as the essentials of a healthy culture. Perverse as this may seem, it allowed Russians to develop a pride in their nation, a welcome recovery from the failed Petrine project; the collapse of Soviet communism in recent times has again brought Russia to a similar position at the close of the twentieth century, as Russians were forced to consider their failure to better, or even equal the West's achievements. The Slavophiles went on to construct an ideal image of original innocence (rather than mere brutish ignorance) in pre-Petrine Russia, an image derived from convenient fantasies rather than any historical researches. The arrival of Peter the Great on the scene was now painted as Russia's greatest tragedy, when a noble nation was forced to develop artificially, according to an alien and pernicious Western model, causing the nation to lose sight of its own origins and values. The appeal to return to these essentially Russian foundations was passionately reiterated by the Slavophiles and their followers throughout the second half of the nineteenth century. An independent mind such as Dostoyevsky's, even though steeped in Slavophile thought, could not help voicing a note of scepticism:

> I certainly wish – I still wish with all my might that the precious, firm and independent principles which are characteristic of the Russian people would become reality. But wouldn't you agree: what kind of principles are these . . . that they are hidden – have hidden themselves – and don't want to be found?[34]

Rationality vs insight

Ivan Kireyevsky saw the root of Western rationalism in the Classical world, characterized by "the triumph of formal reason over everything that is inside and outside man – pure, bare reason, founded upon itself and refusing to recognize anything superior to itself or outside itself".[35] According to Kireyevsky (and contrary to Chaadayev), it was Russia's good fortune to inherit none of this from the Greeks and Romans. While the Western church, inspired by syllogism, was emboldened to seek rational explanations for the mysteries of religion, and to usurp Christ's headship of the church in the institution of the papacy, Russia, under the wise ministrations of the Eastern church preserved the "inward reasoning of the spirit" by holding fast to the tradition (*predaniye*) of the Greek Fathers from generation to generation, a tradition which remained unquestioned, untouched by the corrosive force of reason. The most characteristic features of modern Europe, features which Russia had fortunately failed to replicate, could be traced to this disobedience of reason, according to Kireyevsky:

> That same Protestantism which Catholics reproach for its rationalism can be traced back to the rationalism of Catholicism itself. In this last triumph

of formal intellect over faith and tradition a sharp mind could already foresee, in embryonic form, the entire destiny of Europe [as unfolded up to the] present as a consequence of this futile starting point: Strauss and all the new philosophy; the shaping of social relations by industrialization; philanthropy founded upon calculated self-interest; a system of education stimulated by the power of aroused envy; Goethe, in whom the new poetry found its consummation, changing the idea of beauty just as Talleyrand changed his governments; Napoleon; a heartless search after gain – the hero of the new times; the material majority, the fruit of rational politics; and Louis Philippe, the most recent result of such hopes and such costly experiments.

Of course many of Kireyevsky's Russian contemporaries still held that the very things he condemned were to be valued as essential features of any civilized modern society. Kireyevsky had to make great efforts to turn Russia's apparent failings into advantages; in the following passage, he requires his reader to take much on trust, since he speaks largely of intangibles, and his concepts are vague:

In the West, theology became rational and abstract, while in the Orthodox world it retained the inner integrity of the Spirit; in the West the forces of intellect are sundered, while here there is a striving for a living whole [zhivaya sovokupnost']; there you have mind moving towards truth through a logical chain of ideas, here, a striving for truth through the inner elevation of consciousness towards integrity of the heart and intellectual concentration; . . . there you have scholastic and juridical universities, while in ancient Russia there were monasteries of prayer that enjoyed a concentration of the supreme knowledge within their walls . . ..

While Western rationality brought rich material rewards, Russia's contrasting poverty had to be explained and excused:

Russia did not shine either in the arts or in scientific invention, having no time [?!] to develop in an original way and rejecting foreign developments as based on an erroneous outlook and therefore hostile to the Christian spirit. But to compensate for this, Russia preserved the first conditions of true development, a development that required only time and favourable circumstances: here the structural foundation of knowledge was assembled and preserved – the philosophy of Christianity that is alone able to provide the right basis for the sciences. All the Greek Fathers . . . were translated, and copied, and studied in the silence of our monasteries, those sacred embryos of unborn universities . . . And these monasteries were in live, permanent contact with the people ... this kind of education was not brilliant, but profound; not splendid, not material, not aiming at the comforts of external life – but rather internal, spiritual ...

The individual versus the community

Kireyevsky saw the foundation of Western private and social life in the notion of the private individual. Individuals are accorded rights qua individuals, the foremost of these being property rights, which according to Kireyevsky are deemed "sacred". Not so in Russia:

Man belonged to the community, and the community to him. The land which was in the West subject to individual property rights, here belonged to all of society.[36]

While in the West society consists, therefore, of isolated individuals, in Kireyevsky's fantasy Russia there existed a kind of superior organic unity (Berdyayev later noted, in relation to this, that in talking of organicism the Slavophiles were in fact merely following the German Romantics):[37]

Countless numbers of these small communities of which Russia was comprised were connected by a network of churches, monasteries, and hermits' dwellings, out of which emerged the same ideas on how public and personal relations were to be conducted. Gradually these notions were to become common convictions – custom in place of law – establishing in the whole expanse of lands subject to our church the same thinking, the same outlook, the same striving, the same way of life.

As a result of these firm, homogeneous and universal customs, any change in the structure of society that did not agree with the order of the whole was impossible. Everyone's family relationships were predetermined prior to their birth; in the same predetermined order, the family was subordinate to the community [mir], the larger community to the skhodka [assembly], the skhodka to the veche [a larger popular assembly] etc., until all the individual bodies came together in a single centre, in the single Orthodox church. No personal opinion, no artificial agreement could found a new order, or invent some new rights and privileges. Even the very word pravo [law] was unknown to us in its Western sense, but rather meant "fairness" or "truth".

This characteristically Russian way of life, according to Kireyevsky, was destroyed among the upper classes by Petrine reforms, but was left unaffected among the lower classes. It is curious that when Khomyakov addressed the same issue, he was able to come up with only one example of such communal spirit, which we find, bizarrely, in his description of a typical quiet Sunday in London. Khomyakov was amazed to see that the English refrain from normal weekday activities and spend the day at home (apart from church attendance), and remarks upon the deep-rootedness of the custom, and its religious meaning:

> There was no traffic on the streets . . . There was a strange silence in this enormous, noisy, always boiling city . . . I was glad to see that; it was a joy to witness the determined morality of the people, their nobility of soul.[38]

Remarkably, Slavophiles were prepared to see England as a model for Russia, therefore excepting it from the hated West; even the most zealous of them were still able to delight in English civic institutions, or in England's self-respect and independence as a nation. Of course, there was no large English-speaking community in Russia, nor any class striving to imitate English manners, so there were no grounds for resenting the English in the way that the Germans and French were resented. England also stood as a model of cultural confidence, since it remained independent from French manners to an extent which Russians thought only a vain hope for their own country.

Old Europe versus young Russia

Since the Slavophiles had to concede that Russia had contributed little to European history and had not yet excelled in arts and sciences, they adopted another opposition congenial to their cause: old, corrupt, sickly Europe against a young, innocent and fresh-blooded Russia that had everything ahead of her. This idea appears quite early on in Kireyevsky's writings:

> The time of Childe Harolds, thank God, has not yet come to our father-land: young Russia has not partaken of the life of western states and other people, as a personality, is not getting old under the weight of other's experiences. A brilliant career is still open to Russian activity; all kinds of art, all branches of knowledge still remain to be mastered by our father-land. Hope is still given to us: what is the disillusioned Childe Harold's business among us?[39]

Vladimir Odoyevsky, who was strongly influenced by Slavophile thought, often made use of this opposition in his prophesies on the future of Russian music. He viewed Glinka as an injection of young, healthy blood into a decrepit European musical culture:

> We are placed on the border between two worlds, the past and the future; we are new and fresh, we have nothing to do with the crimes of the old Europe; we are only spectators to its strange, mysterious drama, whose clue is perhaps hidden in the depth of the Russian spirit; we are only witnesses; we are indifferent, for we have already grown accustomed to this strange spectacle; we are unbiased, for we can often anticipate the dénouement – we often recognize parody together with tragedy . . .

> . . . you will be astonished to learn that there exists a people that understands musical harmony naturally, without material study; you will be astonished to learn that not all melodic paths have been trodden over, and that an artist born from the Slav spirit [namely Glinka], one of the members of the triumvirate [together with Mendelssohn and Berlioz] that is guarding the shrine of art (the art that was debauched, debased, humiliated in the West) – this artist has found a fresh and untrodden path . . .[40]

Many later thinkers used the "old–young" opposition and its messianic promise as the basis of more ambitious visions: Dostoyevsky spoke of a Russia capable of uniting all humanity, and Sergei Solovyov, developing the old idea of Moscow as the Third Rome, thought that Russia should be able to reconcile Catholic Rome and the Orthodox Constantinople (he even made a curious practical step towards this noble goal by converting to Catholicism himself). Even official Soviet rhetoric, from the mid-'30s to the '80s, preserved a prominent strain of Russian messianism.

From tractates to poems

At no time was Slavophile discourse restricted to the pages of their journals: discussion of the Russian national character and Russia's destiny entered the salons and spread throughout the intelligentsia; its enduring influence was assured through the work of many novelists and poets. Admittedly, the contours of the discussion in the more learned journals were not fully preserved in transmission; more important, ultimately, was assimilation of such ideas through the appeal of poetic images, or of sympathetic Russian types in novels – and so a certain picture of Russianness was firmly embedded in the minds of the populace of the cities at least. To see how Slavophile discussion trickled down, we shall return for a moment to Kireyevsky and his attempt to justify the poverty of Russian material culture; in comparing

Russian monastic learning (or contemplation) to Western university education, he said that

> this kind of education was not brilliant, but profound; not splendid, not material, not aiming at the comforts of external life – but rather the inner and spiritual . . .[41]

The same ideas later found their way into some well-known verses of Fyodor Tyutchev (1855). In their letters and diaries, Russian gentlemen who travelled around Europe often compared the splendour of Italian landscape to the humble charm of the Russian expanses, the prosperity of German homesteads to the wretchedness of Russian hovels. Here, in Tyutchev's poem, everything is explained: suffering is ennobled by references to Christ, and poverty itself becomes the sign of a chosen, holy people.

Eti bednïye selen'ya,	These poor dwellings,
Eta skudnaya priroda –	This meagre landscape –
Kray rodnoy dolgoterpen'ya,	My native land of long-suffering,
Kray tï russkovo naroda!	You the land of the Russian people!
Ne poymyot i ne zametit	The proud gaze of the foreigner
Gordïy vzor inoplemennïy,	Will not see, will not understand
Chto skvozit i tayno svetit	What secretly glows through
V nagote tvoey smirennoy.	Your humble barrenness.
Udruchennïy noshey krestnoy,	Oppressed by the burden of the cross,
Vsyu tebya, zemlya rodnaya,	The Heavenly Tsar in the guise of a slave,
V rabskom vide Tsar' Nebesnïy	Wandered all around you and
Iskhodil, blagoslovlyaya.	Blessed you, my native land.

The oppositions of the material and the spiritual, the external and the internal, acquired colourful details through Russians' observations of neighbouring cultures. The Germans were perhaps most heavily exploited in the process of constructing Russian national identity (as a negative image, of course). One did not have to travel far to encounter a German, for St Petersburg was home to a substantial and distinct German community since its foundation, and comparisons of the two lifestyles were unavoidable. Germans came to be associated with action, Russians with contemplation; Germans were seen to act upon reason, Russians acted impulsively. Yet in the representative sample of passages examined below, we shall see that the passive and unpredictable Russians invariably emerge superior to the active and logical foreigners.

Observing Germans: against philistinism

Russians observed that traits such as orderliness, economy and decency were conspicuously absent from their own lives, but thrived among their German neighbours; rather than emulate the latter, Russians preferred to dismiss these qualities as symptoms of mere philistinism (*meshchanstvo*). The following selection of extracts from a varied group of writers, journalists and philosophers illustrate how Russians searched for various positive qualities they could ascribe to their own people, in opposition to *meshchanstvo*. The first of our extracts, from the radical activist Alexander Herzen, takes a satirical look at this project, since Herzen was himself a Westernizer rather than a Slavophile:

[Baltic Germans] are deeply offended by our carelessness, our habits, our neglect of etiquette, our pride in our semi-barbaric, semi-perverse passions. They bore us to death, with their bourgeois pedantries, their emphatic purism and the impeccable triviality of their behaviour. Finally, they view a person who spends more than half of his income as a prodigal son, a squanderer, whereas here a man who exhausts only his own income is considered a monstrous miser. . . . This difference between Russia and the Baltic provinces, which is so sharp, . . . exists also between the whole of the Slav world and Europe.[42]

Lev Shestov's irony towards his fellow-countrymen is rather more rueful:[43]

The Westerner relies on himself and only on himself. He is firmly convinced that if he does not help himself, no one will help him. Accordingly all his thoughts are directed towards organizing his life better. A certain limited time is measured off for him; if he does not manage to sing his song, it will remain unfinished . . . not a second of his life will be wasted . . . Counting out the days, the very hours and minutes – try finding a single Russian who would demean himself with such philistine activity! We look around, stretch our limbs, rub our eyes; first, we want to decide *what* to do and how, and only then do we want to start living . . . Minutes, seconds, measures – all this is so insignificant, so worthless . . . We would like to draw generously from the bottomless well of eternity; everything limited is the lot of the European philistines . . .[44]

Ivan Ilyin sought out the tacit assumptions behind the characteristics which Russians liked to ascribe to themselves, characteristics such as hospitality, generosity and warmth of feeling. He concluded that the guiding sentiment was that Russia is rich in resources, both human and material: that there are plenty of Russians, that they have plenty of everything, and that there will be enough for everyone and still plenty left over. But this feeling left no room for the Western notions of economy, conscious investment of effort, or perseverance in striving towards a goal, as Ilyin pointed out with some bitterness:

> Russians are gifted, they can make wonders out of nothing. But everything they do somehow works out by itself, unexpectedly and without effort, and is therefore easily abandoned and forgotten. Russians do not value this gift; they squander their fortune, they don't like the strain; they become distracted and forget, plough up the land and then abandon it; in order to cut down one tree they destroy five. It is "God's" land for them, and "God's" forest, and "God's" means no one's.[45]

It might seem that no one could turn Ilyin's Russian vices into virtues. Yet one need look no further than Dostoyevsky to find just such reversals. On the one hand, the characters, their utterances, and narrative paradoxes were designed to shock and offend. But on the other hand, one cannot fail to perceive in them a genuine contempt for the predictable patterns of proper, decent but dull behaviour, contempt for the "comme il faut". In *The Gambler* we witness a conversation started by the main character, Alexei:

> "Historically, the ability to acquire capital entered the civilized Westerner's catechism of virtues and merits at the top of the list . . . whereas Russians are not only unable to acquire capital, but they squander most disgracefully whatever they have."

Up to this point Alexei's companions are sure that he is simply opposing a Western virtue to a Russian vice, and they rally to defend their nation. But hear what develops next. Alexei says:

> "But can anyone really say that Russian waste and indolence is worse than German parsimony and honest labour?"
> "What a repugnant suggestion!", cried the General.
> "Ah, but how very Russian!", exclaimed the Frenchman.

And after this, Alexei describes how a German father saves his money by subjecting his own children to great hardships, until we are finally ready to be persuaded that playing roulette is the more honourable course.[46]

Another example from Dostoyevsky is even more grotesque and even more telling, for now it is not one of his characters, but the author himself speaking from the pages of *The Writer's Diary:*

Take a Russian drunkard and, let's say, a German drunkard: the Russian is fouler than the German, but the German is undoubtedly more stupid and more ridiculous than the Russian. Germans are largely self-satisfied and proud. In a drunken German these principal traits grow in proportion to the amount of beer drunk. A drunken German is undoubtedly a happy man: never does he weep, but sings boastful songs and is proud of himself. A Russian drunkard likes to drink from sadness and weep. If he swaggers, there is no triumph in it, just rowdiness. He would always remember some insult and reproach the offender, whether he was there or not.[47]

A sociopathology of drunkeness might suggest that Germans go no further than the phase of jollity and boastfulness, while the Russians move quickly onward to the maudlin and lachrymose phase, there to linger for much of their waking lives; or a clinician might show that the contrast in behaviour is due to chemical differences between each nation's preferred poison. But none of this for Dostoyevsky, who is determined to convince his readers that the German is merely a smug philistine drunk or sober, while the Russian, even in the degradation of advanced inebriation, remains humble and weeps over human suffering, thus exemplifying Dostoyevsky's ideal of the simple Russian who bears Christ in his soul.

It may well be said that Russian nineteenth-century writers made a cult out of suffering and perpetual self-torment with the burning questions of existence. If Gogol invented the mysterious Russian soul, Dostoyevsky made it the tragic soul. Andrei Bely, for one, spared no effort in establishing the superiority of the Russian tragic soul:

The hub of the universe, for Europeans, is not in Goethe, Nietzsche or other luminaries of culture: a European has nothing to do with them. Goethe and Nietzsche are being experienced in Russia; they are ours, because we, Russians, are the only people in Europe who search, suffer, and torment ourselves. In the West they are happy growing flabby; rosy-cheeked Mr Bowler-Hat and ivory Mrs Toothpick – those are the real *Kulturträgern* of the West.

Soon Bely is excitedly opposing the characteristic Russian striving after ultimate truth to the European cult of the toothpick. A modicum of critical distance allows us to see that Bely merely projects whatever he sees as virtues and vices onto Russia and Europe respectively. He concludes "Our pride lies in the fact that we are not Europe," and then perhaps looking anxiously over his shoulder at Asia, "or that we are the only true Europe."[48]

Stolz vs Oblomov

In 1859 the publication of Alexander Goncharov's *Oblomov* reinforced this virtue-in-vice aspect of discourse on Russian identity. The novel's eponymous hero is a Russian gentleman who languishes on his sofa dreaming of the great things he could achieve. His idleness is contrasted with the busy life of his friend Stolz, who is, of course, German. At the crisis of the drama, Oblomov hovers on the brink of proposing to the girl he loves and who seems to share his feelings, but he simply cannot bring himself to act decisively, and so he eventually pretends to be unwell; as a result, he soon finds that he has lost his beloved to Stolz. Although Oblomov is weak and idle, Goncharov presents his unlikely hero in such a way that we cannot help sympathizing, while Stolz, full of conventional virtues, in the end irritates us with his cool, business-like, tedious and ultimately meaningless activity. Oblomov is "kind, intelligent, affectionate, noble"; he has "an honest and faithful heart" within his inactive body, while Stolz, outwardly fit, active and successful, has nothing of interest within. Through Goncharov's efforts, the arguments of the Slavophiles were transformed into highly memorable images of enormous expressive power. Vladimir Solovyov considered the character of Oblomov the first "all-Russian" type in Russian literature, as opposed to the heroes of Pushkin and Gogol who had only a limited significance.[49] Solovyov made his judgement twenty years after the appearance of *Oblomov*, by which time the hero's name had been turned into a common noun, "oblomovshchina" (Oblomovism). Critics acquired the habit of measuring new literary heroes against the yard-stick of Oblomov's Russianness. Apollon Grigoryev, for example, in discussing the main characters from Turgenev's *Nest of the Gentry*, finds it most helpful and natural to draw parallels with *Oblomov*:

> The humility of Lezhnev and Lavretsky . . . is real humility. By nature they are simpletons, I dare say laggards . . . or slobs . . . Their intellectual and ethical progress is crowned by humility, because there is more nature in them, more . . . personality, if you will, than in Rudin and Mikhalevich – more . . . unity with the soil that produced them, with the environment that educated their first impressions. . . . They are, if you will, Oblomovs . . . but in no way Stolzes, which does them great honour, for Stolzes are artificial growths among us.[50]

> Lavretsky and his Lisa, and the priceless Marfa Timofeyevna, all this is Oblomovism; they are all Oblomovs, and what Oblomovs, tightly, physiologically bound not only to the present and future, but to the long past of Oblomovka![51]

Panshin is an active man, a reformer from the heights of a bureaucrat's outlook, a leveller who believes in abstract law, in abstract justice. He is offensive to our Russian soul ... And what do we know about him? Nothing except those features which show him to be a ... merely superficial, vacuous man. ... Is it that his nature is purely superficial, superficially clever, superficially brilliant, and so forth, in contrast to the sincere, but in appearance far from brilliant, personality of the main hero?[52]

[Lavretsky] is a man of our soil, he is, if you will, an Oblomov. . . This is his weakness, but thus far, like the Oblomov, he does not exactly belong to action; but he is our defence against the Panshin-reformers, against the Kostanzhoglo-organisers [Kostanzhoglo is a character of the unfinished second part of Gogol's *Dead Souls*, often considered to be Stolz's direct predecessor], finally against the aimless activity which Goncharov. . . harshly but correctly presented in the freak Stolz (for I cannot call him a person).[53]

These words immediately betray Grigoryev's Slavophile bias; a Westernizing critic would invert most of his arguments. We find just such Westernizing criticism in Dobrolyubov's celebrated essay *What is Oblomovism?* (1859), which reprimands Goncharov for furnishing his undeserving hero with a "crystal-clear soul" and an honest heart that "cannot be bought at any price".[54] He thinks Oblomovism is a real, but diseased Russian characteristic, and that Goncharov's attempt to present such behaviour in a winsome guise is pernicious. Dobrolyubov wanted to see a positive model replace Oblomovism in Russian society, but he does not try to elevate Stolz to this role.

The brilliant type versus the meek type (observing the French)

The perceived national character of the French was another perennial point of reference. In this case the foreign culture was represented not so much by any community of Frenchmen in Russia as by the French culture of the Russian upper classes. The gentry communicated in French and had adopted what habits they could afford, but only the higher nobility and imperial court could avail themselves of all the requisite paraphernalia – the French cooks, dressmakers, dancing masters and so on. At the beginning of the nineteenth century, Paris was the unquestioned arbiter of taste, but with Napoleon's Russian campaign of 1812, the glamour of all things French was gravely tainted, and initial defeat brought a temporary abandonment of French luxuries. True the aristocracy returned to their pre-war behaviour after victory had been secured (only the Bolshevik revolution eradicated French culture entirely); but the gentry was increasingly impressed by the barrage of ridicule heaped upon French culture by nationalist writers. German culture had been attacked for its supposed philistinism, but any such charge against French culture would not have been credible, so emphasis was laid instead upon its artifice and superficiality.

Tolstoy provocatively began his *War and Peace* with a brilliant salon dialogue in French that continues for several pages. The perfectly balanced conversation flows, artfully directed by Anna Scherer, the hostess of a brilliant salon. Suddenly Pierre Bezukhov appears, and his figure seems too large, too awkward for this refined environment – and this is how Tolstoy introduces his favourite hero. Later on Pierre finds himself completely out of place in the salon of his own wife Hélène, where Duport leads the dancing and Mlle George gives her recitations, and in the dazzling Hélène herself he finds only vice under the shine of glamour. In his analysis of *War of Peace* the critic Strakhov articulated his argument around the opposition between "meek" types and "brilliant" or "predatory" types. According to Strakhov, not only individual characters, but the warring nations themselves fall into this opposition:

> In the person of Napoleon the artist wanted, as it were, to unmask and dethrone the brilliant type – to debunk it through its greatest representative. . . . (T)he power of Russia of that time rested much more on the endurance of the meek type than on the actions of the strong. There are no brilliant aspects in Kutuzov himself – the greatest force depicted in *War and Peace*. He is a sluggish old man whose greatest power is manifested in the ease and freedom with which he carries the heavy burden of his experience. His slogan is "patience and time".[55]

> Is it not clear that Tolstoy strives to elevate the simple man, rather than any other, to the level of the ideal? What is *War and Peace* – this vast and multicoloured epic if not the apotheosis of the meek Russian type? Are we not here told . . . how the predatory type lost out to the meek type, how the simple Russian people defeated on the battlefield of Borodino, all that can be thought of as heroic, brilliant, passionate, strong, and predatory – that is, Napoleon and his army?[56]

In portraying the victorious nation, Tolstoy does not conform to any heroic typology. Captain Tushin, for example, is anything but a mighty Russian warrior: he is short, painfully shy, and gauche; he prefers to go into battle barefoot because he feels clumsy in boots (he came from peasant stock); and he is transfixed with terror at the sight of his commanding officer. Yet among all the soldiers on the field, it is the same Tushin who refuses to retreat and saves the day. Another unforgettable "simple" man is Platon Karatayev, whom Pierre encounters in captivity. Tolstoy describes this peasant as "the personification of everything Russian, kindly and round".[57] Everything in his figure is indeed rounded, from his head to his arms ("as if ever ready to embrace something") to his wrinkles; there is some simple harmony in him with no sharp edges to disturb it. His strength lies in his ability to adapt, to protect his little world in hostile circumstances, to endure hardship by repeating his homely proverbs and songs. Tolstoy clearly takes Platon to be a symbol of the Russian nation (*narod*), as he evokes notions of community and organicism that we encountered earlier in the Slavophiles:

> Sometimes Pierre, struck by the meaning of his words, would ask him to repeat them, but Platon could never recall what he had said a moment before, just as he never could repeat to Pierre the words of his favourite song: *native* and *birch-tree* and *my heart is sick* occurred in it, but when spoken and not sung, no meaning could be got out of it. He did not, and could not understand the meaning of words apart from their context. Every word and action of his was the manifestation of an activity unknown to him, which was his life. But his life, as he regarded it, had no meaning as a separate thing. It had meaning only as part of a whole of which he was always conscious. His words and actions flowed from him as evenly, inevitably, and spontaneously as fragrance exhales from a flower. He could not understand the value or significance of any word or deed taken separately.[58]

It is this collective spirit that Napoleon has to fight, and his "brilliance" and "genius" (the two words Tolstoy repeatedly uses) prove to be powerless before it.

Unlike Tolstoy, Dostoyevsky makes no clear statements about national identity in *Crime and Punishment*, but he still alludes to the opposition of the predatory and the meek types. Raskolnikov's hero is Napoleon, and, inspired by his example, he attempts to become a superhuman, not merely by breaking the law, but by overstepping the bounds his own conscience. He is soon unable to live with what he has become, until Sonechka saves him with her infinite meekness. While in Dostoyevsky's novel humility is Christian and universal rather than specifically Russian, the wider context of his writings demonstrates the relevance of this idea to Russian nationalism. According to Dostoyevsky, the self-effacing character of the Russian nation means that Russia could be all-embracing, and that its messianic role would involve uniting all other nations around her and leading them towards a better future.

Chekhov's underachievers

Throughout his work, Chekhov developed an opposition that was direct heir to those mentioned above: that of the noble underachiever to the morally suspect success. Although both types in Chekhov are usually exemplified by Russians, the reader's sympathy is carefully directed towards the weak and unhappy character, while the confident and successful character is made to seem foreign and even repulsive; thus worship of success, a supposedly Western trait, is shown as worthless. We should note here that the Russian word normally translated as "underachiever" is *neudachnik*, which more literally means the unfortunate one: the Russian word emphasizes the whims of fortune rather than the individual's responsibility for success or failure.

In shaping the familiar opposition Chekhov is never crudely schematic; indeed his subtlety is such that the opposition is difficult to recognize in his first major play, *Ivanov*. The principal character, Ivanov, a gentleman in his thirties, is a permanent topic in his neighbours' idle and sometimes malicious exchanges. His wife, Anna, had been disowned by her wealthy Jewish parents when she showed herself determined to marry the gentile Ivanov (the neighbours assume that Ivanov must still have expected her to inherit when he entered into the marriage). Anna, now dying of consumption, is unloved and unhappy; her husband, who had long since stopped loving her cannot now bring himself to feign affection in front of the doctor, Lvov, not even for her sake. While Lvov had not intimated to Anna that her death was imminent, Ivanov, brutally reveals this to her during the course of a row, whereupon she faints. In the next act, a year after Anna's death, Ivanov is ready to marry again (his neighbours note that he has chosen another wealthy young lady). The prospect of Ivanov taking another wife so angers Doctor Lvov that he publicly denounces him in the midst of the wedding preparations. Ivanov shoots himself.

Watching the first rehearsals, Chekhov realized that the actors had seriously misinterpreted him; they had overlooked many subtle details which had been provided to show that Ivanov was not the man his neighbours thought him to be, that his torments should win our sympathy, and that we should see events through his eyes, rather than the doctor's. Instead, the actors imagined that Ivanov was simply an understated villain and the doctor an understated "great man".[59] Chekhov wrote to them, pointing out that the play has little artistic merit if it is understood thus; he explained the intended import of the conflict between Ivanov and Lvov:

> Ivanov is a gentleman, a university graduate, quite unremarkable, but like
> the majority of the educated gentry, an honest character, ardent, easily

excitable, and strongly driven by his passions. . . . But upon reaching his thirties he begins to experience fatigue and ennui. . . . He starts to look for external causes but finds none; then he starts looking inwards, but discovers only an undefined feeling of guilt . . . Such people as Ivanov don't solve problems but collapse, rather, under their weight. They lose their bearings, shrug their shoulders, become nervous, whining and foolish, and in the end, letting their loose, unrestrained nerves go, they lose the very ground under their feet and join the ranks of the "broken" and "misunderstood".

[Doctor Lvov's] type is [again] honest, direct, and ardent, but [unlike Ivanov] narrow-minded and bluff. . . . Anything that looks like breadth of outlook or immediacy of feeling is foreign to Lvov. . . . He looks at everything in a blinkered fashion; he is full of prejudice. He worships those who cry out, "Let honest hard work prevail!". He thinks that everyone who doesn't cry out thus is a scoundrel and a kulak. For him, there is nothing in between.[60]

Chekhov wished to oppose a man of broad horizons, good intentions, and a troubled conscience on the one hand to a self-righteous philistine on the other; *Ivanov*, in effect, followed the typology of *Oblomov*. Though Chekhov did not choose to inject any nationalism into such oppositions, all his later Ivanov types were perceived to be characteristically Russian, by Russian and foreign audiences alike. Uncle Vanya is another such unhappy and passive underachiever, punished for his selflessness by the more prudent professor. In *The Cherry Orchard* the opposition lies between the passive, useless Gayev and active, sensible Lopakhin. Chekhov, ever avoiding the schematic, endows both characters with noble qualities, and not only Gayev, but also Lopakhin shows signs of developing the tragic Russian soul, oppressed by the weight of existence. Yet still there is some lack of sensitivity, lack of *intelligentnost'* in Lopakhin, and so the audience is led, in the end, to resent him. The consensus of Soviet critics held that the conflict of *The Cherry Orchard* was only historically possible at one moment, namely the beginnings of Russian capitalism; Russian audiences have nevertheless continued to see the play as a general exploration of the Russian national character.

Vasily Rozanov took the latter approach in his portrait of Chekhov; in the passage below, he even begins to sound like a creation of Chekhov himself:

In Chekhov Russia came to love itself. No one had expressed her collective identity as he did, not only in his works, but ultimately in his face, his bearing, his manners, and, it seems, in his lifestyle and behaviour. . . . Things happened to him just as they happen to any Russian. He studied one thing, but ended up doing another; and, of course, he didn't reach old age.

And who [in Russia] does? He did not have his own nest, he was a wanderer
... [He produced] neither harsh sounds, nor grand thoughts. But a certain
something is present in all this, something that one cannot find anywhere
else. What would it be? Well, without this something life would be boring.
With someone else [life] would be more successful, happier, more prosperous, but also more boring. And when you listen to him [Chekhov] – you
listen and you forget that it is raining, and that everything is so stupid, and
you – no, you don't reconcile yourself to this stupidity, there isn't any of that
– but in this immeasurably stupid and rainy era you find the strength to
exist somehow, to drag yourself along with it.[61]

Contradictions

The search for the perfect definition of Russianness led to some oddities. In
the early days of Russian self-stereotyping, a writer could throw together
several rather arbitrary adjectives (for example, characterizing the Russian
people as kind-hearted, patient and peaceful) without expecting serious
scrutiny. But later in the century, successive attempts at comprehensive and
systematic description made it dishonest, rather than merely careless, to
ignore evidence to the contrary, such as acts of great cruelty and aggression in
Russian history. Russian thinkers were too much entrenched to abandon the
notion of a national character, and so they decided to embrace contradiction.
At the turn of the century, diligent seekers after Russianness like Nikolai
Berdyayev or Nikolai Lossky tried to turn this apparent flaw in the structure
into its most crucial insight.

In his collection of essays *The Destiny of Russia* (1918), Berdyayev set out
several paradoxical features of "the soul of Russia": Russia is the most anar-
chic, yet also the most bureaucratic of states; it is the least chauvinistic and yet
the most nationalistic; it is a nation both submissive and arrogant; it enjoys
great freedom of spirit, and great oppression. These contradictions Berdyayev
attempts to explain on a higher and somewhat mystical level; he invokes the
conflict between the masculine and the feminine, and between the Apollonian
and the Dionysian. But Berdyayev's main opposition is as old as the debate on
Russian's destiny: it is the opposition between West and East, the two worlds
which messianic Russia would bring together and reconcile.[62]

Lossky wrote his treatise *The Character of the Russian People* after the
Revolution, as an émigré; his work wends its way through a series of oppositions, attempting to find a single quality which will generate each pair of
extremes. Lossky took his task very seriously, and expended much effort, but
his project was ultimately futile; if it served any purpose, it was one far from
its author's intentions, namely to demonstrate conclusively that the subject-

matter is much too thin for serious philosophical investigation as opposed to lightweight journalistic musings.

The post-perestroika period has seen the rehabilitation of émigré thinkers such as Berdyayev and Lossky, as well as a renewed passion among Russians for understanding themselves as a nation, and so it was hardly surprising to see a resurgence of these polemics in the 1990s. Here is one of the most unabashed examples, a 1994 attempt to inspire foreign students of the Russian language with heady ideas of Russianness:

> Regarding Russian national character, we think that contradictoriness is its dominant feature.[63]

> On the one hand, the free expanses of the flat terrain formed the expansiveness and openness of the Russian soul, as well as its most essential feature, a disposition to contemplation. On the other hand, these immense expanses – the fields covered with snow, the thick forests – oppressed and enslaved the soul. As a result Russians did not acquire the European thrift, the economy of time and space, the intensity of culture. For the broadness of the Russian land opened up the possibility of extensive, rather than intensive work.[64]

Thus the ideas of Herderian nationalism appropriated by Slavophile and post-Slavophile thinkers, and clothed by Russian literature, still persist at the time of writing. In the following section we shall compare this picture of the national character with that constructed by Russian music during the course of the nineteenth century.

Musical Russianness and Russian music

Protyazhnaya, or the sorrowful face of Russia

We saw earlier, in passing, that there had been discussion of a Russian national character from the late eighteenth century onwards, but that this had been limited in scope, was never more than a minority interest in the world of Russian letters, and had no political consequences. Nevertheless, this discourse is still of significance for our present purposes, and we shall now examine it in detail. The eighteenth-century stimulus was Herder's theory that folksong (the very concept dates back to him) provided the evidence necessary for building up a correct picture of a given nation's character. His Russian followers therefore began to investigate folksong, but their methods and conclusions were very different from those of Russian ethnomusicologists a century later.

These Herderian investigations soon discovered and adopted a single folk-song genre, the *protyazhnaya* [literally "drawn-out song"], and from then on all discussion revolved around this one genre until halfway through the nineteenth century. The *protyazhnaya* came to be seen as a paradigm for all Russian folksong, or even as the essence of Russian creativity and the "Russian soul" itself. N. A. Lvov, compiler of the first substantial folksong collection in Russia, wrote in his introductory remarks that:

> Perhaps this collection will not be without usefulness even for philosophy itself, which seeks to draw conclusions about national character from folk song. Taking account of the minor modality of the majority of *protyazhnïye* songs, which . . . comprise the characteristic Russian song, philosophy will perceive, of course, the tenderness and sensitivity of the Russian people and also that inclination of the soul to melancholy . . .[65]

Lvov had some knowledge of the enormous variety of music practised by the Russian peasantry, but he still bases his conclusions about national character exclusively on the *protyazhnaya*. In doing so, he fell into line with his contemporaries among the urban literati, who knew only this genre; even those who spent part of the year on their country estates were unlikely to attend a peasant wedding or any seasonal festivities – this would have been considered improper on both sides. Russian gentlemen did, however, hear individual servants or coachmen singing, and these songs were almost always *protyazh-nïye*, precisely because this genre was independent of any work-related or ritualistic context.[66] These, long, slow songs with elaborate melodies now found many receptive listeners among a gentry that was newly interested in discovering (as they thought) what Russianness was. Such listeners all noticed a general mood of melancholy, although there is little to suggest that they were interested enough in the lyrics to follow the slow unfolding of the entire narrative in each *protyazhnaya* – the mood set by the music was enough to take root in their imaginations, so that they could spin their own fantasies about the meaning and cause of the songs' melancholy. Thus the *protyazhnaya* became urbanized and began to influence Russian art song (then at an early stage of its development). In this manner, the art-songs which came under the influence of the *protyazhnaya* formed a link, however tenuous, between the gallant Francophone salon of the Russian gentry and the coarse and pungent hut of the Russian peasant. Listening to the sounds of *protyazhnaya*, the gentleman pitied the peasant and himself at the same time, the two distinct classes coalescing into one Russian people in his imagination. A perfect illustration of this can be found in *The Singers*, a short story by Turgenev (written in 1850, but reflecting attitudes typical of the 1830s and '40s). The story gives an account of a rare meeting of the two distinct worlds, when a gentleman at sport seeks refreshment in a rural tavern. He witnesses a competition between two folk singers, where the first sings a dance-song which brings his listeners to their feet, while the second sings a *protyazhnaya*, and makes them weep. Of the latter, he says:

> I should confess that I have rarely heard such a voice: it was slightly broken and rang as if cracked; at first it even seemed somewhat sickly, but it also had a genuine deep passion, youth, strength, sweetness, and some enticingly careless, melancholy sorrow. A true, ardent Russian soul sounded and breathed in it, and it gripped your heart, gripped the very Russian heart-strings.[67]

The simple people, after a wave of emotion, resume their drinking, their banter, and their dancing as if nothing had happened, but the cultivated sportsman cannot bear to stay, since he is afraid of "spoiling the impression". This moment of melancholy must have matched his image of the soul of Russian people, and he wanted to preserve it, removed from its context. The dance song of the first competitor and dances that followed the competition are forgotten, and only the *protyazhnaya* stands out as the climax of the story. The *protyazhnaya* is romanticized and thus incorporated into the gentleman's version of Russianness, while the dances are filtered out to satisfy his romantic sensibilities.

It is telling that in the original, Turgenev made a glaring mistake in choosing "Pri dolunushke stoyala" to serve as the melancholy song of the story. His friend V. A. Insarsky pointed out the error: that the song Turgenev had casually chosen was in fact joyful and dance-like – on no account could it have made the impression the story ascribes to it. Turgenev accordingly exchanged this song for "Ne odna vo pole dorozhen'ka", a well-known *protyazhnaya* of a more appropriate cast. The reader should realize at this point that Turgenev's source, Kireyevsky's folksong collection, supplied the enquirer only with a fragment of the lyric, usually the opening, but there was no synopsis of the entire lyric, nor any musical information whatsoever.[68] Turgenev had simply assumed that any folksong he plucked from the collection would be suitably melancholy – Russian folksongs were *supposed* to be melancholy, after all; Turgenev and the gentleman hunter of his story had more in common than he perhaps realized. Just as characteristic was Turgenev's attempt to stage the events of the story, perhaps in an attempt to experience for himself the emotional sequence he had so powerfully represented in *The Singers*: he recreated the singing competition at his own home by inviting . . . no, not peasants, but two educated connoisseurs of Russian song, the painter K. Gorbunov and the writer A. Zhemchuzhnikov, who later related this anecdote in his memoirs.[69] So much for authenticity.

As it happens, we can obtain a good idea of the yawning gap between "Ne odna vo pole dorozhen'ka" as performed for Turgenev, and typical peasant performances, since we not only possess harmonized arrangements of this song from Turgenev's time, but also some early ethnomusicological transcriptions from phonograph recordings, made by Yevgeniya Linyova in 1909 (Ex.1.1a). The version Turgenev heard in the comfort of his drawing room was probably taken either from the arrangement of Ivan Rupin (1831–6; Ex.1.1b), or of Gurilyov (1849; Ex.1.1c); at best, he might have heard a single melody line sung without the piano accompaniment included in these collec-

1.1a "Ne odna vo pole dorozhen'ka" from Linyova's collection

1.1b "Ne odna vo pole dorozhen'ka" from Rupin's collection

tions. Luckily for our comparison, we are definitely dealing with the same regional version of the song, as every section of the "original" finds its way into the urban arrangements, remaining more or less recognizable. But the song's highly melismatic character is toned down in the urban versions, as the text unfolds at the twice the original speed, and the highly characteristic breaking off in the middle of a word are ignored. Of course there is also the gap between the folk hetero/polyphony recorded by Linyova and the textbook harmonizations of the folk melody supplied by the urban arrangers. In a rural tavern such as that of Turgenev's story, the peasant singers would not have sung solo in the company of others (even given the competitive context in the story); the collectors of Turgenev's time, however, only heard less characteristic solo versions, since they approached individual peasant servants in the towns and cities. If Turgenev's huntsman encountered a genuine peasant performance of the song, he would in fact have found the vocal timbre, intonation, and clashing harmonies alien in the extreme, more likely to invite feelings of repugnance than melancholy.

It should not be imagined that Russian peasant songs travelled along a one-way road from field to townhouse; nor should we assume that their representation in art music moved progressively from gross distortion to an ever more accurate picture. We shall look at three telling examples now, in order to see

1.1c "Ne odna vo pole dorozhen'ka" from Gurilyov's collection

how these complications arose. One of the earliest appearances of the *protyazhnaya* in art music was in Yevgeniy Fomin's opera *Yamshchiki na podstave* (Coachmen at the inn, 1787), where it features prominently as the opening chorus (Ex.1.2); the writing would seem to indicate first-hand knowledge of the genre – a rare thing indeed – and there is even some attempt to recreate the hetero/polyphony of peasant ensemble singing within the musical limits of the day. Yet some sixty years later, we can find representations of the *protyazhnaya* which do not begin to approach Fomin's accuracy: one such is Gurilyov's arrangement of "Uzh kak pal tuman" (The fog has fallen, Ex.1.3), which works its material into a straightforward Italianate romance, with square phrasing and regular cadences, and even a refrain in the tonic major. Only certain lines of the text (*Tï vzoidi, vzoidi, krasno solnïshko, Tï sgoni*

1.2 Fomin, opening chorus from *Yamshchiki na podstave* (Coachmen at the Inn)

1.3   Gurilyov, "Uzh kak pal tuman" (The fog has fallen)

tuman, tuman s sinya, s sinya morya), both in their imagery of the sun, sea and fog and its repetition of the words, hint at the song's previous life as a peasant *protyazhnaya*. Gurilyov, who published this song in 1849, wrote at the top of the score "as sung by Stesha, the Gypsy, in the 1820s" reminding us that the ever-popular gypsy choirs played their part in the urbanization of the Russian folksong. But the extent of Stesha's contribution would be would be difficult to establish, since the gypsy choirs, needful of an income, reshaped their performances as much as they needed to maximize the response of their urban audience. Purists and connoisseurs of the "true" peasant song (as they liked to believe), such as Balakirev, would have considered this source impossibly contaminated and thus unsuitable for inclusion in any serious folksong collection. But Balakirev was blind to other forms of urban influence; take, for example, song No. 36 of his own folksong collection, *Chto na svete prezhestokom* (Ex.1.4). While the melody shows no obvious signs of urbanization, the text follows the regular metre of art poetry and contains such pearls of sentimental rhetoric as "Chto na svete prezhestokom prezhestokaya lyubov'" (That in this cruellest of worlds, love is the cruellest thing), entirely alien, of course, to the character of peasant texts. Since Balakirev recorded the rural origin of this song, it furnishes us with an example of the two-way traffic in songs between town and village, for a thoroughly salon-style urban text has been attached to an unaltered peasant melody. Evidently, the urban text has travelled from town to the village attached to an urban melody, whereupon peasant listeners, finding the text attractive, have attached it to an existing melody of their own. Ethnographers have been complaining about such two-way traffic since the dawn of song-collecting – it only demonstrates the difficulty of finding a pure culture to examine. Balakirev, however, appeared to be ignorant, or at least unconcerned by such mixtures, his strictures on authenticity notwithstanding

1.4 "Chto na svete prezhestokom", No. 33 from Balakirev's collection

(he only saw the inauthenticity of others' efforts). Indeed, to look back to the *protyazhnaya* of Turgenev's story, it would be quite plausible to suppose that the huntsman would have encountered the urbanized version at the gathering in the inn; this, of course, would have spoilt altogether the supposed authentic melancholy that Turgenev sought to inject into this scene.

Apart from the actual blending of the rural and urban idioms, the perceived melancholy of Russian folksong perfectly resonated with the sentimental mood of the salon verses and romances. To a foreign observer, it might well have seemed that the entire Russian nation was united in melancholy – such was the impression created by the urban élite; as Pushkin said, mockingly, in *Eugene Onegin*: "From the coachman to the greatest poet, / We all sing of our gloom" . . .[70]

But even Pushkin's highly developed sense of ironic detachment could desert him: Gogol reports that after he had read out the first chapters of his *Dead Souls*, Pushkin cried out, "How sad is our Russia!"[71] Gogol's celebrated work is indeed a turning point: no one managed to embody vague Romantic philosophizing about Russia, its people and its destiny in images so powerfully vivid and so highly poetic. The image of Russia as a flying troika became a cornerstone of emergent Russian self-consciousness and to the present day remains one of the nation's favourite images of itself.

Let us examine these famous lines:

Hey-ho, troika, you fly like a bird! Who thought you up? You could only have been born from a bold race living in a land that doesn't fool about, but stretches out its plains over half the world, a land where you can count out the milestones until they begin to blur before your eyes. It's quite a simple contraption really. It didn't need any iron bolts to hold it together, since it was thrown together quickly, with just an axe and a gouge, by a skilful fellow from Yaroslavl. The driver isn't wearing any fancy German boots, but he does have a beard and thick gloves, and he's perched upon goodness knows what. Now he rises up and swings his whip, breaking into song – the horses become a whirlwind, and the spokes a solid circle, while the road shakes, and a passer-by cries out in fear as he jumps aside. There it goes, dashing headlong. And now you can only see that something on the horizon is raising a swirling cloud of dust.

And you, Russia, aren't you flying along like a bold troika, never to be overtaken? The road beneath you is burning up, the bridges shudder, and everything else falls behind. The onlooker is amazed: "Is this a bolt flung from heaven? What is the meaning of this terrifying commotion? And these horses, like nothing else known on earth, what mysterious force animates them?" Hey-ho, my beauties, hey-ho! How your manes twist in the wind!

You listen keenly to the driver, and your every vein burns with his song. In unison you tense up your brassy necks, and your hooves scarcely touch the ground. You become mere lines, extended through the air, and the troika dashes on, inspired by God. "Russia, where are you flying? Answer me!" But she gives no reply. The bells on the harnesses ring out wondrously. The air is torn to shreds, and becomes a roaring wind. All the world hurtles by. All other states and peoples stand aside, casting back envious glances.[72]

It is remarkable that the lingering song of the coachman becomes one of the most important components of Gogol's rich image of Russia, together with the troika and the journey without end. It is the *protyazhnaya* that imparts a poignant sense of longing into these lyrical soliloquies; it becomes a double metaphor: as the song stretches out, so too do the expanses of the Russian soil and the Russian soul:

But what is that inexplicable force that draws me to thee? Why does thy plaintive song, which rises all over the length and breadth of thee from sea to sea, constantly resound in my ear? What is there in it, in that song? What is there in it that calls, and sobs, and grips the heart? What are those strains that poignantly caress and torment me, that stream straight into my soul, that entwine themselves around my heart? Russia! What dost thou want of me?[73]

In a later explanation of these lyrical digressions which Gogol attempted in his *Selected Passages*, his direct experience of Russian peasant song manifests itself even more clearly:

Even today I still cannot bear those plaintive, heart-rending sounds of our song, the song that streams all over the limitless Russian expanses. These sounds hover near my heart, and indeed I am amazed that everyone else does not feel the same. Those who look at this desert, until now an uninhabited and shelterless space, and yet do not feel melancholy, those who do not hear painful reproaches to themselves in the plaintive sounds of our song, . . . those are the people who have either fulfilled their duty already or who have nothing of Russia in their souls.[74]

Dostoyevsky, Tolstoy and Chekhov all followed Gogol's example in expressing a burning concern for the destiny of Russia. But Pushkin was different; it never struck him that the Russian nation was pervaded by melancholy. Nikolai Berdyayev attempted to explain this gulf between Pushkin and the following generations; the key, he believed, was the emergence of the intelligentsia in the first half of the century:

Pushkin was not an *intelligent* yet . . . he had something of the Renaissance in him, and the whole body of great nineteenth-century Russian literature is completely unlike him in this respect. . . . The great Russian writers of the nineteenth century were to create not out of joyful creative abundance, but out of a thirst to save the people, out of sorrow and suffering caused by untruth and human slavery.[75]

Berdyayev also alerts us to the first instance of a writer's grief and concern for the people displayed by Alexander Radishchev as early as 1790:

The forerunner of the Russian intelligentsia was Radishchev, he anticipated and determined its main features. When Radishchev in his *Journey from Petersburg to Moscow* wrote, "I looked around myself – my soul was stung by the sufferings of humanity", the Russian intelligentsia was born.[76]

If the birth of the Russian intelligentsia is associated with the first pangs of conscience the upper classes experienced when contemplating the plight of the lower classes, then we may consider the Russian *protyazhnaya* an important agent of this process. The same Radishchev made the crucial connection between the songs of a people and the character of that people; and in a characteristically Enlightenment manner he even tried to derive a principle of good government from this idea:

Those who know the sound of Russian folksongs will admit that there is something in them signifying a grief of the soul. Nearly all of these songs are in the minor mode. One ought to learn how to set the style of government according to this disposition of the people's ear. It is here that the soul of our people is to be found.[77]

In contrast to Radishchev, later commentators were drawn by the Romantic notion that music was able to grasp the ineffable. And if the Russian national character could not be encapsulated in words, then a song would have to do the job instead. Ivan Kireyevsky found no words appropriate to express their character:

an ineffable quality, comprehensible only to a Russian heart: for what name can you give to the feeling with which the melodies of Russian songs are imbued, to which the Russian people most frequently resort, and which can be regarded as the centre of their spiritual life?[78]

To Gogol, Russian folksongs also suggested *razgul*: this is a Russian concept which is especially difficult to translate – in this context implies both freedom and aimlessness, derring-do and a devil-may-care attitude, perhaps associated with the unbounded play of some elemental force. "In old folksongs", he wrote,

> there is little attachment to life and its objects, but a strong attraction to some unbounded *razgul,* a desire to be carried far away by the sounds.[79]

> this inexplicable *razgul,* that is heard in our songs, flies somewhere past life and past the song itself, as if driven by the burning desire of a better fatherland . . .[80]

Scholars and music critics were no less ready to indulge in romanticizing the *protyazhnaya*: in 1837, Professor O. M. Bodyansky confirmed that the genre contained "gloom" and "a great expanse", as established by previous writers, but also claimed to detect "the utmost oblivion" and "submissiveness to fate".[81] Bodyansky traces these qualities to the landscape (the flatness of the plains, the gloomy forests etc.) and climate (the long winters) of Northern Russia, and also, more interestingly, to its people's detachment from the real world, their indifference all that happens around them. The music critic F. Russo, writing some fifty years later, was able to accept Bodyansky's characterizations as given, adding that the majority of Russian folksongs, excluding wedding and game-songs, are "filled with some deep fatalistic grief".[82]

As we have seen, the *protyazhnaya* was widely perceived throughout the nineteenth century as a paradigm for all Russian folksong and as a Romantic image of all that was essential to the Russian soul. Novelists were faithful to the notion that Russian music is necessarily melancholy – so much we have established, but did Russian composers follow suit? Glinka did indeed assent to this at the time of *A Life for the Tsar*; the first notes we hear in the overture are an imitation of *protyazhnaya* (see Ex.3.9a). His use of the Russian romance style at the crucial points of the opera such as Susanin's aria (Act IV) confirm his belief in Russian melancholy. Contemporary audiences made no distinction between folksong adaptations and salon romance, and so they perceived the opera as homogeneous in style and sorrowful in overall mood; less sympathetic commentators even detected a certain monotony of expression. Glinka's dependence on song caused many to question the viability of such method for creating a dramatic work. "His drama is too doleful," wrote Alexander Dargomïzhsky in a letter to Odoyevsky (3 July 1853), hoping that he himself could provide both Russian comic music and Russian dramatic music in his *Rusalka*.[83] But most of Glinka's contemporaries agreed that *A Life for the Tsar* successfully encapsulated the notion of musical Russianness current at that time.

It was Glinka's second opera that ultimately led to the change of direction in the development of Russian musical identity. *Ruslan and Lyudmila*, misunderstood and undervalued at the time of its première in 1842, laid the foundations of a very different musical image of Russia. The following section outlines the creation and acceptance of this new image; later chapters will cover this area in greater detail.

Ruslan *and the change of direction*

Both the critics and the public at large considered Glinka's second opera to be less Russian that the first; to this extent, it was a disappointment. Indeed, all traces of Russian folksong seemed to have gone, and the romance idiom lost its prominence to other styles. The music of *Ruslan* came from a variety of sources: Mozart was distinctly in evidence (*Zauberflöte, Figaro*), as was Italian opera; there were also various folksongs of non-Russian provenance. But most important was the original idiom which Glinka brought into being specially for *Ruslan*; this provided a joyful and harmonious image of Russia very much in keeping with the young Pushkin's *Ruslan*, the effervescent *jeux d'esprit* which provided Glinka with his scenario.

Through the tireless advocacy of Vladimir Stasov, Glinka's oeuvre in general and *Ruslan* in particular was mythologized and adopted as an infallible model by the composers of the Kuchka.[84] The genres of fairy-tale and epic opera, both suggested by *Ruslan*, became central for Rimsky-Korsakov, whose fifteen operas constitute the main body of the Kuchkist operatic legacy (especially if we disregard the work of Cui, who belonged to the Kuchka circle mainly as a critic, but who was not very representative of the Kuchka as a composer). Borodin's *Prince Igor* is undeniably another of *Ruslan*'s offspring, perhaps the most faithful of all Glinka imitations. Glinka's introduction of the fantastic and Oriental elements in *Ruslan* made an even stronger impression on the Kuchkists: they expanded these topics into rich and distinctive styles, both of which became an integral part of the Russian musical identity. In the details of its musical technique, *Ruslan* was again a source of inspiration, above all for its use of changing-background variations, which were now seen as the characteristic method of Russian musical development, in opposition to German methods.

Another model adopted by the Kuchka was Glinka's *Kamarinskaya*, a short orchestral piece based on two Russian folksongs. On the one hand, it gave rise to the infinite string of overtures and fantasies on Russian themes (Glinka's Spanish overtures played a similar role in generating pieces based on foreign material); on the other hand, it pointed in a new direction through its choice of folk material: instead of taking the expected *protyazhnaya* as its basis, it used instead a wedding song and a fast dance. In the 1860s, inspired by Glinka's earlier example, there was a general shift away from the *protyazhnaya* as the genre most representative of Russianness to other genres of a very different mood. Richard Taruskin here refers to this change:

> Not that the use of folk song was dead in Russia by any means. But "progressive" interest had shifted to the short-breathed "calendar song" (a shift best traced in Rimsky-Korsakov's operas), and Stravinsky, for example, who based his whole "Russian period" style on the calendar song, imitated the *protyazhnaya* only once – Ivan Tsarevich's theme in *The Firebird*.[85]

While the *protyazhnaya* was a lyrical genre expressing personal emotions, songs connected to seasonal rituals as well as *bïlinï* (epic songs) were collective expressions of a whole community: the "Farewell to Shrovetide" scene from Rimsky-Korsakov's *The Snowmaiden* or the fourth tableau from his *Sadko* were clearly modelled on such songs. Unlike *protyazhnaya*, other groups of songs had not been and could not be absorbed into the salon romance; in the eyes of a new generation of enthusiasts for peasant culture, this was now a positive feature: the *protyazhnïye* were contaminated by urban culture, while other folk genres had retained their purity. (It was not even a matter of finding unadulterated examples of *protyazhnaya* – the whole genre was now associated with a past generation of song collectors which the new generation wished to supplant.) Since most of the ritual songs were considered (speculatively) to be in the oldest cultural stratum, they were of course perfect for archaic colouring.

The range of expression available within this new Russian musical style was, however, severely circumscribed; if passion, or any kind of romantic sensibility was to be conveyed, then the Kuchka often retreated to the idioms of European Romantic music; even the rolling on of the drama had to eschew the new Russian style, which was best suited to static tableaux. Stasov and Balakirev both saw the communal songs as the authentic expression of Russianness, and the Kuchkists accordingly provide far fewer personal outpourings of emotion than was normal for their European contemporaries. The absence of any love interest in the first version of *Boris Godunov* was highly symptomatic of this, and when Musorgsky finally added love interest, through the new prima donna role of Marina Mniszek, the resulting passages were the least Kuchkist of the entire opera, and indeed the least characteristically Musorgskian. Rimsky-Korsakov's *May Night* constitutes another exception that proves the rule: because he placed the emotional lives of individual characters in the foreground, the other members of the Kuchka notably withheld their praise – and this at a time when they were still tightly knit and mutually supportive.

One pervasive characteristic of the Kuchka's new musical image of Russianness is that of the *bogatïrsky*. A *bogatïr'* was a Russian warrior of folk epics, and *bogatïrskaya sila* (strength of *bogatïr'*), conveyed weight, might and courage. Stasov applied this cluster of associations to Borodin's Second Symphony, claiming that Borodin himself had indicated its programmatic content to him (the portrayal of an epic singer in the slow movement, and of a joyful *bogatïr* feast in the finale).[86] Glazunov's symphonies also draw on this tradition of *bogatïrsky* music, marked by solemn hymns and heavy dances; although non-programmatic, they have likewise been described as portraying pagan Russia. The closing movement of Musorgsky's *Pictures* is "The Bogatir Gate (at Kiev, the ancient capital)", and both the music and the Hartmann drawing which inspired it illustrated the concept well.

And so by the time the Kuchka had become entrenched as the musical representatives of Russianness, a great gulf had developed between the images of Russia propagated in music and in literature. Of all the members of the Kuchka circle, only Musorgsky's thinking had much in common with the ideas that preoccupied his literary contemporaries. *Boris Godunov* and *Khovanshchina* demonstrated that Musorgsky was a true *intelligent*, characteristically tormenting himself with the crucial questions posed by Russia's history. He clearly wanted to explore the issues such as the relationship between the tsar and the masses, and the competing interests behind tradition and progress. The weeping Yurodivïy at the end of the Kromï scene in *Boris*; the Petrine troops coming to witness the self-immolation of the Old Believers in the final scene of *Khovanshchina* – both these scenes provide symbols of Russia's tragic destiny to rival those found in the most powerful contemporary Russian novels. The other Kuchkists preferred, like the Slavophiles, to paint an idealized or fairy-tale world of pre-Petrine Russia; but unlike the Slavophiles, the Kuchkists generally favoured the paganism of the epics as the authentic expression of the Russian spirit.

1842 was a watershed year in Russian culture, for it was in this year that the two works which established the conflicting images of Russia in music and in literature both appeared: in music Glinka's *Ruslan and Lyudmila*, and in literature Gogol's *Dead Souls*. They both shared an epic element, so that the audience/reader was led to feel that the agent behind the peripeteia of the plot was in fact the Russian nation, travelling towards its destiny. But here the similarities end. If *Ruslan*, in the best traditions of the epic genre, glorified Russian might, *Dead Souls*, on the contrary, satirized the horrors of the Russian present; but true to the epic, it prophesied a glorious future for Russia, all the more striking because of the surrounding blackness. And while *Ruslan* begins and ends with a wedding feast – a symbol of stability, community and confidence in the future, *Dead Souls* leaves in our memory the image of the troika flying into the unknown – an image of dynamism, loneliness and an unknown future. While the music of the Kuchkists and their followers abounded in portrayals of festivities, the image of the troika was constantly repeated and commented upon in Russian literature and criticism. It is enough to recall the many festivities enacted in Russian opera, or the carnivalesque symphonic pieces in the wake of *Kamarinskaya*, or the festive finales of Glazunov's symphonies, to see that this is an indispensable element of Russian music in the second half of the nineteenth century. And it was this colourful festive image that Diaghilev considered eminently marketable in the West (and, of course, he was proved correct).

There were, of course, other composers who did not follow the Kuchka line; even then, Glinka was of foundational importance, but as the composer of *A Life for the Tsar* rather than *Ruslan*. Alexander Serov's opera *Power of the Fiend* (1871), is one such successor to Glinka's first opera: a drama which is carried by music in a familiar idiom that his audience would perceive as unmistakably Russian (the Kuchka had not yet established their own brand of musical Russianness in the public's mind). The musical idiom he chose for this work was neither from the village nor the salon, but rather the streets and taverns of the city. Unfortunately for Serov, Russian music criticism was already dominated by Stasov and Cui, who allowed nothing but their own narrow doctrines on musical Russianness. Such criticism effectively resulted in praise for the Kuchkists alone, while Serov was dismissed as a purveyor of pseudo-Russian music (note that Serov was the most popular composer of Russian opera at the time, and not the obscure figure he is today).

Tchaikovsky also faced criticism from the Kuchka that his music was not authentically Russian. In *Eugene Onegin*, Tchaikovsky, like Serov, drew on the older melancholy Russianness of *A Life for the Tsar*, and the salon romance style, and it could very plausibly be argued that this, if anything, was the most authentic approach for an opera based on Pushkin's verse-novel. But Stasov seems not to have considered this, and instead gave the badge of Russianness only to the decorative pastoral choruses of Act 1 and to a few phrases in the recitative of Tatyana's peasant nurse. After Tchaikovsky's death, Stasov conceded that the composer had been "a sincere patriot and an ardent admirer of all things Russian", but he immediately qualified this by arguing that his "musical nature lacked the national element"; it is not long before his ruminations over this qualification lead him effectively to withdraw his initial statement, and he suggests that Tchaikovsky's apparent sympathy for all things Russian was merely self-deception.[87]

Cui's *La musique en Russie*, published in 1880, carried the Kuchkist orthodoxy to Paris, and by the turn of the century its ideas were common currency among musical circles across Europe. Even Riemann tacitly acknowledged this

Kuchkist onslaught, since he classified Tchaikovsky (and Anton Rubinstein) as composers of the German school – this, of course, carried no derogatory import for Riemann, but it does indicate how the Kuchka had won the battle to claim Russianness for themselves alone.[88] But both *Eugene Onegin* and *The Power of the Fiend* present an alternative Russian musical style to that offered by Kuchka, and it is absurd for us today to submit to Kuchka rhetoric and reject these operas as inauthentic. Tchaikovsky's Russianness in *Onegin* is the musical portrait of the gentry of Pushkin's time; Serov's *Fiend* depicts the contemporary life of the Russian merchants who inhabit the opera's literary source, a play by Alexander Ostrovsky. Both operas are remarkably homogeneous in style, and because their musical idiom was so familiar to audiences at that time, one could plausibly argue that they had better claims to the status of Russian national opera than any Kuchka fantasy about the Russia of fairytales and epics. But given the environment created by Cui and by the critics who successfully propagated his views in the West, Serov and Tchaikovsky were now unsuited to be representatives of Russia in the West, as Diaghilev was soon to find out.

Diaghilev's image of Russia

Composers who set out to develop a Russian national style were not satisfied with recognition within Russia alone: they also craved acknowledgement in the West – they wanted the West to acquire a new image of Russia through their music. Odoyevsky, Stasov, and Cui, the prophets of musical nationalism, indeed wrote that European musical culture was decrepit, urged Russian composers to "part forever with the general current of European music", and even announced "the new period in art history" that was "the era of Russian music". But this was merely a public façade.[89] When they stepped down from the soapbox, they were all too aware that Russia's position on the European musical map was marginal at best. When planning concerts at the Free Music School, Balakirev made sure that the names of his disciples were always to be found alongside those of Schumann and Liszt. Musorgsky greatly feared the prospect of meeting Liszt on a planned trip to Europe (in the end he never went); after hearing that Liszt admired his *Nursery*, he said: "[F]ortunate is Russian music to win such sympathy from a star like Liszt."[90]

But the hour of recognition was slow to come. In the 1850s Berlioz organized performances of Glinka's works, in the 1870s and '80s Borodin held meetings with Liszt, and in the same period the countess Mercy-Argenteau supported both Cui and Borodin; but none of this had any lasting impact on the larger Western public. For the Kuchkists such a situation was all the more disturbing since Anton Rubinstein's operas were regularly produced on

European stages – Rubinstein was of course third-rate and not authentically Russian in their eyes. Rimsky-Korsakov's appearance at the 1889 Paris Exposition passed almost unnoticed (Debussy and Ravel were among the handful that took note), and his Brussels concerts a year later only brought him local repute. Yet it is in his report on the Brussels concerts that we find the gateway to his later successes, for he had now discovered what music most interested European audiences. Rimsky-Korsakov's Spanish Capriccio and Easter Overture enjoyed the warmest reception; Musorgsky's *Night on the Bare Mountain* (as recomposed by Rimsky-Korsakov), Borodin's Second Symphony and Glazunov's *Lyrical Poem* were also well received, but the audience was much cooler towards Balakirev's Overture on Three Russian Themes and remained totally unmoved by the fragments from Cui's opera *Flibustière*. Rimsky-Korsakov was thus able to conclude that "the Belgians mainly seek originality in the Russians, and Cui does not satisfy them in this respect."[91] The originality of the music which most struck the Belgians was in particular a strong exotic flavour and sumptuous orchestral attire; the Balakirev and Cui pieces which failed to find favour both lacked these properties.

It is notable that Tchaikovsky's successes in England and the United States did not bring him automatic success with Parisian audiences. Rimsky-Korsakov's friend Kruglikov reported to him that there was considerable interest in Russian music in Paris, but, as it turns out, this interest was restricted to the Kuchka:

> Tchaikovsky is more of a European and an internationalist and therefore less interesting; as for Glinka: well, Papa Glinka is simply out of date. They need something more *à la russe*. Let it be bold, strange, unusual . . .[92]

The desires of the Paris audiences were finally satisfied in 1907, when Sergei Diaghilev, that entrepreneurial genius, showcased Russian music, after great success with Russian painting. Fyodor Shaliapin called the series of concerts "an examination of Russian maturity and originality in art, an examination we had to pass before the eyes of Europe".[93]

Diaghilev's five "historical concerts" of 1907, which purported to represent Russian music from Glinka to the present day, in fact offered a largely Kuchkist portrait of Russia to Paris audiences. Glinka, for example, was characteristically represented by the overture and Act I of *Ruslan* and *Kamarinskaya*, the very works which had inspired the Kuchkist departure from the former melancholy musical image of Russia. Then there was a selection of operatic excerpts from Borodin, Musorgsky and Rimsky-Korsakov: a number of Russian-style (Kuchkist) scenes such as Varlaam's Song from *Boris* or Lel's Song from *The Snowmaiden*; an array of Oriental pieces such as the

Polovtsian Dances or the Dance of the Persian Maidens from *Khovanshchina*; there were also several scenes from Rimsky-Korsakov united by their fairy-tale character. The second generation of Kuchkists – Lyadov, Lyapunov and Glazunov – were also represented in the programme, and, to be fair, so were two non-Kuchkist composers of the same generation, namely Rakhmaninov and Scriabin. But it was Rimsky-Korsakov who received all the laurels from an enthusiastic Parisian public; it was not that he was the only composer who had travelled from Russia to attend the performances: Glazunov and Scriabin both appeared, and Rakhmaninov took the solo part in his own Second Piano Concerto and conducted his cantata *Spring*. Rimsky-Korsakov, nevertheless, was seen as the leading light of Russian music.

In the *Saisons Russes* each year thereafter Diaghilev capitalized on the music which followed the pattern of these initial successes: there was more Rimsky-Korsakov and Musorgsky, more fairy tales with Oriental colour and, of course, more dance. But it is important to realize that the music did not stand alone: the element of spectacle contributed much to the success of the enterprise. Diaghilev himself believed that the *Saisons Russes* created less of a revolution in music (*The Rite of Spring* notwithstanding) and choreography (Isadora Duncan had already laid the groundwork) than in set design and costume. This side of the production was assigned to the best and most forward-looking Russian artists, who were generally allowed great licence to make strong artistic statements of their own. The music of Rimsky-Korsakov, Borodin and Musorgsky, and later Stravinsky became indelibly associated the exotic, garish colours and exaggerated shapes of the productions. One of the witnesses, Anatoly Lunacharsky, who was to become the first Soviet Minister of Education, described the sets for *Khovanschina* in the following way:

> The sets by Fedorovsky were fantastic or symbolic, rather than historically realistic; they gave us a vision of some cyclopic land that was nevertheless nothing but Russia ... Everything, including the goblets on Khovansky's table and even his comb, was gigantic. The boyar costumes were monstrously conceited and splendid. In a word, this was the wild beauty and the previously unseen picture of a European barbarism.[94]

(Note that the Russian word conveying "barbarism" is *aziatchina* – literally "Asianism".) Fairy-tale material prompted even bolder flights of the imagination. The sets for *The Golden Cockerel* were painted by Natalya Goncharova and reminded Rimsky-Korsakov's widow of an enormous childrens' book (this, together with the fact that the opera was presented as a ballet with singing, led her to contemplate legal action against Diaghilev). How the composer himself would have reacted to the production had he lived to see it is not hard to imagine, for he many times expressed his irritation at those "decadent" painters whose sets (much more moderate than Goncharova's) he had to tolerate in the last decade of his life. The tolerance of the Grand Opéra administration was also put to test when the sets for *Boris Godunov* arrived in the theatre; according to Ravel, their bold colours were so startling that for a while the première was under threat.[95] Needless to say, the audience loved them. At the same time, Diaghilev claimed to know the tastes of the Parisians well enough to withdraw the Inn scene from *Boris Godunov* on the grounds that its "coarse realism" might prove unpleasantly shocking. He also created lavish spectacles from the Coronation and the Kromï scenes: the first featured a grand procession of church dignitaries, while the second included falling snow and a horse-drawn sleigh for the Pretender.[96]

The Oriental side of Russian music enjoyed still greater popular success. Borodin's Polovtsian Dances, Stravinsky's *Firebird*, and ballets employing the music of Rimsky-Korsakov's *Sheherezade* and *Golden Cockerel*, and Balakirev's *Tamara* all achieved something that Russians could never have dreamed of hitherto: they influenced Paris fashion. In all the excitement of dressing up in Orientalist garb and chattering about those famous Russians, Parisians had no time to draw careful distinctions between Near East and genuine Asiatic cultures, and so the image of Russia as an exotic Asiatic country was only reinforced. For the French, and later for the English and American audiences of Diaghilev's *Saisons*, Russian music was forever associated with its colourful packaging, and this image was passed along to later generations. This music was itself heard as bright, decorative, exotic and fantastic; no Russian tragic soul was in view.[97]

Music meets literature

It is important to realize that the *Saisons Russes* were entirely conceived for the export market; no such venture could have been undertaken in Russia, not only for fear of heavy-handed censorship, but also because of the conservatism of the public, a lack of money and institutional inertia. But in order to pass an exam under the invigilation of the West, Russia mobilized all its artistic powers and was able to attract more capital than it could have done for any internal undertaking. Shaliapin commented that the Coronation scene in *Boris Godunov* could never have been staged so splendidly in Russia: the expense would have been deemed prohibitive, and of course there were restrictions on the representation of clergy on stage, while in Paris all the bishops and metropolitans could parade in glittering robes.[98] But more importantly, the image of Russia that the *Saisons* projected was not merely more and better: it was essentially an export, in that Russia was consciously presented as something exotic. It was as if the Russian artists involved were able to view the motherland with detachment, and (from a safe distance) to delight in its lack of European civilization. This new perspective momentarily coincided with new literary developments, as Vladimir Solovyov, Alexander Blok and Andrei Bely sang of the rising might of . . . no, not Pan-Slavism, but now Pan-Mongolism. The poets provocatively replaced the meek image of an all-embracing Slavonicism by the terrifying savagery of the Asian tribes, as in Blok's *Scythians:*

> There are millions of you,
> But hordes and hordes and hordes of us.
> Just try to fight us!
> Yes, we are Scythians, yes, we are Asians,
> With squint and greedy eyes.[99]

The "we" of this poem is the same Russian nation which had at first eagerly learnt from Western civilization, then searched for a native alternative; having failed in both tasks, it now threatened to destroy the West by brute force:

> You old world! While you have not perished,
> While you are still tormented by sweet pangs,
> Stop, you wise one, like Oedipus
> Before the Sphinx with an ancient puzzle! . . .
>
> We love all things, both the heat of cold numbers
> And the gift of divine apparitions.
> We comprehend all things, both sharp Gallic sense
> And gloomy Germanic genius. . . .
>
> We love flesh, both its taste and colour,
> And love the stuffy, deathly odour of flesh.
> Are we to blame if your bones crack
> In our heavy tender paws?
>
> Russia is a sphinx. Rejoicing and mourning,
> And shedding black blood,
> She looks and looks into you
> With hatred and with love.[100]

The genesis of the shocking new identity Blok created for Russia in this poem can be seen as twofold: first, the poet attempted to look at his country through

Western eyes, grotesquely playing upon the Western image of Russia the bear, and second, he provocatively followed the logic of the Slavophile reversal of Western values *ad absurdum*. The development of musical Russianness followed a parallel course: we have already noticed the self-conscious exoticism of Diaghilev's *Saisons*, and a parallel to the transformation of Slavophilism can be seen in *The Rite of Spring*. As Slavophiles turned into Mongolophiles, the Kuchkist folk rituals turned savage.

CHAPTER 2

THE PUSHKIN AND GLINKA MYTHOLOGIES

There is no better description of Glinka than "our musical Pushkin".

Hermann Laroche

The giant Pushkin is our greatest pride and the fullest expression of Russia's spiritual strength; next to him stands the magician Glinka.

Maxim Gorky

Nationalist historiography of Russian music takes the première of *A Life for the Tsar* as its inaugural moment; 1836 is therefore Year 1, and everything before this is relegated to the so-called pre-Glinka period. This scheme was proposed at a surprisingly early stage: just before the première, Nestor Kukolnik, a friend of Glinka, wrote in his diary:

A new dawn for Russian music is beginning. Tomorrow the sun will rise, and Glinka will become immortal.[1]

A few days later, such sentiments were expressed before the public, in a review of the opera by the critic Odoyevsky.[2] And so the myth of Glinka as the founding father of Russia's national music was already established among growing numbers by the end of 1836. We shall now compare the development of this founding-father myth to another such myth that had been established a few years earlier: Pushkin, as the founding father of Russian national literature. The Pushkin myth has always enjoyed much wider acceptance – it was almost universal among all subsequent generations of literate Russian speakers (only the cult of Lenin that Stalin created a century later was able to overshadow it). The elevation of Pushkin became the model for later, smaller cults: not only were lesser figures likened to Pushkin in their own sector of the arts, but any chance personal connections to the great poet were also eagerly sought out. Glinka's status, as we shall see later, benefited from one such connection.

The Pushkin myth

Perhaps the first hint at Pushkin's special status appears in Ivan Kireyevsky's article, "A few comments on the nature of Pushkin's poetry" (1828), where the works of Pushkin's third, "Russian" period (following the "Franco-Italian" and "Byronian" periods) are presented as an embodiment of the national character:

> The characteristic traits of [this period] are: the picturesque, a certain nonchalance, a certain special pensiveness, and, lastly, some ineffable quality, comprehensible only to the Russian heart – for what name can you give to the feeling with which the melodies of Russian songs are imbued, to which the Russian people most frequently resort, and which can be regarded as the centre of their spiritual life?[3]

Kireyevsky is only tentatively suggesting that Pushkin might become the national poet because he expresses "the hopes, strivings and losses of his fatherland ... unwittingly, through self-expression". But Kireyevsky's discussion is couched in a vague, Romantic style; by the 1830s, however, the concept of nationality (*narodnost'*) had become common currency among officials and liberals alike, and the honorific "national artist" was bestowed on artists quite promiscuously. After the 1830s it was no longer possible to discuss and criticize Pushkin as a human being with both personal and artistic failings. In 1835 Vissarion Belinsky, in one of his earlier reviews, criticized the folk-style tales, mocking Pushkin and other exponents of this genre for their shared delusion that an educated gentleman can transform himself into a naive peasant at will. But in the same year, Gogol already places Pushkin above criticism, in the manner of later writers:

> On hearing the name of Pushkin, one immediately thinks "the Russian national poet". Indeed, none of our [other] poets is superior to him, none deserves to be called national poet more than he; this right positively belongs to him.[4]

For Gogol, Pushkin's verses reflected "the Russian landscape, the Russian soul, the Russian language, the Russian character", and even the poet's life was "utterly Russian". In Chapter 1 we have already noted Gogol's foundational role in various aspects of national mythology, and with Pushkin too, he offered us one of the earliest and best formulations of the nascent myth. Pushkin's untimely death in a duel in 1837 was bound to accelerate the process of myth-creation; the memorable announcement of his death began with the words, "The sun of our Poetry has set!"

During the following two decades, however, Pushkin's mythologizers found that they had been set adrift by the most powerful nationalist current: the Slavophiles were busily establishing a Russian identity which was humble, pious and suffering, while Pushkin's work was witty and irreverent, playful and brilliant. How could Pushkin be the representative of the nation portrayed in the Slavophiles' writings? The "prophets" of the Russian nation sensed the conflict, and not wanting to abandon either side, they set out to reconcile the two. The solution was already present in embryo in the same Gogol essay of 1837, where Pushkin was situated in an ideal Russia of the future:

> Pushkin is an extraordinary phenomenon, perhaps a unique phenomenon of the Russian spirit: it is the Russian at a stage of development he may reach in two hundred years' time.[5]

This notion was still in circulation in 1880, when a statue of Pushkin was erected in Moscow. The cult of Pushkin was then at its height, and at the unveiling ceremony, the following verses were read:

We are greeting you,	My privetstvuyem tebya –
Our pride, as a foretaste	Nashu gordost' – kak zadatok
Of those wonders which may be	Tekh chudes, shto, mozhet bït',
– which we in our full bloom	Nam v rastsvete nashem polnom
Are destined to display.	Suzhdeno yeshcho yavit'![6]

The other problem besetting the mythologizers of Pushkin was the poet's unashamed cosmopolitanism: most of his work was written within imported genres, and there were countless references to foreign poets from Homer to Goethe. This was a lurking embarrassment for nationalists until Dostoyevsky cut the Gordian knot in his celebrated dedicatory speech at the unveiling. Pushkin's "universal susceptibility" is now turned into a national virtue, and linked to Russia's role as messiah of the world's nations:

> to become a complete and genuine Russian means . . . to become brother of all men, a universal man.[7]

Again, Pushkin was found a place in the grand edifice of Russian nationalism: he was a sign of future times, when other nations would look towards Russia to save them.

The reception of individual works was soon transformed by the nationalist rhetoric of the critics. *Ruslan and Lyudmila*, for example, was a youthful skit, wittily alluding to the quest for a Russian epic that other Russian poets had undertaken; it was a satire on Russian epics, not a sincere Russian epic itself. Among *Ruslan*'s many sources of inspiration, Ariosto's *Orlando furioso* is foremost, and, as Belinsky said, the poem is 'no more Russian than it is German or Chinese'.[8] Yet from the moment of its publication in 1820, wishful thinking turned it into the long-awaited Russian epic. Significantly, Gnedich, the Russian translator of the *Iliad*, bestowed high praise upon Pushkin's youthful effort:

Tï zhe, postignuvshiy tainstva russkogo dukha i mira,
Tï – nash Bayan: nebom rodnïm vdokhnovennïy,
Tï na Rusi nash pevets nesravnennïy! [9]

You, who have comprehended the mysteries of the Russian spirit,
    the Russian world,
You are our Bayan, inspired by native skies;
In Russia you are our incomparable singer.

This unexpected reception of the mock epic even influenced Pushkin himself, for in 1828, after immersing himself in the study of Russian folk tales, Pushkin brought out a new edition of *Ruslan*, now with a much more folk-style Prologue, as if he sought to justify the work's reputation:

U lukomor'ya dub zelyonïy;
Zlataya tsep' na dube tom:
I dnyom i nochyu kot uchonïy
Vsyo khodit po tsepi krugom;
Idyot napravo – pesn' zavodit,
Nalevo – skazku govorit.

By a curving shore a green oak; and night and day a learned cat walks round and round on a chain: when it goes to the right it strikes up a song: to the left – it tells a tale.

Another passage from this Prologue, "'Zdes' russkiy dukh, zdes Rus'yu pakhnet" (There's Russian spirit here, there's Russia in the air), has become proverbial, and is applied with inappropriate generality to all Pushkin's works. But *Ruslan* above all, because of the critics' claim that it was a true Russian epic, lost its associations with Ariosto and its other foreign influences. By the time Glinka started writing his opera in 1837, Pushkin had already become the national poet; to choose *Ruslan* now as the opera's subject was unavoidably a nationalist gesture, and Glinka glorifies Pushkin in Bayan's second song. Similarly, when Rimsky-Korsakov and his librettist, Belsky, set to work on *The Golden Cockerel*, there was no question of viewing the Pushkin source as anything other than a cultivated appropriation of the Russian folk tale. Belsky, in his preface to the score, even traced Pushkin's *Cockerel* back to particular Russian fairy tales. The fact that Pushkin borrowed the plot wholesale from Washington Irving, the early American short-story writer, had been conveniently forgotten.

The Moscow monument initiated the tradition of regular Pushkin celebrations. But while in 1880 the intelligentsia had paid for the statue and organized the celebrations, the events marking the hundredth anniversary of Pushkin's birth, nineteen years later, were overseen by Nicholas II himself; now the state and commerce were heavily involved in promoting Pushkin for their own interests. The state established a dedicated branch of the Academy of Sciences (now known as the Pushkin House), purchased the Pushkin country estate, and commanded performances of Pushkin's works in the imperial theatres; all over the country, there were special services in churches and in all educational establishments, including readings with magic lantern slides for the simple folk, and the distribution of a new illustrated edition of selected works, free of charge to schoolchildren.[10] An epidemic of re-naming streets and institutions broke out – to this day, there are, confusingly, two "Pushkin museums" in Moscow. Private societies held their own celebrations, including the Pushkin bicycle race and a banquet consisting exclusively of dishes and beverages mentioned in *Eugene Onegin*. Commerce added its own kitsch flavour to the festival by producing a range of Pushkin goods, including the perfume "Bouquet de Pouchkine" and a bad-taste novelty board game, "Pushkin's Duel".[11]

The intelligentsia greeted the repackaging of Pushkin with considerable distaste, objecting especially to the insinuation that Pushkin had been a loyal servant of the monarchy. The journal *Mir iskusstva* (The World of Art) devoted a whole issue to the defence of Pushkin against such co-option by the state. The "Silver Age" poets continued the counter-offensive over several years by issuing a series of "My Pushkin" essays, in which they dwelt on their artistic relationships with Pushkin, often picturing encounters with him in some timeless literary netherworld. A number of these essays were celebrated not simply as attempts to reclaim Pushkin's reputation, but as literary achievements in their own right (the contributions by Valeriy Bryusov and Marina Tsvetayeva were probably the best known). Pushkin's life and violent death were sentimentalized in a hundred different ways, and since there were no longer any first-hand memories of Pushkin to be canvassed, every place associated with Pushkin – his apartments, houses, favourite cafés and even park benches – was able to speak to Pushkin's true devotees. Pushkin was presented as a living presence, foreshadowing the Stalinist cult of Lenin ("Lenin lived, Lenin lives, Lenin will live"). Even the few who refused to worship implicitly acknowledged Pushkin's stature. The critic Dmitry Pisarev, for example, who was a well-known literary figure from the 1860s to the '80s, argued that Pushkin had to be toppled from his pedestal in order to make room for the new realism (dubbed "nihilism" by its detractors, then adopted by the artists for themselves). He encouraged a "disrespect for art", and the most effective way to show this was by insulting Pushkin, "the decrepit idol".[12] A couple of decades later, Pisarev's tactic was revived by the Futurists, who in their manifesto voiced the desire to "throw Pushkin off the steamboat of modernity". Thus the irreverent Pushkin came to stand, in spite of himself, for all the pieties of high art.

The October Revolution looked poised to realize the Futurist manifesto, but the Pushkin cult soon made a comeback after war against the Whites and foreign armies had ended. A curious celebration of the eighty-fourth anniversary of Pushkin's death was organized by the small circle of remaining Symbolists, whose enthusiasm for the Revolution had by now waned. Alexander Blok and other speakers used much apocalyptic imagery. "The death of the poet" (after Lermontov's verse obituary for Pushkin) became a pervasive symbol for the death of Russian culture, the death of the Pushkin era under the onslaught of "the crowd" and bureaucracy. Khodasevich's prediction was typical: "Led away into the 'smoke of centuries', Pushkin will rise up as a gigantic image. Through him national pride will pour out into indestructible bronze moulds – but that direct closeness, that emotional tenderness with which we loved Pushkin, future generations will not know."[13]

Khodasevich's prophecy of the "indestructible bronze moulds" came true in 1937, the centenary of Pushkin's death, when the poet was recruited to serve the Stalinist regime. The 1937 festival was very similar to that of 1899 in many respects, and Pushkin was again a pillar of the state ideology; of course all the details of Pushkin's life which had earlier been ignored were now emphasized and exaggerated. Pushkin's friendship with some of the Decembrists and his troubled relations with Nicholas I provided the Stalinist literati with fertile ground for cultivating the new image of Pushkin the anti-monarchist revolutionary, persecuted and destroyed by the tsar. A calendar published at the time laid out the new terms:

On 10 February 1937 the peoples of the Union of the Soviet Socialist
Republics commemorate the hundredth anniversary of the death of
Alexander Sergeyevich Pushkin, that genius among their compatriots, who
was killed by an obedient agent of the autocracy and reactionary aristocracy. The bullet of the hired assassin cut short the noble path of he who
throughout his life held up to shame the Russian "crown-bearers" and their
courtly and priestly lackeys.

Pushkin died, but up to the very last moment he passionately, "with an
impatient soul", awaited the moment when the shackles of violence and
oppression would fall . . .

This dream of the great poet was realized by the Great Proletarian
Revolution under the banners of Lenin and Stalin.[14]

In 1936–7 alone, about 13.4 million volumes of Pushkin's works and Puskin
criticism were published in the Soviet Union, compared to 1.5 million during
the first post-revolutionary decade.[15] The image of Pushkin the great citizen,
Pushkin the Decembrist, and Pushkin the favourite of Marx and Lenin was fed
to successive generations of Soviet schoolchildren. Surprisingly, however,
Khodasevich's "indestructible bronze moulds" did not destroy "that direct
closeness, that emotional tenderness" which earlier generations had felt
towards Pushkin, for many readers now looked to the national poet as a source
of private strength in withstanding the pressures of the regime. Memorizing the
whole of *Eugene Onegin* became the supreme goal for some members of the
intelligentsia; there were rumours of some staving off insanity in prison by
repeating the beloved lines and thus keeping their private world alive.

The arrival of *perestroika* in the mid-1980s prompted a revival of the "My
Pushkin" style of essay. But at the same time, a minority also revived the irreverent spirit of Pisarev and the Futurists: Abram Tertz's "Strolls with Pushkin",
for example, was a mock "My Pushkin" essay which aroused particularly
fervent controversy and accusations, in effect, of blasphemy. But the official
publications for foreign consumption were wholly reverent: the bicentenary
collection of English-language essays, *Alexander Pushkin: A Celebration of
Russia's Best-Loved Writer*, begins with a sugary preface by Mikhail Gorbachev,
and contains essays such as "Pushkin for Me", "My Life with Pushkin",
"Pushkin Under Our Skin", "Russian is, Pushkin is", and many others of this
kind.[16] The cult is still very much alive today.

Glinka's tsarist opera

The story of Glinka's elevation runs parallel to that of Pushkin's (although,
granted, he is regarded as a luminary of the second rank). As we have already

mentioned, he, too, was promoted to the rank of national artist during the weeks following the première of A Life for the Tsar on 27 November 1836.[17] The circumstances could hardly have been more favourable. The opera was supposed to open the newly rebuilt Grand [*Bolshoy*] Theatre in St Petersburg, so public expectations were already heightened. The presence of Nicholas I contributed further to the excitement; he was not merely attending out of duty, but he had personally encouraged the project: Baron Rosen, the tsar's secretary, had been given leave to write the libretto, and the tsar had attended some of the rehearsals. The date of the première was itself connected to the historical figure at the centre of the opera, for 27 November was the anniversary of Ivan Susanin's heroic death, which lent further solemnity to the event (or so it was declared; at any rate, the public was willing to make the association). The conception of the opera can probably be traced back to the Tsar's pilgrimage, two years earlier, to the site outside Kostroma where Susanin's self-sacrifice was thought to have occurred. The presentation of the Poles as an enemy nation was also topical, since the Polish had only recently tried to throw off the yoke of their Russian masters. The work itself was the first Russian-language opera to be sung throughout – a decisive step upwards which had taken place in Germany only a decade earlier.[18] Everything told the assembled public that this was to be a momentous event. The opera's nationalism was acknowledged and praised by the court, intelligentsia and public. All agreed, though for different reasons, that this was how Russianness should be represented: for the court the opera was a glorification of autocracy and orthodoxy; for the intelligentsia it was the distinct voice of Russia, heard at last within Herder's family of diverse nations; for the general public, the opera took the familiar and intimate sounds of the Russian drawing-room romance, and elevated it too a grander plane. The official report on the production stated that

> all the spectators feasted their eyes on the construction and beauty of the new temple of the Muses; everyone was delighted by the sounds of our native, national Russian music . . .[19]

The liberal critics seemed to agree: "Glinka's opera is a purely Russian, national, native work";[20] "there is not one phrase which does not sound familiar to Russian ears".[21] They also provide us with some idea of the opera's impact on public consciousness (perhaps we should allow for a degree of exaggeration):

> Scarcely three weeks have passed since the first staging of A Life for the *Tsar*, and already phrases from the opera can be heard not only in the

drawing-rooms (where it is the main topic of conversation), but even in the street – a new proof of the national spirit embodied in that opera.[22]

No other major Russian work was ever received with such universal acclaim; but even in this case, tastes changed. The general public, after the initial excitement had subsided, returned to the prior, more easy-going Russian style, which was unencumbered with the complexities of Glinka's score. Perhaps most tellingly, instead of being displaced, Catterino Cavos's *Ivan Susanin* emerged unscathed, retaining its prominent place in the repertoire as if nothing had happened. The court's love affair with *A Life* was equally superficial and short-lived, and the resident Italian company was once again in much greater demand than their Russian counterparts; nevertheless, *A Life* retained its privileged position as season-opener at the Mariinsky, and was used for court festivals (such as the tsar's name day and birthday).

The liberal intelligentsia was less fickle, but by the 1860s the vigorous patriotism of *A Life* had become offensive; Stasov expressed the changed mood in uncompromising terms:

> Perhaps no one dishonoured our people so much as Glinka, who, through his music of genius, put forward the base serf Susanin as a Russian hero; that Susanin who is loyal as a dog, narrow-minded as an owl or a deaf grouse and who sacrifices his life in order to save a youngster who ought not to be saved at all, and whom he, it seems, had never even met. This is the apotheosis of the Russian swine, particularly that of the Moscow type and the Moscow era.[23]

However, the resentment of some was balanced by the desire of others to co-opt *A Life* to new causes: the Slavophiles, for example, who based their ideal of Russian statehood precisely on the same "Moscow era", were only too happy to cite the opera in their polemics. Their outlook had not changed significantly since one of their number, Alexei Khomyakov, wrote in 1844, just after seeing *A Life*:

> It was a time of troubles for Russia. There was no state, for there was no sovereign to be the expression of the state. There was no state, but family and community remained – they saved Russia. [. . .] The vote of the people elected the tsar by the Zemsky sobor; the great community closed its ranks and became a state again. [. . .] Centuries have passed. The Russian state has become stronger, but the new invasion from the West requires new resistance. This invasion is not of the sword and of power, but of learning and thought [. . .] Now the danger is not to the state, but to the community and

the family. Family and community once saved Russia: shall we be able to save family and community now?[24]

The 1860s also saw critics and composers line up behind the rival claims of *A Life* and *Ruslan*; the course of Russian opera was shaped thereafter by these divergent ideals of Russian opera and Russianness in music. The Kuchka, as we have already seen in Chapter 1, united behind *Ruslan*, while Serov, Rubinstein, and Tchaikovsky remained faithful to *A Life*. But this meant that for all of them, as well as their followers, Glinka was the uncontested source of Russian music – its Pushkin. The decline of musical nationalism by 1900 brought with it the decline of the Glinka cult; this was not paralleled in literature, for the Russian symbolists never demoted Pushkin, while the Scriabinists had no time for Glinka. Not until we arrive at Stravinsky's *Mavra* can we find anything like a musical equivalent to the "My Pushkin" essay; the work carries a very personal dedication to Pushkin, Glinka and Tchaikovsky.

The Soviet *Susanin*

During the first years after the Revolution Glinka enjoyed no special favours, and was simply lumped together with other "bourgeois" composers. His status was further compromised by the inescapable monarchism of *A Life for the Tsar*, which made the opera, unlike most Russian classics, completely unusable after 1917. And yet it was the virtues of his first opera that allowed him to rise from this disadvantageous position to the absolute top of Soviet musical hierarchy twenty years later. The story of the transformation of *A Life* into the Soviet *Ivan Susanin* is remarkable enough to be told in more detail.

In the more liberal climate of the NEP years, voices were first heard in support of bringing *A Life* back to the stage. While at the former Mariinsky, they were vaguely discussing the possibility of staging the unadulterated original,[25] in the provinces there were two attempts to salvage Glinka's music by altering the libretto and scenario. The first adaptation, produced in Odessa in 1926 under the title *Hammer and Sickle*, turned the opera into a tale of the recent Civil War. The other adaptation, produced in Baku in 1927 under the title *Minin*, with a libretto by Nikolai Krasheninnikov, was much less radical and retained the original historical setting, with the expedient of replacing references to the tsar with references to the eponymous Minin, who led the Russian army to victory in the original story. Although Krasheninnikov's libretto was originally derided in Moscow as "illiterate in every sense",[26] his adaptation was given serious consideration for a much more prestigious production at the Bolshoi Theatre, planned for the 1927/28 season under the title *Smutnoye vremya* (The time of troubles).[27] It seems that this could have become the moment of Glinka's complete rehabilitation, judging also from a very positive essay on Glinka by Ye. Vilkovir in the journal *Music and Revolution*, where his first opera, referred to as *Ivan Susanin*, was highly praised for its "progressive" nationalism.[28] The production, however, never took place, possibly because of rather low historical status of Minin at the time, who was then viewed by Soviet historians as the financier for a gang of mercenaries that installed the dictatorship of the Romanovs – at least this was cited by Nikolai Krasheninnikov, the author of the adaptation, as the principal reason for the rejection. With the end of the NEP and introduction of stricter control of the arts, the project had to be shelved. In 1929 a party functionary for music, Viktor Gorodinsky, announced that "*A Life for the Tsar* cannot be staged under any sauce".[29] As late as in 1934 Soviet critics were still obliged to lump the opera together with the tsarist national anthem as an example of the "sugary-patriotic".[30]

But in the very different climate of 1937, when Stalin was carefully cultivating a new Russian nationalism, the right moment for reviving the opera had finally come. The Committee for Artistic Affairs instructed the Bolshoi to prepare a new production under the title of *Ivan Susanin* and set up a team to carry out the task: Boris Mordvinov, who was to be the director, Samuil Samosud the conductor, and Sergei Gorodetsky was to write the new libretto in consultation with Samosud. The idea of the project could have resurfaced as an offshoot from the Pushkin celebrations, as the following statement from the team suggest:

> By the production of *Ivan Susanin* we are fulfilling on the music drama front the same task that in 1937 was given by the Soviet public and Soviet government to Soviet literature, namely to grow and develop under the banner of Pushkin. . . . Glinka is the Pushkin of Russian music.[31]

When Krasheninnikov heard of this, he complained that Gorodetsky was plagiarizing his idea. Gorodetsky had assisted Krasheninnikov at the time of the earlier, failed bid to mount a production at the Bolshoi, so he had clearly been familiar with Krasheninnikov's work. In a desperate gesture, Krasheninnikov even offered to produce a rival version for Leningrad, but this only showed how little he appreciated the situation. The Bolshoi's forthcoming *Susanin* was being presented as the true and authentic *Susanin*, as somehow closer to Glinka's intentions than the version of 1839. There was therefore no possibility that a rival version could be allowed to challenge the *Susanin* sanctioned by the highest authorities – what was unexceptionable in the late '20s was unthinkable a decade later.

According to the new official account of the opera's history, Glinka's original conception of the opera had been "brutally distorted" by the original librettist, Baron Rosen; the new version was effectively a reconstruction of that original conception. But there was hardly a shred of evidence to back this up: for example, the report written by the director, Mordvinov, could only point to the fact that in the Glinka's original plan for the opera's choral introduction, the tsar is not mentioned, while in Rosen's libretto the people celebrate the tsar's return from captivity in Poland. But this could only appear significant to someone who knew nothing else about the opera, since the drama in all three acts revolves around Mikhail Romanov: the news of his election to the throne is the most important dramatic point of Act I, and the rest of the plot is built upon this event; the only dramatic event of Act II is the hatching of the Polish conspiracy to capture the new tsar; while in Act III, the Poles attempt to execute their plan. Whether Glinka intended the first reference to the tsar to appear at the beginning of Act I or a little later is therefore of little consequence – even if Glinka's original conception of the opening chorus had been retained, the opera's strident monarchism would scarcely have been diminished.

In fact, the design of the plot was canny and sufficiently tight to deter even superficial changes. Gorodetsky's first suggestion was simply a return – unacknowledged, of course – to Krasheninnikov's version of 1927, with Minin replacing the tsar. There was now no objection to Minin, since the debunking of nationalist myths that marked '20s historiography was now determinedly forgotten. The suggestion was rejected this time on the grounds that Minin in the 1930s would provide nothing comparable to the symbolic power of Mikhail Romanov in pre-1917 productions. It was certainly not acceptable to produce a version of the opera that exuded less grandeur than the tsarist version – this would defeat the purpose of the exercise. The character of Susanin was accordingly given the role of saving the entire city of Moscow (and, by implication, all of Russia). This certainly gave him a suitably grand purpose, but made nonsense of the original scenario, so that more drastic alterations were now needed. The Poles had originally been searching for the tsar in the Kostroma district two hundred miles to the east of Moscow, but this was entirely incompatible with the new scenario. Susanin's village of Domnino had to be relocated to the outskirts of Moscow, and all references to the swamp that supposedly swallowed up the Poles was removed, since the dacha-strewn environs of Moscow are not normally associated with lethal swamps. The date of the story was also changed: the original libretto was based on events that took place in the first half of 1613, hence the spring symbolism in several numbers of Act I; the historically more vague Stalinist version is set in the autumn and combines events that took place in late 1611 and late 1612.[32]

This solution was only available at the cost of substantial damage to the opera's dramatic integrity The simple and elegant intrigue of the original libretto was based on the connection between the two *venchaniya* (a term that covers both "coronation" and "wedding"): until the lawful tsar was wedded to his country, the two young lovers, Sobinin and Antonida, could not marry – such was the arbitrary ruling of Susanin, Antonida's father.[33] The rumour of the tsar's election changes Susanin's mind, but the wedding celebrations are brutally interrupted by the appearance of the Poles, who take Susanin captive. The two desired outcomes can only take place after Susanin's self-sacrifice: then the tsar is crowned, and the newly-wedded couple joins the large public celebrations. These close parallels between the public and the private were destroyed by the plot changes of the Soviet version.

On a smaller scale, the greatest casualty was the dramatic coherence of Act I. In the original, Sobinin delivers two items of news. The first item, the victory of a Russian division in battle, is certain, but the second is only a rumour: the election of Romanov as tsar. Sobinin is hesitant to reveal this, in case it turns out to be untrue, but once the words are out, everyone celebrates, and Susanin declares that the wedding can proceed. In Gorodetsky's version. Sobinin also delivers two pieces of news: first the Russian victory, as in the original, followed by the news that Russian armies have laid siege to Polish-occupied Moscow. But now the two items are related, the first making the second possible, so there is no longer any reason for Sobinin's reluctance to divulge the second item (although this expression of reluctance remains in Gorodetsky's version). The moment of revelation thus loses its power, for both before and after, Susanin, Sobinin and the choir are given bland incantations on Russia's final victory. The Introduction to Act I was already static, more oratorio than opera, but the Stalinist version pushes this section over the brink into tedium. Act II in the original depended for its impact on the staging and choreography of a series of dances at the Polish court, a tableau between the more dramatic outer acts. But since Gorodetsky's version undermined the drama in Act I, there is no significant drama to be found in the opera until the second half of Act 3. Even then Gorodetsky was ambiguous: it is not clear whether the Polish division simply wanted Susanin to show them the way to Moscow, so that they could liberate their besieged compatriots, or to show them the way to Minin's camp some distance from the capital, in order to demoralize the Russian forces by capturing or killing one of their leaders.

Emptied of its dramatic momentum, the opera was now filled with the new Stalinist patriotism of the late '30s through the constant references to motherland, Moscow, and the Kremlin; admittedly this had a parallel in the original's constant and obsequious invocations to the tsar, but these were minor blots on the landscape, rather than a wholesale substitute for drama. Interestingly, the new libretto tilted the opera towards the Soviet oratorio genre of the '30s, of which Prokofiev's *Alexander Nevsky* is the most celebrated example.

For the officials, Glinka's music was the essential core of the opera, and the guarantor of authenticity for the new version of *Susanin*, whatever drastic changes had been wrought upon the libretto and scenario. Music itself, according to Stalin-era aesthetics, had a definite paraphrasable content (or "image", to use the Russian parlance), and it was argued that Rosen's libretto was not a true reflection of the music. Basing their argument on the contention that Glinka composed much of the music before he had a libretto, the Soviet team claimed that it was a crude, distorting *podtekstovka* – the term means "words written under the existing music", but it implies a slapdash approach. "For a century", they wrote, "this *podtekstovka* has deprived the people of a work of genius by Glinka". Thus Gorodetsky's job as the new librettist was, as he himself put it, "to guess at and to convey through words what is expressed in the sounds [of Glinka's music]", and to bring about an "emotional and stylistic equivalence between the words and the music".[34]

Here is an example of Gorodetsky's reasoning:

For example, Rosen's false words that "the people have earned their tsar" ["zasluzhili mï tsarya"] through their victory over the enemy, was accompanied in Glinka's score by a mighty allegro in an ancient mode (which begins the Finale of Act 1) – this does not correspond to the content of these words.

In this allegro, which has the remark "deciso", I read other words:

Soon our Ivan the Great	Skoro nash Ivan Velikiy
Will ring its bells	Zazvonit v kolokola,
Soon the savage enemy will perish!	Skoro sginet vorog dikiy!
Russia has gone into battle.	Rus' na boy poshla.[35]

But Gorodetsky is being disingenuous here. It was not for him alone to determine what words would best reflect Glinka's music. According to the transcripts, Pavel Kerzhentsev, chair of the Committee for Artistic Affairs, took part in the discussions over the libretto; since Kerzhentsev reported directly to Stalin, it is possible, although not confirmable, that the latter also contributed to the outcome. The archive materials testify to the enormous amount of work that went into the new text. This work occupied more than a year, and in the space of that year Gorodetsky submitted four (!) complete versions of the whole text. The evolution of the libretto moved from a relatively light revision of the existing text to a freer and more literary rendition; since this was too colourful by Socialist Realist standards, the final version was blander and historically more vague. Especially impressive is the record of Gorodetsky's work on the final hymn, "Slav'sya"; the many versions of this short chorus occupy no less than 98 pages of manuscript.[36] To show briefly how much the libretto changed during this period, let us compare one of Gorodetsky's earlier versions of the "Slav'sya" chorus with the version that was finally accepted.

[early version]

Rejoice, my Russia, in your strength	Raduysya, Rus' moya, sile svoyey
Rejoice, Motherland of the *bogatïr*s [legendary epic warriors]	Raduysya, Rodina bogatïrey
And if the enemies brew up a storm	Grozu li podnimut vragi nad toboy,
You will go into battle, terrible but full of light.	Grozna i svetla, vïydesh' smelo tï v boy.
Your rivers will foam their waves in their wrath	Reki vo gneve zapenyat volnu,
The grumbling of the forests will smash the silence	Ropot lesov sokrushit tishinu,
And your unbounded breadth will tremble	I drognet tvoya neob'yatnaya shir',
And from the heart of the earth a Bogatïr' will appear.	I vïydet iz serdtsa zemli bogatïr'.
He will look around himself without fear	Vzorom besstrashnïm vokrug povedyot,
He will breathe his soul into the breast of the people	V grud' svoyu dushu narodu vdokhnyot,
And he will joyfully rush into raging battle	I radostno brositsya v yarostnïy boy,
Taking victory as his comrade-in-arms.	Pobedu v tovarishchi vzyavshi s soboy.

[final version]

Glory, glory to you, my Russia!	Slav'sya tï, slav'sya tï, Rus' moya!
Glory to you, my native land!	Slav'sya, rodnaya moya zemlya!
Let our beloved native country	Da budet voveki vekov sil'na
Be strong for all time!	Lyubimaya nasha rodnaya strana!

Glory to the great Russian people!	Slav'sya, russkiy velikiy narod!
Glory to you for all time, from	Slav'sya voveki iz roda v rod!
generation to generation!	
Strike down with your merciless	Vragov, posyagnuvshikh na kray
mighty hand	rodnoy
The enemies who encroach upon	Razi besposhchadnoy moguchey
the native land.	rukoy!
Glory, glory to our dear warriors	Slava, slava rodnïm boytsam!
To the brave sons of our	Nashey Otchiznï otvazhnïm
motherland!	sïnam!
Who spills blood for his fatherland,	Kto krov' za otchiznu svoyu
	prol'yot,
Will never be forgotten by the people!	Togo nikogda ne zabudet narod!

The earlier version is quite colourful and rather mysterious, harking back to Gorodetsky's earlier work as a symbolist in the pre-revolutionary period. The final version, by contrast, is utterly bland and forgettable, and therefore an ideal Socialist Realist text. The lines which follow the chorus underline this: they are deliberately anachronistic, and draw the scene into the Socialist Realist present:

Here is our Kremlin!	Vot on, nash Kreml'!
All Russia is with it!	S nim vsya Rus'!
The whole world is with it!	S nim ves' mir!
Sing, the world!	Poy, ves' mir!
Be merry, Russian people!	Veselis', russkiy lyud!
Sing your songs!	Pesni poy!
A bright day, a joyful day has come	Svetlïy den', vesyolïy den' dlya nas
for us!	nastal!

Even after the final version was accepted in principle, there were further changes, and Stalin's involvement here was publicly acknowledged. The early production history of the new *Susanin* was strange. There was an initial première in late February of 1939; this was soon followed by a private showing for various dignitaries including Kalinin, Voroshilov, and Litvinov, but not Stalin himself. After this showing, the production was suspended, only to reappear in two months later with changes affecting the Introduction and Epilogue. The number of superlatives the critics showered on this "second première" already indicated that they were aware of Stalin's involvement, and a few years later this was openly stated in one of the published accounts of the production.[37] These final changes set the seal on the Socialist Realist character of the new *Susanin*, establishing it as the ideal Soviet opera. In the Epilogue, the more modest and generalized set "At the Kremlin Gates" was now replaced with a very imposing and realistic set showing Red Square, with St Basil's on the left and the Spasskiye Gates on the right. From the gates, the leaders of the Russian army, Minin and Pozharsky rode out on horseback – these two characters only existed offstage in all previous productions. The heroic appearance of these two figures, rather than a single tsar, may seem strange today, but Soviet audiences would have been aware of the iconographical references here, since they were surrounded by paired portraits, whether of Stalin and Lenin, Stalin and Marshal Voroshilov, or Marx and Engels.[38]

The transformation of the Epilogue into an almost Soviet-style military parade entailed the sacrifice of a passage which had strengthened the scene both musically and dramatically, namely the lament for Susanin, sung by his family between the two renditions of "Slav'sya". Susanin's sacrifice is no longer remembered, but Stalin had in any case placed himself at the centre of the Epilogue, in a masterful theatrical gesture. Here is the account of Elena Bulgakova, who attended the April première:

> Before the Epilogue, the government [including Stalin] moved from its usual box into the large central box formerly reserved for the tsar, and watched the rest of the opera from there. When the audience noticed this, they began to clap, and continued clapping throughout the musical interlude that precedes the epilogue. When the curtain [calls began], and particularly at the end when Minin and Pozharsky appeared on horseback, [the applause] grew ever louder until it became a tumultuous ovation. The government was applauding the cast, the cast was applauding the government, and the audience was applauding both.[39]

The 1939 *Ivan Susanin*, which proved such a perfect vehicle for a Stalinist show, catapulted Glinka into the Soviet pantheon of heroes. He even earned a mention in Stalin's address of 7 November 1941, when the Nazi troops were approaching the Moscow suburbs. As a newly appointed representative of the heroic Russian spirit, Glinka had to undergo a thorough makeover in scholarly works, popular books and films. This was no easy task, for Glinka's biography was full of unhelpful details: while Pushkin had associated with the Decembrists, Glinka socialized with staunch monarchists such as Zhukovsky and Kukolnik. His report on the fateful day of the Decembrist uprising in his memoirs was acutely embarrassing to Stalin's officials:

> Early in the morning of 14 December, the elder son of Lindquist (who was an inspector in our college) called upon us; we went to the [Senate] Square

and watched the tsar set out from the palace. To this day I have retained in my soul the magnificent and awesome appearance of our emperor. I had never seen him before. He was pale and somewhat melancholy. Crossing his arms calmly on his chest, he walked slowly, straight to the centre of the crowd, addressing it with the words, "Children, children! Go!" We spent several hours on the square; then I, spurred on by hunger (for I had not had breakfast) went off to the Bakhturins'. It is possible that this unimportant circumstance saved me from death or injury, for soon cannon shots rang out, fired at the mutineers.[40]

Glinka research reached a peak of activity in the post-war decade, when a number of monographs were published in anticipation of the 150th anniversary of the composer's birth.[41] This coincided with the period when Socialist Realism was most aggressively policed, and so *Ivan Susanin* was treated as if it were simply another Socialist Realist work. By that stage, it was already dogma that

> Pushkin and Glinka were the founders of realism in Russian art, which in this respect was far ahead of the art of other countries.[42]

Alexander Ossovsky, a prominent critic of the time, emphasized the opera's realist qualities, its consciousness of nationality and its symphonic development; but this was not based on Ossovsky's personal analysis, for these were simply three of the four cornerstones of musical Socialist Realism (the fourth was revolutionary subject matter, which Ossovsky was scrupulous enough to omit). At the end of his essay on *Ivan Susanin*, Ossovsky mentions the 1948 Party Resolution against formalism, and he dutifully makes an appeal to those composers who were condemned for their formalism to look to Glinka and learn from him.[43] Those scholars who were conscientious enough to refer to the original *A Life for the Tsar*, nevertheless had to make strenuous efforts to dissociate it from monarchism and from the Official Nationalism of the tsarist state. Glinka's approach to the subject matter, they said, came not from the desire to glorify the Romanov dynasty, but from Glinka's own experiences during the Patriotic "People's" War of 1812. Precisely what these formative experiences were we are left to guess – Glinka was only eight at the time, and beyond the fact that he and his family temporarily left their estate (which was in the path of Napoleon's army), he would not have witnessed any of the effects of the war. Given the fragility of this approach, another means of improving the opera's credentials had to be found; the solution lay in the (doubtful) claim that Glinka's principal inspiration was Kondratiy Rïleyev's verse account of the story, *Ivan Susanin*.[44] A few years after writing the poem, and fortunately for Glinka's Soviet reputation, Rïleyev joined the Decembrist conspiracy (the fact that Rïleyev's poem was recited by Lenin's older brother at the age of ten was also duly noted) – no matter that Glinka had never so much as mentioned Rïleyev's poem in his copious writings. Still worse, Rïleyev's poem was just as rich in sugary monarchism as the libretto of A Life, but fortunately the small extract which was printed in Soviet anthologies gave no clue to this. It was concluded therefore that Ivan Susanin was a true Decembrist opera, or even better, that it was in fact more progressive and democratic than the Decembrists, because of its attention to "the people".[45] Glinka's account of his behaviour and thoughts on the day of the Decembrist uprising (as quoted above) was simply declared "incredible"; this final obstacle out of the way, Glinka emerged from his Soviet makeover not only as a "people's artist of genius" and a "thinker", but also as a "fighter".[46]

Glinka at the movies

There was no better vehicle to popularize the new image of Glinka than film. Remarkably, the post-war decade saw the appearance of two biographical films on the composer: one in 1946 (Glinka, directed by Lev Arnshtam, black-and-white), the other in 1952 (Kompozitor Glinka, directed by Grigoriy Aleksandrov, colour). In the first film, there were already many things that the authors got right: Glinka's foreign travels were almost completely cut out, while his listening to Russian protyazhnïye folksongs occupied much more space. Glinka's permanent companion is a serf musician Yakov Ul'yanov who ensures his continuous connection with the people. The Decembrists' episode is of course completely falsified compared to Glinka's own account. One of the main threads in the film is Glinka's relationship with Pushkin: at the première of A Life, for example, the composer does not so much look onto the stage, as into Pushkin's box, trying to guess from his changing expressions whether his opera is a worthy one. Yet in spite of all these right steps, the film was blighted, in the eyes of Soviet officials, by the miscasting of the hero. In an attempt to bring Glinka closer to the people, the authors went for the demotic charm of Boris Chirkov, an actor famous for playing endearingly down-to-earth proletarians, most famously Maksim in The Trilogy of Maksim. His Glinka was not a believable aristocrat and spoke in a casual manner of a tractor driver. Stalin himself remarked on this: "What is this Glinka? This is Maksim and not Glinka".[47]

This explains to us why the second film had to be made so soon after the first: the canonic image of Glinka had not yet been attained on celluloid. Kompozitor Glinka was produced by an all-star team: the script was by Pyotr

Pavlenko, who previously authored *Alexander Nevsky* and two films canonizing Stalin (*The Vow* and *The Fall of Berlin*); the director was Alexandrov, Stalin's favourite; the cameraman was the masterful Eduard Tisse. The leading female role of Glinka's sister was given to Lyubov' Orlova, avowed the most beautiful woman in the country. Glinka himself was a little-known Boris Smirnov, tall and sprightly (unlike Chirkov), enunciating his lines in a perfect drama-school manner. The role of Glinka, for which he received the Stalin prize, was a great step forward in his career: from there he went on to play Lenin. Compared to the low-budget 1946 *Glinka*, with basic sets and bad lighting, no expense was spared to create a beautiful visual background, from the magnificent panoramic landscapes of Russia to colourful carnival scenes in almost credible Venice, to Orlova's magnificent gowns. Against this background, recognizable cultural luminaries (Pushkin, Dargomïzhsky, Stasov) looking very much like their standard Soviet portraits, pompously recite standard quotes from themselves. Compared to the first film, Pushkin's role as Glinka's guru is further enhanced: the film begins with their chance encounter, later there is a scene at Pushkin's house, where the host introduces Glinka to Rïleyev's *Susanin* (reciting precisely the uncontroversial passage quoted in Soviet textbooks), and in another scene, upon hearing Glinka play *Slav'sya*, seals his blessing of the composer with a kiss.

* * *

While the films impressed the Pushkin–Glinka parallel on the nation's imagination in this direct way, the scholars were busy theorizing it. Their main postulate was that

> . . . like Pushkin, who created the Russian literary language, Glinka created the Russian musical language and composed within it.[48]

The possession of an uncontaminated language had been the most important nation-defining criterion since the early nationalist writings. From Herder onwards, nationalists believed that such a language was a natural phenomenon that guaranteed the organic unity of a nation; this irreplaceable heritage, moreover, had to be protected from the dilution of foreign borrowings – only organic change was acceptable. Soviet criticism was mindful of such strictures, and so the foreign basis of Glinka's art was side-stepped (as was the case with Pushkin also). Glinka's Russianness was supposed to stem from his intimate connections with folk culture, which were grossly exaggerated. Any mainstream Soviet writing on the subject will illustrate the absurd lengths to which this blinkered nationalism was taken; in Yuly Kremlyov's *National Traits of Russian Music*, for example, even Glinka's *Valse-Fantasie*, which is altogether as Western as its name, draws the same automatic nationalism from Kremlyov:

> Where would you find a prototype of that dreamy, anxious, passionate and agitated tone poem, the *Valse-Fantasie*? Nowhere beyond the boundaries of Russian art![49]

Kremlyov brings together all the principal myths of Russian cultural nationalism in the space of a few pages. He claims, for instance, that Glinka had an "absolutely organic ability" to think like simple Russian folk, mirroring the claims made on behalf of Pushkin and other poets attempting a folk style. But as early as 1834, Belinsky had protested against all such claims:

> You will never write your own folk tale, for to do that you would have to become, so to speak, a *muzhik*; you would have to forget that you are a master (*barin*), that you had studied grammar and logic, history and philosophy. Forget all the poets, Russian and foreign: you should be completely reborn, otherwise your creation will lack that essential true naiveté of mind, a mind not enlightened by science. Your tale will lack that sly simple-heartedness which characterizes Russian folk tales. [50]

While Kremlyov's "organic ability" suggests artlessness, he goes on to contradict this by speaking of Glinka's conscious and purposeful activity: Glinka, he says, "persistently cultivated" Russian musical "intonation", borrowing not only from folksong, but also from Russian speech.[51]

The "language of music" figure greatly enhanced the ability of the nationalist Glinka cult to draw upon the more senior Pushkin cult. The Kuchka presented their work as music spoken in Glinka's "Russian musical language", a self-image retained by the Kuchka's heirs at the turn of the century. When Socialist Realism began to reheat neglected nationalist ideas, "speaking Glinka's language" once again became a desideratum for Russian composers, just as novelists and poets had to return to nineteenth-century "classic" literary styles. Khachaturian's Lezghinka from his ballet *Gayane* is very close to its prototype in *Ruslan and Lyudmila* in spite of the hundred-year gap that separates them. The abandonment of Socialist Realism in the 1980s brought the astonishingly long era of Glinka to a close for all but a few ageing professors of composition whose careers began before Stalin's death. As for Pushkin, Russians still claim to speak his language; if this is so, it is strange to find that each new generation requires an ever longer commentary to *Eugene Onegin*.

As we have seen, the Pushkin myth has always helped to feed the Glinka myth; it is rather as if Glinka were Pushkin's younger brother, elevated by the incantation, "like Pushkin, he too . . ." And not only were the artistic similarities cited, but also the biographical connections: the two artists had overlapping circles of friends and acquaintances; better still, they knew each other personally; they even collaborated on a song or two (how fitting, then, that the pinnacle of Glinka's achievement, *Ruslan*, should have been based on one of Pushkin's best-known works). Even their romantic affairs were interlinked: Pushkin had a brief, passionate affair with one Anna Kern, to whom he dedicated the lyric "Ya pomnyu chudnoye mgnoven'ye" (I recall a wonderful moment), while Glinka set the same lyric to music while he was in love with Anna's daughter, Yekaterina. These connections were sentimentalized endlessly: the hand of destiny had clearly yoked these two men of genius together, etc. But then there was a genius of still higher order – Mozart – who could elevate both Pushkin and Glinka, were they to be associated with him. It was their supposed possession of a specifically Mozartean genius that led them led them to produce works that are consistently harmonious, clear and bright. And so, like Mozart, Pushkin and Glinka were granted the rank of universal artists; this made the West's lack of interest in the two Russian artists all the more puzzling and hurtful a snub. But then again, the Russian nationalist can say that the West's lack of comprehension is a sure sign of that untranslatable mystery at the heart of Russia.

CHAPTER 3

GLINKA'S THREE ATTEMPTS AT RUSSIANNESS

A Life for the Tsar

From the critical reception of *A Life for the Tsar* it is clear that the discourse of cultural nationalism was already widespread and well developed in the Russia of 1836. In contemporary reviews we find nearly every theme of later-nineteenth century nationalist writings already in place: there are countless evocations of the Russian soul or spirit, blatant exaggeration of the original "Russianness" of the work in question, and prophesies of "the era of Russian music . . . when Russia will be able to offer Europe the fruits of her spiritual life"[1] and thus "renew the senescent artistic life of its mentor".[2] But it should not be imagined that Glinka's opera initiated the discourse of musical nationalism; for decades preceding its appearance, critics had been searching assiduously for signs of Russian identity in operas, and they were unsparing in their praise whenever they found any signs of this. As early as 1808, an anonymous critic wrote thus about Sokolovsky's comic opera, *The Miller – A Sorcerer, Cheat and Matchmaker* (first produced in 1779):

> [I]t was performed nearly two hundred times in a row at a time when we had already become familiar with many foreign spectacles. And even today we still watch this old opera. But are our ears and hearts instinctively attracted to it? Without a doubt because *The Miller* is a native Russian work.[3]

Another perennial success, *Starinnïye svyatki* (*Old Christmastide*), an opera by F. Blyma (first produced in 1798 or 1800 according to different sources) was also praised by an anonymous reviewer in similar terms:

> Why does the audience always watch it with great pleasure, even though the action is very slow and not very engaging? – because the songs and choruses

in the *Old Chrismastide* are made for Russian ears; because the spectators see in it honesty, hospitality, mores and customs . . . in a word, everything as it used to be long ago in Russia and in white-stone Moscow.[4]

And so we see that Glinka's opera was not the first to be regarded as specifically Russian in its design and style, nor was Glinka the first to be called a national (*narodnïy*) composer: according to the mid-nineteenth century historian V. Morkov, such an honour was bestowed on the Russified Italian Cavos, after his opera *Ivan Susanin*.[5] But while critical reaction to *A Life* was couched in familiar rhetoric, many of its reviewers were nevertheless at pains to emphasize that this opera was a watershed, a new beginning that superseded everything that came before. One of these critics, Feofil Tolstoy, recalled his first impressions of Glinka's opera thus:

> When I heard [*A Life*] for the first time, in its entirety and on stage, I was so astonished by the depth and breadth of its conception – which sought to elevate Russian folk tunes into a jewel of Nature – that all music which had been written prior to this on Russian texts seemed like childish babble.[6]

Other contemporary reviewers – Odoyevsky, Yanuary Neverov and Nikolai Melgunov – were of like mind.[7] In Neverov's review, for example, a distinction is made between the inferior Russianness of Verstovsky and the superior Russianness of Glinka: while Verstovsky's operas "consist of nothing more than a collection of mainly charming Russian motives joined together by German choruses and quartets and Italian recitatives", Glinka "has delved deep into the character of our nation's folk music, observed all its characteristics, learned and mastered the music, and then has given complete freedom to his own fantasy, which has created images which are purely Russian and symbolize our homeland".[8]

Melgunov wrote along similar lines, but made even more far-reaching claims for Glinka's Russianness:

> [Glinka] had a different understanding of the terms "Russian music" and "Russian opera" from his predecessors. He did not limit himself by imitating folk tunes more or less closely; no – he has deeply studied the makeup of Russian songs, the exact manner of their performance by the people, those shrieks, those sudden changes from grave to lively, from loud to soft, the chiaroscuro, surprises of every kind, the peculiar harmony which does not follow any accepted rules and the peculiar development of musical periods. In a word, he discovered the whole system of Russian melody and harmony, drawn from folk music itself and different from any of the old schools.[9]

With no apparent concern for consistency, the reviewers also took delight in the fact that Glinka's opera was technically and artistically on a par with Western European music. Odoyevsky praised Glinka's initiation into "all the secrets of Italian singing and Germany harmony"[10] as well as his "skilful counterpoint and musical intricacies".[11] Moreover, Glinka not only managed to emulate various Western techniques, but, according to Neverov, he produced a score that was "new, fresh and original, from the basic idea through to the last details of its realization".[12] This gave Neverov reason to hope that Europeans "will be able to take advantage of the new ideas developed by our maestro".[13]

While most of the contemporary reviews of *A Life* placed equal emphasis on Glinka's Russianness *and* on the fact that his compositional technique stood up to the highest European standards, Stasov's obituary of Glinka, twenty years later, ditched the latter in order not to compromise the explicitly Slavophile cause to which he had enlisted Glinka posthumously; it was this obituary which set the tone for what was to become the mainstream view of Glinka. Stasov was solely concerned with the opera's place in the history of Russian music; accordingly, he heaped praise on Melgunov's exaggerated nationalist claims while ridiculing those who imagined they were honouring Glinka by ranking him alongside Bellini or Meyerbeer. Nor was Stasov's perspective restricted to bourgeois criticism of the tsarist era: the commentators who served Stalin's bureaucracy were still more diligent in avoiding any mention of possible Western influences upon Glinka; for them, the opera stood as the foundation of a Russian musical culture that had developed independently of the West. The next section will question the various nationalist claims made on behalf of *A Life*, while the section that follows will assess the opera as a progressive work fully within the European tradition.

"Russian through and through"

Although Neverov's description "Russian through and through"[14] was accepted from the start by Russian critics and public alike, no Western listener coming to the opera for the first time would notice anything to distinguish the work as Russian – there is nothing exotic or un-Western to suggest a distinct national identity. The Russian features of Glinka's style in fact stem largely from urban culture, rather than peasant culture. While Glinka only quotes popular melodies twice within *A Life* (and elsewhere only in *Kamarinskaya*), the details of his many Russian-style melodies indicate a keen observation of all that was most characteristic of the popular melodies.[15] The popular models for the women's chorus of the Introduction and the Wedding Chorus have been pointed out by Russian scholars V. Protopopov and Ye. Kann-Novikova and reproduced by David Brown.[16] Richard Taruskin has also found a most convincing correlation between Vanya's Song and two songs from the Lvov-Prach collection (Nos 21 and 25).[17] The latter collection was widely known: even Beethoven had used it when composing his *Rasumovsky* quartets; it was not, of course, a set of transcriptions of credible ethnomusicological standing, but a book of melodies at several removes from the peasant originals, supplied with conventionally harmonized piano accompaniments.[18] Aside from one solitary, and very modest case, which we shall discuss later, Glinka never came closer to Russian peasant music than Lvov-Prach; or to put it another way: throughout his career Glinka barely advanced beyond Beethoven as a scholar of Russian peasant music. Although one would hardly know it from the existing literature, both Russian and Western, Glinka's Russian style in *A Life* was not a breakthrough, but simply a continuation of the Russian operatic tradition, perhaps better executed but no closer to peasant life.

The first chorus of the Introduction "V buryu vo grozu" (In storm and gale) provides the opera with an opening that genuinely reflects one aspect of peasant practice: the alternation of tenor solo and male chorus (Ex.3.1). But Glinka had not hit upon anything novel. This form, a chorus in which a soloist (*zapevala*) sings the first lines of each strophe, was used in Russian opera as early as 1787, in Fomin's *Yamshchiki na podstave* (Coachmen at the Inn). The attempt to represent folk polyphony by employing a changeable number of voices, as well as bringing voices into the unison at cadences, had also previously been explored by a number of composers, an early example being the women's a cappella chorus from A. Titov's *Devichnik* (The Bride's Party) of 1809 (Ex.3.2). In Glinka's harmonic scheme, a full "Western" cadence is attached to every modal centre of the folk-inspired melody (I, vi and V in G

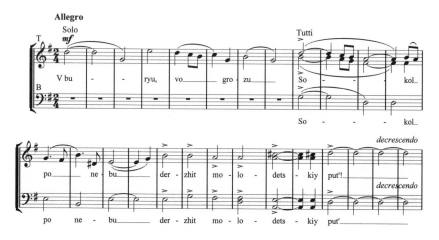

3.1   Glinka, opening chorus from *A Life for the Tsar*

3.2 Titov, women's chorus from the opera *Devichnik*

major), but this is in fact very similar to Fomin's chorus, which briefly modulates onto the same degrees. The idea of coupling a *protyazhnaya* with a fast dance-like song was also familiar to Glinka's audience, thanks to Daniil Kashin's very popular "air russe national" of 1829, "Luchina, luchinushka" (O torch, my little torch) which employed this combination within a standard cavatina-cabaletta design (Ex.3.3). The device of developing folk-style themes contrapuntally (as in the fugal chorus from the Introduction) was already featured in the opening chorus of Cavos's *Ivan Susanin*, the immediate precursor of Glinka's opera (see Ex.3.4). In short, Glinka's opening fell within well-established traditions of evoking Russianness in music.

3.3a Kashin, "Luchina, luchinushka" – Introduction

3.3b   Kashin, "Luchina, luchinushka" – Beginning of the slow section

3.3c   Kashin, "Luchina, luchinushka" – Beginning of the fast section

The following number, Antonida's cavatina (Ex.3.5), once again begins with a *protyazhnaya*, but much of the vocal writing stands fully within the Italian coloratura tradition. Russian commentators preferred to ignore the latter, and focused on the *protyazhnaya* aspect of the number, as did the nineteenth-century music-historian Mikhail Ivanov:

[T]he cavatina was doubtless a novelty at the time: there Glinka felicitously employs florid passages characteristic of our lyrical folksongs. The cavatina ought to have amazed the audience through its similarity to folk tunes, and

3.4   Cavos, opening chorus from the opera *Ivan Susanin*

3.5   Glinka, Antonida's cavatina from *A Life for the Tsar*

indeed Arnold, Serov, Tolstoy and other contemporaries agree that this was the case.[19]

But Ivanov exaggerates when he speaks of a "novelty" which would have "amazed the audience", since Glinka's cavatina appears to be modelled on Kashin's "Luchina" (Ex.3.3), even down to the prominent use of solo clarinet.[20]

The drawing-room folklore style, which was based on the *protyazhnaya*, assimilated a certain amount of the Italianate operatic style; in most songs within the genre, it would be difficult to declare any particular phrase to be either Italianate or folk-like. It is instructive in this respect to compare Glinka's *protyazhnaya*-like cavatina with two contemporary transcriptions of a *protyazhnaya* (Ex.3.6; the *protyazhnaya* is "Akh, ne odna vo pole dorozhen'ka"). The melodic motion in the chosen phrase is a typical *protyazhnaya* melisma, a decorated linear descent from 5 to 1. First we have a version by Rupin which slightly pre-dates *A Life* (Ex.3.6a); Rupin's melisma is not notably Italianate, but neither is it incompatible with the drawing-room style of the time. We can check Rupin against a much later transcription from a phonographic recording by Linyova (Ex.3.6b); this is significantly more alien, but demonstrates that Rupin's approach was scrupulous by the standards of his time (its melodic contours are close throughout to Linyova). Then we have

3.6   Examples of decorated linear descent from $\hat{5}$ to $\hat{1}$ in Russian and Italian music

the version by Gurilyov (Ex.3.6c), written a few years after *A Life*, which is much further from Linyova, and which incorporates a feature which is nowhere to be found in Russian folk music: the diminished fourth at the end of the phrase. Similar phrases are, on the other hand, easy to find in Italian opera, for example a phrase from Bellini's *Norma* (Ex.3.6d) includes the same descent from 5 to 1 with the final note immediately preceded by the same diminished fourth. The Gurilyov and Bellini are in turn very similar to the opening phrase of Glinka's cavatina (Ex.3.6e); again in the descent from 5 to 1, the final note is preceded by a diminished fourth. And what applies to this short phrase applies equally to Glinka's adoption of the drawing-room folklore style for *A Life*.

A particularly subtle illustration of the Italian–Russian amalgam can be found in the numerous upward octave leaps in the Introduction. In the short orchestral ritornello between the strophes of the men's chorus (Ex.3.7a), an ascending octave leap is used mid-phrase as part of the approach to the cadence; octave leaps used in a similar way are a common feature of Italian opera (Ex.3.7b). In the theme of the women's chorus, however, an ascending octave leap appears *after* the cadence, as a decoration of the final tonic note (Ex.3.7c); this is certainly not a feature of Italian operatic writing, but it is, in fact, idiomatic within Russian folksong, as some of Glinka's predecessors had evidently noticed (see Ex.3.7d, the peasants' chorus from Verstovsky's *Askold's*

3.7a Glinka, opening chorus from *A Life for the Tsar* (orchestral ritornello between two of the verses)

3.7b Rossini, *Mosé in Egitto*, Act I, duet of Osiride and Elcia

3.7c Glinka, *A Life for the Tsar,* women's chorus from the Introduction (orchestral parts omitted)

3.7d Verstovsky, *Askold's Tomb*, peasants' chorus (solo part only)

Tomb).[21] As we saw earlier, Glinka generally prefers to avoid unresolved eclecticism and merges the two styles, but here, exceptionally, he plays the two styles off against each other.

A further aspect of *A Life*'s Russianness is the Glinka's prominent use of the romance style, which is to be found in the Trio of Act I, Antonida's romance, Susanin's aria and some shorter arioso passages. The Russian romance style was a distillation of influences from French chanson, German lied and Italian opera, so that any Western listener unfamiliar with the Russian genre would simply register a cosmopolitan mélange on hearing these numbers from *A Life*.

To the Russian listener, however, these passages sounded characteristically Russian, because this particular combination of harmonies, melodic figures and formal schemes had become firmly associated with the romance since the early 1820s; since the ability to produce competent examples of the genre – both lyric and music – was considered a standard gentlemanly accomplishment, it is not surprising that a narrow repertoire of devices was soon established, for originality was not of the essence, and romantic doctrines of genius were entirely out of place. (One might say that this was the closest Russian equivalent to Biedermeier.) Most romances are ternary in form, the overwhelming majority beginning and ending in the minor mode with a middle section in the relative major; the first eight bars usually outline the progression I–iv–V–I, and this is soon followed by a modulation. The phrasing is regular, and the accompanimental texture characteristically guitar-like, or piano-like (this feature survives in Glinka's orchestral accompaniments to the romance-type numbers in *A Life*). Virtuosity was by no means a defining feature of the romance vocal line, but a moderate amount of display was considered acceptable. The romance was primarily for private, domestic performance, and pitched at the level of practised amateurs. The characteristic mood is homely sentimentality. Just as we saw with folksong, Glinka was not the first to introduce this genre to opera, but was following familiar precedent. Indeed, the romance style was already a default in the operas of Verstovsky, to be found not only in the many numbers expressly labelled as romances, but also in many of the arias and ensembles. Glinka is more sparing: in *A Life*, the romance style is reserved for moments of intense emotion; evidently he considered the romance more suitable for expressing the emotional states of an individual, whereas folk styles were more communal, and therefore less personal.

Amidst the Russianness of the romance style and the drawing-room folklore style, only one passage stands out as something quite different: this is the music at Susanin's entry, known in the literature as the "song of a Luga coachman", which Glinka had transcribed himself. It stands in sharp relief to the melodies of the drawing-room folklore style through its remoteness from conventional melodic figures and conventional phraseology. According to Levashev, the melody was associated with an indecent text, and since this was well known to the public, Glinka's choice caused some embarrassment.[22] While a phrase once uttered by an unknown aristocrat in connection with Glinka's music – "C'est la musique des cochers"[23] – has frequently been mocked within Glinkiana, Levashev's observation suddenly casts new light upon it. One can only suppose that Glinka was sufficiently proud of his solitary exercise in transcription to insert the melody in the opera without any attempt to assimilate it to the drawing-room folklore style.

The mere presence of Russian-style material in *A Life* (whether romance or folklore) would not have been worth remarking upon at the première, given the many precedents over the previous decades. It was rather the *consistency* of Glinka's Russian style throughout the opera that invited so much interest. In the Russian scenes of the opera, almost every number, and even the orchestral interludes were united by the Russian style, and the stylistic connections were further strengthened by the repetition of characteristic melodic patterns in different parts of each scene (Ex.3.8). The result was perceived as a change in quality, not merely a change in quantity, for the Russian style was now available as a default, sustainable over the course of an entire opera, whereas before it had only been used to give local colour to particular numbers. Critics such as Odoyevsky and Neverov saw the possibility of Russian opera becoming an equal counterpart to Italian opera, instead of a mere national offshoot. Their hopes were not fulfilled: Glinka's second and last opera abandoned the Russianness of *A Life*, and those composers of the next generation who looked

3.8 Glinka, *A Life for the Tsar*, similar melodic patterns – (a) Orchestral link to Antonida's cavatina (b) Introduction to Antonida's cavatina (c) Antonina's cavatina (the cabaletta section) (d) Sobinin's solo in Act I (e) Susanin's solo in Act I

to *A Life* as their model, like Rubinstein in his *Kulikovskaya bitva*, Villebois in his *Natasha*, or Napravnik in his *Nizhegorodtsï* were by general assent much less successful.

The continuity and coherence of the Russian style in *A Life*, although a very significant advance on earlier Russian opera, was exaggerated by the critics. In the less inspired numbers, Glinka did indeed produce some rather conventional Italian writing, especially in the part of Sobinin, the dashing character who came closest to the Italian heroic tenor. Melgunov's claim that "Glinka discovered the whole system of Russian melody and harmony" was typical in this respect,[24] and these words set Stasov and other nationalist commentators on the search for folk-based modal harmony in *A Life*.[25] Yet for the most part Glinka follows the practice that we have described earlier, to represent the modal features of folksong by the means of conventional harmony, modulating conventionally to whichever scale degree seems like a local tonic. Glinka turned this existing practice into his own persistent stylistic feature, and used it in a wide variety of contexts. In Ex.3.9a, b, and c we can see that Glinka's favoured harmonic canvas (the tonic major/relative minor pair, with their respective dominants and occasionally subdominants) can form the basis for everything from a short *protyazhnaya*-style duet up to an entire *scena*. Though each cadential progression sounds perfectly Western in isolation, the continual re-circulation reflected the peculiarities of Russian popular song, already familiar to Glinka's audience; and in turn, these patterns in popular song reflected a characteristic of peasant singing, albeit filtered through triadic tonality.

A Life offers us only a single brief example of a modal melody prompting a modal progression: this occurs in the so-called "song of a Luga coachman" (Susanin's entry, Act I) already discussed above. Glinka's problems in arriving at a suitable harmonization are suggested even by the finished score: on its first statement, the melody is left unaccompanied; the second statement is modified so that it can be accommodated to standard harmony (Ex.3.10a); only the third statement offers a harmonized version of the unaltered melody, and this is only achieved through the modal progression just mentioned (Ex.3.10b). And whenever the melody reappears later (in the same scene and then in the recollection of this material in Act IV), Glinka truncates it, removing the characteristically modal features, so that the harmonization is unproblematic. Nationalist commentators following Melgunov's claim that *A Life* presents "the whole system of Russian melody and harmony" have to fight shy of details, for if they did not, they would have to admit that Glinka only provided harmony to one folk melody that had not already been assimilated to drawing-room tastes by collectors, and on that occasion he proved much more willing to sacrifice the melody to harmonic conventions than the

3.9a Glinka, *A Life for the Tsar*, beginning of the overture

reverse. Let us be clear: this cannot be regarded as the foundation stone for the "system of Russian melody and harmony", but, on the contrary, it is evidence that Glinka, for one, had no interest in any such thing.

The critics often tell us that they are praising this or that aspect of *A Life*'s Russianness, when in fact their comments are only general tributes to Glinka's refined compositional technique. Thus Odoyevsky on the rowers' chorus:

> You need to listen to this chorus in order to understand the effect it produces. In the instrumentation [the use of] pizzicato is especially remarkable, separating itself completely from the singing: here the balalaika is elevated to the level of art. The effect produced by this chorus is simply beyond description.[26]

3.9b Glinka, *A Life for the Tsar*, Act III, quartet

3.9c   Glinka, *A Life for the Tsar*, Act III, duet of Vanya and Susanin

Odoyevsky appears to be praising the Russianness of Glinka's balalaika imitations using pizzicato strings. But as Odoyevsky well knew, this had already been done just as effectively nearly half a century earlier, in Fomin's *Coachmen* (the Trio with Chorus), and again in various operas of the intervening decades. What Odoyevsky is admiring here, is rather the independence of the busy orchestral part from the slowly flowing choral melody (Ex.3.11), in the

3.10   Glinka, *A Life for the Tsar*, scene with Susanin and chorus from Act I

3.11   Glinka, *A Life for the Tsar*, rowers' chorus from Act I

manner of the Guards' duet in Glinka's favourite, *The Magic Flute*. It is not the balalaika imitation in itself that intrigues Odoyevsky, but rather Glinka's ability to transfigure the raw material of folk art into high art. Let us now explore this other side of *A Life*'s reception – the claims that it was the equal or superior of its European counterparts.

"Europe will be amazed"

In his review of *A Life*'s première, Neverov boldly predicted that "Europe will be amazed" and will "take advantage of the new ideas developed by our maestro";[27] but Europe, on the contrary, has still barely noticed, even after the best part of two centuries.[28] The planned simultaneous publication of the score in Russia and in Germany (with a performable translation) collapsed on

the German side. The excerpts from the opera that were performed before the
Paris public under the baton of Berlioz were ill selected: they were not the
most striking passages, and failed to give a fair impression of the opera. In
general, Russian opera was overlooked by Western audiences throughout the
nineteenth century, and by the time Diaghilev's *Saisons Russes* finally reversed
the situation, Glinka's opportunity to capture the West had long since passed:
his music could no longer sound sufficiently progressive or exotic at a distance
of eight decades. But although Neverov had failed to predict events, his judgement of the opera's potential was not amiss. We shall now examine *A Life* in
the context of European opera, to see what contributions it made to that
tradition, and why it could have made an impact in Europe if only the circumstances had been more propitious. At the same time, this exercise forces us to
set aside the Russian context that has dominated all previous literature on
A Life.

Two musical languages

The struggle between Russians and Poles in *A Life* is reflected in the music:
against the backdrop of the default Russian style, the Polish scenes stand out
in bold relief. The Russian style is dominated by duple time, whereas the
Polish scenes are largely cast in triple time. The Polish style already appears in
the overture, but Glinka chose not to follow the model provided by Beethoven
in the *Egmont* Overture, where the Spaniards and Netherlanders are given
thematic material of equal importance; instead, he relegates the Polish style to
non-thematic passages in the transition and at the beginning of the coda,
leaving all the themes in the Russian style – this is, of course, in keeping with
the subordinate role of the Poles and their music in the main body of the
opera.

In order to make the Polish style sufficiently distinct, Glinka had to purge
the Russian style of any obvious Polish dance idioms, for the polonaise,
mazurka and krakowiak were mainstays of the ballroom repertoire in St
Petersburg, and had already become embedded in Russian opera. The great
majority of Glinka's audience would have found these just as familiar as
romances and drawing-room folklore, but within the frame of the opera,
Glinka had to persuade that audience, by musical means, to hear the dances as
specifically Polish. His task was therefore more difficult than the Kuchka's, a
few decades later, when the music of Russian opera often hinged around the
opposition between the Russian style and the Oriental style, where the latter
was heard as something exotic and outside everyday life. Glinka did make one
exception: the lyric polonaise. This genre that had been established in Russian
music as early as the 1790s, by Michal Oginski, and many of his polonaises

remained popular well into the nineteenth century – indeed, the "Farewell to the Motherland", is still well-known today. The genre soon became assimilated within the romance and opera; Verstovsky's operas contain many sung numbers *alla polacca,* such as the girls' chorus from *Askold's Tomb,* Act III (Ex.3.12a). In *A Life,* we find two passages in this style (both from Act III): the middle section of Antonida's romance (Ex.3.12b) and the chorus "Mï na rabotu v les" (We are off to work in the wood) (Ex.3.12c). Fortunately, these two passages do not jeopardize the distinction between Polish and Russian styles, since the Russian polonaises lack the characteristic dance rhythms of the Polish polonaises. At the risk of being pedantic, the final chorus "Slav'sya" (Glory) also has Polish connections, since it has been shown that the eighteenth-century part-song genre on which it is based, *kant,* is Polish in its origins;[29] Glinka's audience, of course, would have known nothing of this. In general, the Polish side is represented only by dance music of the three types mentioned, either orchestral or with the addition of chorus where needed; this is easily sufficient to distinguish the Polish scenes from the rich and variegated Russian style heard in the rest of the opera.

The distribution of the Polish scenes across the opera was carefully planned: Act I is entirely Russian, establishing the work's musical default; Act II is entirely Polish, but largely given over to dances – a possibility offered by the French divertissement tradition; Acts III and IV both contain a mixture of Russian and Polish scenes. Although the Polish music remains subordinate within this scheme, it still occupies a substantial proportion of the opera, forcing Glinka to produce something more sophisticated than the occasional formulaic splash of local colour; we therefore find a wide variety of Polish themes, many of which are subjected to symphonic development (recall the restriction of Polish material in the Overture to developmental or transitional passages). This symphonic approach in the Polish scenes is at its most complex in the mazurka-finale of Act II, which builds up into something akin to a large truncated sonata form. This is in clear contrast to the rest of the opera, for Glinka chose not to subject the Russian themes to symphonic development. Glinka also succeeded in moulding the Polish dance types to varying moods: in Acts III and IV, we find apposite mazurkas to complement characters displaying aggression, cunning, or weary clumsiness.[30] If we compare this to other European operas that contain musical depictions of foreignness, we find that the subsidiary exotic colour, while often striking enough, is much more restricted in scope: it is less adaptable to different dramatic situations, and not absorbed into symphonic development (this applies even to such a sophisticated example as *Aida*). Because *A Life* was never able to influence the wider European tradition, we have to look to the next generation of Russian composers to find obvious successors. Musorgsky's *Boris Godunov* draws from

3.12a Verstovsky, *Askold's Tomb*, girls' chorus from Act III

A Life in its depiction of the Poles in Act III, as does Rimsky-Korsakov's *Pan Voyevoda*, which follows Glinka in presenting the Poles as a dancing nation. Borodin's *Prince Igor* even surpasses *A Life* in the imaginative and varied treatment of the enemy camp's distinctive music. Rimsky-Korsakov tried to recreate Glinka's musical delineation of two nations at war in *Kitezh*, reinforcing a Russian tradition which extends as far as Prokofiev's *Alexander Nevsky*.

3.12b Glinka, *A Life for the Tsar*, Act III, Antonida's romance

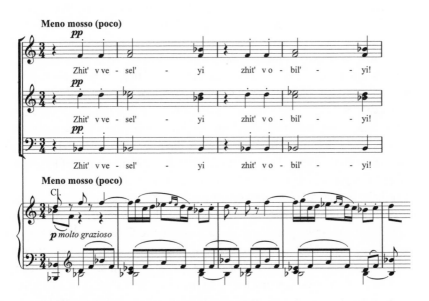

3.12c Glinka, *A Life for the Tsar*, Act III, Peasants' Chorus

Recitative and characterization

[Glinka] has also created a unique type of recitative and has thus enriched art with new ideas. His new recitatives are unlike either German or Italian ones; they combine the expressiveness and the dramatic variation of the former with the melodiousness of the latter . . .[31]

Glinka did not merely eschew spoken dialogue for the first time in a Russian-language opera – he also chose not to avail himself of the obvious replacement: standard recitative. In its place, he employed what he called "recitative *chantant*": a flexible arioso, sometimes used throughout a number, and on occasion incorporating the chorus in a dialogue with soloists; in general, there is little that resembles normal parlando recitative.[32] Glinka's recitative *chantant* should not be regarded as a precursor of the innovations found in the recitative of Dargomïzhsky or Musorgsky; Dargomïzhsky's recitative was intended to reflect the smallest nuances of the text, while Musorgsky's recitative was designed to reflect the intonational patterns of Russian speech. Glinka's concern was twofold: the avoidance of parlando recitative would distance his work from Italian opera, and at the same time promote greater musical continuity across the span of each act.[33] In Ex.3.13, we can see from a number of Susanin's recitative *chantant* phrases how a family resemblance is maintained: witness the two-quaver upbeat at the beginning of some phrases, or the three-quaver upbeat pattern at the end of phrases, together with a stepwise descent of a fourth. Recitative *chantant* also allows Glinka to provide each of the four main characters with a distinctive voice throughout the opera, and not merely in arias: Susanin is *vazhnïy* (weighty, solemn), Antonida tender and gracious, Sobinin *udalïy* (daring, bold, dashing), and Vanya simple-hearted, or naïve. Sobinin, for example, often sings phrases in the manner of Russian soldiers' songs, wholly appropriate for his *udalïy* character. Remarkably though, when the situation calls for a different emotion, he changes his tone but preserves his characteristic melodic features, for example, when Sobinin has to console his distraught fiancée after Susanin's departure with the Poles (Ex.3.14b illustrates the tender Sobinin of this scene, against Ex.3.14a, which shows us the usual dashing Sobinin).

Glinka's "recitative *chantant*" sometimes continues into ensemble passages, and even here characterization is preserved. Sobinin's return in Act I illustrates this: the melodic phrases given to Sobinin and Susanin are kept distinct throughout, even where a convergence in mood is eventually required for dramatic reasons. At the beginning of the scene, Sobinin sings longer, song-like phrases with wide upward leaps, appropriate to his youthful excitement on seeing his fiancée once again (Ex.3.14a); Susanin soon interrupts Sobinin's

3.13 Glinka, *A Life for the Tsar*, Act I, Susanin's phrases in the scene with Sobinin and chorus

3.14a Glinka, *A Life for the Tsar*, Act I, Sobinin's entry

brillante, demanding news from the front – his shorter, more weighty phrases are marked *maestoso* (Ex.3.13a). Sobinin fails to reply, and returns to the subject of his forthcoming wedding; here his coloratura is, appropriately, very close to passages in Antonida's cavatina. But Susanin persists, and Sobinin finally speaks of the war; at the same time, his music shifts to the *maestoso* character previously reserved for Susanin. Now that the minds of both characters are focused on graver matters, Glinka quickly distinguishes the parts again, in new, more subtle ways. Sobinin gives his account of the battle in short *risoluto* phrases, but still using the same dotted rhythms we saw in Ex.3.14a, while Susanin expresses his concern through material of his own (*marcato assai*); finally Antonida joins them with a flowing romance-style melody marked *spianato*.

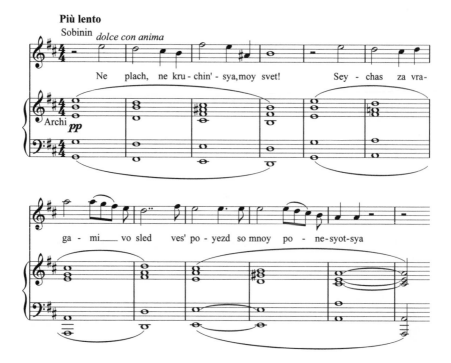

3.14b   Glinka, *A Life for the Tsar*, Act III, Sobinin's solo

Dramatic sophistication

A Life has many more static scenes than any contemporary French opera: the principal conflict is kept simple and the drama only begins to unfold near the end of Act III. Nevertheless, the efficient organization of the dramatic scenes and the deft coupling of the music with the action compensate for the fact that only a small proportion of the opera moves the plot forward. One of these couplings is to be found at the arrival of the Poles, disrupting the benign calm of Susanin's home: by using the principal motive from the Act II polonaise, Glinka warns the audience of the Poles' lurking presence, before Susanin, Antonida and Sobinin are aware of the danger. Later in the same scene, when Susanin is surrounded by the Poles, he agrees to their conditions; we know that he is feigning only because he sings entirely out of character, specifically by adopting the main theme from the Act II mazurka. After Susanin has been led away, leaving behind a distraught Antonida, the bridesmaids arrive, expecting the nuptials to begin; since Russian tradition calls for ritual lamenting and weeping from the bride, the bridesmaids think nothing of Antonida's tears. For this reason, the Wedding Chorus the bridesmaids sing is not a dramatic mismatch, as some Western listeners might imagine, but a reflection of the bridesmaids' understandable misinterpretation of the evidence before them. Glinka then adapts a melancholy romance from his earlier years as a vehicle for Antonida's explanation; a refrain in the original is now given to the chorus of bridesmaids, as they react to Antonida's account of recent events.

We have already noted that Glinka allowed Susanin to sing against type for straightforward dramatic reasons, namely that he was dissembling before the Poles. In Susanin's final scene, however, the course of the drama requires something much more ambitious. Susanin, after all, is facing a terrible death at the hands of his captors, and Glinka prefers to follow the inner thoughts of his character at such a moment rather than the unflinching courage Susanin maintains in front of the Poles. The latter would have allowed Glinka to remain within the musical vocabulary he had already created for Susanin, whereas the former requires music that reflects first Susanin's anguish, and then his rallying as he remembers the grander scheme that requires his death. Thus in the arioso, "O stormy night", Susanin is tormented by the thought that he shall never see his family again, and for a moment succumbs to despair. Then the arioso is transformed as Susanin experiences an ecstatic vision of the tsar restored to his throne with divine blessing.

Technical prowess

Before *A Life*, Glinka's accomplishment as a composer was by no means unique within Russia. He had written many songs and variations on popular operatic themes; the height of his ambitions had been chamber works, written in an accomplished but unoriginal Biedermeier style. Other composers of the Russian gentry had equalled him in these respects, and those who had also written operas enjoyed far greater public renown. After *A Life*, this was no longer true. It was not only the scale of the opera, but also its density: *A Life* was a sustained exercise in compositional virtuosity; Russia had never produced anything remotely similar, and if *A Life* had gained a European audience, it would still have been considered an extraordinary feat. The romance genre had precluded large-scale development and technical display, and even Glinka's chamber works give little warning that such a work as *A Life* could be produced by the same hand. Glinka's oeuvre up to this point leaves the emergence of this opera a mystery, but if we turn to his biography, we find some details which offer a partial explanation. Glinka had always been fasci-nated by technique, and his desire for self-improvement led him to study harmony and counterpoint under Siegfried Dehn in Berlin during the mid 1830s; the composition of *A Life* followed immediately on his return to St Petersburg, and the fruits of his many exercises for Dehn are evident.

But if Glinka had merely returned with academic techniques, he could have turned his new opera into a dry Kapellmeister's oratorio; crucially, he also had the imaginative resources to translate academic techniques into fresh and engaging music that enhanced the dramatic impact of his opera. Let us take the chorus of the Introduction, which has been misconstrued, for opposing reasons, by Russian and Western commentators alike. Russian commentators call the chorus a double fugue, and emphasize the learned aspect to the exclusion of everything else, so eager are they to rebut Western accusations that Russian music is devoid of intellectual substance. Western commentators have rightly dismissed the idea that the chorus constitutes a true double fugue; like their Russian counterparts, they assume that Glinka intended the number to be a contrapuntal tour de force throughout, but criticize Glinka for failing to live up to these aspirations.[34] In fact Glinka never described the chorus as a fugue, double or otherwise; the most he ever said was that "the chorus proceeds fugally", which it certainly does, for substantial passages.[35] A fortiori, he did not think of the chorus as a double fugue. There are two themes heard prior to the beginning of the fugal passages, the first allocated to the male voices, the second to the female voices. The men's theme returns as the subject of a fugal exposition, but the women's theme remains homophonic on every reappearance. The form of the chorus is strophic variation: every strophe beginning with the men's theme varied fugally, followed by the women's homophonic refrain, which now employs only the second half of the original melody (Ex.3.15). Both themes contain a shared motif, which Glinka exploits fully by the end of the number. Once this framework is accepted, Glinka's large-scale handling of the fugal passages turns out to be quite ingenious: in effect, he does write a complete single-subject fugue, but this is periodically interrupted by the women's refrain, which stands outside the fugal structure. The first fugato serves as a three-voice exposition, the second a counter-exposition with two entries, the third, a development with modulations into minor keys and stretto entries, the fourth a reprise with initial entries in closer stretto. Both the third and the fourth fugatos begin early, overlapping with the women's chorus, but only in the fourth is material from the women's theme reincorporated in the orchestral contribution to the counterpoint. The fugal part of the number closes with two final entries in the subdominant and tonic, with the shared motif in the orchestral counterpoints. After the music is brought to a temporary halt, on low octave Gs, the number ends with a homophonic coda which develops a new theme that bears some relation to the foregoing (the quavers from the women's theme, and the descending leap of a

3.15 Glinka, *A Life for the Tsar*, Introduction, two themes from the fugal chorus

fifth from the men's theme). The final passage, using orchestra only, both looks back to the earlier fugatos and foreshadows both tonality and melody of the following number, Antonida's cavatina and rondo.

The Act III chorus, *Mï na rabotu v les*, displays a similar degree of ingenuity.[36] One nineteeth-century commentator, Ivanov, who, unlike Stasov, gave an unprejudiced and perceptive account of the opera, called this number "a most refined work of art, quite without rival in the operatic literature of the time".[37] The chorus is a pastoral 3/4, with elements of the "Russian polonaise" style providing it with a clear Russian identity. The orchestra carries the burden of musical development rather than choir or soloists, which are only given inessential melodic phrases, often with repeated harmony notes, or outlines of more elaborate phrases heard in the orchestra at the same time. While the peasants discuss their plans for the day with Susanin – first their work, then the wedding celebrations – and accept some wine from him to mark the occasion, the orchestra proceeds through a full-scale sonata form. The large-scale harmonic structure is unorthodox: after an unusual modulation through iv, the second subject arrives in ♭II; the brief development features material from both subjects, in counterpoint, after which the recapitulation moves from I, for the first subject, to an unexpected V for the second subject. Even in the coda, which re-establishes the tonic, the second subject makes a brief return in ♭III.

This chorus is by no means an isolated example of elaborate formal and harmonic schemes in Glinka's operas: the overture and an important aria in *Ruslan* also follow unusual sonata-based schemes, while the Act II Mazurka finale in *A Life* follows an equally elaborate, but non-sonata procedure. In the *Ruslan* Overture, the main keys of the exposition are D and F major, while the recapitulation restates the material in D and A major, leaving the coda to re-establish D major. In Ruslan's Aria in Act II, this scheme is reversed: we have E and B major in the exposition, then E and G in the recapitulation. The Act

II Mazurka finale in *A Life* transforms what could have been a conventional dance suite into a piece of symphonic scope, with careful correlation of music and drama at the main points of articulation. The first theme, in E flat major, which is followed by a chain of contrasting new themes in a colourful sequence of keys: D flat major, A major, C major, and F major. The dancing is brought to a sudden halt by the arrival of a messenger with bad news from the battlefield. His recitative with choral interjections is set against a long and unsettled orchestral development, mainly devoted to the first mazurka theme. A group of officers within the chorus then rallies the spirits of all assembled, and here the first theme reappears in its original, confident version, but in the subdominant rather than the tonic. The task of re-establishing the tonic is reserved for the Presto coda.

In the Act II mazurka-finale, the Act III chorus and the two *Ruslan* examples, Glinka's purpose is evidently to avoid large-scale harmonic resolution until the last moment, to save it for the brilliant Presto coda. In both *A Life* and *Ruslan*, Glinka was confidently re-fashioning existing "Western" forms to suit his musical and dramatic purposes, displaying the same spirit of invention that gave us numbers in 5/4 metre, found in both operas, and numbers making prominent use of the whole-tone scale in *Ruslan*.

A symphonic opera

The unprecedented degree of unity in *A Life* was noticed and analysed at quite an early stage; Serov's essay on the opera, which explored the role of a single motive in its construction (1859), was the first published piece of motivic-thematic analysis in Russian music criticism.[38] Serov had already carried out motivic analyses of Beethoven for his own purposes; unsurprisingly, he was later to become Russia's foremost advocate of Wagner. Indeed, *A Life* provides fertile ground for exercises in tracing motivic reminiscence, development and transformation; Glinka's consistency and subtlety in this respect makes him one of most diligent disciples of Beethoven and perhaps the earliest to apply Beethoven's symphonic methods to opera (remarkably enough, with few stylistic borrowings).[39]

We have already discussed some manifestations of this unity when considering the transformations of the mazurka, and in our observations on Glinka's recitative *chantant*. While the Poles are characterized through the fixed genres of mazurka and polonaise (Russian scholars have inelegantly called them leit-genres), the characterization of the Russians through character-specific recitative *chantant* is one step further away from leitmotivic technique, and in a way more flexible. A number of themes that had already been encountered only become assigned to individual characters in the final scene of Act IV. The preceding scene, where Susanin, in his only formal aria, reflects at midnight upon his impending death, is worth discussing in detail at this point, since it constitutes a kind of reprise within the opera. At the beginning of the scene we find Susanin recalling the recent times of family happiness; the music here is very close in spirit to the celebrated reminiscence passage from Beethoven's Ninth: themes from the previous acts are stated by the orchestra, alternating with Susanin's recitative.[40] Glinka recalls no less than seven themes, three taken from the family quartet in Act III and four referring to particular characters (one for Antonida, one for Vanya and two for Sobinin). Susanin thus bids each of them farewell and after a short outburst of fear and despair lies down to sleep. Against the background of the snowstorm fugato, we hear Antonida's theme once again, as if in Susanin's dreams. Then we hear the mazurka, Susanin's first recitative from Act I, and the theme of his Act IV aria, now stated in augmentation by way of an apotheosis. The momentum of thematic recapitulation continues even beyond the end of the fourth act and thus beyond the drama proper: the following entr'acte bridges the gap between the tragic ending and the celebratory epilogue by bringing in further thematic recollection, and even in the Epilogue itself another new reminiscence is heard – the melody of Susanin's farewell arioso from Act III.

Although by 1836 the reminiscence technique had become widespread in French, German and Italian opera, Glinka's use of it was a very significant advance in terms of consistency, variety and thematic transformation. Unity-enhancing devices can be found on every level: on the smallest scale, the repeated melodic figures that ensure the stylistic coherence; on a larger scale, the consistency of the contrast between the Russians and Poles, which benefits the clarity of the dramatic conflict; and on the largest scale, various meaningful correspondences which straddle the opera. The most important high-level connection can be found at the climax of the drama, in Susanin's confrontation with the Poles in Act III, where he sings both the melody of the chorus from the Introduction and the "Slav'sya" theme that is to appear in the epilogue. The first signifies the Russian people, while the second refers to the glory of the tsar; in this scene, the two ideas are brought together, Susanin's heroic deed linking people and tsar. In structural terms, the beginning and the end of the opera are both reflected at this climactic moment.

To summarize, A Life represents Glinka's assimilation of Beethovenian symphonic procedures. It was a bold attempt to create an opera as a coherent, integrated artwork, at a time when the audience for opera was more apt to see a mere lack of invention in any re-use of material. Glinka also enjoyed remarkable artistic freedom for an operatic composer of the period, conceiving the scenario, planning the central dramatic conflict of the opera in musical terms, composing much of the music in outline prior to the completion of the libretto, and exercising authority over the librettist's decisions; Glinka's Italian and French contemporaries did not approach this degree of autonomy for decades.[41] This ought to have ensured *A Life* a prominent place in any history of Western music of the nineteenth century, especially given the centrality in many narratives of progressive unification of the work leading to the mature music-dramas of Wagner. But *A Life*, far from being central to such histories, rarely even rose to the level of the marginal, due to the contingencies of marketing the work in Europe, rather than because of anything intrinsic to the work. No Russian music prior to the Kuchka made any serious impact on European operatic and concert life, and even there, the celebrity of the music long post-dated the act of composition, and indeed was posthumous for Musorgsky and Borodin. Our account of *A Life* was aimed to demonstrate that its early Russian reviewers were fully justified in assessing the opera as a work of utmost importance and a major Russian contribution to the European stage. That their predictions of Glinka's imminent fame across Europe proved false was through no fault of the composer.

Ruslan and Lyudmila

In search of Ruslan's *Russianness*

Six years after *A Life for the Tsar*, Glinka's admirers eagerly awaited a still more consummate embodiment of Russianness in the master's new work. But they were disappointed by *Ruslan and Lyudmila* (1842). "What manner of music is this? Neither Italian, nor German, but at the same time not Russian?"[42] – this reaction, voiced by one of the opera's early commentators sums up the initial public response. Those enchanted by the music of *Ruslan*, who saw it as Glinka's gigantic step forward rather than an "une chose manquée", had to dig deep, and interpret the evidence creatively, in order to establish it as a worthy successor to *A Life for the Tsar* – failure would have meant the exclusion of *Ruslan* from any future canon of national art. Since then, attempts to demonstrate *Ruslan*'s Russianness have taken up hundreds of pages. Sometimes the discussion involved technical details, but more often a moral tone prevailed. As the Russian critic Hermann Laroche wrote in 1867–8, in a major article entitled 'Glinka and his Role in Music History':

> Our connoisseurs, self-confidently condemning *Ruslan and Lyudmila* as 'German" music and with the same self-confidence defending *A Life for the Tsar* as "Russian" music, are in truth offending the shade of the great artist.[43]

Yet many remained unconvinced, among them Musorgsky, who called *Ruslan* a creation of the Glinka's "Europeanized" side (he made this term sound more derogatory by means of an unusual prefix and suffix).[44] It seems that anyone writing about *Ruslan* who was not satisfied with tired clichés about the Russian spirit had to address the issue of its Russianness afresh.

Glinka's two operas are indeed strikingly different. The stylistic coherence of *A Life for the Tsar* gave way to a dazzling mélange, with Italian *buffo*, various European dance idioms, and genuine folk tunes of non-Russian provenance, as well as the expected Russian romance and Italian coloratura idioms. Undeterred by this diversity, critics kept searching for demonstrably Russian melodies, treating *Ruslan* as if it were another *Life for the Tsar*. Laroche, for example, tried to demonstrate that nearly every melody in Glinka's second opera somehow bore the imprint of Russian nationality (*narodnost'*). Even in those cases where the music is used to depict something non-Russian, Laroche convinced himself that the melodies still followed the patterns of Russian song while their harmony and orchestration give them their Oriental colour.[45] Let us examine the passages he chose to support his thesis: "I zhar, i znoy" (Ratmir's aria: Ex.3.16a); "O moy Ratmir" (Gorislava's aria: Ex.3.16b); "Mirnïy son" (Chorus of the invisible nymphs: Ex.3.16c); and Turkish dance (Ex.3.16d).

The only characteristic uniting these songs is their diatonicism, and so Laroche pounced on this as proof of their thoroughgoing Russianness. No matter that these passages did not sound remotely like any Russian folksong, for Laroche's ideas on folksong were speculative – he had little or no direct knowledge of folksong. As it happens, we can identify the theoretical source of these speculations, even though Laroche does not mention his debt, for these ideas had all been set out previously in a series of essays by Odoyevsky. These essays propounded a dichotomy in Russian music between the rural and the urban, in which the former was associated with diatonic, ancient, and truly Russian music, while the latter was associated with non-diatonic, relatively new and merely pseudo-Russian music.[46] Laroche followed Odoyevsky's scheme, placing the melody of Lyudmila's second aria "Akh tï, dolya-dolyushka", which struck other commentators as the most Russian of all, among the list of the non-Russian exceptions. The melody in question was indeed firmly within the drawing-room romance tradition, and so the wider audience, untroubled by any such theories, recognized it to be Russian, while doctrinaire nationalists like Laroche could allow only that it was pseudo-Russian.

The partisans of *A Life for the Tsar*, who used it as a weapon against *Ruslan*, were soon to be confronted with a counter-argument that seemed unimpeachably rigorous, based on the new theory of "Russian harmony". The

3.16a   Glinka, *Ruslan and Lyudmila*, Act III, Ratmir's aria

3.16b   Glinka, *Ruslan and Lyudmila*, Act III, Gorislava's cavatina

harmonic procedure in *A Life for the Tsar* that some critics had labelled as Russian (modulation onto a range of modal centres), was all but absent from *Ruslan*. The apologists for *Ruslan* had to dig deeper in their search for harmonic Russianness, and eventually they arrived at the theory of plagalism. In short, the theory stated that Russian music was pervaded by the IV–I progression, and was thus distinguished from Western music, which was articulated by the V–I progression. Plagalism was usually accompanied by the

3.16c   Glinka, *Ruslan and Lyudmila*, Act IV, chorus of the invisible nymphs

3.16d   Glinka, *Ruslan and Lyudmila*, Act IV, Turkish dance

thesis that Russian folk music employed the ecclesiastical modes known from Western music theory; these had died out in the West, to be replaced by the major/minor system in which the perfect cadence played a commanding role; Russia – so the theory went – had preserved the modes, hence the lesser importance of the perfect cadence. Russian plagalism, together with its accompanying modal contention, although utterly misguided on various levels, has managed to retain some influence up to the present day.

In 1858 Vladimir Stasov, the Russian critic who later became the ideologist of the Kuchka, wrote an open letter to Liszt and A. B. Marx that was published in the *Neue Zeitschrift für Musik*.[47] The letter chiefly concerned Marx's *Allgemeine Musiklehre*, in which the modern use of ecclesiastical modes was restricted to the harmonization of old chorale tunes. Stasov pointed out that from Beethoven onwards, the deployment of modal harmony had been much wider and had contributed significantly to the development of harmonic resources. Stasov saw modality in every progression not based around V–I, and focused especially on supposed plagal cadences, which took in any incidence of IV–I in the middle of phrases; Stasov, in his blind obsession, even placed some I–V half cadences under the same rubric of "plagal", disregarding the key to suit his purposes. Chopin was the modal hero of modern times, since, according to Stasov, he had used "medieval harmony" to support his "Oriental" melodies (Stasov, of course, had no idea what, if anything, "medieval harmony" might mean, while he used "Oriental" to mean anything folk-like). In the course of Stasov's longish letter, Glinka was mentioned but once, at the very end, but a year earlier, in an article on Glinka, Stasov again touched on the issue of modality.[48] He said that Glinka's intuitions had, remarkably, led him along the very same path that Beethoven and Chopin had taken before him (Stasov misleadingly implied that Glinka had largely been ignorant of European developments), and without knowing the names of the modes, Glinka had nevertheless used an increasing number of modal progressions in his compositions. This early appearance of plagalism was as yet free of the exclusively Russian associations it would later accrue; in any case, this would not have been appropriate in the context, since Stasov wished to persuade Western readers that Glinka merited comparison with Beethoven and Chopin – that he had been inspired by the same spirit that had led them towards modality.

It was not long before the connection was made between the ecclesiastical modes and Russian folk song. Before Balakirev founded the Kuchka, he and Stasov had become close friends through the convergence of their interests in the future of Russian music. In 1860, Balakirev spent a vacation in his home town on the Volga, using the opportunity to collect folksongs. In one of his letters to Stasov, he reported his discovery of "a Russian minor scale"; Stasov, in his reply, pointed out that this scale was identical to the Dorian mode (Stasov was always better acquainted with music-theoretical terms and concepts, although he had none of Balakirev's abilities as a practicing musician). This led Stasov to speculate that both Russian church and folk music must operate within the system of ancient Greek modes (to compound the error). In his excitement, he wrote to Balakirev:

Imagine how well-armed you will be when you come back from your trip, for instead of having just the two old scales, a whole new music will be yours, since you will now be in possession of seven! What a fine new source of melodies and harmonies![49]

Unfortunately, Balakirev's reply has been lost, so we do not know whether his practical musicianship might have allowed him to retain some scepticism about his friend's theoretical fantasies. But Stasov needed little encouragement once he had embarked on these speculations. Three months later, he updated Balakirev on his thinking:

> Please listen carefully and transcribe the hawker's cries. I've often noticed that they are also very old, and probably belong to the same system of church modes as our folksongs and ecclesiastical music – in a word, everything that is being sung and has ever been sung in Russia.[50]

A few years later, the Laroche article referred to above (p.104), supplies the final connection. Laroche tells us that Glinka was entirely justified in harmonizing Russian folksongs with progressions drawn from the ecclesiastical modes; but, Laroche reasons, since the father of Russian music knew nothing of Renaissance church music when he was writing his operas, he must have extrapolated the modes from Russian folksong. So impressed was Laroche with this argument that he promiscuously extended his insight to all of Glinka's harmonic peculiarities alike: even a passage in which B flat major and D major triads were juxtaposed supposedly bore the unmistakable imprint of Russian folksong.[51]

Stasov's hasty speculations, Odoyevsky's misplaced erudition, and Laroche's wayward polemic all contributed to the development of a collective nationalist line on Russian plagalism and modal harmony. And as I mentioned at the outset of this discussion, plagalism was used to articulate an opposition between the West and Russia: where Westerners use the dominant, Russians use the subdominant. And the entire precarious edifice of Russian plagalism was built upon the shallow foundations of a single musical passage, namely, the opening of the overture to *Ruslan* (Ex.3.17a).

The exponents of Russian plagalism argued that Glinka could as easily have used I–V–I in this passage, but his instinct for essentially Russian harmony led him to write I–IV–I instead.[52] If we eschew the obscurantism of nationalist explanations, we do not have to look far to find Glinka's probable source for the idea: during his stay in Italy, Glinka attended a performance of Rossini's *Mosè in Egitto*, and here we find the same progression at the opening (Ex.3.17b) – even Rossini's key of D major is preserved in Glinka's version.

3.17a   Glinka, Overture to *Ruslan and Lyudmila*

3.17b   Rossini, opening of *Mosè in Egitto*

Stasov had a remarkable knack for coining ideas which embedded themselves in the minds of later critics and scholars, and plagalism was foremost among these; it remained a nugget of unassailable wisdom in Soviet musicology, and was credulously imported to the West.[53] The doubts voiced by Boris Asafyev in the 1940s seem to have passed unnoticed:

> the so-called plagalism of Glinka's harmony is strongly exaggerated . . . It is not possible to explain its presence by invoking the characteristics of Russian folksong, just as one cannot consider 5/4 metre to be the national property of Russian music.[54]

So much for the popular myth. But what does a critical examination of the evidence have to say? The influence of urbanized folk music in *A Life for the Tsar* is undeniably present, but in *Ruslan* it is hard to detect. Granted, Glinka's favourite modulatory device, which uses the subdominant as a pivot, frequently appears in *Ruslan*, and this is generally cited as an example of Russian folk influence; but when we see much the same device in Schubert and Schumann, and recall Glinka's own musical education and knowledge of the German concert repertoire, we cannot place any confidence in such assertions (even leaving aside the question of whether Russian folk music, urbanized or not, provides a model for this type of modulation). Glinka's harmony has been called so novel and fresh because it has been measured against a straw man of Western harmony, which degenerated in the course of the polemical onslaught to a mere alternation of tonic and dominant chords. Glinka's respect for Chopin's music, for example, was obliterated in the effort to account for his novelties with reference only to Russian genius.

The proportion of modal harmony to be found in Glinka has also been exaggerated. Let us examine one controversial instance: the chorus "Lel' tainstvennïy" from Act I of *Ruslan* (Ex.3.18 – the choral parts, all doubled in the orchestra, are omitted here).

This has always been listed among Glinka's modal melodies: Laroche claimed to have found Dorian cadences (at the end of the present extract and in analogous passages),[55] while Olga Levasheva recently argued that the chorus was basically Mixolydian.[56] Both these interpretations result from wishful thinking: while we might entertain ourselves by imagining possible modal harmonizations during the initial *unisono* statement of the theme, its subsequent harmonization is not modal at all; indeed, Glinka later offers us some re-harmonizations of the theme, but not once does he draw on modal harmonies. Again, considering Glinka's own musical background, we can properly trace the few modal inflections in *Ruslan* back to the sophisticated harmonic palette of Glinka's Western contemporaries (which included some

3.18 Glinka, *Ruslan and Lyudmila*, wedding chorus from Act I

conventionalized exotic elements). There is no need to resort to Russian folk-song for such harmonies, given that Glinka knew almost nothing of this music, and given that folk hetero/polyphony is very distant from harmony in nineteenth-century concert music. And the kind of nationalist essentialism which alleges that Glinka had no need of direct knowledge, but that the music of the Russian folk flowed in his veins is wishful thinking so feeble-minded that we need not construct any counter-arguments.[57]

A similar myth grew up around Glinka's variation technique, known variously as "changing-background" or "ostinato" variations (to Russian and Soviet musicologists simply "Glinka variations"). This technique pervades *Ruslan*, in both arias and choruses, accommodating both repetitive incantation and the telling of narratives.[58] Russian critics, of course, declared that the device was somehow essentially Russian; some said that its origins lay in folksong, while others argued instead for instrumental folk idioms (there was no settling the matter, since both parties preferred speculation to field research). The folksong explanation is dependent upon a tendentious comparison between the changing-background technique and the appearance of new (improvised) variants at every repeat in a strophic folksong; note that only monodic performances of folksongs were heard, so these critics had nothing but melodic variation in mind, whereas Glinka's device involved an *unchanging* melody with varied harmony and texture. And if we seek out the professional opinion of Soviet music theorists, half a century and more afterwards, we are still offered the same baseless account of changing-background variations. Admittedly, it was probably wise in the late 1940s and early '50s to leave these relics of nineteenth-century nationalism unchallenged; to do otherwise was to risk the charge of "rootless cosmopolitanism".[59] But even after this danger had passed, scholars went no further than mild qualifications, such as "partly prompted by folk tradition".[60]

This feature of the Russian/Soviet musicological tradition also made some impression in the West, for we read in David Brown's *Tchaikovsky*, that "to think in terms of variations is one of the most deeply rooted instincts of Russian musical creativity"; to illustrate this, he compares some folksong patterns with Glinka's folk-based symphonic fantasy *Kamarinskaya*.[61] It was, no doubt, *Kamarinskaya*, that prompted the critics to entertain the idea that another supposed source of Glinka's variation technique was Russian instrumental folk music. Indeed, in the fast section of *Kamarinskaya*, Glinka imitates the improvised accompaniment to a folk dance that endlessly rotates a short phrase with slight variations. But although Glinka clearly employs the changing-background device here, we must not jump to the conclusion that the folk practice was the source of the device. Firstly, the fast section of *Kamarinskaya* is not the first, but the *last* example of the device in Glinka's oeuvre. Secondly, this passage is far from typical of Glinka's changing-background variations, since the repeated unit is much shorter than the usual full-fledged rounded strophes (as in every example from *Ruslan*), and the melody itself undergoes some variation (in fact, melodic variation is at the heart of *Kamarinskaya*, in which one folk theme is transformed into another). Thirdly, if we still wished to insist (in the face of my previous arguments) on the centrality of *Kamarinskaya* to changing-background variation, we would have to deny Glinka the priority claim, since many earlier Russian composers (including the immigrant John Field!) composed their own variation sets on the *Kamarinskaya* tune, with strikingly similar patterns of melodic variation. In the fast section of his *Kamarinskaya* Glinka was, therefore, following a tradition already established within Russian art music, while in his earlier examples of changing-background technique he was more original.

As for David Brown's suggestion that there is something essentially Russian about changing-background variations, he seems to ignore certain awkward facts: that the technique of extending a musical passage by means of repeating a melody in one part while the other parts change had existed since *cantus firmus* composition; or, more to the point, that the layout of the variations in the slow section of *Kamarinskaya* closely shadows the first section of purely instrumental variations on the Joy theme in the finale of Beethoven's Ninth Symphony. As for the basic idea of writing variations on a folk melody, the early nineteenth-century European piano repertoire would have furnished Glinka with a great many examples; since this was part of the musical tradition in which he was thoroughly schooled, we have no reason to turn to the music of the Russian peasantry of which he knew little or nothing. Finally, the defining characteristics of Glinka's changing-background variations were re-harmonization and re-orchestration, and these have no counterpart in Russian folk music; Glinka's variation technique was certainly idiosyncratic and inventive, but it was his own development from European art music sources, not the result of folk inspiration, or the manifestation of his Russian soul.

It is no surprise that we can find nothing of substance in these blindly determined attempts to trace the music of *Ruslan* back to a barely known Russian folk music – indeed the fact that it was barely known was its most important feature, otherwise speculation would have been constrained by facts. But we also find statements which locate *Ruslan*'s Russianness in its characters, which allegedly follow the typology of Russian folk tales and epics. There must have been something, we might think, that prompted Stasov to write the following lines:

> I happened to have spent . . . recently a lot of time . . . over Russian tales, folk verse-narratives etc. And after this I cannot stop marvelling at the

extent to which Glinka grasped the spirit – the character of our ancient nation. Pushkin was unable to do that. Both he and Lermontov were only good for recent times, the Moscow era, and even then, only for the times of its rot – Boris Godunov, Kalashnikov. But then Glinka equalled this in *A Life for the Tsar*, while they have nothing to compare with *Ruslan*.[62]

Ruslan himself, critics invariably said, is a Russian warrior, a *bogatïr'* from the ancient epic songs. But what is the difference between this Russian *bogatïr'* and a conventional dashing operatic hero/lover? When we dispense with the bluster, all we have left is Glinka's choice of bass instead of the normal tenor. Nor was there any deep significance in Glinka's eschewal of convention, certainly no intention to tap the wellsprings of Russian epic to create an authentic Russian operatic type. The train of events was simply this: in *A Life for the Tsar*, the part of the father was set conventionally enough for bass voice; however, the first singer to play the part, Osip Petrov, won such acclaim in this role that when Glinka came to compose *Ruslan*, he was eager to fashion the part of his new hero as a showcase for Petrov. And because of *Ruslan*'s later status for nationalists such as the Kuchka, the bass voice soon came to figure very prominently in Russian opera. There is, admittedly, one aspect of this which is not Russian merely by convention, for low voices are statistically more prevalent among men in Russia than in much of Europe; this explains the ready supply of fine Russian basses for these operatic roles, and the relative scarcity of good tenors. But the part of Ruslan did not always offer the nationalists exactly what they wanted. To achieve the status of a model national hero, Ruslan would have been better advised not to depart from his operatic type at any point; but those occasions when the character temporarily becomes three-dimensional (as at the start of his Aria in Act II when he contemplates death and oblivion, or in Act III where he forgets his heroic goal under the influence of Naina's sorcery) only work against the monolithic *bogatïr'* figure the nationalists would have preferred; Laroche, for example, complained of Ruslan's anachronistic display of Romantic frustration.[63]

Lyudmila's role clearly belongs to the soubrette type, and this failed to offer anything distinctive to those in search of *Ruslan*'s Russianness. Her actions might seem to offer more: her stand against the temptations of Chernomor's castle in Act IV improve her candidacy as a model for Russian womanhood, but even this is problematic, for her behaviour smacks more of stubbornness than dignified courage; worse, Glinka had a clear model in creating a soubrette part with just such a response to a similar predicament, namely Rosina, in *Il barbiere*. And so, for various reasons, the two leading characters fell short of the nationalists' requirements.

Of the more important characters, the only other Russian is Gorislava, to whom the critics now turned in desperation. Gorislava is a soprano role, but the writing is less virtuosic than Lyudmila's, more lyrical and earnest. Gorislava's one solo number, her Act III cavatina, was written in a romance style; one might have thought that the Ruslanite nationalists would have been deterred, since they had already dismissed such writing as urban pseudo-Russianness in *A Life for the Tsar*, in opposition to the authentic Russianness of the peasantry which was supposed to characterize *Ruslan*. Laroche, however, was not to be so easily discouraged, and he unflinchingly pronounced the cavatina as folk-like as everything else in the opera. A generation or so later, when the opera's reputation was firmly established so that no further polemics were needed, critics were prepared to be more frank in acknowledging the romance elements in *Ruslan*, which, although not pervasive as in *A Life*, were nevertheless unmistakably present. This permitted a closer examination of Gorislava, who was now seen as a worthy precursor of Tchaikovsky's Tatyana (*Eugene Onegin*). First it was noticed that Tatyana's famous letter-scene contained some melodic writing very close to that of Gorislava's cavatina (Tchaikovsky had deliberately evoked the romance style of the Pushkin era). Asafyev repeatedly mentions the connection, finding some grounds for essentializing Russianness in music: he claimed that one of the features shared by Gorislava and Tat'yana, the chromatic step from sharp $\hat{4}$ to natural $\hat{4}$ in minor-mode melodies, is "primordial in Russian lyricism".[64] Once the musical kinship had been noted, the discussion turned to the characterization of Gorislava and Tatyana, which brought their original creator, Pushkin, into the arena: it was decided that the two women were united in serving as models of marital loyalty. Since Belinsky had once called Tatyana "the ideal Russian woman" (in Soviet times his words became a textbook cliché), Gorislava was likewise hailed as "the most wholly Russian character" of the opera.[65] We should note, however, that Tchaikovsky's *Onegin* had already been subjected to laborious re-interpretation as a profoundly national work, and Tatyana's elevation was an important part of this process. Gorislava's similar elevation brought *Ruslan* into a later phase of nationalist discourse, in which the notion that Glinka had drawn the opera's music directly from the Russian soil gave way to an emphasis on the Russianness of the character-types; music now played a more indirect and supporting role.

Since the two main characters were found unsuitable as Russian archetypes, and since Gorislava's reputation was only built up later in the century, where else did the early Ruslanites hope to find a solid basis for the opera's putative Russianness? They based their strongest case on the nature of the opera as a whole, which they saw as a monumental Russian epic. The Pushkin original for *Ruslan* was a youthful *jeux d'esprit* altogether too light-hearted and completely lacking in solemnity; accordingly, these critics could not celebrate it as the source for the opera's folk-epic character. Laroche, for example, wrote that the poem was Pushkin's weakest, and that it had only acted as a framework for Glinka's much grander project of uncovering the roots of the Russian national character.[66] This perspective caused him to hear the first chords of the overture as "mighty and joyful, but also simple-hearted and a little coarse"; amusingly, he interpreted their "parallel movement" as "that of the kind that was used in the oldest period of harmony".[67] Of course, if his prior choices had been different, he could just as easily have found the overture a perfect reflection of the Pushkin poem: light, energetic and elegant.

From magic opera to epic opera

As we have seen, the apologists took *Ruslan* to be the inaugural work of a new epic-opera genre (many later examples were supplied by the Kuchka and their followers). Glinka himself, however, considered *Ruslan* to be an example of the pre-existent genre of magic opera. In the present section we shall first examine *Ruslan's* magic-opera origins, and then consider whether its eventual status as the paradigmatic epic opera led to a *Ruslan* far from its creator's intentions.

Ruslan was, indeed, firmly rooted in the traditions of the Russian stage, but this was remote from the kind of Russianness its apologists sought. They were primarily interested in the music, and they wanted to find a Russianness that somehow emanated from the folk, rather than something so prosaic as a set of conventions consciously developed in urban theatres. In any case, they were concerned to present *Ruslan* as a solitary act of genius without precedent, so far above other Russian operas that it would be impertinent to talk of influence. But *Ruslan* was in many respects a more traditional work for the Russian stage than *A Life for the Tsar*. Its genre, *volshebnaya opera* (magic opera) had met with particular favour from the Russian public from as early as 1803, when F. Kauer's *Die Donauweibchen* was first staged in its Russian version, *Dneprovskaya rusalka* (The Dnieper Mermaid). The story of the opera, in which a young girl who is wronged by her lover, throws herself into the river, becomes a mermaid and in this form exacts her revenge, held a lasting fascination for the Russian audience; spectacular stage effects in the first production increased the impact of the story. To satisfy public demand three sequels were created, turning the mermaid into the equivalent of a soap-opera heroine. Even Pushkin was sufficiently interested to write his own version of the story, although he left it unfinished; in spite of the existence of the original two versions (both the German and the Russian had long runs in Russia) and the three sequels, Dargomïzhsky saw fit to set Pushkin's version as a fifth opera on the subject (*Rusalka*, 1856). This enduring interest in mermaids is also evident in *Ruslan* (the opera, not the original poem), in which a chorus of mermaids persuades the captive Lyudmila not to drown herself.

Soon after the advent of magic opera on the Russian stage, dramatists and composers started using Russian fairy tales, as in Cavos's *Ilya-bogatïr'* (Ilya the Mighty Warrior, 1806), and *Zhar-ptitsa* (The Firebird, 1823). *The Firebird* in particular anticipates *Ruslan* in its combination of the heroic, the comical and the Oriental. The magic plots also began to appear in ballet when, in 1810, the Petersburg-based ballet-master Charles Didelot decided to use fairy tales (some of them Russian) in addition to his customary Greek myths. His *ballets-féeries* are of some importance in the genesis of *Ruslan*, because Pushkin's poem was apparently influenced by Didelot's balletic novelties. According to the early Soviet scholar L. Grossman,

> Pushkin's first narrative poem is theatrical throughout. The impressions of a yesternight's performance were clearly reflected in the morning work of the poet. No one noticed that the great poet's début was a ballet-poem.[68]

Grossman singles out one passage in Pushkin's *Ruslan* which even recalls one of Didelot's trademark balletic "transformations in flight":

V okno vletayet zmey krïlatïy;	A winged dragon flew in through
Gremya zheleznoy cheshuyoy	the window;
On v kol'tsa bïstrïye sognulsya	Rattling his iron scales;
I vdrug Nainoy obernulsya	He quickly bent into coils
Pred izumlyonnoyu tolpoy.	And suddenly turned into Naina
	Before the astonished crowd.

Given its inspiration, it was fitting that the publication of Pushkin's *Ruslan* should have been followed swiftly by a magic ballet based on the poem, advertised as a "grand heroic-magic pantomime ballet in 5 acts, with battles, character dances and magnificent spectacle".[69] The two lengthy balletic divertissements in Glinka's *Ruslan* therefore reflect the tradition from which the opera emerged; they should not be regarded as mere impositions on an essentially musical work.

Magic opera turned to national mythology after the first Russian production of *Der Freischütz*, in 1824, hence the "Slavic" operas of Verstovsky, such as *Vadim* (1832) and *Askold's Tomb* (1835), which used freshly written mythologies set in late pagan/early Christian Russia. These operas can properly be regarded as *Ruslan*'s immediate precursors; *Vadim* in particular has close links with both Pushkin's and Glinka's version. The literary source of this opera, a romantic ballad by Zhukovsky, had influenced Pushkin, (a debt irreverently acknowledged through parody). The influence of *Vadim* on Glinka is also much in evidence. Verstovsky's opera opens with a feast at the palace of the Kievan prince; the scene is dominated by an epic song presented by the character Stemid and a chorus, with harp accompaniment, and in true epic fashion the song contains premonitions of the story's outcome. This is all carried over into the opening scene of Glinka's *Ruslan*; even the key of Verstovsky's scene is retained by Glinka (see Ex.3.19), but while Verstovsky's setting clearly evokes the *protyazhnaya*, Glinka attempts to create music which is free of strong generic associations (for which his nationalist apologists were grateful, since the *protyazhnaya* had become too tainted by urban pseudo-Russianness in their eyes, as we saw earlier in this chapter). A quick glance at the dramatis personae of *Vadim* yields a female character named Gremislava, who is given a romance which foreshadows Gorislava's cavatina in *Ruslan* (Ex.3.20).

Although Glinka advertised *Ruslan* as a magic opera, it frustrated any expectations of light entertainment which this might have encouraged; its large scale, slow pace and musical complexity all placed it outside the normal bounds of the genre. These aspects of the work go some way to justify the desire of *Ruslan*'s apologists to reclassify it first as *sui generis*, and later as the first example of epic opera, in spite of the fact that it drew very heavily on the magic ballet/magic opera tradition, as we have just seen. We should not forget, however, that these critics also had an overwhelming interest in effacing the connections between *Ruslan* and the magic genres, for if *Ruslan* belonged to this urban tradition (which had been dominated, moreover, by foreigners), it would be difficult to argue that it was also an authentic utterance by the spirit of the Russian folk.

The anonymous critic "O***" was the most important of the early apologists, arguing his case concisely and strongly in 1843, shortly after the opera's première.[70] O*** emphasizes the epic qualities of *Ruslan*:

In the plot of *Ruslan and Lyudmila*, [Glinka] saw not an opera buffa, but a serious opera, whose idea lies not only in the magic, but in the elemental struggle of different peoples, who are ready to merge in an indissoluble whole . . .

The main idea – Finnism and Tartarism enclosed in the magic ring of Slavism – is clearly developed in the form of an intricate fairy tale. . . .

It is strange to hear the libretto of the opera being attacked for its lack of action and distinctive characterization, whereas the dramatic nature of this opera lies in the unprecedented struggle of its musical elements, rather than in the interaction of its characters; he portrays whole peoples living

3.19 Verstovsky, Stemid's song from the opera *Vadim*

through their fiery music, rather than individual characters. To attack
such an opera for its lack of drama and for the inconsistency of its character-
drawing is to attack an epic for failing to be a drama or a novel. It is
superior to all of this![71]

3.20   Verstovsky, Gremislava's romance from *Vadim*

O*** situates the Slavs of *Ruslan* in the geographic centre. To the West is
Farlaf, represented by Italianate buffo writing. To the South is Ratmir – O***
tells us that both the South and the West, like Lyudmila's suitors, "wanted to
become family to Russia". To the North is Finn, and to the East, Chernomor.
Dramatically, all these peoples find themselves enclosed within the framework
of the majestic Russian scenes – within "a magic ring of Slavism", O*** says.
This is certainly an elegant interpretation of *Ruslan*'s topography: it dissolves
most of the controversies and reveals the underlying strength of the structure;

where characters were thought to be under-written, O*** shows how this two-dimensionality assists their symbolic purpose, as representatives of their respective nations.

Some might think O***'s scheme too neat a package for *Ruslan*'s five-act sprawl, but we find corroboration in the composer's conception of the final scene. As it happens, the eventual staging of this scene did not fulfil Glinka's wishes, otherwise O***'s scheme would have seemed more obvious and uncontentious to other critics. Alexander Serov, in his memoirs, recalls Glinka complaining that

> At the end of the opera, during the Finale, I desired that a number of *tableaux-vivants* should be presented, characterizing the different regions of Russia. I was told that it would be impossible, and that even without it God only knows how much the production was going to cost.[72]

This journey through the expanse of Russia, displayed in all its variety, would have explained perfectly some musical details in the Act V finale which puzzled many of *Ruslan*'s critics. One of them is the use of the Lezghinka from the Act IV Oriental dances (Ex.3.21a); this theme was originally associated with the enemy kingdom of Chernomor, so its reappearance in a scene glorifying Russia appears to be a musical gain purchased at the price of dramatic absurdity, casting doubts on the composer's competence in stagecraft. But in the light of that explanation, we can see how the reappearance of the dance was perfectly in accord with the composer's imperial-epic conception of the Finale. Another apparent dramatic miscalculation, even more striking, is the reappearance of the Turkish dance theme (again taken from the Act IV divertimento), now sung by Ratmir and Gorislava (Ex.3.21b). Why should these characters appear in the Act V finale at all? Why are they given the same prominence in this finale as Antonida, Vanya and Sobinin were given in the finale of *A Life for the Tsar*, where they introduced a note of grief into the general rejoicing? In the context of the latter opera, this was a fine dramatic stroke, but in *Ruslan* it seems entirely out of place. It might seem that Glinka mechanically re-deployed this scheme simply because it had worked so well in his previous opera. But the imperial-epic conception of the finale, including the intended *tableaux-vivants*, prophesies a glorious Russia of the future, uniting under its aegis the many nations that had long warred with it. Within this conception, the reappearance of Ratmir and Gorislava would then serve several – entirely appropriate – purposes. Firstly, as a couple, they represent Russia (Gorislava) and the Caucasus (Ratmir) drawn together in bonds of love. Secondly, Ratmir alone of all the characters has been undergone a substantial change in the course of the drama: the lecherous Khan of

3.21a Glinka, *Ruslan and Lyudmila*, the Lezghinka theme in the Finale of Act V

Poco meno mosso

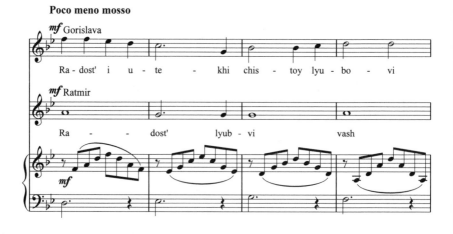

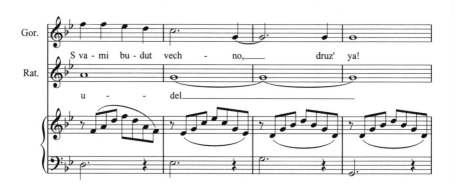

3.21b   Glinka, *Ruslan and Lyudmila,* the Turkish dance theme in the Finale of Act V

Khazaria has now become a faithful husband to his Russian wife, and in the process has become Ruslan's loyal friend, though they were once bitter rivals in love. Thirdly, the fact that the couple sings a version of the Turkish dance, associated with Chernomor's kingdom, rather than one of Ratmir's own native melodies, allows the Khazar to represent the outlying nations in general, universalizing the message that Russia's former enemies have now become its loyal provinces. Indeed, loyalty appears to be the main moral force driving the plot: Ruslan and Lyudmila make their entry while pronouncing their vows; in Act II, Ruslan succumbs to regular fits of jealousy, doubting the faithfulness of his betrothed; Acts III and IV present Ruslan's and Lyudmila's trials of loyalty respectively. By the end of the opera, when Ratmir demonstrates his faithfulness to Gorislava (the bonds of love) and to Ruslan (the bonds of friendship), we are to recall that Russia has always presented itself in relation to the surrounding nations as an elder brother, with familial responsibilities and intimate ties. The fraternal love of Russia towards the other nationalities of its empire was always given much emphasis, lest anyone should be inclined to see nothing but raw imperial might. Thus the finale of the opera elevates the tale of Ruslan and Lyudmila, making it a parable of Russia's own carefully-constructed imperial self-image.

While it is a solid tradition of Russian musicology to describe *Ruslan* as an epic opera, its imperial pathos has been largely overlooked or deliberately underplayed. This tradition was initiated by Stasov's defence of *Ruslan*, which was garrulous and inconsistent, by contrast with O***'s elegant and cogent interpretation – O***'s essay was unfortunately forgotten soon after its publication, and it was unknown to later generations until its eventual recovery in the 1960s.[73] There was good reason for O***'s lapse into obscurity, since the imperial interpretation (corroborated, as we saw, by Glinka) had no appeal for the liberal nationalists who constituted Stasov's intended audience, indeed, the adoption of O***'s interpretation would have made *Ruslan* as offensive to them as *A Life for the Tsar*, whereas Stasov's very purpose was to praise the later opera as a model for a new nationalism, to the detriment of *A Life*. Although the Russian empire had always incorporated territories inhabited by non-Russian peoples (to say "nations" would be anachronistic), the "Eastern issue" was a permanent source of disagreement in the mid-nineteenth century, occupying many column inches of the newspapers. An imperial epic would only possess a factional appeal, whereas Stasov and his fellow critics wanted to present a *Ruslan* which was not rooted in contemporary controversy, but which could appeal to all Russia. In the following decades, a consensus formed around Stasov's interpretation; only the conservative Dostoyevsky chose to view the characters as nations and plot as a political allegory, which shows that productions of the opera still offered sufficient evidence to suggest an interpretation like O***'s to other minds.[74]

In Soviet times, Stasov's interpretation was upheld (although given a characteristic tilt): *Ruslan* was to be regarded as "national, but not patriotic" (the latter word carried reactionary connotations in the Soviet lexicon), and as "an objective refusal to serve the foundations of autocracy".[75] Only Asafyev, in one of his early articles, styled *Ruslan* "a national-*state* epic", but he never mentioned this again, no doubt for fear of causing *Ruslan* to undergo the same distortions that *A Life for the Tsar* had suffered, in order to render it ideologically suitable for Soviet audiences.[76] Without its imperial ingredient exposed, *Ruslan* as a national epic was allowed to flourish. Indeed, *Ruslan* was upheld as the paradigm for all music which displayed "epic dramaturgy" (*epicheskaya dramaturgiya*, a very common positive epithet employed by Soviet musicologists), which included not only the Russian operas evidently modelled on *Ruslan*, but also the symphonies of Borodin, Glazunov, Bruckner and Sibelius.

Unfortunately for Glinka, acceptance of *Ruslan* as a model national epic came too late for him to see. *A Life for the Tsar* had enjoyed immediate success; why did it take so long before *Ruslan* was received warmly, by the wider public, court circles, or the nationalist intelligentsia? Firstly, the public did not expect to encounter a work of epic character in the opera house, and were more likely to regard it as an excessively ponderous magic opera than a successful example of something substantially new. They had not been prepared: unlike Wagner a few decades later, Glinka had never clarified his intentions in writing, let alone commissioned a special opera house for his creation. Operas were not expected to articulate serious cultural or political statements; although *A Life for the Tsar* had done so, it did not demand reception on this level, since it possessed the qualities which normally signalled an opera-house success – it had a compelling dramatic sweep, and a musical style which was fresh enough to distinguish itself, but familiar enough to be easily assimilated. *Ruslan*, on the contrary, was uncompromising: it required a longer attention span without any compensatory features, since it eschewed dramatic attention and used musical material which was more demanding throughout. Secondly, the production had already jettisoned half of the epic features which Glinka had planned, rendering the composer's intentions opaque to most in the audience (who lacked the insight of an O***). For example, the epic time-frame emerges most strikingly in "Yest' pustïnnïy kray" (There is a desert land), Bayan's second song, which contains a prophecy concerning Pushkin; this is a remarkable external reference of a kind that Glinka's contemporaries welcomed in literary epics. Yet this telling detail was one of the first cuts made. Even most of *Ruslan*'s defenders seemed unable to see the significant loss inflicted, since they failed to understand it in the context of the epic: Laroche, for example, calls the song a grievous and insensitive blunder, precisely because the prophecy can only be understood by the audience, but not by any of the characters on stage (!).[77] The cuts were thus sufficient to prevent the epic nature of the work from being conveyed, but not enough to transform *Ruslan* into anything resembling a standard magic opera. Thirdly, the national character of the work was not appreciated; as we have seen above, the public understood the romance in general and the *protyazhnaya* in particular (in its digestible salon form) to be distinctively Russian, but since the music they heard in *Ruslan* was much less reliant on this familiar Russianness, they were unsure of the composer's intentions. As a corollary of this, court circles also failed to perceive the patriotic intent behind the opera, and so Glinka did not receive any of the official recognition or rewards he might otherwise have enjoyed (this is not to suggest any ulterior motive on his part). Lastly, the première was blighted by the fact that the Tsar walked out before the end of the performance; this was, of course, noticed by everyone present, and made acceptance of the opera at court a most unlikely prospect, whatever the reviews might have said. Imagine for a moment, counterfactually, that Glinka had taken some intelligent critic such as O*** into his confidence before the première, so that public expectations about *Ruslan* could have been shaped in advance – the critic would have explained in the pages of some respected journal that the new opera was a great national epic, an unprecedented event in Russian opera. If such action had been taken, it is likely that Glinka would have been spared the blow which destroyed his ambitions as a composer, and which drove him to find solace and distraction in Europe.

The music of Ruslan: new horizons

Having stripped away the layers of mythology which *Ruslan* has accrued, we can now examine for ourselves whether the epic character of the opera has any bearing on Glinka's choice of musical material. The fact that an epic is unfolding is first signalled by the two songs given to the epic singer, Bayan, in the opening scene. To represent Bayan's bardic strumming, Glinka modifies an existing convention, adding the sound of the piano to the usual harp, and thus creating a strikingly apt imitation of the *gusli*, a plucked string instrument that Russian epic singers were supposed to have used. The way Glinka particularized, Russianized bardic strumming may suggest to us that he was searching for a more authentic representation of Russia's epic past, but this is hardly borne out by the rest of Bayan's material, which could be loosely described as being in romance style. If Glinka had any interest in excavating authentic Russianness, he could have turned to a readily available source, namely Kirsha Danilov's notated collection of *bïlinas*, i.e. Russian epic folk songs, (Rimsky-Korsakov later used *bïlina* material from this volume in *Sadko*).[78] But neither the music nor the texts which Glinka provided for Bayan's songs resembles anything contained in Danilov's collection. Glinka was interested not in recreating the *bïlina* on the operatic stage, but rather in adopting a number of musical strategies which would defamiliarize Bayan's music (and indeed much else in *Ruslan*), which the listener would soon recognize on repetition, and accept as signifying the strangeness and dignity of the mythologized past presented in *Ruslan*. In the harmony, we find an insistence on certain progressions, not especially unusual in themselves, but certainly striking when repeated a number of times: thus, for example, at the end of every strophe we have a cadence on the dominant minor in the first song, and a minor plagal cadence in the second. The initial phrases of each strophe, on the other hand, provide an example of a melodic feature used to defamiliarize:

in both songs the melody rotates within a narrow melodic range; the same device can be found in the melody of the Head's Tale. As it happens, this melodic device was probably folk-inspired, but it is likely that the source was Finnish, not Russian, for the device figures prominently in one of the opera's other epic numbers, the Finn's Ballad, which Glinka based on a Finnish melody (Ex.3.22). It seems that Glinka decided to accept the characteristic narrow ambit of the Finnish song as a marker for the other epic numbers;[79] the issue of authentic Russianness was clearly of little moment to Glinka if he could allow a Finnish melody to determine the music of the Russian characters when singing their own epic songs.

We shall look briefly at some of Glinka's other constructions of Russianness within *Ruslan*. From the Ruslanites onwards, the chorus "Mysterious Lel" has always been seen as the epitome of Glinka's "ancient Russian" music. This chorus uses repetition, exact or sequential, of simple melodic phrases, which suggest the intonation of natural speech. Most of the chorus proceeds in 5/4 metre, which Glinka had already used in the wedding chorus of *A Life* (it also

3.22   Glinka, *Ruslan and Lyudmila*, Finn's ballad

appears in a short choral interpolation within Lyudmila's cavatina). While the poetic metre was influenced by the folk models, the music Glinka sets to it, one crotchet per syllable, has no parallel in folksong. In other words, Glinka's settings are entirely a personal construct of musical Russianness, not a reflection of existing folk practices, and in *Ruslan* he obviously prefers such constructs to the quotation of Russian folksongs. This approach of simply inventing Russianness characterized the practices of the Kuchka, and we shall examine this development in the next chapter.

Another gold mine for the Kuchka is found in one of the two funereal choruses sung over the sleeping Lyudmila in Act V. The chorus "Akh tï, svet Lyudmila" ("Oh you our light, Lyudmila") introduces a new type of folk-like melody, with short motives that are repeated and varied (Ex.3.23a). Although we would stop short of connecting this melody to any particular folk prototype or even genre, it definitely does not belong to the sphere of the *protyazhnaya*, but instead evokes dance songs or *naigrïshi* (repetitive, often improvised instrumental tunes), akin to the material of the fast sections in *Kamarinskaya*. In this chorus, Glinka immediately goes beyond simple repetition, ingenuously playing with the durations of the opening few notes of the initial motive. In the course of the changing-background variations, the melody appears, ostinato-like, in the bass. Glinka's employment of such material for a ritual lament was followed by Rimsky-Korsakov in his first opera, *The Maid of Pskov*, where very similar material and even phrase structure appear in a chorus of the people lamenting the imminent arrival of Ivan the Terrible (Ex.3.23b). The use of such motives for lamentations, incantations and, when

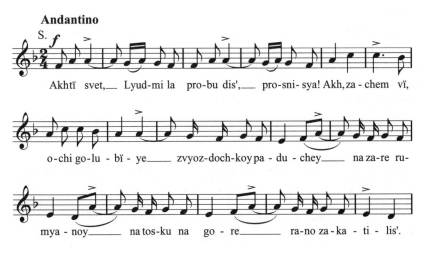

3.23a Glinka, *Ruslan and Lyudmila*, chorus "Akh tï, svet Lyudmila" from Act V (melody only)

3.23b Rimsky-Korsakov, *The Maid of Pskov*, chorus "Grozen tsar'" from Act III (melody only)

speeded up, folk-style dances was to become a staple part of the Kuchka style and was later assimilated and transformed by Stravinsky.

Although Glinka did not quote any Russian folksongs in his representation of Russians in *Ruslan*, quotation played an important role in the representation of non-Russians in the opera. We have already discussed Glinka's quotation of a Finnish folksong, but the composer lavishes special attention on the musical representation of the Oriental characters. *Ruslan*'s Orientalism is strikingly unusual for its time; for a representative point of comparison, we might set the "Turkish music" of *A Life for the Tsar* against the Georgian Lezghinka in *Ruslan*. The former (Ex.3.24a) is written well within the bounds of the pre-existing conventions for exoticism, while the latter (Ex.3.24b) is an original melody which followed no existing conventions. Indeed, most of the Oriental melodies in *Ruslan* are original, which results in a freshness and diversity which is immediately apparent (in contrast to later Russian Orientalism, which eventually became bogged down in stale mannerisms). It is true that the use of a flat sixth degree in major key contexts is a common

3.24a Glinka, *A Life for the Tsar*, Act II, "Turkish music" section from Krakowiak

3.24b   Glinka, *Ruslan and Lyudmila*, Lezghinka from Act IV

feature of the Oriental scenes, but this cannot have functioned as an Orientalist device for Glinka, since he is equally happy to use it in the Russian scenes.

Another feature of *Ruslan* which later became a cliché in Russian opera was the use of the whole-tone scale in association with the fantastic; within *Ruslan*, this scale was used exclusively as a leitmotif for the evil sorcerer, Chernomor. It is usually noted that Chernomor's leitmotif appears in the opera only three times: in the overture, at the moment of Lyudmila's abduction and in the chorus "He will perish" which reports on the battle between Ruslan and Chernomor.[80] The whole-tone scale indeed appears only in these instances, but other versions of Chernomor's leitmotive, now interspersed with semitones, also appear when Chernomor is mentioned or hinted at, in the Introduction, in the Head's Tale and in the Slaves' Chorus recounting the second abduction of Lyudmila. The distinction between the whole-tone scale proper and its paler shadows seems to make clear dramatic sense: the might and terror of Chernomor's sorcery cannot be recounted – it is incomparably more striking in action. But there is also another Chernomor, a strange and comical mute character, a dwarf with a beard seven times his size. He appears without his scale in his March, although the two tonal centres of C and E (as in the battle chorus) make a clear connection between Chernomor on his day off and on business. In other words, although Glinka's use of leimotive in *Ruslan* is generally more straightforward than the system of reminiscences in *A Life*, the meaning of the scale motif is vexed: rather than attaching it specifically to Chernomor, it should perhaps be understood as a theme of an evil fate that will surely come to pass, but which will just as surely be overridden by the good.

The diversity of Glinka's means which we have been discussing has led some commentators to complain that Glinka never developed an individual style. David Brown, for example, blamed this supposed failure on the humdrum nature of Glinka's life as depicted in the composer's own memoirs. Let us pause to analyse this notion of an individual style: clearly original ideas are required for individuality, and a reasonable size of oeuvre in order that we may trace the emergence of a style if there is any. But Glinka passes on both counts. What he lacked was the habit of *repeating* himself, of picking out the most felicitous of his original ideas and reusing them until listeners could smile and say, "Ah, Glinka!". This did not pass unnoticed during the composer's lifetime, indeed Berlioz expressed his amazement at this trait. Not only was Glinka's second opera very different from the first, but within *Ruslan* itself the rule was stylistic contrast. The more familiar stylistic ingredients of *A Life for the Tsar*, such as Russian romance or Italianate coloratura were carefully assimilated and blended in that opera, whereas in *Ruslan*, the use of such pre-existing styles (outside the many passages which are stylistically novel) is governed by an avoidance of any higher stylistic unity – they are presented in deliberate contrast to each other. It is important that we have the example of *A Life* before us, otherwise we might suspect that Glinka was merely incompetent in this respect. Lyudmila's cavatina in *Ruslan* is more purely Italianate than its nearest counterpart in *A Life*, namely Antonida's cavatina. *Ruslan*'s Act I finale has an unabashedly Italian drive, while Farlaf's rondo is a model example of the buffo style. And the Russian romance style is given the same treatment: the central part of Lyudmila's Act IV aria outdoes any of the romance-style numbers of *A Life*; one can almost imagine Glinka ticking off items on a check-list of romance characteristics – there is even a solo violin interlude as a vestige of the genre's domestic provenance.

In this conscious gathering together of everything in the world that seems of worth, and claiming it for Russian culture, Glinka was following in Pushkin's footsteps. Some Ruslanites, such as Laroche, tried to sift out the best features of the opera, which were to be considered organically Russian, while the rest was rejected on the grounds of its foreign-ness. Others, instead, rejoiced in *Ruslan*'s eclecticism, and a number of Russian composers were only too happy to accept it as a licence to incorporate Western operatic idioms freely, even assimilating aspects of Italian opera, their arch-rival. Rimsky-Korsakov, for example, populated a Ukrainian village with a basso buffo and a coloratura soprano in his *Christmas Eve*, but in this he was only creating counterparts to Glinka's Farlaf and Lyudmila. The balletic scenes, divertissements and spectacle of *Ruslan* proved to be another licence: Russian nationalist opera, for all its seriousness of purpose, did not abandon entertainment.

Ruslan's Russianness was retrospective: it came to play a crucial role in the formation of a Russian art-music idiom even though neither the composer nor his public would have perceived the music as distinctly Russian. *Ruslan* was influential, rather, because Glinka had mastered those idioms which he had inherited, and invented much that was striking and memorable, resulting in work which stood so high above the achievements of other Russian composers that Glinka was adopted as a national standard. And like Pushkin he was soon mythologized to fit the requirements of nationalist agendas.

Glinka's "Testament"

The final years of Glinka's life, although musically unproductive, have always received special attention from nationalist commentators, who argued that his silence was due to his extensive preparatory work towards the next great step in Russian music. And although he died before his new ideas could bear fruit, his searches were regarded as prophetic of late nineteenth- and early twentieth-century developments. It was in this context that Boris Asafyev, for example, entitled his chapter on the final years "Glinka's Last Testament".[81]

After the meagre success of *Ruslan* (especially dispiriting after the triumph of *A Life for the Tsar*), the composer sank into deep compositional lethargy. Disappointment need not have been the sole reason, however, since he had always been reluctant to repeat himself, preferring to wait until he had found fresh ideas. His prolonged stay in Spain gave him the inspiration for his two Spanish overtures, and these, in turn, provided a model for his celebrated orchestral piece on Russian themes, *Kamarinskaya*. But a change of scenery did not always inspire new music: Glinka's visit to Paris and even his friendship with Berlioz failed to spur him towards any new endeavours. Glinka seemed to have retired to the sidelines, and found more satisfaction in studying the music of his new-found idols, Handel and Gluck, than in adding to his own oeuvre. In 1855 he even expressed some revulsion at the thought of writing more music in the service of the Russian nation:

> Even if my muse were suddenly to awaken, I should rather write something textless for orchestra; I am rejecting Russian music as well as the Russian winter. I don't want any more of Russian drama – it has given me enough bother![82]

Glinka had nevertheless toyed with the idea of another Russian opera (*Dvumuzhnitsa*, The Bigamist), but eventually abandoned it for fear of repeating himself:

> [I]t is difficult and nearly impossible to write an opera in the Russian style without borrowing at least the general qualities of my old woman [i.e. *A Life for the Tsar* – this was Glinka's pet name for that opera].[83]

With these words, it appears that Glinka has submitted to the public verdict that *Ruslan* lacked any clear Russian qualities, and accordingly he feels that he had exhausted all the possibilities of musical Russianness in his first opera. However, his other letters of the same period hint that the idea of turning towards Russian church music was already stirring in his mind.

Glinka first came into close contact with official church music in 1837, when he was appointed the Kapellmeister of the Court Cappella in the wake of *A Life for the Tsar*'s success. But at that time, the music he heard in the course of his work had not inspired him to set out on any new musical path, and the very few liturgical pieces he wrote in these years did not break any new ground. In 1854, however, he was much impressed by the singing of the celebrated Sheremetev Choir then directed by Gavriil Lomakin, which had diverged significantly from official liturgical style; Lomakin instead had the choir sing harmonizations of the oldest stratum of church music, the *znamennïy* chant.[84] The following year, after the winter had passed, Glinka set out for the Sergiyev monastery, eager to deepen his acquaintance with this music. Glinka still knew little about the modes used in *znamennïy* chant, and little more about the modes of Renaissance theory; nevertheless, he believed that their similarities might allow him to create a new polyphonic music based on old Russian church music, using Western Renaissance polyphony as his model; with this in mind, in 1856 he made the startling decision to resume the study of counterpoint with his old teacher Dehn in Berlin, more than two decades after his last lesson.

And so the fifty-two-year-old composer, his health declining, set out to investigate a new repertory and to perfect his compositional technique. His first reports from Berlin convey his excitement:

> Apart from my health, I was attracted here to Berlin by my desire to study church music in depth with Dehn, and to become proficient at canons, so that later I could make an attempt (I don't say a model) at setting the liturgy of John Chrysostom in Slavic-Russian Orthodox style, in 2 and 3 parts, for junior deacons rather than for choir.[85]
>
> The main thing is that Dehn and I have already started working towards the liturgy, and it seems that this enterprise would be possible, for those ancient Greek modes over which I took so much futile trouble in Petersburg, still offer wide possibilities and are in fact nearly the same as our church modes.[86]

But the progress was much slower than Glinka had expected, partly due to the limitations his ill health placed upon him, but more importantly because he had seriously underestimated the scale of the task:

My studies with Dehn have been interrupted for nearly two months now. Tomorrow (1 October [1856]) we shall get back to business. Dehn intends to ... lead me gradually to the composition of a double fugue ... whose theme should be based on the church modes – I still haven't the slightest idea about them. In general, I must admit that I've never studied any real church music as yet, and so in such a short time I can't expect to grasp everything that had been worked out over several centuries. Dehn offers me Palestrina and Orlando di Lasso as examples.[87]

Although working on canons and fugues throughout this time, Glinka never lost sight of the purpose behind this industry: his letters are full of exclamations such as "May God Almighty let me produce Russian church music".[88] One of his last known remarks on the subject displays a new, hard-won certainty:

I am nearly sure that it is possible to tie Western fugue to our kind of music by bonds of lawful marriage.[89]

This quotation became especially widely known among Russian musicians and was perceived as Glinka's testament for generations to come.

Aside from the remarks in his letters, there is little evidence to tell us what kind of music Glinka hoped to write. In Ex.3.25 we can see a fragment from his 1856 notebooks that contains preliminary sketches for a double fugue using a *theme russe* (a *protyazhnaya*-like melody), but this does not reveal any novel approach to counterpoint that might be traced to the characteristics of the Russian theme. Indeed, Glinka could have produced much the same sketch twenty years earlier, as demonstrated by the fugal chorus from *A Life for the Tsar*. More interesting are two sacred pieces that Glinka wrote for the Sergiyev

3.25   Glinka, a sketch for a double fugue, dated 1856; published in Glinka, *Polnoye sobraniye sochineniy*, vol. 17 (Moscow: Muzïka, 1969)

monastery just before he left for Berlin. The first of these, "Yekten'ya pervaya" (First Litany), appears to be purely liturgical in its intent, although it is interesting for its determined re-harmonizations of the repeated interjection "Lord, have mercy". Also notable is Glinka's avoidance of the leading note in minor-mode harmonizations: here, he employs plagal cadences (Ex.3.26), foreshadowing the practice of many Russian composers at the end of the century (see Chapter 5). His desire for exclusive heptatonicism indicates that he thought the leading note (when requiring an alteration) was inauthentic within Russian church music. Overall, however, Glinka's approach is as conservative as possible – he is certainly not attempting to personalize or modernize the liturgical style.

3.26 Glinka, First Litany (fragment)

The other piece, the three-part *Da ispravitsya molitva moya* (Let my prayer be answered, see the extract in Ex.3.27) is a setting of a chant melody in strophic form which Glinka treats with some harmonic variation. Like the Litany, it is also completely heptatonic, and again uses plagal cadences when finishing a phrase on a minor triad. Without speculating on the extent to which this piece was influenced by Glinka's experiences in the Sergiyev monastery, we may note that the three-part male-voice texture is in keeping with the monastic tradition. The doubling of the chant melody in thirds or sixths was a common feature of chant arrangements, both earlier (e.g. Bortnyansky), and contemporary (Alexei Lvov),[90] although Glinka's writing is more distant from standard chorale harmony. The absence of bar-lines may indicate Glinka's familiarity with Lvov's essay "On free and non-symmetrical

3.27 Glinka, *Da ispravitsya molitva moya* (fragment)

rhythms", which was being prepared for publication at the time. The strict heptatonicism of the piece may reflect the practices of the Sergiyev monastery, but could just as well be the result of Glinka's theoretical conjectures about how Russian Orthodox church music ought to sound. Whatever the case, the monks eagerly accepted the pieces; three of them came to St Petersburg to rehearse at Glinka's apartment, and the pieces were sung at the monastery during Lent 1856.

Later nationalist commentators considered *Da ispravitsya* to be uncannily prophetic of the late nineteenth-century New Trend school of liturgical composers (which included Kastalsky and Rakhmaninov). But there is no mystery: Glinka's piece was published posthumously by Jurgenson in 1878, and the nationalist composers of the New Trend could hardly be expected to remain uninfluenced by it, let alone to be unaware of it. More difficult to unravel is the mystification surrounding Glinka's piece and the indigenous Russian polyphony to which it is supposedly related. Olga Levasheva, for example, tells us that *Da ispravitsya* was written "strictly in the tradition of ancient Russian polyphony, the so-called 'troyestrochnoe singing'" [i.e. three-part singing].[91] This alleged tradition of *troyestrochnoye* singing is especially dear to the heart of nationalist commentators; it supposedly flourished for a short time in the early seventeenth century just prior to the arrival of Western polyphony. The purpose of the story is clear: Russia had already developed polyphony before the Western polyphonic tradition was imported, and so Russians should not consider themselves indebted to the West in this respect, but instead recover and celebrate their indigenous polyphonic tradition. Unfortunately for the supporters of this account, the only evidence that has ever been adduced to prove the existence of such a tradition is unlikely to convince any scholar who was not already predisposed to belief by national-istic considerations; all the manuscripts which supposedly constitute a record of the tradition are in neumatic notation, leaving the pitch relations and rhythmic alignment of the parts undetermined (see Chapter 5 for further discussion). Odoyevsky had in his possession an early eighteenth-century manuscript which recorded an attempt to realize the neumatic polyphony in modern notation; this was the only example which could have been known to Glinka.[92] But Odoyevsky himself had very little regard for the transcription and in 1867, he made the following highly sceptical inscription on the manuscript:

> The supposition that at any time these three parts could have been sung together, simultaneously, is absolutely out of the question. There is no harmonic correlation between them whatsoever; these parts are completely independent; no human ear could possibly tolerate the chains of seconds which you meet at every step. [The passage continues in a similar vein.][93]

A modern transcription of the same *sticheron* was made by Nikolai Uspensky from a neumatic manuscript that had clearer indications of pitch. The alignment of parts is slightly different from Odoyevsky's version, but this does not render the style any less dissonant; even if we granted the existence of this tradition, and the treatment of seconds as consonances, this is not remotely similar to Glinka's consonant, functional-harmony based polyphony. Having established this, it is hardly worth adding that we have no evidence to indicate that Glinka had ever heard of *troyestrochnoye peniye*.

* * *

In conclusion, the issue of Glinka's Russianness is of paramount importance for the history of Russian musical nationalism. Not only was he was accorded the mythological role of founding father for Russian national music, but Glinka also consciously embarked on the project of creating Russian national music. This he did in three different ways. The first is represented by *A Life for the Tsar*: the assimilation of popular styles that already carried associations of nationality. For a time, Glinka saw this as the only way of achieving Russianness in his music; as he said, "It is difficult and nearly impossible to write an opera in the Russian style without borrowing at least the general qualities of my old woman [i.e. *A Life*]"). But towards the end of his life, Glinka sought a new path to Russianness by essentializing a certain tradition (chant or folksong) that would somehow transmit its Russianness to any art music that incorporated it, whatever the specifics of the treatment. Conveniently, he viewed Palestrina-type counterpoint as a neutral, universal method, which he hoped to apply to the raw material of Russian chant and folksong to create the foundation of a new, "truly Russian" music. Where *A Life* sought Russianness through public consensus, the project of Glinka's last year sought Russianness through a mystified archaeology. The third way was found in *Ruslan*, although only after the composer's death. When Glinka wrote the opera, he was unfettered by either of the above nationalist approaches; instead, he sought only to provide imaginative, novel music, avoiding so far as it was possible any obvious duplication of idioms that belonged recognizably to the oeuvre of any particular composer (his own previous works included). In the hands of the Kuchka, however, this path of negation was chosen as the new way to create Russianness in music. On the one hand, they avoided idioms that belonged too recognizably to "the West", while on the other they accumulated characteristic features of *Ruslan*, which were retrospectively essentialized as markers of Russianness; to these, they added a repertoire of further devices, sometimes of their own devising, but sometimes – covertly – from Schumann or Liszt. The music (as opposed to the scenario) of *Ruslan* was therefore only heard as an expression of Russian nationhood after the Kuchka had adopted its characteristics in their own music, which was carefully marketed as nationalistic.

These are the three ways to Russianness in music. Since Glinka's death, generations of Russian composers have followed one or other, following the common perceptions of the audience, looking ever deeper for the authentic, uncontaminated source of the nation's music, or simply honing their individual styles in the hope that marketing will ensure that the music is eventually heard as Russian. As Russian art music matured and accumulated the baggage of tradition, the three ways became ever harder to distinguish.

CHAPTER 4

THE BEGINNING AND THE END
OF THE "RUSSIAN STYLE"

Nationalist critics had long nurtured hopes for an autonomous, distinctively Russian line of operas and concert music, to be produced by a recognizable Russian school of composers. They believed that *A Life for the Tsar* was the inaugural moment of this school, and they leapt upon each new Russian work that had received some acclaim, proclaiming it the next great deed of the Russian School. Serov also claimed that Dargomïzhsky wrote his opera *Rusalka* in the "independent Russian style", disregarding the fact that it was substantially different in style from either of Glinka's operas, or that the two Glinka operas were stylistically different from each other.[1] It was not until the 1860s that the terms "Russian style" and "Russian school" acquired real content, through the activities of the Kuchka, which was united by its common goals and shared stylistic features. And it is the style of the Kuchka and their successors that is still recognized as the "Russian style" by the international audiences.[2]

In the present chapter we shall examine some features of this Russian style. Rather than attempt any exhaustive survey of this vast topic, we shall restrict ourselves largely to the Russian style as exemplified in the works of Rimsky-Korsakov. The choice is by no means arbitrary: to see how central Rimsky-Korsakov was in the formation and dissemination of the style, let us imagine for a moment that his ambitions had been satisfied by his naval career, and that he never found time to indulge any musical yearnings. In this case, we would scarcely have had any Russian nationalist school to talk about: without the prolific Rimsky-Korsakov, with his fifteen operas and numerous symphonic works (and discounting the prolific, but bland Cui), the Kuchka's entire output could be counted on the fingers. Works now considered central to the Kuchka canon would have remained as sketches, fragments, partial drafts or short scores – among them *Khovanshchina*, *Prince Igor* and *A Night on the Bare Mountain* – had it not been for the selfless industry of Rimsky-Korsakov, who brought many such works to completion, endowing them with the brilliant orchestral clothing that helped ensure their success. Without Rimsky-Korsakov's revision of *Boris* (controversial as it remains), and his advocacy of the opera, the Western première in Paris, and the subsequent surge of interest in the work would not have taken place (revival, if it had ever come, would have been left to a later generation). Without Rimsky-Korsakov's own works and his conducting activities, the Kuchka would never have achieved such renown within their own country, and Diaghilev's entrepreneurial feelers would not have detected a corpus of dazzling Russian works which could be taken on tour to the West. Without the composer of *Sheherezade*, the Spanish Capriccio and *Kashchei*, the musical styles of Ravel, Debussy, and early Stravinsky would have been substantially different: in effect, we would not have the *Rhapsodie Espagnol*, *La mer* or *The Firebird*. And finally, without Rimsky-Korsakov's work as a teacher to three generations of composers (including Glazunov and Stravinsky), and his establishment of a school that prolonged the life of the Russian style well into Soviet times, nearly a century of Russian/Soviet music history would look very different.

By the sheer quantity of his output, Rimsky-Korsakov consolidated his own and his friends' musical inventions into the coherent style we now know as that of the Kuchka. Granted, the discerning ear is often able to trace various ideas in his music to a particular piece of Balakirev, Borodin or Musorgsky; but even if they have priority claims, it was Rimsky-Korsakov who rescued their often fragmentary or undeveloped ideas from oblivion, and brought them to fruition. And thus it was Rimsky-Korsakov who brought us, the operatic and concert audiences, to perceive these features of the music as unmistakably Russian. Therefore we may see him not merely as one more composer who contributed to the familiar Russian style, but in a sense its architect, who painstakingly built up the edifice of Russian national music with the stones rough-hewn or carved to varying degrees by his fellow-composers.

For all these reasons Rimsky-Korsakov will act as our guide to the Russian style, his works the starting points of the discussion. The fact that he was continuously reflecting on his work and work of others (and that his ruminations are preserved in his *Chronicle of My Musical Life* and in Yastrebtsev's *Reminiscences of Rimsky-Korsakov*), makes him all the more useful as a guide. We shall attempt to identify the main sources of the Russian style through one of its first manifestations, in Rimsky-Korsakov's first opera, *The Maid of Pskov*, and we shall see Rimsky-Korsakov's farewell to the Russian style in his last opera, *The Golden Cockerel*. But our discussion will begin with one of the most easily identifiable idioms of the Russian style and its connotations.

The "Kuchka Pattern"

Of all the musical habits formed collectively by the members of the Kuchka, one in particular is so often found and so prominent that it can be regarded as the Kuchka calling-card: namely, the melodic pattern 5–#5–6–♭6–5 over a static bass, normally heard in an inner voice. Since we shall be examining this pattern throughout the present section, we shall call it the Kuchka Pattern for convenience, hereafter to be abbreviated as KP. The influence of the Kuchka can indeed be monitored by noting occurrences of the KP, which are frequent and widespread; even in a harmonic idiom more complex than that of the Kuchka, the KP remains immediately recognizable, as in the opening theme from the second movement of Rakhmaninov's Fourth Piano Concerto (Ex.4.1a), or in the third theme (Très rythmé) from Debussy's *La Soirée dans Grenade* (Ex.4.1b). The pervasiveness of the KP was noticed by Gerald Abraham, in his essay "Evolution of Russian harmony", who wrote that "the use of this particular chromatic effect is one of the commonest characteristics of nineteenth-century Russian harmony; one finds it on page after page of any Russian 'nationalist' score and on a good many of Tchaikovsky's".[3]

4.1a   Rakhmaninov, Piano Concerto no. 4, second movement

4.1b   Debussy, *La soirée dans Grenade*

The next scholar to pay attention to this idiom was Richard Taruskin, who brought it up in his discussion of Russian Orientalism.[4] While Taruskin also discussed other Oriental markers, such as the *cor anglais*, melismatic melodic patterns, or drum-like rhythmic patterns, he makes the KP central to his argument.[5] He calls it "the essential *nega* undulation"[6] or "the very morpheme of *nega*"[7], *nega* being a Russian term for sexual pleasure (the word has fallen into disuse, but the standard nineteenth-century Russian dictionary defined *nega* as "complete sensual contentment and enjoyment").[8] Taruskin traced the KP qua Orientalist marker back to Glinka, passing forward "optionally" (as he says) through Balakirev but "necessarily through Borodin and *Prince Igor*".[9] Borodin is especially important for his argument, since both his opera and his concert piece *In the Steppes of Central Asia* places representations of Russians and Orientals in opposition to each other. The languorous East, Taruskin says, is feminine and seductive: it is "no match for the purposefully advancing Russians",[10] but at the same time it presents a sexual threat to them. After recounting the story of Vladimir, the son of Prince Igor, who was ensnared by Konchakovna (daughter of Khan Konchak), Taruskin reflects on the ending of their love duet:

> And while they hold their final notes the orchestra harps repeatedly on the hypnotic undulation of fifth degree and the flattened sixth. Vladimir is now thoroughly lost: Ratmirized, his manhood *nega*ted, rendered impotent with respect to his (and his father's mission), he must be left behind. No less than Ratmir, he has been the victim of a sinister Oriental charm.[11]

It is indeed in this Oriental context that the KP would most readily be recognized today, whether in the Polovtsian Dances or *Sheherezade*. But does this mean that we have any right to view it as an exclusively Orientalist trope on "page after page" (Abraham) of Russian scores? It would seem extremely convenient to use it as supporting evidence in the interpretation of programmatic symphonic scores (which Taruskin does with the love theme from Tchaikovsky's *Romeo and Juliet*), and perhaps even as an interpretative clue for non-programmatic symphonic music – Glazunov's symphonies, for example. However, a more comprehensive account of the KP and its associations than Taruskin provides will demonstrate that the KP was not "the very morpheme of *nega*" but a generally unmarked feature of the Kuchka style (this is not, of course, to deny that the KP occurs, sometimes prominently, in Orientalist contexts).[12] In the discussion that follows, various reasons for the idiom's ubiquity in Russian music will be uncovered, and this will feed into some more general conclusions about the evolution of the Russian style.

The origins of the KP and its Oriental associations can indeed be traced back to Glinka, as Taruskin has said, and in particular to *Ruslan*. Many numbers associated with the East, such as the section of Lyudmila's cavatina which is addressed to Ratmir, or either of Ratmir's solo numbers, contain in isolation either the ascent or the descent from the KP, but they are never heard together in the full form of the KP, that is, against a static bass, with the ascent immediately followed by the descent in the same voice.

Nevertheless, the instances of #5/♭6 chromaticism in *Ruslan* are by no means limited to the representation or evocation of the Orient. Indeed, there are simply too many of these non-Oriental occurrences for us to be able to say with any confidence that contemporary audiences would have interpreted this harmonic feature as an Oriental marker. Why should they, if they heard the same feature in a number of purely Russian contexts? Or, for that matter, why should we imagine that Glinka intended the feature as an Oriental marker? It would have been very simple for him to restrict its use to Oriental contexts, if this had been his purpose. Aside from this consideration, the use of ♭6 in major-mode passages was in any case a standard feature of Russian music in the decades before *Ruslan*: it can be found in abundance in the Russian romances of the 1820s and 1830s, including Glinka's early songs. It was used in diminished seventh, augmented sixth chords, and in minor subdominant chords, especially to strengthen modulations via the subdominant. The outer sections of ternary-form romances were most often in the minor, and the middle sections in the relative major; composers of romances often placed the leading note of the minor and the ♭6 of the major close to each other (as in Glinka's early romance "Ne iskushay" – Do not tempt me, Ex.4.2a). Harmonic progressions playing with reversible #5/♭6 chromaticism could often be encountered in the post-cadential prolongations of the final tonic, as in another romance, "Razocharovaniye" (Frustration, 1828, Ex.4.2b). The melodic alternation of natural and flat 6 in cadential areas was in fact typical of Italian-influenced songs and arias. Far from springing to life as a special marker of the Oriental, *Ruslan's* #5/♭6 chromaticism belongs to the world of

vse o-bol'-shche - nya prezh-nikh   dney!   Uzh   ya   ne ve-ryu u-ve - ren' - yam, uzh

4.2a Glinka, *Ne iskushay*

4.2b   Glinka, *Razocharovaniye*

the early nineteenth-century romance, the world from which Glinka, the composer, had himself arisen. It should therefore be no surprise that #5/♭6 chromaticism is put to many different uses in *Ruslan*, as a standard harmonic device. We find it in the service of *peremennost'* (changeable modal centres) in the folksy choral interjection within Lyudmila's cavatina. We also encounter it as one of the many devices called upon for re-harmonizing a melody within changing-background variations, as in Finn's ballad or the chorus "Akh tï, svet Lyudmila" from Act V (see Examples 4.3a and b). And in the Naina–Farlaf scene, Glinka clearly opposes the two resolutions of the augmented triad, which takes us one step closer to the full KP. But none of these examples represents the Orient or *nega*. In other words, #5/♭6 chromaticism in Glinka's works is semantically unmarked; *Ruslan* is no exception, but later audiences, including the Kuchka, might indeed have found the many occurrences of #5/♭6 chromaticism alongside Glinka's genuine markers of the Oriental (such as the cor anglais, and certain ornamental melodic patterns) sufficiently memorable

4.3a   Glinka, *Ruslan and Lyudmila*, Finn's ballad

that in time it became associated with the complex of musical devices used to represent the Orient.[13]

The chorus "Akh tï, svet Lyudmila" (Act V), is a particularly instructive case of #5/♭6 chromaticism occurring outside Oriental contexts. The chorus features a diatonic melody subjected to changing-background variation procedures, in the course of which it is supplied with numerous chromatic countermelodies. In the fifth variation, the diatonic melody is caught up in a chromatic tangle of voices (Ex.4.3b; Farlaf's interjections are omitted), with two instances of 6–♭6–5 followed by three instances of 6–♭6–5–#5–6 and a final 6–♭6–5. There is a simple pragmatic explanation for the appearance of #5/♭6 chromaticism here: once Glinka had run out of simpler re-harmonizations, he would turn to chromaticism. The KP was a useful resource in this technical context, and evidently Glinka did not himself associate it so strongly with the Orient that he saw any reason to exclude it here. Now if this incidence of the KP can be accounted for on purely music-technical grounds, what of its occurrence in the Persian Chorus? For this is Taruskin's prime example from *Ruslan* of the KP as a designator of the Oriental, yet the KP once again appears in the later stages of a set of changing-background variations. Now if the KP was used in precisely this way during the course of "Akh tï, svet Lyudmila", a chorus with no Oriental associations, then we might ask whether there are any compelling grounds for arguing that the use of the KP in the Persian Chorus is Orientalist. Even if we widen the scope of our inquiry to embrace chromaticism of any sort, and not merely the #5/♭6 variety, we find that the progressive chromaticism of "Akh tï, svet Lyudmila" is equally a feature of the other changing-background numbers: the chorus "Mysterious Lel", Finn's Ballad, and the Head's Tale, all of which likewise occur outside any Oriental context. Set alongside these four numbers, the chromaticism of the Persian Chorus is seen to arise simply by virtue of its changing-background variations, not as an Oriental marker. In *Ruslan*, chromaticism is thus found in Oriental and non-Oriental scenes alike, sometimes for technical reasons in changing-background variations, and elsewhere merely because it was a general feature of Glinka's style, drawn from the inherited harmonic reper-

4.3b Glinka, *Ruslan and Lyudmila*, Chorus "Akh tï, svet Lyudmila" from Act V (vocal parts omitted)

toire of the Russian romance. A generation later, much had changed, for we see Stasov expressing some disappointment that Glinka had allowed chromaticism into the accompanimental harmonies of the Finn's Ballad: he found this inappropriately "iznezhennaya" (i.e. too delicate, or effeminate; the word is related to *nega*).[14] Where Taruskin overlooks the fact that chromaticism is a general feature of Glinka's style in *Ruslan*, Stasov acknowledges the fact, but wishes it were otherwise.[15]

From this perspective, we can approach the controversy over Ratmir's waltz in the cabaletta section of his Act III aria. Laroche and Cui held that Glinka had simply miscalculated in giving a blatantly "Western" number (as they heard it) to an Oriental character.[16] Taruskin takes the opposite course, defending the waltz on the grounds that is in fact appropriately Oriental; his argument stands on the waltz's abundant chromaticism in general, and on the presence of #5/♭6 chromaticism in particular. Since Laroche and Cui were so much closer to *Ruslan*'s first audiences in time and place, we might ask whether their opinion should not carry more weight. In the light of the discussion above, we also know that neither #5/♭6 chromaticism nor the other chromatic features were out of place in a non-Oriental scene; indeed, we even happen to have another of Glinka's waltzes, this time from *A Life for the Tsar*, to prove the point: the scene provides no reason for evoking the Orient, and everyone on stage is Polish, yet we find the same degree of chromatic activity as in Ratmir's waltz (Examples 4.4a and b). We have no reason to suppose, therefore, that Glinka thought he had supplied Ratmir's waltz with Oriental markers, nor that contemporary audiences would have perceived the waltz as characteristically Oriental. Contemporary critics did not see anything wrong in giving a Western dance, the waltz, to an Oriental character, nor did they object that the dance had not been transformed to sound Oriental; the conventionalized presentation of the Orient in music was rudimentary and piecemeal at this stage, and audiences were quite accustomed to hearing Oriental characters sing minuets, sicilianas, and other European dances (for example, in Alyabyev's *The Captive of the Caucasus*, a melodrama of the late 1820s). It was only when Orientalist musical conventions were better established in the minds of composers and audiences that Laroche and Cui could

4.4a   Glinka, waltz from *A Life for the Tsar*

4.4b   Glinka, *Ruslan and Lyudmila*, Ratmir's aria

complain that the waltz was *inappropriately Western*. The critic Senkovsky, writing just after *Ruslan*'s première, even suggested that Ratmir's waltz was much more successful than the preceding slow section, yet it was this slow section which later became a paradigm of Orientalist music. The languorous dialogue between Ratmir and the cor anglais left Senkovsky cold, while the waltz is described as invoking "desire, voluptuousness, violent passion . . . a storm of passion in sound, something completely understood by every listener".[17] The markers of sexual passion were much more basic than #5/♭6 chromaticism, and readily understandable to all members of the audience: the ever-increasing tempo and, indeed, the breathless whirlwind of the waltz itself. We should remember that the waltz was still celebrated (or notorious) at this time for its lack of formality, and its power to awaken the passions of the dancing couples. Glinka must have thought it a perfect vehicle of representing passion: on another occasion, he used the waltz to set a text similar to Ratmir's, in his romance "V krovi gorit ogon' zhelan'ya" (the text begins, "My blood is burning with desire, my soul is stung by you; kiss me more – your kisses are sweeter than myrrh and wine"). For later critics such as Laroche and Cui, the waltz was already a more formal genre, and its European, ballroom associations would have overridden whatever signs of the Orient might have been present (such as the cor anglais).

We should realize, then, that in *Ruslan* the Oriental style is only detectable retrospectively, because the Kuchka took up the characteristic features of these scenes and continued to use them in association with the Oriental. Glinka offered many different possibilities for representing the Orient (among them the modal diatonicism in the Turkish dance and the accumulation of open-string fifths in the Lezghinka), rather than a handful of fixed progressions or melodic phrases. As it happens, we have a useful test case to prove that Glinka had not established an Oriental style in the minds of musicians, critics or the public. Rubinstein's *Persian Songs* of 1854, a cycle of 12 romances, presents a wide array of possibilities for representing the Orient – any scale degree can be altered, and irregular phrasing becomes the norm; indeed, anything slightly out of the ordinary could be enlisted in the cause of exoticism. Among critics, the *Persian Songs* won Rubinstein the reputation of the Oriental composer *par excellence*; but if they had already accepted the devices in *Ruslan*'s Oriental scenes as the touchstone for musical Orientalism, they would have been bound to reject Rubinstein's own attempt at Orientalism, since it shared little with Glinka (even in the case of altered scale degrees, ♭6 in the major mode only appears once, in the first song). The Kuchka, however, established the Oriental style once and for all from the starting point of Glinka, rather than Rubinstein; eventually, we see Rubinstein concede the point to the Kuchka, for in a later Orientalist work, *The Demon*, he adopts wholesale the Kuchka's repertoire of devices for representing the Orient.

The establishment of the conventions which constituted the Oriental style did not take place until the 1860s and owed much to Balakirev. Nevertheless, Balakirev's appropriation of #5/♭6 chromaticism from Glinka, and his derivation of the KP initially had nothing to do with the representation of the Orient. From the early songs of the 1850s to late works like the Piano Sonata, the KP remains a pervasive feature of Balakirev's individual style, and not an Oriental marker. The texts of the songs clearly indicate that the KP did not carry any essential Oriental associations for Balakirev; for example, he used the figure in his setting of Koltsov's "Russian" lyrics in "O come to me" (1858, Ex.4.5). But if Balakirev's KP is not Orientalist, what of the remainder of Taruskin's contention: that the KP signifies *nega*? If we seek our answer in Balakirev's romances, the contention might seem to find support, since the context is always love and desire; but then we must remind ourselves that this was a defining characteristic of the genre. If we turn to the instrumental music, however, we find the KP persisting through a great variety of moods, a many of which seem remote from *nega*; this indicates that the KP was simply a topic-neutral feature of Balakirev's compositional vocabulary.

There is another, more oblique piece of evidence which should warn us against associating the KP with the Orient, *nega*, or any other idea. Rimsky-Korsakov once pointed out to his biographer Yastrebtsev that the passage in Ex.4.6, from Glinka's song "The Gulf of Finland", "had left a deep impression on new Russian music", especially on Balakirev and on Rimsky-Korsakov

4.5   Balakirev, *Pridi ko mne*

4.6   Glinka, *Finskiy zaliv*

himself.[18] The passage chosen by Rimsky-Korsakov shows the ascending form of #5/♭6 chromaticism, extended diatonically: 5–#5–6–7–8. We find such variants quite often, as, for example in Balakirev's song "O come to me", which also features the standard KP (see Ex.4.5 above). Rimsky-Korsakov fails to mention any Oriental associations, and indeed we find that the frequent use of the KP in his own early works is a general, unmarked, stylistic component, just as in Balakirev. It appears, for example, at the start of the First Symphony's robust Scherzo, and in the harmonization of a Russian folksong "Kak po sadiku" (No. 79 from the *100 Russian Folksongs*). Rimsky-Korsakov's first opera, *The Maid of Pskov*, likewise contains many examples of #5/♭6 chromaticism; the opera's plot concerns Russian characters entirely, with no mention of the Orient. The full KP even appears in a passage which is intended to suggest Orthodox liturgical music: the chorus of the people, in Act III, sung in praise of the tsar (Ex.4.7); once again the musical context is a set of changing-background variations. An especially telling demonstration that Rimsky-Korsakov considered #5/♭6 chromaticism unmarked at this stage of his career occurs in the romances of 1866, when his music was closest to Balakirev's. #5/♭6 chromaticism can be found in both the Oriental "Plenivshis' rozoy, solovey" (A nightingale captivated by a rose, subtitled "Eastern romance") and in the non-Oriental "Iz slyoz moikh" (a translation of Heine's "Aus meinen Tränen", which also appears in *Dichterliebe*). But it is the latter, non-Oriental song where #5/♭6 chromaticism is not only much more prominent, but also takes the form of the KP proper.

4.7 Rimsky-Korsakov, *The Maid of Pskov*, Act III, chorus "Tsar' nash" (vocal parts omitted)

It was not until the late 1860s that Oriental associations began to adhere to the KP. Balakirev was again the source of this change, in spite of the fact that the KP remained an unmarked stylistic device within his own oeuvre. This has an air of paradox about it, but there is a simple explanation: it was not Balakirev's oeuvre in its entirety, but only a handful of individual works which made a great impact upon the other members of the Kuchka, and indeed upon the concert-going public, and if some of these works carried Oriental associations by virtue of their titles, then the KP, as a distinctive element of Balakirev's music, was more likely to acquire such associations itself, even if this was remote from the composer's own intentions. During his three trips to the Caucasus (1862, '63 and '68), Balakirev listened to the folk music of the various peoples of the region, and returned with many rough-and-ready transcriptions. These melodies soon began to appear in his music, and such passages were inevitably imitated by the other members of the Kuchka. Balakirev, in his letters, tells us how Lermontov's descriptions had impelled him to visit the Caucasus, and how the music, peoples and landscapes were etched in his memory. His visits were not, however, informed by any serious ethnographical interests, and he was little concerned to distinguish between the different peoples and their distinct musical cultures. His memories of the music he had heard, assisted by the transcriptions, were soon translated into a set of conventions for use in his own music, such as drones, representations of percussion patterns, and a certain type of florid ornamentation. Because of his direct experience of Caucasian music, there was always some fresh variation in Balakirev's use of these conventions; the other members of the Kuchka, lacking such memories, were only able to reproduce what they found in their teacher's music, and so in their hands the conventions became more rigid and circumscribed. If we compare, say, Balakirev's "Georgian Song" with Rimsky-Korsakov's "A nightingale captivated by a rose", we can readily see that the latter simply follows the model provided by the former.

Aside from his symphony, the other major works which occupied Balakirev during the 1860s were evocations of the Orient: the virtuosic piano piece *Islamey*, the symphonic poem *Tamara*, and a projected opera *The Firebird*, which never moved beyond sketches, although he claimed much of the music was in his head.[19] Although the Firebird fairy tale was Russian, Balakirev stated that the music was to be thoroughly Oriental in style. Why should he want to present the Russian through the Oriental? For Balakirev and Stasov, this was by no means arbitrary or eccentric, for in 1861 they had discussed some putative connections between Russian mythology and certain Eastern mythologies.[20] This exchange was prompted by Stasov's dissertation, "Proiskhozhdeniye russkikh bïlin" (Genesis of the Russian *bïlinï*),[21] which had just been submitted to the Academy of Sciences for the Uvarov Prize competition. In this work, we see not the familiar face of Stasov the unflinching nationalist, but rather a disinterested scholar excited by the newest developments in comparative mythology and philology, hence the following uncharacteristic remarks:

Bïlinas do not contain anything Russian in their foundations.[22]

The architecture and painting that we, in the fatherland, inherited from Byzantium met the same fate as the *bïlinas* (epic poems) that we received from the Mongol and Türk tribes. In each case, ancient Russia added nothing essential to the inheritance: its only contribution was the transmission of foreign legends [or architecture, or painting] as accurately as possible, adding only a very few insignificant, second-rate or third-rate details.[23]

Among Stasov's examples of connections between Russia and the Orient, two featured prominently: Yeruslan Lazarevich, a hero of Russian mythology (and a precursor of Pushkin's Ruslan), undertook much the same exploits as Rustem in the Persian epic *Shah-Name*; Stasov also claimed that the Russian Firebird was a version of the Indian Golden Bird. Balakirev received all this information with delight.

Thus Stasov and Balakirev both believed that the Russians shared a common ancestor with the peoples of the East. This is crucial to our understanding of Balakirev, and to some extent the other members of the Kuchka, within the context of the Orientalist debate. For Balakirev did not see the Oriental style as means for representing a separate, alien people, an Other, in current parlance, but as an essential component of musical Russianness. The use of the newly-constructed Oriental style was thus for Balakirev (and for the rest of the Kuchka in their earlier years) the easiest way to assert a distinct, non-European identity.[24]

Most strikingly, for Balakirev, the Oriental style became a default style, so that he ceased to perceive it as Oriental. The first signs of this development appeared as early as 1867, in his concert overture *In Bohemia*. This work contains a substantial section which is based on a Moravian folksong, startlingly presented in a full-blown Oriental style, with a battery of percussion delivering the characteristic rhythms which Balakirev had explored earlier in his "Georgian Song" (the KP, already part of his general style, is also present of course). When puzzled listeners requested an explanation for such an apparent geographical mismatch, Balakirev was baffled and could only say that he had not intended to insert any Oriental colour in the Overture.[25] We should not jump to the conclusion that Balakirev was using the Oriental style indiscriminately for the exotic, for Caucasian and Czech alike; the Czechs were not perceived as exotic in Russia, at this time especially, for Pan-Slavism was then at its height. The Czechs were therefore seen as Slav brothers, and Balakirev himself had participated in a Pan-Slavic project which brought him to Prague to conduct in performances of Glinka's two operas. Apart from the collapse of the Oriental style into Balakirev's general compositional vocabulary, a further issue is involved here. The Moravian folksong in question could be confused with Caucasian melodies (by the non-ethnomusicologist) even without Balakirev's Oriental-style orchestration. Folk melodies from two musical cultures with very different performance practices can often look very similar to the non-specialist when presented as a single line in standard notation (with discrete pitches, no indication of tuning norms, and all other aspects of performance stripped away). Balakirev, on another occasion, was intrigued by the similarities he had found between three melodies: one was Caucasian, another Russian, and the third a Spanish tune which had been transcribed by Glinka. Balakirev chose to interpret these similarities, as a proof of the underlying unity of disparate cultures, as in the case of fairy tales.[26] While Balakirev was no doubt misguided in drawing such conclusions, his mistake is instructive in the present context, since it demonstrates that his thinking was not dominated by Orientalist binary oppositions.

The influence Balakirev exerted on his disciples during the 1860s would be hard to overestimate. Rimsky-Korsakov, in a conversation with Yastrebtsev, readily admitted this:

> [Balakirev's] *Tamara* and "Georgian Song" introduced into contemporary art the new, so-called "Balakirevian" East, reflections of which we can find in "Egypt" (from *Mlada*), in the Indian Dance with chorus (also from *Mlada*), in the third movement of *Sheherezade* (when the queen is carried out on her litter), etc. Apart from this, in *Tamara* you can already see the outline of the future clarinet cadenzas from *Sheherezade* . . .[27]

On many other occasions, recorded both in his *Chronicle* and in Yastrebtsev's *Memoirs*, Rimsky-Korsakov recalled that he and his friends admired Balakirev as a man of genius, and that they were particularly struck by *Islamey* (completed in 1869) and the material for *Tamara* (composed in the 1860s but not fully scored until 1882); they eagerly absorbed all the most memorable features of these works. Since the KP was omnipresent in *Islamey* and prominent in *Tamara*, its Oriental associations were, it would seem, largely fixed by these works (even though, as we saw above, the KP was a feature of Balakirev's style, and not an Oriental marker). Another work that helped fix and disseminate the KP as an Oriental marker was Rimsky-Korsakov's symphonic suite *Antar* (its first version was completed in 1868 and performed in the Russian Musical Society Concerts of 1869). As mentioned above, Rubinstein had developed his own vocabulary of Orientalism in his *Persian Songs* (1854), but he eventually acceded to the Kuchka's Orientalism; it was specifically from *Antar* and *Islamey* that he learnt the characteristic repertoire of devices (we know that he keenly played *Islamey* to his students in 1869).[28] By 1871, when Rubinstein composed his opera *The Demon*, he had accepted that the Kuchka had firmly established their Orientalist vocabulary in public consciousness; we therefore find a complete assimilation of the KP in the many Orientalist numbers of that opera (for example, Synodal's Romance in Act I, or the Oriental dances of Act II).

From the 1870s onwards, Rimsky-Korsakov and Borodin generally used the KP as an Oriental marker,[29] but a number of counter-examples prevent us from saying that the meaning of the KP was now irrevocably fixed. In *Prince Igor* we find the KP dominating the non-Oriental Act I scene in Prince

Galitsky's palace (Examples 4.8a and b); if the KP represents anything here, it would seem to be the struggle between drunks and the force of gravity. In another non-Oriental scene from Act I, the KP serves a very different purpose: it assists Yaroslavna, in her recitative, to give voice to her sufferings. Among Borodin's songs, Taruskin finds a prime example of Oriental eroticism in the KP-laden "Arabian Melody", but the KP is no less prominent in the non-erotic and non-Oriental "U lyudey-to v domu" (In other peoples' homes, Ex.4.9), which features a rather coarsely comic account of the problems besetting a Russian peasant household (including infestation by cockroaches). Perhaps "U lyudey-to v domu" was regarded as an unsuccessful portrayal of Russian life, due to its use of the KP? No, for instead we find Rimsky-Korsakov singling out this as a model of its type (the comic Russian peasant song). The KP there-fore remained open to a variety of expressive uses. Moving on to Borodin's *Petite Suite*, none of the titles suggest any Oriental associations, although four of the Suite's seven pieces prominently feature the KP. Sometimes, as in the Reverie, the music seems to fall well within the Orientalist conventions, at other times, as in the C-major mazurka, Occidental associations prevail. Is the

4.8a Borodin, *Prince Igor*, Act I, end of chorus in Galitsky's palace

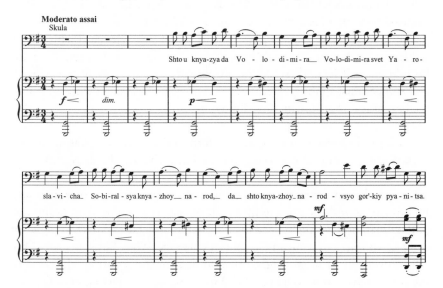

4.8b Borodin, *Prince Igor*, Act I, song of Skula and Yeroshka

4.9   Borodin, *U lyudey-to v domu*

KP just as much a part of Borodin's style as it is of Balakirev's? In some of Borodin's instrumental works, we find other features pointing to the East, as in the celebrated nocturne from the Second Quartet, or in some of the lyrical themes from his Second Symphony. But if we hear these melodies as Oriental, then what of Yaroslavna's Lament in *Prince Igor*? This is no less Oriental, with its arabesque melody and even an augmented second, yet we do not hear it thus because we know it to be the expression of a Russian woman's grief. Unlike Balakirev, Borodin had never visited the Caucasus or heard Caucasian music at first hand, and so his contemporaries sought to explain his unmotivated use of the Oriental style by suggesting that he had inherited an Oriental sensibility from his father – Borodin was the illegitimate son of a Georgian prince. Unfortunately for this ludicrous genetic thesis, Borodin's Orientalism surfaced only *after* his exposure to Balakirev's Eastern pieces, whereas before this, one might have conjectured that his blood was German (Schumann's influence) or Franco-Polish (Chopin), but certainly not Georgian. As for Borodin himself, he understood the purpose of Russian Orientalism very well: a weapon against all things Germanic. In a review of a concert which featured the Lezghinka from *Ruslan*, Borodin wrote:

> Now you can really hear those "Eastern hordes", whose invasion of the routine German music is so much feared by our musical Lohengrins.[30]

When we think we detect hints of the east in the music of Balakirev and Borodin, or after the Kuchka in the music of Glazunov, Kalinnikov, Lyapunov, or Rakhmaninov, we might need to pause before using the #5/♭6 chromaticism as a peg on which to hang an Orientalist narrative. What Taruskin called "the very morpheme of *nega*" might prove to be something entirely different in the slow movement of Tchaikovsky's First Symphony ("The Land of Gloom, the Land of Mist", its original subtitle, was meant to refer to a bleak landscape of the Russian North). The slow movement of Rakhmaninov's Fourth Piano Concerto seems to reminisce about that Tchaikovsky movement, and thus inherits the cold and gloomy associations. By contrast, but equally remote from Taruskin's *nega*, is the association of the KP with drunkenness, as already mentioned in connection with *Prince Igor*. One fascinating offshoot of this "drunken KP" complex is the solo piano piece *In a Vodka Shop*, by Arnold Bax (published in 1915). In spite of the lighthearted title, Bax took his task seriously, and produced a set of changing-background variations in the best Kuchka manner, albeit with his own freer treatment of dissonance. In Bax's hands, the KP is generalized to become chromatic movement between any adjacent scale degrees, not merely 5 and 6, and such chromatic movement often takes place in parallel triads (although movement between 5 and 6 is certainly prominent).

What, then, of Taruskin's putative discovery of Oriental colouring in the love theme of Tchaikovsky's *Romeo and Juliet*? On the surface, this would appear to be a very successful application of his argument. Taruskin claims that Tchaikovsky "used the orientalist trope metonymically, to conjure up not the East as such but rather its exotic sex appeal".[31] The two Oriental indicators Taruskin finds here are the "strongly marked chromatic pass between the fifth and sixth degrees, and . . . the equally marked English horn timbre" (Ex.4.10).

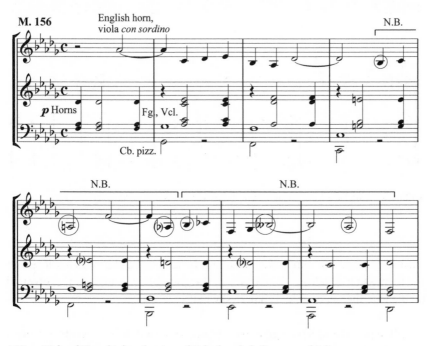

4.10a   Richard Taruskin's reduction of Tchaikovsky's *Romeo and Juliet*

4.10b   Richard Taruskin's reduction of Tchaikovsky's *Romeo and Juliet*

Taruskin appears to clinch the argument by calling Balakirev as a witness to
the theme's Orientalism; Balakirev was the grateful dedicatee, and, captivated
by the love theme, he told Tchaikovsky that:

> I often play it and have a great wish to kiss you for it. It has everything: *nega*,
> and love's sweetness, and all the rest. . . . It appears to me that you are lying

all naked in the bath and that Artôt-Padilla herself is rubbing your tummy with hot scented suds. I have just one thing to say about the theme: there is little in it of inner spiritual love, only the physical, passionate torment (coloured just a wee bit Italian). Really now, *Romeo and Juliet* are not Persian lovers, but European.

The appearance of *nega* together with the Persian lovers is a real gift to Taruskin, and might, at first, seem to settle the matter. But we need to pay closer attention to the rest of the quotation. The only direct reference to the musical style of the love theme is that it is "coloured just a wee bit Italian". And indeed, if we look back over the theme without assuming that it is a prime example of musical Orientalism, we will find the first series of "chromatic passes" are merely the upper members of 7–6 progressions within a chain of fifths sequence – this could hardly be more routine and therefore unmarked, for Orientalism or any other quality (which is not to say that the passage as a whole sounds merely routine). For Taruskin to extract his "essential *nega* undulation" from such conventional material is more than a little reminiscent of the Procrustean-bed approach to motivic analysis. The motivation for the colourful modulation from D♭ major to B minor (i.e. C♭ minor) lies in its role as a tribute to Balakirev, since these were his favourite keys (although their juxtaposition was Tchaikovsky's idea). Then from B (or C♭) in the bass, we descend through B♭, B♭♭ and A♭ to cadence back in the tonic D♭ major; the B♭♭ functions as a ♭VI approach to a cadential 64, but again this is entirely routine and common practice – there is nothing in the chromaticism here that would compel us to look any further than the Italian style that Balakirev himself found in the passage. The only chromatic writing that alludes to characteristic Kuchka harmony occurs in the *pp* passage for strings con sordino – here we have the only example of what I call the KP in this chapter. Whether or not these few bars should be heard as Oriental takes us back to the issue I have dealt with at length: that the KP, as I argue, is too habitual a feature of the Kuchka's house style, and occurs too often in contexts that have nothing to do with the Orient for it to be regarded automatically as Oriental, in the present instance and elsewhere. Since, as I have argued, there is nothing else in the harmony that pushes us towards an Orientalist interpretation, there would seem to be much stronger justification for seeing this merely as a Balakirevian feature – and indeed it occurs precisely where Tchaikovsky makes his reference to Balakirev in the use of D♭ major and B minor, as already mentioned.

What, then, of the cor anglais? The solo cor anglais timbre was, from time to time, used in Orientalist contexts, particularly in imitation of the zurna. But if this had ever been Tchaikovsky's intention, he seems to do his best to undermine it, since he doubles his cor anglais with the entire viola section, and places this hybrid timbre in the midst of three part harmony in the horns, outlining a conventional Western harmonic sequence. When the D♭ pedal point arrives, Tchaikovsky could finally have consummated the Orientalist potential of his cor anglais, but this is exactly the moment when Tchaikovsky removes the cor anglais from the scoring.

This is not to argue, of course, that the *Romeo and Juliet* theme is not sensuous or erotic. The "Italian" chromaticism can work in this direction, too, as can the markedly Italian throbbing horns, and of course, the general intensity curve of the theme – its orgasmic climax. But when did a Tchaikovsky "love" theme lack such qualities? I am happy to agree with Taruskin that this is as steamy as Russian music gets before Scriabin, but Tchaikovsky hardly needs the Orientalist trope to achieve that. He is able to conjure up physical love without it, and if Balakirev, in a racist manner, wishes to find such unspiritualized emotion "Persian", then that is a matter for him, but the Orientalism in that case is in the mind of the beholder, and not encoded into the music.

I realize that those who have already been persuaded to hear the *Romeo* theme as Oriental, will hardly be able "unhear" it as such. But I hope to have shown that the issue of colouring here is by no means straightforward, and that the referential suggestiveness of the #5/♭6 chromaticism should be treated with care. A cool assessment of the possibilities might well uncover nothing more than a favourite Kuchka idiom.

The beginning of the Russian style: *The Maid of Pskov*

The Maid of Pskov, the first (1868–72) of Rimsky-Korsakov's fifteen operas, pays little heed to operatic convention; it is thus the least characteristic of the fifteen, since the composer afterwards made a fluent mastery of the conventional and normal his business. *The Maid* was shaped throughout by Stasov's precepts, namely that opera should be Russian, progressive, and realistic. But after *The Maid*, as Rimsky-Korsakov gradually asserted his independence from Stasov and Balakirev, he revised or rejected these precepts. Realism, which for Stasov entailed a declamatory style and through-composed scenes, left hardly a trace in his later operas. His dedication to technical progress was intermittent, and only his desire to compose specifically Russian operas remained with him, apart from a more cosmopolitan period around the turn of the century. But precisely because *The Maid* was inspired by the aesthetics of Stasov (and thus of the Kuchka) rather than by any muse Rimsky-Korsakov later turned to, it is ideal for present purposes – to capture the Russian style in the making. *The Maid* presents the Rimsky-Korsakov of the Kuchka without his later polish and concern for conventional correctness – all the new and radical ideas discussed by the Kuchka at the time are present on the surface, realized at best with a fresh boldness, at worst with the gaucheness of inexperience. They are also realized with a consistency typical of the composer, which makes them easier to isolate, than would have been possible with *Boris*. We are also fortunate in having Rimsky-Korsakov's later revisions of *The Maid*, which confront us with his mature attitude to the Kuchka principles he once shared; and the remainder of his operatic legacy demonstrates the choices the composer made in retaining some features of *The Maid* and dropping others, as the Russian style crystallized.

Thanks to Rimsky-Korsakov's detailed memoirs, and the substantial amount of surviving correspondence between the members of the group, we can reconstruct much of the context in which *The Maid* was composed, and from which the Russian style emerged. The members of the Kuchka were in closest contact during the 1860s, and accordingly this was the period of their most intense collective creativity. Stasov and Balakirev exercised their authority over the younger composers, but while Stasov pushed the Kuchka towards unrestricted experimentation, Balakirev, as a practising composer, was concerned that their innovations should not leave behind all respect for principles of good voice-leading and harmonic progression. The Stasov/Balakirev conception of progressive music was drawn from the works of three Western composers: Berlioz, Schumann and Liszt. For realism, Dargomïzhsky's "melodic recitative" was taken as a model, and Glinka was the foundation for musical Russianness.

Balakirev, as later became apparent, had all but exhausted his stock of ideas in the 1860s, for most of his later pieces are based on material from sketches and drafts from this period. This vocabulary was considered common Kuchka property, due to Balakirev's selflessness as a teacher, for instead of completing his own work, he devoted most of his time to the correction and revision of his disciples' material to the extent that he was often the unacknowledged co-author of many of their early works. In short, he gave away not only his time and creative energy, but his entire compositional style. Because of this generosity, it has always been difficult to identify a Balakirev style distinct from that of his disciples; in one passage we hear Borodin, in another Rimsky-Korsakov, or even Glazunov, since we have learnt all his idioms from the better-known works of these others. Indeed, if we were only to take publication dates as evidence, we would soon be convinced that it was Balakirev's music which was derivative. But in truth his name also ought to appear on the title page of Rimsky-Korsakov's and Borodin's First Symphonies, and he was the inventor of the many idioms and procedures which the Kuchka lived off.[32] Much later, in the 1890s, Stasov recalled with amusement how Balakirev had recommended that "everyone should compose collectively, because only music thus filtered can truly be good".[33] But Stasov's laughter was misplaced, for this was the reality behind the activities of the Kuchka in the early years.[34] Balakirev's revisions and effective co-authorship were thus of great importance in the formation of a collective style, but there were also constant exchanges of ideas among all the members of the Kuchka, of critical opinion, suggestions for plots and libretti, or the circulation of interesting folksong melodies for possible use in composition.

But as the four younger composers matured under Balakirev's tutelage, they became capable of making substantial contributions to the collective style: Borodin's most daring harmonic innovations, such as the free use of parallel fifths and seconds, appeared in his songs of 1867–8; Musorgsky, in *Boris*, introduced his celebrated "bell harmonies"; Rimsky-Korsakov developed the use of the octatonic scale in *Sadko*; the continuous recitativo style was developed in different ways by Musorgsky in *The Marriage* and *Boris*, and Cui in *William Ratcliffe*. The notion of a Kuchka style is therefore much more than the aggregate of five individual styles united arbitrarily under a collective name: the style was genuinely a collective product emerging in the 1860s, and even though the members of the Kuchka eventually went their separate ways, they never jettisoned what they had learnt in this period.

Rimsky-Korsakov, in his conversations with Yastrebtsev, specified several ingredients of the Kuchka style. He mentioned the following:

1) tritones
2) the juxtaposition of keys in augmented-fourth (or diminished-fifth) relationship . . .
3) parallel fifths, thrown around with profligacy, even where they are completely undesirable and serve no artistic purpose [Rimsky-Korsakov was by this time unsympathetic to various Kuchka habits which he now considered naive or crude rather than bold or progressive] . . .
4) Borodinian epic parallel seconds, and
5) the Balakirevian keys of B minor and D flat major, which were so prominently and purposefully introduced in the early works of the Russian school and undoubtedly left traces in all later Russian music [a list of examples ensues].[35]

We shall now attempt to expand this list, and, following Rimsky-Korsakov's lead, we shall concentrate on features of the musical surface, which is likely to be more fruitful than any more nebulous discussion of operatic aesthetics. Our main examples will be drawn from the first version of *The Maid of Pskov*, and reference shall be made to other relevant Kuchka material along the way.

Folksong's new look

I'm always amused when they claim that I made a study of folk song. Believe me, my friend, this supposed "study" boils down to the fact that, thanks to a certain gift, I could simply remember and assimilate what was most characteristic in these tunes – that's all.[36]

Thus Rimsky-Korsakov, with the frankness characteristic of his old age, relieves us of the need to debunk this nationalist claim made by others on his behalf. There was a second myth which fulfilled the same purpose: that the composers of the Kuchka had thoroughly absorbed folk music during their (allegedly) rural childhoods, and that their compositions were inescapably imbued with these deep-rooted memories; this claim is commonly found in popular writings.[37] But why should the same composers have needed to make any study of this folk music in their adult life, if it had already been imprinted on their minds? Not that the conflict between the two claims seems to have bothered those who were determined to establish that the Kuchka was authentically Russian. Although not designed as a rebuttal, a sentence in Rimsky-Korsakov's memoirs effectively pours cold water on this myth also: he recalls how in 1866 he watched Balakirev harmonizing and arranging Russian and Caucasian folksongs.

My discovery of Russian and Oriental songs at this time laid the foundation for my love of folk music, music to which I devoted myself later.[38]

It was Balakirev who directed the Kuchka towards folksong as an inexhaustible pool of fresh musical material. And it was Balakirev's folksong harmonizations which showed his disciples how to assimilate folksong melodies within their own compositions. But behind Balakirev's approach to folksong harmonization stood Odoyevsky, who in 1863 had published an influential essay on the presentation of folksong material in anthologies. In the essay he emphasizes the difference between folksongs transmitted in authentic versions, and those which had been "corrected" by their transcribers:

More and more of these primordial melodies are lost every day, for either no one transcribes them, or when they are transcribed, it is by people who think it their duty to correct them as if they were barbarian; that is, they refashion them in the Western manner, regrettably, most often in an Italianate way (so foreign to the character of purely Russian melodies). This was done from the times of Prach up to Varlamov, and he was the most culpable for distorting our folk tunes.[39]

Odoyevsky is nevertheless wrong to blame transcribers for Westernizing folk-songs, for people like Varlamov were only following the existing non-notational practices of semi-folk entertainers, such as the popular gypsy choirs. Former peasants who had been brought to urban centres as servants all soon succumbed to this kind of Westernization; Odoyevsky could not have been unaware of this fact, but for the sake of his polemic he chose to ignore it.[40] What is most interesting for our present purposes is that Odoyevsky continues his argument by invoking Balakirev, to whom he effectively issues an appeal:

> We have heard that one of our gifted musicians, M. A. Balakirev, collected a substantial number of hitherto unknown Russian melodies during his travels, and we are convinced that he, with his deep musical sensibilities, will not fall into the strange delusions of the Shpreviches, the Praches, the Kashins of the Varlamovs.[41]

Odoyevsky also offers his own practical advice for harmonizing folksongs, and supplies an illustration (Ex.4.11), to which is appended the following explanation:

> The present melody has been transcribed with great precision; the changing metre, which is so often found in our old songs, is here preserved; we tried to compose the piano accompaniment in the simplest manner possible (*sine quarta consonante* [from his harmonizations Odoyevsky evidently means the cadential six-four]), which corresponds well to the kind of harmony that can be heard in the folk choral performances; we dared not introduce any seventh chords, which had not yet been invented in the era when our ancient songs were created; their use would utterly disfigure the character of Russian singing, sacred as well as secular (this had already been observed by our unforgettable Mikh[ail] Iv[anovich] Glinka, although under the influence of common opinion and modern taste, even he, as if against his will, would now and then introduce seventh chords in the accompaniments to Russian melodies).[42]

Glinka had used seventh chords in such harmonization much more frequently than "now and then" would suggest; "as if against his will" merely indicates Odoyevsky's desperation in trying to make the evidence conform to his thesis. Odoyevsky's own choice of chords is, of course, quite arbitrary: his avoidance of cadential six-fours, and seventh chords were part of an attempt to create a style which Odoyevsky could find un-Western; he still sought a result which seemed pleasing to his ears, but since his musical values were entirely conditioned by his Western musical training, and not by Russian folk practices (of

4.11   Odoyevsky's harmonization of the folksong "Vozle rechen'ki"

which he was ignorant), his harmonizations were no better an approximation of non-urbanized Russian folksong than the harmonization of his predecessors. Odoyevsky's innovation lay primarily in the self-deception of his claim to authenticity. Even his conviction that seventh chords and six-fours are anachronistic was derived from his reading of Western music histories rather than from any ethnographic field studies. Even if we were to concede the possibility that he might at some time have heard genuine folk polyphony, it is readily apparent from his triads and his half-concealed Alberti figurations that he was altogether unable to construe what he heard in notational terms.

Did Balakirev heed Odoyevsky's appeal? Only in part. He would have pleased Odoyevsky by retaining the metrical irregularities in his sources; and he even outdid Odoyevsky in the austere harmonies of his accompaniments: sometimes a static fifth drone would suffice (e.g. No. 33), and Balakirev made greater use of secondary triads, to distance the songs further from standard Western harmony (which in the course of these polemics soon became an absurdly simplified fiction). Balakirev even managed to rid himself of the dominant function in "minor-mode" songs by placing another minor triad on the fifth degree. But Odoyevsky would have been disappointed by the frequent and prominent use of dominant seventh chords, albeit generally unprefaced by a six-four (No. 18 is one exception). Indeed Balakirev even saw fit to include occasional chromatic countermelodies in the manner of Glinka (e.g. No. 38), including the KP (Nos 38 and 39). Balakirev was evidently interested in the model Odoyevsky offered, but he refused to adopt it as a rigid doctrine; this divergence was hardly surprising: Balakirev was a practising composer who was ultimately concerned to produce pleasing results, whereas Odoyevsky, as a music historian and theorist, could afford to produce harmonizations which were blander and more uniform. Ultimately, of course, Odoyevsky's harmonic doctrine was dependent upon his own tastes, since he certainly did not derive it from any serious researches into folk hetero/polyphony; his rigidity in employing the doctrine was motivated by the need for scholarly appearances, and lacking Balakirev's musical imagination and talents, he would not have felt unduly shackled by his rules. We do not have any statement from Balakirev which would determine whether he shared Odoyevsky's authenticist outlook, but the music offers considerable indirect evidence to the contrary. In addition to the many prominent departures from the letter and spirit of Odoyevsky's harmonic principles, we also have the clear witness of textures and figurations which are often overtly pianistic to prove that Balakirev was not seeking to participate in any authenticist enterprise.

Nevertheless, the features of Balakirev's accompaniments which most interested the other members of the Kuchka were precisely those which were inspired by (if not directly borrowed from) the Odoyevskian doctrine: diatonicism, the emphasis on secondary triads and sparse textures (i.e. where Balakirev's writing was not especially pianistic). Inevitably, these features were soon accepted as properly Russian, even though Balakirev had not attempted to emulate the purism of Odoyevsky's supposed authenticism. With this in mind, we shall now return to *The Maid of Pskov*. Rimsky-Korsakov mentioned that the opera contains only three deliberate folksong quotations,[43] but there are also many quite plausible imitation folksongs – and Rimsky-Korsakov acquired this facility from his study of Balakirev's collection, rather than from any independent research. The two songs given to the opera's protagonist, Mikhailo Tucha, are both clear examples of the *protyazhnaya* genre: one of them, the "Farewell to Pskov" (Act II, Ex.4.12a), is taken from a known *protyazhnaya* melody, while the other, "Raskukuysya tï, kukushechka" (O cuckoo, continue your song!, Ex.4.12b), is Rimsky-Korsakov's own invention. The freshly composed melody seems to have been modelled carefully on the genuine folk melody: both have phrases which end on the flat seventh degree in the "minor" and in both the leap of a fifth is pervasive. And indeed both are reminiscent of Glinka's less urban-sounding *protyazhnïye*, such as the Rowers' Chorus from *A Life*. Perhaps the chromatic slide in the transcribed

4.12a Rimsky-Korsakov, *The Maid of Pskov*, Tucha's song from the Veche Scene, Act II

genuine folksong, representing the typical portamento of Russian folk practice, is the only feature which is not to be found in Glinka – *pace* Melgunov, who imagined he could hear the "shrieks" of rural singers in *A Life for the Tsar*. But when we turn from the melodies to the accompaniments we find much which is foreign to Glinka. Tucha's "O cuckoo" has three strophes. The first of these is a monody, which was not uncommon in Glinka, but the remaining two are treated quite differently. The second is given only a bass line, largely of pedal notes, but with stretches which constitute a true counter-melody. The third is a four-part harmonization which is diatonic throughout, including a prominent minor triad on the fifth degree and accordingly an unconventional cadential gesture. Glinka had never gone so far in the modal direction. The other song, the "Farewell to Pskov", which closes Act II, is based on a folk-like alternation of solo and chorus, a familiar pattern in Glinka's folk-like passages (e.g. the opening chorus of *A Life*). The choral texture is not unlike Glinka's, but the harmony behaves very differently: it eschews the leading note, simply by avoiding the seventh degree (the more common Kuchka practice was to flatten the seventh degree); this in turn

4.12b   Rimsky-Korsakov, *The Maid of Pskov*, Tucha's song from Act I

leads to an avoidance of modulation, for which Rimsky-Korsakov evidently thought the leading note essential. In the second strophe the orchestra provides a single-line accompaniment to the chorus, again, a texture foreign to Glinka's folksong or folk style numbers. Finally, the third strophe is crowded with new events: the texture becomes more complex, as additional recitative-style choral interjections are added, a theme heard earlier appears in the orchestra, but most importantly the leading note and the dominant chord are reinstated in the orchestra and part of the chorus, while the remainder of the chorus continues to sing the folksong over this new harmonization – the dense activity befitting the end of an act. This example demonstrates the limitations of modal harmony for the Kuchka: they can use it with conviction when it is a temporary, colouristic feature, but for structural purposes (here the closure of the act), there is always a return to normal tonal harmony, including the leading note and dominant function. The Kuchka thus succeeded in creating novel, "non-Western" harmonic procedures on the small scale, but failed to find any replacement for the large-scale pillars of Western musical practice.

Such half-hearted modalism is characteristic of all the Kuchka; and indeed Musorgsky, contrary to his radical reputation, does not even go as far as Rimsky-Korsakov in his treatment of folk melodies. At the opening of *Boris Godunov*, a very plausible imitation *protyazhnaya* boasts a conspicuous flattened seventh degree. The second strophe, with a pedal and a pizzicato counter-melody, succeeds in maintaining the modal flavour, but the melody in the third strophe begins a fourth lower, like a fugal entry, which immediately dissolves whatever non-Western colour there had been, for this feature is entirely alien to Russian folksong, whether authentic or urbanized (due to his lack of contrapuntal technique Musorgsky could not have proceeded with a fugato; in any case, if he had noticed any disruption of the "Russian" style, he could simply have removed the pseudo-fugal entries). In general, Musorgsky's folksong harmonizations follow Glinka's example much more faithfully than those of Rimsky-Korsakov, modulating with conventional cadences onto the various modal centres of the melody (e.g. "Ne sokol letit" from the Kromï Scene in *Boris*, and Marfa's Song in *Khovanshchina*); chromatic counterpoints to folk melodies were also retained from Glinka, even though Stasov had complained that these undermined the folksongs' Russian character (e.g. Marfa's Song, or "Slava" from the Coronation Scene of *Boris*). In Borodin we also find a retreat from Aeolian mode at structural points, as in the Chorus of the Peasants from Act IV of *Prince Igor*. At the beginning of the second strophe, Borodin effects a shift from one modal centre, F#, to another, E, by means of a conventional cadence; this requires a D# leading note which is absent from the subsequent passage in the E mode.

Borodin, however, was in one respect far in advance of his Kuchka colleagues in his representations of folk music, for in this chorus, he makes a conscientious attempt to reflect folk hetero/polyphony. As we saw above, the representation of hetero/polyphony had begun as early as the 1780s, with Fomin's *Coachmen*, but until Borodin's chorus, this aspect of folk practices had failed to register in the music of Glinka and the Kuchka (although Rimsky-Korsakov claimed otherwise in the case of his Troitskaya Song from Act I of *May Night* – see below).[44] If authenticists lived up to their own claims, this would have to be regarded as a regression, but of course they select, modify, disregard and even cultivate ignorance according to their own needs. They could reduce the orchestra to a pedal note, and introduce some imitative writing in the choir; they could vary the texture from one to four parts and even break one or two rules of standard Western harmony, but nowhere do we find any convincing evidence that they had actually heard peasants singing in ensemble. Granted, Borodin's chorus does not meet the standards of modern ethnomusicological scholarship, but given the limits of what was musically conceivable for someone in Borodin's historical position, and given the gulf that separates his chorus from the folk representations of his contemporaries, his asynchronous setting of the text with many repeated words would indeed appear to indicate some direct experience of peasants singing *protyazhnïye* in ensemble. Observe, for example, the following short passage, where the altos temporarily move into the foreground while the sopranos retreat (Ex.4.13); those readers familiar with Russian folk hetero/polyphony will readily discern the signs of direct experience here that are conspicuously absent from Glinka, or the rest of the Kuchka.

To summarize, the Kuchka supplied the folksongs with harmony that was no less artificial than Glinka's. Their choice of chords was not directed not by any analysis of genuine folk singing, but by the model handed down by Balakirev, which was an uneasy amalgam of Odoyevsky's arbitrary theories and Balakirev's personal preferences. If they had ever been aware that the method of harmonization was based on artifice, any such thoughts were soon lost in the thick fog of nationalist rhetoric which soon gathered; in time, the method was taken to be a touchstone of authentic Russianness. Hence Rimsky-Korsakov's shocked reaction to the first published folksong transcriptions (by Melgunov) which reproduced the *podgoloski* (the "undervoices" which accompany the primary melody – the term is used by the peasant singers themselves). At first the composer simply could not believe his eyes, for the resulting harmony was too irregular and bizarre, bearing no resemblance to the Kuchka's conception of Russian folk polyphony. Although he eventually conceded that Melgunov's *podgoloski* did in fact reflect folk practices

4.13   Borodin, *Prince Igor*, Act IV, chorus of villagers

with accuracy, he was evidently still smarting from embarrassment as late as 1894:

> Do you know what part of the affair causes me most offence? It's the fact that not one of those who cried out in support of, or against Melgunov, ever took the trouble to look at the score of *May Night*, where in the Trinity Song (Act I), before Melgunov's collection was published, I had already employed – quite artistically – the same notorious *podgoloski* which he had supposedly discovered; but, I repeat, no one took any notice of this; no one so much as hinted that they were there, as if in fact they weren't there at all.[45]

And even in his *Chronicle*, a quarter of a century later, Rimsky-Korsakov's had lost none of his contempt for Melgunov: he is "a dry theorist and the compiler of a barbaric collection of Russian songs"; there is the same note of jealousy in his comments on the "undeserved" attention Balakirev had devoted to the young folksong collector.[46] But Rimsky-Korsakov's representation of folk practices in *May Night* is no better a reflection of genuine hetero/polyphony than the music of his Kuchka colleagues (and as we saw, falls short of Borodin's chorus from Act IV of *Prince Igor* in this respect). If he could claim in all sincerity that the Trinity Song pre-empted Melgunov's transcriptions, he was suffering from profound self-delusion. To move from the particular to the general, the Kuchka always claimed that their arrangements of folksongs were an enormous advance on those of Prach, with regard to their authenticity.[47] But Balakirev and Rimsky-Korsakov always followed the same method as Prach: they followed the current harmonic practices of art music, tempered by their own arbitrary preferences.

Another item in the Kuchka's collection of "authentic Russian" devices used in the setting of folksong melodies (and folk-style melodies) within operatic and orchestral concert works was the changing-background variation technique. Each strophe of the song was a new variation, texturally more complex, re-orchestrated and often re-harmonized; no matter that this bore no resemblance to folk practice, which varied the melody itself, which was precisely the element that remained constant in changing-background variations. But leaving aside the accompaniments, one might at least expect that the folk melodies used by the Kuchka were reliably transmitted, and treated with more respect than in the Lvov–Prach collection (which, as we saw above, the Kuchka claimed they had left far behind in their quest for authentic Russianness). Let us investigate the matter. In Ex.4.14, two versions of the same song are shown: (a) is Musorgsky's own transcription, with singer

4.14a Musorgsky's transcription of a folksong marked "Russian song in 13/4". Heard from M.O. Shishko in Belorussia

4.14b The same song as used in Musorgsky's *Khovanshchina*

and location noted, while (b) is his adaptation of the song for use in the opera *Khovanshchina*. A common cadential melodic figure was removed by Musorgsky, and replaced by a pentatonic figure which removes the leading note – evidently he wanted something which sounded more exotic than the folk melody itself. So much for authenticity. Of course, a composer is free to alter a folk melody as he sees fit within the context of his own works (although it helps if he doesn't associate himself with a strident authenticist polemic at the same time); but it is quite another matter when the altered version is presented later as the sedimentation of peasant singing over countless generations. This is precisely what happened when Rimsky-Korsakov left aside the original (which was available to him if he wanted it) and instead chose Musorgsky's version of the melody when he was compiling his folksong collection (it appears in the collection as song no. 92).[48] This should be kept in mind when we hear Soviet/Russian ethnomusicologists claim that Rimsky-Korsakov's collection is a reliable work of scholarship.[49]

While unpicking the new nationalist myths created by the Kuchka, it is worth recalling that they only displaced earlier myths, rather than any more clear-headed conception of Russian folk music. Through the greater variety of folksong genres they employed in their works (by quotation and imitation), the myth of Russian folksong's essential melancholy was forever dispelled, a myth which had arisen through the near exclusive use of the *protyahznaya* in the art music of the previous generation. The balance was already tipped in *The Maid*, where *protyazhnïye* are outweighed by *khorovod* songs – a much more light-hearted genre sung by girls in the course of collective activities, from berry-picking to dancing. "Po malinu" (After the raspberries) from Act 1 and Olga's theme from the love duet are both genuine examples of the genre, while an imitation can be found in "Akh tï, dubrava" (Oh, thou oak-grove) from Act IV. In most of his subsequent operas, Rimsky-Korsakov increased the range of folksong genres further: *May Night* introduced the spring calendar song genre, *The Snow Maiden* wedding songs, *Sadko* the *bïlina*, and *Christmas Eve*, predictably, the carol. Musorgsky, in *Boris*, found a wealth of inspiration in children's songs (Act II), and was the first to use a *bïlina* (in the Kromï scene), having been inspired by Trofim Ryabinin, an epic singer from the north of Russia who performed in St Petersburg in 1871. The other members of the Kuchka never crowded their works with folksong to this extent, but they all drew freely from the many genres untouched by Glinka. In other words, nearly all folksong genres found their way into the music of the Kuchka. Conversely, they studiously avoided urbanized folksongs, as well as the street and tavern songs popular in the towns; consequently, they condemned Serov for "pseudo-Russianness" when he used such material in his *Rogneda*. These familiar songs seemed merely vulgar to them, and disturbed their picture of Russianness which they promoted: the dignified, communal life of the peasantry, following ancient traditions, and preserving Russian virtues lost to the cosmopolitan inhabitants of the towns and cities.

Evocations of church music

While the influence of folksong on the Kuchka style has received extensive coverage from scholars (usually credulous, occasionally sceptical), the barely less important influence of Russian church music has usually been passed over in silence. This is largely due to Stasov's outspoken atheism and anti-clericalism; since he was the Kuchka's mouthpiece, his own presentation of the Kuchka's interests and motivations has become embedded in the historiography of Russian music. Stasov undoubtedly exerted great influence over the younger composers, and even to some extent over Balakirev, so his account of the Kuchka contains much that was true; nevertheless, he was prepared to iron out anything that might jar with his own ideas, so the influence of Orthodox music was expunged from the record. Indeed, Orthodox music not only offended Stasov's anti-clericalism, but also his nationalist sensibilities, since unlike secular peasant music it had its roots in music from the near West, namely the *partesnoye peniye* borrowed in the seventeenth century from the Ukraine and Poland. In the course of the intervening centuries, through everyday use by inexpert musicians, it had largely degenerated into a very narrow repertoire of harmonic progressions (and so it remains to the present day). Tchaikovsky was clearly unimpressed by the result:

> During the last century, Europeanism invaded our church in the form of assorted banalities ... even in the villages, in the remotest places, ... the singing of the deacons is very close that of St Petersburg's Kazan cathedral, ... the disgracefully vulgar dregs of European clichés.[50]

Thus Orthodox music, by the mid-nineteenth century was not only thought to be insufficiently Russian, but also of low musical standards, even an offence against musicianly good taste. Even in the absence of these three disincentives against advertising the influence of Orthodox music (including Stasov's anti-clericalism), there would have been no reason to expect Stasov or the Kuchka to draw attention to the fact: unlike many of the folk genres they used, Orthodox music would have been entirely familiar to their public, and recognized as such wherever it appeared in the Kuchka's music (Western commentators, on the contrary, have been silent because they do *not* recognize these musical topics).

Ex.4.15a is entirely characteristic of everyday liturgical practices at that time; it is a faithful transcription made by Glinka, who supplied it with the disclaimer "*Hymne russe de la Ressurection telle qu'elle est chantée ordinairement par les diacres et peuple*"(sic).[51] The conventions of voice-leading are observed until the last four bars, which feature parallel octaves; on the same page of the manuscript, Glinka provided the melody with an altered version of the two lower parts, eliminating the octaves (see Ex.4.15b). However, in "Slav'sya", the final chorus from *A Life for the Tsar*, he incorporated precisely this "solecism" from the *Hymne russe* transcription in order to invoke the liturgical style (Ex.4.15c); there are also rhythmic and melodic similarities between "Slav'sya" and the *Hymne russe*. Nevertheless, Stasov ignored this evident source for reasons of his own, and later commentators were largely unaware of it.[52] The most obvious

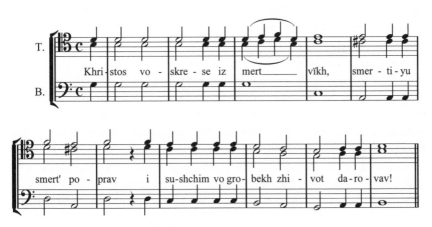

4.15a   Glinka's transcription of a Resurrection hymn published in *Polnoye sobraniye sochineniy*, vol. 17 (Moscow: Muzïka, 1969)

4.15b   Glinka's own version of harmonization published in the same source

4.15c   Glinka, final chorus from *A Life for the Tsar* (voices only)

successor to "Slav'sya" is the opening chorus of *Prince Igor*, which combined parallel movement with Kuchka harmonic features such as an emphasis on secondary triads and diatonicism (i.e. exclusive heptatonicism). This new combination defamiliarized the style, rendering it more archaic (according to the Kuchka's constructions of the archaic, of course).

Ex.4.16 is a setting of a chant melody in the so-called "monastery" style of harmonization; the arranger, Bortnyansky, was too well-schooled in Western rules of harmony to allow parallel perfect consonances, and so he added an independent bass line that still allowed the characteristic doubling in thirds of the chant melody to be preserved. Here, as in Glinka's transcription, we also encounter the characteristic dactylic rhythm; other notable features include the reiteration of I–V–I in the tonic and related keys, and the melodic motion 2–3–4 or 4–3–2 over V in each key. These are all features of church harmoniza-

4.16   Bortnyansky, *Pomoshchnik i pokrovitel'*

tion that have survived up to the present. In the works of the Kuchka, these features certainly appear, but on almost every occasion there is some additional complication. In Musorgsky's *Boris*, for example, the chorus of blind pilgrims in Act I (Ex.4.17a), while displaying the same liturgical features, is harmonized

4.17a   Musorgsky, *Boris Godunov*, chorus of the blind pilgrims from the Prologue

quite idiosyncratically; the composer is representing here the religious folk tradition of wanderers performing chants outside churches and adapting them to the available forces.[53] When Rimsky-Korsakov came to write the chorus "Tsar' nash gosudar'" (Our tsar, our sovereign, Ex.4.17b) in *The Maid*, he turned not only to liturgical traditions, but also to the version of those traditions heard in the chorus of blind pilgrims. The similarity with the latter is clear in Rimsky-Korsakov's first statement of the melody in the basses against a dominant pedal. Although Rimsky-Korsakov uses the changing-background variation technique to defamiliarize his borrowings from the church style (as in the third statement, where the KP appears – see Ex.4.7), the characteristic melodic motions of liturgical music are prominent.

4.17b   Rimsky-Korsakov, *The Maid of Pskov*, Act III, Chorus "Tsar' nash" (vocal parts omitted)

There are other evocations of contemporary church practices in *The Maid*, but these are no more than fleeting references to liturgical recitation: in the last scene of Act III, Tsar Ivan mutters a prayer for the late Vera Sheloga; in Act IV Scene 5, he reads from a book of prayers; and in the Act IV Scene 7, Olga tells the tsar of her prayers for him. Rimsky-Korsakov professed indifference towards religious ritual at this stage of his life, and this is reflected in his presentation of Olga's death at the end of the opera: instead of music based on Orthodox liturgical practices, we have a mourning chorus that lacks any Russian markers; in fact, the chorus was inspired by the ending of Liszt's *St Elizabeth* (we shall discuss the Liszt connection later).

The church style left a much deeper imprint on *Boris* than on *The Maid*.[54] Aside from the blind pilgrims' chorus already discussed, here are just a few examples which show traces of the church style: "Mï da vse tvoi sirotï" (the first chorus of the Prologue), "Tsarya na Rusi khotim postavit'" (the basses interjection in the Prologue), "Teper' poklonimsya" (Boris's first monologue), "Bozhe krepkiy" (the off-stage singing of the monks during the scene in Pimen's cell), "Startsï smirennïye" (Varlaam's and Misail's song in the Tavern scene), "Vechnuyu pamyat'" (Mityuikha's interjection in the St Basil's scene), and "Plachte, plachte, lyudiye" (Weep, weep, O people) in Boris's death scene. It is readily apparent from this list that the church style is not restricted to those scenes in which the drama requires liturgical singing; in fact, of the passages listed above only two are representations of liturgical singing (the off-stage monks, and "Plachte . . ." for Boris), and only one other is devotional (the blind pilgrims' chorus). Musorgsky used the church style flexibly, evoking different ideas according to the local context; to take one example not already mentioned, the instrumental introduction to the scene in the Granovitaya chamber, the music may be heard as a representation of the tsar's divinely-bestowed power, as a premonition of Boris's death or as a direct anticipation of the priests' singing at the end of the scene. But whatever the church style suggested in each of its appearances, one thing was constant: Musorgsky's audience would always have heard such passages as specifically Russian. In this way, the contemporary church style in *Boris* and other Kuchka pieces plays a role similar to that of popular song and the romance style in *A Life for the Tsar*: it was a representation of Russianness guaranteed to be heard as such by the audience (whereas the Kuchka's various non-*protyazhnaya* folk-music references had to be taken on trust as Russian, and likewise the attempts to recreate earlier, long defunct Russian liturgical styles).

In the 1860s Odoyevsky categorized church melodies as pure or Western, just as he had done with folk melodies, on the basis of his belief in the common modal system governing not only both Russian church and folk music, but also ancient Greek and medieval European music.[55] But while his categorization of folk melodies was assisted by the many song anthologies which were available to him, his thoughts on church music lacked any such guidance, and followed only from his assumptions regarding the common modal system. Understandably, the members of the Kuchka, as practical musicians, showed little interest in Odoyevsky's speculations on church music, since his abstract theorizing was not by itself sufficient to inspire any new musical developments; given a wealth of concrete examples, as in the case of folk music, they were much more open to Odoyevsky's thinking, as we saw above. But the early stratum of liturgical music – *znamenniy* chant – had largely disappeared from the church before the nineteenth century, and its rediscovery required painstaking scholarship which was not carried out until the turn of the century (we shall discuss this in Chapter 5). *Znamenniy* singing could be heard only in remote locations, either among the exiled communities of Old Believers, or in a few monasteries. Musorgsky had intended to include an Old Believers' chant melody in the finale of *Khovanshchina*, but death intervened. Rimsky-Korsakov, after *znamenniy* chant had been rediscovered, claimed that the theme of Ivan the Terrible

4.18a   Rimsky-Korsakov, *The Maid of Pskov*, Ivan the Terrible's theme

4.18b   Rimsky-Korsakov chant transcription

4.18c   Balakirev, a theme from Symphony no. 1

from *The Maid* (Ex.4.18a) was "derived . . . from the singing of the monks in the Tikhvin Monastery of Our Lady and, in general, from *znamennïy* chant like this" (see Ex.4.18b).[56] It might be tempting to think that Rimsky-Korsakov retained in his memory these impression from the days of his Tikhvin childhood; but given the fact that he only mentioned this after research on *znamennïy* chant had been carried out, we might suspect that this was merely a chance resemblance which he was now able to adduce, years after he had written the theme, as further evidence of how his music was rooted in the Russian soil. Fortunately, we are not left in this quandary, since the theme in question closely resembles material from Balakirev's First Symphony, and we know that Rimsky-Korsakov, together with Borodin, Musorgsky and Cui, heard Balakirev play the symphony on the piano during their formative meetings of the 1860s (Ex.4.18c). Given this obvious source, we need not take the putative *znamennïy* chant connection very seriously. Nevertheless, while we need not accept Rimsky-Korsakov's account of a direct connection, there may indeed be an indirect connection, of which Rimsky-Korsakov may or may not have been aware, for in a letter to Cui (August 1864), Balakirev wrote:

> I hope, although I'm not yet sure, that I'll bring the complete first Allegro [of the First Symphony] to [St Petersburg]. It will introduce another new Russian element, that is, . . . a religious, Molokan element.[57]

Had Balakirev completed the symphony in the 1860s, it might have prompted some interest in old chant melodies among the rest of the Kuchka; but the symphony had to wait many years, like so many of Balakirev's works, for its eventual completion in the 1890s, by which time chant scholarship was already underway.

The characteristic music of Russian Orthodoxy contained another ingredient which the Kuchka were happy to appropriate: the ringing of the bells.[58] For the purposes of musical nationalism, the bells were ideal, for here was an ancient Russian tradition which was quite free of Western influence. Glinka wanted a set of small church bells to be played in performances of his "Slav'sya" (as an external sound source, not an integral notated part of the score), but instead of following this example, the Kuchka preferred to represent the bells through suggestive figurations using normal orchestral instruments, and so assimilated the Orthodox bells in a way that Glinka had never attempted. The imitation of complex non-harmonic bell timbres by orchestral instruments and normal performance practices posed a formidable problem, of course, but the Kuchka, in its most dynamic period, was always willing to experiment. Musorgsky should probably be credited with making the breakthrough in *Boris*, when in the Coronation scene he represents the bells through the non-functional alternation of two dominant-seventh type chords a tritone apart. Serov had in fact used the same harmonies in the Royal Hunt from *Rogneda*, and this might have been Musorgsky's inspiration, as Taruskin suggests;[59] if not, there is a similar device in Glinka which Musorgsky would certainly have known: namely, the celebrated "torpor chords" (*akkordï otsepeneniya*) from Glinka's *Ruslan* overture, consisting of two dominant-seventh type chords a minor third apart (Ex.4.19a). These possible sources only offered Musorgsky the harmonies; the use of these harmonies for the representation of bells was Musorgsky's own idea, which other members of the Kuchka were quick to adopt. Rimsky-Korsakov borrowed the device for the beginning of the *Veche* scene (Act II) of *The Maid* (Ex.4.19b), although he used the "torpor chord" version; Borodin, in the Finale of Act I of *Prince Igor*, used a slight variation on the same kind of progression for the alarum bell (Ex.4.19c). But while Musorgsky supplied the harmonic device for representing bells, it was

4.19a   Glinka, overture to *Ruslan and Lyudmila*

4.19b   Rimsky-Korsakov, *The Maid of Pskov*, Veche scene

4.19c   Borodin, *Prince Igor*, finale of Act I (vocal parts omitted)

Rimsky-Korsakov who provided it with its characteristic orchestral clothing, with the chords in the brass accompanied by gong strokes and violin figurations in a high register – just the sort of mélange which Rimsky-Korsakov alone could have concocted. As he put it in one of his conversation with Yastrebtsev:

> By the way, since you are so interested in discovering my supposed innovations, here is one: I invented the orchestral representation of bells, for I orchestrated the bell sounds in the Easter Overture, *The Maid*, *Prince Igor* (in the scenes with the alarum bell and with the *skomorokhi*), and even in *Khovanshchina*, *Boris Godunov*, and *Night on the Bare Mountain*.[60]

Of all the works in the Kuchka canon, it is the Easter Overture which most consistently enters the sound-world of Russian Orthodoxy: aside from the bells, there is an authentic chant melody, which is eventually harmonized in the four-part church style. The Easter Overture also appears to be the foundation of Rakhmaninov's style, for in his works we similarly find chant-like melodies, piano textures that evoke the Kuchka's orchestral bells, and, most prominently, the characteristic reiteration of I–V–I which stems from church singing.

"Progressive" harmony

The first version of *The Maid* is a compendium of the Kuchka's experimental harmonic techniques of the 1860s and '70s. The Kuchka's progressive and nationalist tendencies converged in the area of harmony: their continuous search for fresh harmonies was undertaken so that their music would never degenerate into a trivial imitation of established Western styles. Even so, one might well protest that any frank assessment of the Kuchka's harmonic innovations would reveal the crucial influence of Liszt, both in spirit and content.[61] In the discussion which follows, we shall use the *The Maid* to illustrate the Kuchka's quest for new harmonies, and in particular, we shall see the extent to which the enterprise falls under Liszt's shadow.

The beginning of *The Maid* Overture is still striking for its harmonic inventiveness; it was probably this passage (Ex.4.20) which prompted Cui to remark that the Overture's harmony was "cruel and unbridled" (the comment appears in the midst of praise for the opera, but given Cui's own musical preferences we might suspect a lurking note of disapproval).[62] Rimsky-Korsakov took pains to defamiliarize the opening chain-of-fifths sequence: at first we have a chromatic progression onto V^4_3 of D major, then to V of A and V of E, finally settling onto a long pedal on V of B, at first suggesting the major, then the

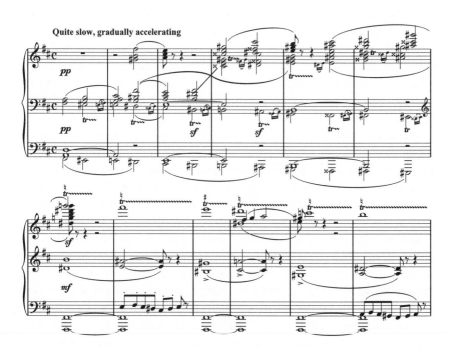

4.20   Rimsky-Korsakov, Overture to *The Maid of Pskov*

minor. While this level of invention is not to be found on every page of the score, there are many other passages which witness to Rimsky-Korsakov's restlessness in his search for new harmonies.

The overture was cast in sonata form with a slow introduction; in itself, this is quite unremarkable, but Rimsky-Korsakov had in fact set himself a major formal problem: how to articulate this well-established framework without recourse to any structural V–I cadences. Early in the Kuchka's existence, the V–I cadence was singled out as the essential gesture of Western music; it should therefore be eliminated from the Kuchka's music, and indeed from any music which would claim to be truly Russian. The initial impulse for such a project came, of course, from Stasov's theory of an essential Russian plagalism in opposition to the V–I of Western music, but the Kuchka now sought out any device which could be used to modify the characteristic sound of the V–I cadence without altogether obliterating the cadential function of the gesture. In the overture to *The Maid*, Rimsky-Korsakov sometimes adds a sixth or a ninth, or flattens the fifth of his dominant seventh chord before proceeding to the tonic triad; elsewhere he may leave the dominant seventh undisturbed but cadence onto scale degrees other than the tonic (on one occasion, the dominant chord in an apparent cadential approach moves to an augmented triad). This is representative of what the Kuchka saw as the avoidance of the Western perfect cadence; evidently, they failed to see how superficial these devices were, for they never displayed any awareness of the roles of V and I on a larger scale. And so, in the overture to *The Maid*, we find that a long dominant pedal precedes the allegro, its second subject, recapitulation and coda. This was far from the radically new harmonic language which Stasov's (baseless) theory of Russian plagalism entailed.[63]

Like *Boris*, *The Maid* attests throughout to the Kuchka's fascination with the augmented triad, not merely as momentary colouring but as the doorway to a new harmonic world. For example, in one of Matuta's scenes (Act IV Scene 4), Rimsky-Korsakov constructs a three-chord progression which interposes a passing chord between two augmented triads and then supplies an augmented triad as the "resolution" of the final cadence (see Ex.4.21; in the final version of the opera, however, this augmented triad is dutifully resolved onto the tonic major chord). On a larger scale, the orchestral conclusion of Act III consists of sequences whose periods are transposed by major thirds; in the '90s, when Rimsky-Korsakov came to revise the opera, he considered this a tiresome device: "the music [at the end of Act III] is as mannered as can be, . . . a kind of continuous augmented triad".[64] On the largest scale, the second half of the Act I duet of Olga and Tucha proceeds by major thirds, beginning in A♭ major, then shifting to C, E, and finally back to A♭.

4.21 Rimsky-Korsakov, *The Maid of Pskov*, ending of Act IV, Scene 4 (vocal parts omitted)

Glinka's use of the whole-tone scale and of major-third key relations in *Ruslan* prepared the ground for Dargomïzhsky's freer employment of augmented triads at the end of *The Stone Guest* in the scene between Don Juan and the Statue (Ex.4.22).[65] The Kuchka revered Dargomïzhsky's opera, and were particularly diligent in appropriating the novelties of this scene. Rimsky-Korsakov was the most enthusiastic in exploring the augmented

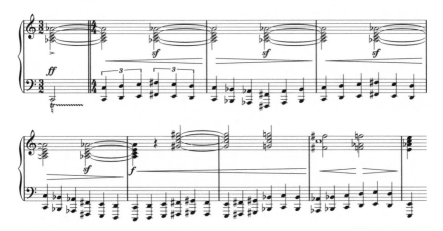

4.22 Dargomïzhsky, *The Stone Guest*, scene with Don Juan and the statue (vocal parts omitted)

triad's possibilities; the fact that he had orchestrated *The Stone Guest* no doubt had some bearing on this propensity. Glinka, Dargomïzhky and the Kuchka all linked the whole-tone scale or augmented triad with the fantastic and the sinister in their operas and programmatic music. Glinka used the scale for the evil magician Chernomor in *Ruslan*, and Dargomïzhsky for the Statue. In *The Maid*, this harmonic sphere is connected, on the one hand, to Ivan the Terrible's violence and his malicious henchman Matuta, and on the other hand, to fantastic images that appear in The Tale of Tsarevna Lada (Act I). Borodin had used the whole-tone complex in his song of 1867, "Spyashchaya knyazhna" (The sleeping princess), and it is this song that served as a model for the Tale of Tsarevna Lada: Rimsky-Korsakov not only used the whole-tone scale to depict similar circumstances, but also made free use of seconds in conjunction with it, as a modification of Borodin's trademark.

The Kuchka also had frequent recourse to a harmonic palette consisting of many minor seventh chords, or of half-diminished seventh chords. Although their significance was much more modest than that of the augmented triad, they, too, were enjoyed for the freshness of sonority and were often used in non-functional contexts. The main choral theme of the Veche scene ("Za Pskov nash rodimïy", For our native Pskov, Ex.4.23a) is based on a half-diminished chord; instead of contextualizing the chord within a functional harmonic progression, Rimsky-Korsakov transposes the chord, thereby suspending tonality in parts of this scene. There was, indeed, a general tendency among the members of the Kuchka to dwell on sonorities of such chords for long passages, thereby weakening the listener's sense of their harmonic function. Voice-exchange was commonly used to create some degree of harmonic movement within such passages, as in the Veche Scene chorus or the middle section of "Slava" in *Prince Igor* (Ex.4.23b). Ivan the Terrible's theme in *The Maid* also

4.23a   Rimsky-Korsakov, *The Maid of Pskov*, Veche scene (vocal parts omitted)

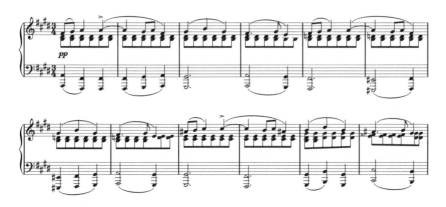

4.23b   Borodin, *Prince Igor*, chorus "Slava" from the Prologue

features this pattern, and because of its many recurrences stamps the whole opera with its characteristic sonorities.

One of the Kuchka's express aims was to be musically progressive, and in *The Maid*, Rimsky-Korsakov certainly achieved this, determinedly avoiding the conventions of operatic structure to produce a work that was unpredictable throughout. He could not, however, claim that his harmonic procedures were entirely independent of contemporary Western practices; and indeed he confessed to handling "stolen goods", as he called them. In the following dialogue with Yastrebtsev, he made no attempt to conceal the inspiration behind his progressive turn:

> "Tell me," I asked, "I've always been struck by one thing: how can you explain the enormous difference in style, music and even orchestration, which is quite astonishing when we compare, say, your First Symphony (leaving aside the Andante) and *Sadko*? One would think these works had been written by different people."
>
> "It's like this," replied Nikolai Andreyevich. "When I was writing the symphony, we knew only Beethoven, Schumann and some Glinka, but when I began *Sadko* and *Antar*, I was already deeply impressed by the beauties of Liszt's *Mephisto Waltz*."[66]

The *First Mephisto Waltz* alone gave the Kuchka much food for thought. The opening tiers of perfect fifths inspired the beginning of the dance from *Sadko* (Ex4.24a, and indeed since Sadko's playing of the *gusli* draws his listeners into an ecstatic dance, much like Mephistopheles's fiddling, the reference was significant). As it happens, Liszt himself had probably developed this passage from a similar idea in *Ruslan* (Ex.4.24b and c); he had played through

4.24a   Rimsky-Korsakov, *Sadko*

4.24b   Liszt, *Mephisto Waltz* no.1

4.24c   Glinka, Leghinka from *Ruslan and Lyudmila*

the vocal score of the opera during his concert tour in Russia and even made a concert arrangement of the Chernomor March. Nevertheless, the *Sadko* passage appears to have been influenced directly by the *Mephisto Waltz*, to which it bears the closer resemblance, rather than by *Ruslan*. Another passage from the *Mephisto Waltz* that served as an inspiration was the chromatic voice-exchange of Ex.4.25: we find its offspring at the beginning of *The Maid* (Ex.4.20) and in Boris's nightmare theme. Another passage from the Waltz, Ex.4.26a, is clearly behind Ex.4.26b in *The Maid*; the pianistic texture of the Liszt is most obvious in the vocal score.

Thanks to Balakirev's worship of Liszt, the members of the Kuchka were intimately acquainted with many other major works from his oeuvre. Rimsky-Korsakov, in a conversation with Yastrebtsev, claimed that he was able to rehearse in his mind all of Liszt's symphonic poems and some of the sacred

4.25   Liszt, *Mephisto Waltz no. 1*

4.26a   Liszt, *Mephisto Waltz no. 1*

4.26b   Rimsky-Korsakov, *The Maid of Pskov*, Act IV, Scene 6

4.27   Liszt, *Ce qu'on entend sur la montagne*

works.[67] *Ce qu'on entend sur la montagne* clearly influenced the beginning of *Sadko*, and also supplied Rimsky-Korsakov with a model for articulating a passage around the octatonic scale (Ex.4.27). The last example is especially enlightening, since the invention of the octatonic scale is often ascribed to Rimsky-Korsakov; this is the textbook consensus in Russia, where it is dubbed "the Rimsky-Korsakov scale". Rimsky-Korsakov claimed to have forgotten whether it was his own or Liszt's invention.[68]

Regarding Liszt's influence on *The Maid* itself, Rimsky-Korsakov again supplies us with a helpful pointer: he tells us that Olga's characteristic music in *The Maid*, like that of Tsarevich Dimitry in *Boris*, was influenced by the orchestral prelude to *The Legend of St Elizabeth*.[69] Rimsky-Korsakov had certainly heard *The Legend* in 1869, when Balakirev conducted it at the Free Music School. As we shall see, he mined it no less thoroughly than the *Mephisto Waltz*. Olga inherited Elizabeth's celestial orchestration of flutes and clarinets, certain textural patterns (as in Ex.4.28), and, most importantly, the characteristic use of secondary triads. Rimsky-Korsakov's mourning chorus at the end of the opera conspicuously follows the closing chorus of Liszt's oratorio; it is just as concise, and contains the same idea of colouring the major tonic by the motion (in the bass or an inner voice) to the submediant and back (Ex.4.29a and b). In Ex.4.30a we can see Rimsky-Korsakov's unusual resolution of the dominant seventh chord into iii6 (which then proves to be an appoggiatura to vi over the dominant pedal); Borodin also used such a progression in the slow movement of his Second Symphony (Ex.4.30b), and so it became a part of the Kuchka style. This progression was in all probability taken from one prominent passage in the orchestral introduction to *St Elizabeth*, shown in Ex.4.30c.

The aura of innocence and devotion characteristic of Elizabeth was directly inherited by Olga; Rimsky-Korsakov evidently wanted music which would

4.28a   Liszt, *The Legend of St Elizabeth*

4.28b Rimsky-Korsakov, *The Maid of Pskov*, Olga's arioso from Act III

win the audience's sympathies for his character. The same borrowing is much more straightforward in the case of Musorgsky's Tsarevich Dimitry, who was a martyr like Elizabeth. There are other Lisztianisms to be found in *Boris* that transmit the expressive connotations of the originals, such as the beginning of

4.29a Liszt, *The Legend of St Elizabeth*, final chorus

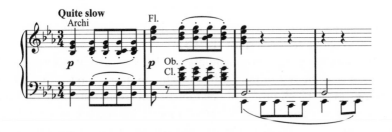

4.29b Rimsky-Korsakov, *The Maid of Pskov*, final chorus

4.30a   Rimsky-Korsakov, *The Maid of Pskov*, Act IV, Scene 7

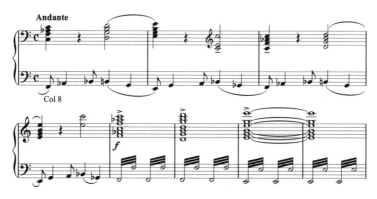

4.30b   Borodin, Symphony No. 2, third movement

4.30c   Liszt, *The Legend of St Elizabeth*

Shchelkalov's arioso, which reproduces a passage from *Vallée d'Obermann* associated with a troubled spirit (Ex.4.31).

The examples given above demonstrate that Liszt's influence on Rimsky-Korsakov and the rest of the Kuchka was by no means limited to chromatic harmony (as the high profile of octatonicism in recent musicological studies might suggest): Liszt's diatonic (often modal) innovations were still more important to the Kuchka. This is essential ammunition for refuting the common notions that the Kuchka's diatonic and modal harmony is somehow

4.31a   Musorgsky, Shchelkalov's arioso from *Boris Godunov*

4.31b   Liszt, *Vallée d'Obermann*

"natural", stemmed from Russian folksong material they used and therefore profoundly un-Western, or at the very least pioneering. We too easily forget that Liszt's *Harmonies poétiques et religieuses*, an encyclopaedia of diatonic and modal progressions, was written twenty years earlier than any of the Kuchka's harmonically innovative pieces.

The Kuchka's assimilation of Lisztian harmony was selective: they avoided the dominant-driven side of his innovations which greatly influenced Wagner, and instead focused on those devices, both diatonic and chromatic, that weakened functional harmony. Without abandoning the structural dominant altogether, they shaped their music around long stretches with very slow or static harmony or attenuated harmonic function. The result was a music that sounded very different from Liszt, but the examples discussed above that this sound was nevertheless achieved through Lisztian devices, and that Liszt should accordingly be considered just as important a source of the Russian style as Glinka or, indeed, the Russian folksong.

From "barbaric dissonances" to "more decent music"

During the 1890s, Rimsky-Korsakov worked on a radical revision of *The Maid*, resulting in the opera's third and final version; the earlier music, he complained, was full of "barbaric dissonances", while through these new revisions, he had transformed the opera into "more decent music".[70] There were, of course, a great many small-scale revisions, but Rimsky-Korsakov also re-orchestrated the entire score, and added new scenes with freshly composed music. For our purposes, however, the small-scale revisions are most inter-esting, for they allow us to draw direct comparisons between the habits and preferences before and after the musical re-education he undertook during the 1870s. After several years of writing fugues and determinedly developing other aspects of his compositional technique, Rimsky-Korsakov was a new composer – facile, expert and polished – who viewed his own earlier works as embarrassingly gauche and, if daring, then only through ignorance. None of these earlier works remained unrevised, and some of them, like *Antar* and *The Maid*, were subjected to further revisions. We shall limit our investigation of Rimsky-Korsakov's revisions to the process undergone by a single number, Olga's Act III solo in the first version of *The Maid* (Ex.4.32a), which became Olga's Act II arietta in the final version (Ex.4.32b); this comparison will also shed more light on the development of the Russian style in general.

In the first version, Olga's Act III solo is prefaced by a remark from the nanny, Vlasyevna – "Don't be so sad, boyarïshnya, my dove" – as if we have entered upon a conversation in progress. In the final version, Rimsky-Korsakov heavily reworked the solo as a self-sufficient "arietta": Vlasyevna's remark is gone, and instead of the very long tonic pedal and inconclusive recitative-like phrase in the original, we have a standard V–I followed by an orchestral postlude. These changes are characteristic of Rimsky-Korsakov's new operatic ideals: instead of Dargomïzhsky's continuous recitative, he prefers Glinka's more closed forms; even before the new version of *The Maid*, Rimsky-Korsakov had demonstrated this change of heart in *May Night* (1879), earning the disapproval of Stasov and Cui. Even the apparently trivial matter of transposition is representative of Rimsky-Korsakov's deviation from the Kuchka's ways: the unusual original key of D flat major was a favourite of Balakirev's and much used by the Kuchka, whereas the G major of the later version removes this link with the past; in addition, the resulting transposition to the head-voice register makes the second version much more idiomatic as soprano writing (the Kuchka had rejected vocal virtuosity as Italianate, and were not particularly anxious to write idiomatically for the different voices).[71]

The original introduction to Olga's solo consisted of dominant preparation for A minor; the leading note then turns out to be $\hat{5}$ of C# major (notated as D♭ major). The connection of distant keys through a common tone is a device found elsewhere in the first version of *The Maid*, and indeed it was a favourite device of the Kuchka at that time. The final version abandons this device: the introduction to Olga's arietta is now dominant preparation for E minor, and the ensuing tonic is the closely related G major. This removes the element of surprise in the original, but allows Rimsky-Korsakov to link Olga's arietta with the preceding number, a chorus in B minor; the arietta's introduction imme-diately follows this with a pedal B, and the arietta proper has two perfect

4.32a   Rimsky Korsakov, Olga's arioso from *The Maid of Pskov* (first version)

4.32a   Continued

4.32b Rimsky-Korsakov, Olga's arietta from *The Maid of Pskov* (final version)

4.32b Continued

cadences in B minor. Rimsky-Korsakov provides some compensation for the loss of his youthful boldness.

The principal melody of Olga's original solo was retained in the final version; it was based on a felicitous harmonic progression (VI_7 $V^6_{\#3}$ I^5_3) with voice-leading smooth enough for Rimsky-Korsakov's mature sensibilities. This was just the kind of progression that the Kuchka, in Balakirev's workshop, delighted in: it contains two of the Kuchka's favoured sonorities, the minor seventh chord and the augmented triad, and the ambiguity of the latter is fully exploited during the course of the number. But having found the prize progression, Rimsky-Korsakov uses it obsessively (twelve times in as many bars) in a sequence moving from D-flat major to F major to A major and back to D flat. While the first section of the solo is therefore a simple circle of major thirds, the middle section and reprise are both heard over a tonic pedal, and so there is an absence of any large-scale harmonic movement. On the small scale the number is characterized by the harsh dissonances of its chromatic appoggiaturas and chromatic voice exchange between the root and the seventh of the local chords (which are themselves already dissonant to the pedal). The reprise of the initial harmonic progression in the tonic minor (more of the same, 8 times in 8 bars) provides only a tenuous sense of closure, given that *harmonic* closure, effected by the tonic pedal, had already occurred long before. The use of a device which normally marks a coda section – the tonic pedal – was no doubt a conscious reaction against Germanic procedures, but it succeeds more in calling attention to what it is not than in providing a convincing alternative; likewise, the rising sequence of the middle section is a standard Germanic device for raising tension, a function that calls for a dominant pedal, whereas Rimsky-Korsakov's tonic pedal leaves the tension unmotivated, and requires mere dissipation at the reprise.

Olga's solo faithfully follows Stasov's call for the dissolution of familiar forms, but it only does this by taking characteristic devices of Germanic music and denying them their normal function. Rimsky-Korsakov, like the rest of the Kuchka, and like Stasov, underestimated the scale of the task they had set themselves, since Germanic forms were not independent properties of pieces, but were articulated through harmony; to remove themselves from the pull of these forms would have required the most radical reworking of harmony. The following extract from Rimsky-Korsakov's Chronicle, which discusses the working preferences of Balakirev's group, further explains how the mismatches of Olga's solo arose:

A certain kind of musical fragment or *period* was held in greatest esteem, variously preparations, extensions, short but characteristic phrases, dissonant progressions (but not of the enharmonic kind), sequential growths, abrupt closures, etc.[72]

This quotation takes us away from Stasov's heady abstractions into the practical needs of the student composers of the Kuchka. While the younger composers were greatly in Balakirev's debt, they also inherited the shortcomings that stemmed from his own haphazard education and *ad hoc* teaching methods. Balakirev, as an autodidact, had learnt composition directly from scores, rather than through a traditional textbook grounding in harmony and counterpoint. His approach, accordingly, was to mine existing scores (including the Kuchka's own) for striking devices which he could assimilate and reuse in new contexts: these were the "short but characteristic phrases" and "dissonant progressions" Rimsky-Korsakov refers to. The next task was to work such material into more extended passages, since a mere patchwork of *objets trouvés* would hardly do; hence the "preparations, extensions, . . . sequential growths, abrupt closures, etc." This is by no means absurd as an approach to composition, and no doubt it constitutes an informal (and usually tacit) part of any composer's learning process, but Rimsky-Korsakov later became dissatisfied with it, complaining, for example, that Balakirev's First Symphony "abounds in a kind of closing statement, yet there is no proper closure at the end".[73] The problem, as he saw it, was that this approach could create a haphazard effect, when little consideration was given to the original contect or function of the "characteristic phrases". It is, of course, possible to argue that Rimsky-Korsakov, later in his career, was merely imposing an alien set of (conservatoire) values on the music of the Kuchka's earlier years, But even if we do not accept Rimsky-Korsakov's evaluation, it is easy to find such devices as the prominent pedal passages in the Symphony turning up in Olga's solo with the same problems (according to Rimsky-Korsakov's new criteria): a lack of larger-scale harmonic motivation or fulfilment. We now turn to Olga's arietta in the final version of *The Maid*, to see how Rimsky-Korsakov dealt with these problems.

The arietta of the final version is at once more sophisticated and less daring (or "less gauche" for those, like the older Rimsky-Korsakov, who saw little virtue in the original version). The harmonically static ternary form now becomes a binary form (the middle section has its own reprise), with much more harmonic movement, and most important of all, a well marked structural dominant. The phrase structure also settles into four-bar units, while the vocal writing becomes lyrical throughout; matching these changes, the original prose text is now versified. The first four-bar phrase modulates to iii, while the second is a transposition of the first, now modulating from V to VII. Instead of the original circle of major thirds decorating the tonic in a static manner, we now have both third-related keys *and* a clear articulation of tonic and dominant in two rhymed phrases. The middle section of the original is now refashioned as a kind of modulating second subject, which moves from F#7 round to dominant preparation for the reprise, while still using melodic material derived from the equivalent section of the original (the modulating phrases hark back to a passage from Schumann's Piano Concerto). In the reprise, the first subject (to retain the sonata-form terminology) is presented with a new orchestral texture but left otherwise unchanged, while the second subject is more radically refashioned, since Rimsky-Korsakov now requires a long dominant pedal instead of modulations. As it happens, this allows him to bring back the original middle section, adapted to the texture and cleaner harmonies of the new version, but crucially matching the tension-building rising sequence to the dominant pedal. A brief sidestep through V of B minor leads us to the highest note of the arietta, and a barer texture, providing a strong approach to the cadence that finally restores the tonic chord. Rimsky-Korsakov provides us with a very artful re-working of his unruly original, introducing symmetry, harmonic direction and a carefully prepared climax.

The comparison we have undertaken is not only indicative of the difference between the young and mature Rimsky-Korsakov, but also reflects the dynamics of the Russian style in general, since the Russian style developed, as we have pointed out, to a great extent through Rimsky-Korsakov's efforts. The students of Professor Rimsky-Korsakov were schooled in his polished style and took for granted the combination of textbook perfection with the now common "Russian" idioms. This was all very distant from the origin of the Russian style in the Kuchka's workshop, where textbook composition was not simply ignored, but seen as a baneful Western influence that would prevent the emergence of any true Russian national music. But a generation later, Rimsky-Korsakov's student, Glazunov, saw no contradiction in combining the Kuchka's national idioms with the polished technique of his teacher, and an additional mastery of thematic development in the manner of the German symphonists. The result was often attractive, and always expertly crafted, but the innovative spirit of Balakirev's workshop in the 1860s was altogether lost for latter-day nationalists such as Lyapunov or Glière.

Rimsky-Korsakov against Russian music

In spite of Rimsky-Korsakov's pivotal position in Russian nationalist music, towards the end of his career he became disillusioned with the very idea of musical Russianness. Most importantly for our purposes, he uncovered the artifices of the music and ideology to which he had contributed so much; in so doing, he demystified not only Russian nationalist music, but the entire notion of national music simpliciter. Translating his new beliefs into actions, he made a conscientious, if artistically flawed attempt to abandon Russianness. After imitating Western models for a time, he finally turned back to the Russian style one last time, in order to satirize it; with this satire, his last opera, he sought to bring the era of Russian nationalist music to a close.

Rimsky-Korsakov communicated his change of heart to his wife, in a letter of August 1891:

> I don't like anything I listen to these days. I heard *The Kremlin* [a symphonic poem by Glazunov] . . . – it is tedious; some songs and a quartet by Sokolov – dry and lifeless . . . I am looking through Glazunov's *Eastern Rhapsody* – it is trivial, of no value; in short, the pretty harmonies, the interweaving of voices, the mellifluous phrases – none of them move me at all: everything seems dry and cold. *Mlada* [his own opera] is positively cold as ice. Now a Beethoven quartet or symphony: that would be another matter. There, technique and development constitute only the form, and everything is permeated by life and soul; the same with Chopin, and Glinka, and (just imagine!) [even] the Italians with the Sextet from *Lucia* and the Quartet from *Rigoletto*, with all their melodies. There is true life here. *La donna è mobile* is music, while Glazunov is merely the technique and conventional beauty acceptable to contemporary fashions and tastes. I think that the main product of the Russian school is not music, but cold and cerebral composition.[74]

And so the Russian school lacks "life and soul"; if Rimsky-Korsakov still attaches any value to the earlier efforts of the Kuchka, he is certain that the project was an artistic cul-de-sac, whose consummation is the bloodless technical perfection of Glazunov. He compares Glazunov unfavourably, and uncontroversially with Beethoven, Chopin and Glinka, but then delivers a shocking *coup de grâce*. Italian opera, say *La donna e mobile*, is worth far more than the vain efforts of the Russian school. The Kuchka had viewed the demotic tunefulness of Italian opera as the most formidable obstacle to the establishment of Russian national opera; the Russian public had made its preference for the Italian product all too clear. Italian opera was the enemy, and in appealing to it, Rimsky-Korsakov signalled his betrayal of all the nationalist ideals he had established and defended. If this outpouring were isolated in the composer's correspondence, we might be able to dismiss it as a passing cloud, but Rimsky-Korsakov's subsequent pronouncements continued along the same lines; we also have the powerful testimony of his compositions from these later years, as mentioned above.

At the outset of Rimsky-Korsakov's musical career, he had worked within the aesthetic framework outlined by Stasov and Balakirev. It was clear to their disciples which composers were to be admired and imitated, and which to be scorned; in opera, they knew which plots they should choose, and which they must avoid. This climate of intense creativity within predetermined limits certainly did not stifle the composers' creative powers; on the contrary, as we have noted earlier, the most daring innovations of Musorgsky, Borodin, Rimsky-Korsakov and Balakirev can be found in their music of the 1860s. But even by the mid-'70s, Rimsky-Korsakov realized that the years he had spent under Balakirev's tutelage still left him without the systematic training that Western composers received; he remedied this through a painstaking private study of counterpoint, until he had achieved the kind of compositional facility that was beyond the reach of his colleagues. Enriched by this experience, Rimsky-Korsakov then returned to the aesthetic premises of the circle and deployed his new skills for the glory of Russian music; he proceeded thus with significant success until he eventually sensed that the range of musical possibilities within these limits was – for him – exhausted. This thought began to disturb him around the beginning of the 1880s, during work upon *The Snowmaiden*, but by the end of the decade, after *Mlada* he was quite certain:

> After the completion of *Mlada*, I have nothing left to write. I have done all I could with my limited talent. Before composing *Mlada*, some themes were still left untouched; now there is nothing. I have everything that suits me: mermaids, wood-goblins, Russian pastoral, *khorovod* dances, rituals, transformations, Oriental music, nights, evenings, sunrises, little birds, stars, clouds, floods, storms, deluges, evil spirits, pagan gods, horrible monsters, hunts, entrances, dances, priests, idolatry, the musical development of Russian and other Slavonic elements, and so on. *Mlada* has filled in all the gaps . . .[75]

(Significantly, *Mlada* was initially intended as a collective project to celebrate the Kuchka's common goals, but it was eventually abandoned; Rimsky-Korsakov's opera was entirely his own work.) Rimsky-Korsakov's ascribes his artistic stagnation to his own "limited talent"; later, however, he decided that it was not so much his own abilities, but the entire Kuchka aesthetic which had caused the problem:

> I am prompted by my pride to think that many facets, devices, moods and styles, if not all, should be within my reach. I would not like to shut myself within the limits set by Stasov, Caesar [Cui], Balakirev and others . . .[76]

Because the Kuchka's inspiration lay in its idealization of the Russian folk, their emphasis in opera lay in the collective, while individuals were presented as types or mere symbols rather than beings with a distinctive emotional life of their own (the psychological explorations of Musorgsky's *Boris* provide the only exception, and even here the avoidance of any love interest is characteristic). The Kuchka thus adopted a certain asceticism towards emotion; Balakirev made this explicit when he criticized Tchaikovsky's love theme from *Romeo and Juliet* as unhealthy, and offered a rather tame and passionless love theme from late Schumann as a corrective.[77] Composers thought to be too lyrical were criticized: Chopin was "sweet and lady-like", while Mendelssohn was "melancholy and bourgeois"; even the Russian romance tradition was disparaged. The Kuchka's various modal novelties were designed to weaken the "Western" dominant; harmonic tension was thereby reduced, and with it the possibility of depicting emotion. Accordingly, the Kuchka gave us few emotional outpourings in music; on those exceptional occasions when they did have to depict intense emotions, they were forced to resort to the familiar devices of European Romanticism: we have already quoted the overtly Lisztian passages from *Boris*, while the love duet from *Sadko* was pronounced distinctly Straussian by a contemporary.[78]

In 1898, nearly a decade after he had first voiced his misgivings, Rimsky-Korsakov decided to make public his break with Kuchka aesthetics and ideology: his new opera, *The Tsar's Bride*, was a thoroughgoing negation of all Stasov's and Balakirev's precepts for Russian nationalist opera. The opera's style was determinedly lyrical, and the drama's mode of presentation emotional. The Kuchka's operatic policies required prose libretti, so Rimsky-Korsakov now turned to a verse drama to provide the basis for his new work. He also decided to organize his material into a thorough-going, old-fashioned number opera, something the Kuchka had long consigned to the dust-heap of history: there is a conventional overture, full-blown arias, and ensembles ranging in size from duets to a sextet. Although the subject was historical, Rimsky-Korsakov consigned this to the background, and moved a love intrigue to the centre of his version, again mocking the Kuchka's principles. We should not imagine that the play upon which the opera was based had in any way dictated this remarkable aesthetic reversal, for Rimsky-Korsakov had earlier turned to the same playwright – Lev Mey – and the same genre – the historical drama – for the *Maid of Pskov*, which was a showcase for every article of the Kuchka's operatic credo. Even the final scene of *The Tsar's Bride*, featuring the poisoned Marfa lost in delirium, falls fully within the conventions of the mad scenes in Italian opera. The style of the opera is a remarkable mixture of Russian romance (as at the beginning of Gryaznoy's Aria, Act I), Tchaikovsky (especially the orchestra's pervasive echoing of the singers' phrases à la *Onegin*) and various idioms from Bach and Mozart (Ex.4.33); all of these ingredients were an offence to the Kuchka's principles. Even in the songs and dances of the peasant girls (Act I), Rimsky-Korsakov stood firm against temptation: he dropped all his Kuchka pretensions to knowledge of authentic peasant music, and instead produced a conventional pastoral scene very similar to its counterpart in Act I of *Eugene Onegin*. The changing-background variations and modal passages which one might have expected were replaced by "Western"-style developmental passages, and the subtitles "Minore" and "Maggiore" appear in the score, as if to advertise further Rimsky-Korsakov's non-Russian sources). Balakirev suggested that the scene also drew inspiration from Liszt's Second Hungarian Rhapsody, given the

4.33a   Rimsky-Korsakov, overture to *The Tsar's Bride*

4.33b   Rimsky-Korsakov, *The Tsar's Bride*, Act I, fragment of Gryaznoy's arioso (voice omitted)

4.33c   Rimsky-Korsakov, *The Tsar's Bride*, final scene (voice omitted)

faster tempo in each successive section, the alternation between major and minor, and even a certain similarity in the themes.[79]

The Tsar's Bride pleased the public, which had yet to be enlisted for the Kuchka cause, but it baffled the critics and even met with resistance from Rimsky-Korsakov's wife (herself a composer), who thought his departure from the Kuchka's principles was wrong-headed.[80] Rimsky-Korsakov was tireless in the defence of his new opera, perhaps over-stating his case at times:

> I think it is the most virtuosic and balanced of my operas, and in its eclectic array of forms it displays the most desirable qualities of modern opera.[81]

Almost all of Rimsky-Korsakov's conversations with Yastrebtsev eventually came round to subject of *The Tsar's Bride*; the composer would then launch into another defence of his contrariness in producing such an opera at a late stage in his career:

> In the future, this opera ... will have much greater importance in the history of Russian music than is imagined by all those musicians today who can't see beyond its old-fashioned forms.[82]

When Yastrebtsev expressed some mild doubt over these words, Rimsky-Korsakov took offence. Stasov, of course, had to commit his own thoughts to print, although he was uncharacteristically tactful on this occasion, perhaps not wishing to write off a composer who had served his cause so ably in the past:

> In the closing years of the nineteenth century, Rimsky-Korsakov created two operas which were diametrically opposed: *Mozart and Salieri* in 1898, and *The Tsar's Bride* in 1899 [in fact 1897 and 1898 respectively] ... The first, the embodiment of contemporary progressive trends, is in the manner of Dargomïzhsky's *Stone Guest*, with its rejection of all the old traditional forms, with its free, most *truthful*, approximation to the intonations of the human speech. The other is a return (albeit a masterly and talented one) to the conventional forms of the old opera, with its arias, duets, etc. It is as if Rimsky-Korsakov said to the coming century: "Here is the new, and here is the old. One can display talent both in chains and without them. Choose whichever you prefer." I think that the twentieth century will choose the absence of those rusty chains.[83]

Rimsky-Korsakov, on the contrary, saw *Mozart and Salieri* as restrictive; given his own artistic frustrations at this point in his career, he wanted to break free from the rusty chains of the Kuchka's "progressive" manner. Any other style of composition was liberating by contrast; Stasov either failed to understand the cause of Rimsky-Korsakov's artistic crisis, or had no wish to undermine his own position by discussing the matter publicly. Stasov clutched at *Mozart and Salieri* as a counterbalance to *The Tsar's Bride*, and for this reason characterized it as the successor to Dargomïzhsky's *Stone Guest*, which had played a large part in the formation of Stasov's doctrines on the composition of Russian opera. This was not implausible, since *Mozart and Salieri* was based on one of Pushkin's "little tragedies" (*The Stone Guest* is another), and like Dargomïzhsky's work, it is written in a continuous recitativo style. But such a characterization fails to mention the stirrings of Rimsky-Korsakov's neo-classical ambitions, which are readily apparent in many passages. Indeed, the plot's ready justification for any pastiche Mozart allowed Rimsky-Korsakov to ease himself into his late eclecticism; after *Mozart*, he adopted whatever styles he wished (after thorough preparatory study) without feeling any need to justify himself.

What is more, Rimsky-Korsakov came to believe that the Russian style was in truth no different from any other style that he might choose to adopt for purposes of local colour, or simply on whim: the Russian style, like any other, was merely a set of conventions. Commenting on the construction of the Russian style in 1908, at the end of his life, Rimsky-Korsakov blithely demolishes the ideological edifice which had sheltered Russian nationalist music over the previous fifty years:

In my opinion, a distinctly "Russian music" does not exist. Both harmony and counterpoint are pan-European. Russian songs introduce into counterpoint a few new technical devices, but to form a new, unique kind of music: this they cannot do. And even the number of these devices is probably limited. Russian traits – and national traits in general – are acquired not by writing according to specific rules, but rather by removing from the common language of music those devices which are inappropriate to the Russian spirit. The method is of a negative character, a technique of avoiding certain devices. Thus, for example, I would not use this turn of phrase

if I were writing in the Russian style, as it would be inappropriate, but in other respects I would act with complete freedom. Otherwise it would not be a creative act, but rather a kind of mechanical writing according to certain rules. To create a characteristically Russian style I avoid some devices, for a Spanish style others, and for a German style others again.[84]

How very prosaic! The composer is not, after all, the conduit for the ineffable groanings of the Russian soul, but merely a practical musician who has learnt the trick of avoiding certain turns of phrase when he wants to create a distinctive stylistic ambience. The New Russian School had thus acquired its identity, we are told, only through self-imposed restrictions and a negation of what came to be seen as characteristically Western, and this process was no different from the steps towards mastering any other local colour. Rimsky-Korsakov cut so deep into the myth that we may even wish to temper his statement by suggesting that in constructing the musical Russianness the "negative" approach was supplemented by the "positive", when certain idioms and techniques became fixed to represent the Russian subject-matter.

Rimsky-Korsakov also punctures the nationalist claims that the music of the Russian School was not merely a dialect of European music, but a distinct language. He speaks of the Russian style as a restriction on the resources of the "common language of music"; the phrase requires explanation: in the 1860s, Odoyevsky had divided all music into "common" and "Russian" varieties, and since then Stasov and Cui had repeatedly upheld this division in their published articles and reviews.[85] To write "Russian music" in this sense, it was not enough to have been born in Russia; it was necessary, first, to share the nationalism of Odoyevsky and Kuchka, and second, to follow their example in embodying this nationalism in music. Tchaikovsky thus wrote music in the "common" language, whereas Rimsky-Korsakov had hitherto been a leading exponent of "Russian music", perhaps the most prominent of all in the public eye. But now Rimsky-Korsakov implies that the division was merely a fiction: Russian music, in whatever sense, was always a part of the common language. What local colour it employed – Russian folksong – was a resource of strictly limited potential; Kuchka ideology, on the contrary, had claimed that folksong was the foundation for Russian music (in the Odoyevskian sense). As early as 1893, Rimsky-Korsakov had told Yastrebtsev that the compositional possibilities offered by Russian folksong had already been exhausted. It was hardly surprising, therefore, that Rimsky-Korsakov could not find any promise in his students, who were dutifully following the Kuchka conception of Russian music; nor did he lend any credence to the prophecies of a new wave of nationalists – ethnographers and theorists like Melgunov, Sokalsky or Arnold – who promised the advent of a true Russian music based on recent advances in the transcription of folksongs, which had shown that the reality of folk practices was remote from the image propagated by the Kuchka. It mattered little to Rimsky-Korsakov whether Russian music was informed by distorted or accurate information on folksong, for Russian music was dead.

At the turn of the century, Rimsky-Korsakov demonstrated that the rejection of the Kuchka aesthetic signalled by *The Tsar's Bride* was not merely a passing phase. For his new opera, *Servilia* (1900–01), he chose another of Mey's dramas, but now of a kind that Stasov's disciples were to shun.[86] The plot was drawn from Roman history, and was perfectly suited to grand opera in the French manner: it featured two dozen characters, a conventional love intrigue underpinned by the conflict between pagans and Christians, a ghost, a fire, a public prayer and other paraphernalia of Grand Opera. The choice of such a plot was already an emphatic rejection of Stasovian aesthetics, but in the music, Rimsky-Korsakov took every opportunity to exacerbate the offence.

A few years later, while trying to defend *Servilia*, he launched into a thoroughly confused disquisition on nationality in music in his *Chronicle*. "Music without nationality does not exist," he began in the best traditions of Romantic nationalism, citing Beethoven and Wagner as the paragons of German national music, Berlioz for France and so on; he conceded that perhaps an international style had existed in the Renaissance, but thereafter no musical style could be innocent of national associations.[87] It follows from this that Rimsky-Korsakov must proclaim his own music Russian, but instead he produces a stunning *non sequitur*:

> Therefore I had to choose some suitable national colour for *Servilia*. A colouring that was partly Italian and partly Greek seemed most appropriate to me.[88]

Once again, the mysterious blood-borne nationality that Russian nationalists fervently proclaimed of their music is treated here, in a blithe equivocation, as a matter of arbitrary local colouring. Of course, many works by Glinka, Balakirev, Glazunov and Rimsky-Korsakov himself had already displayed the similarities between the well-oiled mechanisms of their Russian overtures on the one hand, and their Spanish or Czech pieces on the other. But Rimsky-Korsakov was wrong in imagining that he had succeeded in endowing *Servilia* with suitable local colouring. He had overlooked the problem that the Italian style was a default, which no operatic audience – Western or Russian – could ever experience as exotic (remember that the operatic diet of nineteenth-century Russian audiences was largely Italian); the possibility of creating local colour, on the contrary, required exoticism, and could not operate in its absence.

It is hard to believe that Rimsky-Korsakov had failed to understand this, given his acute observations on the workings of national musical styles. To make some sense of the contradiction, we would perhaps be best advised to understand the supposed need for Italian local colouring as an obfuscatory pretext for Rimsky-Korsakov's adoption of the Italian operatic idiom. The clue lies in his own words, that "the plot untied my hands in terms of stylistic freedom", "the freedom was absolutely complete". He now exulted in all those things from which he had formerly abstained: the sweetest appoggiaturas, Italianate chromaticism and duets written in parallel sixths and thirds. We could even say that the opera's lyricism is often exaggerated, its Italian idiom too concentrated, sometimes teetering on the brink of vulgarity. To define the style as exclusively Italian would also be imprecise, since the Italianisms have been filtered through Chopin, Liszt, and Wagner. For example, the passionate duet of Servilia and Valerius from Act III (Ex.4.34a) seems to recall the Canzona Napolitana section from Liszt's Tarantella (*Années de Pélerinage*, vol. 3, Ex.4.34b; in this piece, we also encounter the cadence that Rimsky-Korsakov considered to be the paradigm of the Italian style.

4.34a   Rimsky-Korsakov, *Servilia*, duet for Servilia and Valerius from Act III

4.34b   Liszt, Tarantella from *Années de Pélerinage*

The freedom Rimsky-Korsakov sought was primarily the negative freedom of relinquishing his obligation to compose, defend and propagate Russian nationalist music to the end of his days; pastiche, or near pastiche of other styles was in this context a liberation, but the choice of those styles towards which the Kuchka were most hostile served a second purpose of repudiating the Kuchka's aesthetic. It matters little whether Rimsky-Korsakov's artistic frustrations led him to view the ideology with scepticism or whether these doubts undermined his confidence as a composer: by the early 1900s, Rimsky-Korsakov's transformation was irreversible. Revealing these matters to his wife, or to Yastrebtsev was one thing, but divulging his new ideas to Stasov, or the surviving members of the Kuchka was quite another. *Servilia* remained a secret during the entire course of its composition, for Rimsky-Korsakov well knew how his colleagues would react to the new work, and he did not want to afford them the opportunity of bullying him into abandoning it.

He was determined to transgress, and was duly punished, not only by the critics but now also by the public. This change in public opinion had been brought about, ironically, by successful performances of Rimsky-Korsakov's earlier operas: the public now had well-honed expectations for any new Rimsky-Korsakov opera, namely that it should possess all the characteristics of the Russian style that Rimsky-Korsakov had now turned against.[89] Even Rimsky-Korsakov had to concede that the music was too pallid, but he still continued to defend his project in principle; it was not surprising, therefore, that shortly after the failure of *Servilia* he persisted with a similar stylistic experiment: *Pan Voyevoda* (*The Governor*, 1902–3), dedicated to the memory of Chopin. Although it is rarely mentioned in the literature, Rimsky-Korsakov had always idolized Chopin from his adolescent years onwards; even the scorn that was poured on Chopin's "feminine" style in the Balakirev circle, failed to cool this attraction. In 1901, in a conversation with Yastrebtsev, Rimsky-Korsakov even went so far as to say the unthinkable: that he valued Chopin more than Glinka.[90] Until *Pan Voyevoda*, though, only occasional references to Chopin's music are found in Rimsky-Korsakov's works; apart from a handful of pastiche piano pieces, there is only the Snowmaiden's G-minor arietta from the eponymous opera (Act I), and a mazurka in *Mlada*. *Pan Voyevoda* was set in Poland, and Rimsky-Korsakov evidently thought that this afforded him sufficient justification for suffusing the new opera with Chopinisms; although much of the opera is through-composed, the larger scenes incorporate closed numbers with titles such as Berceuse, Nocturne, Mazurka, Polonaise, or Krakowiak. Some of the music is a clear pastiche of this or that Chopin piece, as illustrated in Ex.4.35, but Rimsky-Korsakov generally places a little more distance between himself and his model, as he had done in *Servilia*; the passing of the intervening decades is often marked by characteristically modern harmonies, and of course the orchestration does much to assimilate the Chopinisms to Rimsky-Korsakov's own manner. It must be said that Rimsky-Korsakov's historicizing tendencies were not entirely alien to the

4.35a   Rimsky-Korsakov, Polonaise from *Pan Voyevoda*

4.35b   Chopin, Polonaise in A major

4.35c   Rimsky-Korsakov, Polonaise from *Pan Voyevoda*

4.35d   Chopin, Etude in C# minor

contemporary Russian musical scene: outside the nationalist camp, there was the prominent example of Tchaikovsky's *Mozartiana* suite (1887), which consisted of four Mozart piano pieces given attractive orchestral garb; but in 1892, Glazunov, the most eminent of the Kuchka's disciples, had composed the ballet *Chopiniana*, which provides a striking precedent for *Pan Voyevoda*. (Glazunov was later to turn to Haydn in the finale of his Violin concerto). Nevertheless, an opera by a member of the Kuchka carried far greater burdens in the public perception, thanks above all to Rimsky-Korsakov himself, and *Pan Voyevoda* fulfilled none of its obligations.

But in addition to Chopin, the influence of Wagner is also readily apparent in *Pan Voyevoda*. Indeed, while Rimsky-Korsakov was at work on the opera, the *Ring* received its first performance by a Russian company, the Mariinsky.[91] Rimsky-Korsakov and Glazunov sat through rehearsals following the score, just as they had done for the German production. The earlier encounter with Wagner left Rimsky-Korsakov full of praise for the orchestration, but he was not entirely convinced by the music otherwise; after the Mariinsky rehearsals, however, he was no longer a doubter, and he hurried to assimilate Wagner into his own music. There are obvious Wagnerisms in *Pan Voyevoda*, such as the opening theme of Act II (modelled on the Prelude to *Götterdämmerung*) but beyond these surface similarities, Rimsky-Korsakov made a serious attempt to pattern his music according to Wagner's mature leitmotivic technique; Rimsky-Korsakov had already used straightforward calling-card motifs in the 1880s, but now the motives became more integrated and flexible, above all in Act II of the new opera. The main theme of Act II, for example, serves both as a Forest theme and a Destiny theme (Ex.4.36a), and it is the source of all many dotted-rhythm motives which appear during the course of the act. One of the derived motives, Ex.4.36b, suggests a dramatic connection between two very different conspiratorial scenes: in the first, a solo scene, Yadviga, a beautiful aristocratic widow, plots to poison the governor, while in the second, an ensemble scene, several young officers plot to rush upon the same governor with their swords. The two conspiracies are hatched quite independently of each other and for different reasons, but the motive clearly connects them. At the close of the act, the words of the sorcerer Dorosh, the contemplative, omniscient Wotan figure, who had supplied the poison, unite the two conspiracies with a forest metaphor, explaining the appearances of the motive and reminding us of its source:

Tam yad gotov, a zdes' sverkayut sabli.	Here the poison is ready, and there the swords are glinting.
I mshcheniye, i revnost', i lyubov' Pereplelis', kak vetvi v tyomnom lese.	Revenge, and jealousy, and love Are tangled like the branches of a dark forest.
A nado vsem tsarit sud'bï reshen'ye.	And destiny presides over all.

4.36a   Rimsky-Korsakov, *Pan Voyevoda*, beginning of Act II

4.36b   Rimsky-Korsakov, the "poison motif" from *Pan Voyevoda*

Rimsky-Korsakov's enthusiasm for the *Ring* during these years led him to begin work upon a new opera, based on the *Odyssey*.[92] Although this project was never completed, we have a substantial portion of the opera's opening in the form of the prelude-cantata *Iz Gomera* (From Homer). This beginning of *Iz Gomera* is startlingly close to one of Rimsky-Korsakov's favourite passages from the *Ring*: the Storm prelude at the beginning of *Die Walküre*. It seems extraordinary that Rimsky-Korsakov, at the age of 58, should write a blatant pastiche of Wagner as part of a concert work intended for public performance, rather than as a private compositional exercise (he could have withheld the opus number if he had wished to exclude it from his canon). It would seem that Rimsky-Korsakov now considered anything which departed from the Kuchka style as sufficiently original to claim as his own; we can understand this better if we call to mind his own past as a composer, a past well known to the Russian public when *Iz Gomera* was written.

It is no accident that works such as *Servilia*, *Pan Voyevoda* and *Iz Gomera* are largely forgotten today: they fall outside the Russianness which the public, then and now, requires of Rimsky-Korsakov. Russian musicologists, who generally write on the basis of unexamined nationalist assumptions, either ignore these works, or consign them to the margins of the composer's canon, an insignificant diversion before the composition of *The Legend of the Invisible City of Kitezh*, which they see as the culmination of Russian national epic opera. But I will argue that the status of *Kitezh* is, in fact, problematic, representing the Russian style in crisis, rather than in its settled apogee.

Indeed, it would appear that the scenes in *Kitezh* which Rimsky-Korsakov brings off most successfully are those which reflect his recent stylistic experiments, while other sections flag under the weight of Kuchka clichés dating back to the 1860s or '70s. The limitations of the Russian style in the latter sections are made all the more prominent by the un-Kuchka-like modernist libretto, written by Viktor Belsky, a poet familiar with both the new symbolist dramas and with the God-searching tendencies of the Russian Silver Age.[93] Belsky tried to elicit something unprecedented from Rimsky-Korsakov, even demanding "miracles" and an "overwhelming rapture" in the final chorus; Rimsky-Korsakov, however, was reluctant to comply, perhaps out of scepticism, or perhaps simply because he felt unable to provide music that could satisfy such demands. The finale which Rimsky-Korsakov eventually provided must have disappointed the librettist's expectations, for there was neither Scriabinesque, nor Wagnerian ecstasies. The libretto diverged considerably from anything which had in the past fallen within the Kuchka's orbit. For example, Belsky portrayed the Russians' Oriental opponents, here the Tatars, as ruthless and bloodthirsty barbarians of an entirely realistic sort, as no other Orientals had ever been portrayed before in Russian opera. The horror of their invasion was no fairytale, and there was no noble Khan Konchak to alleviate the pain of defeat. This called for something equally novel and shocking in the music, yet Rimsky-Korsakov disappointingly settled for augmented seconds to represent the Orient and diminished sevenths for horror, falling below the level of the much more imaginative solutions he had found in the past. Even the often-played orchestral entr'acte known as "The Battle of Kerzhenets" seems to owe rather too much to Liszt's *Hunnenschlacht*, now half a century old.

Various other aspects of *Kitezh* seem to be trapped in a time warp. The dashing Prince Vladimir recitativo phrases could easily have been sung by Sadko, and the market-place scene of Act II is nothing but a pale copy of the market scene in *Sadko*. The character of the drunk, Grishka Kuterma, who sinks to the depths of depravity, is nevertheless able to inspire some degree of empathy; he is the only character in Rimsky-Korsakov who could possibly be called Shakespearian. Still, the power of Grishka's scenes is largely due to Belsky's libretto rather than Rimsky-Korsakov's music, which uses a Russian folk dance to convey inebriation, following the pattern of earlier Kuchka drunks such as Borodin's Prince Galitsky or the peasant in Musorgsky's *Trepak* from the *Songs and Dances of Death* (see Ex.4.37).

But while Rimsky-Korsakov's imagination remained barren in the areas which had traditionally been the Kuchka's province, he compensated for this by the incomparable lyrical flow of the opera's first act, composed in a manner which would not have been possible without the composer's assimilation of Wagner, or indeed without his slightly earlier search for lyricism and melodic beauty. Owing to the liberating experience of *Tsar's Bride*, *Servilia* or the Wagnerian excursions of *Pan Voyevoda*, the music of Act I flows with remark-able continuity, is singable throughout and is permeated by the tension of its dominant-charged harmony. In *Kitezh*, Rimsky-Korsakov managed to revivify his compositional powers, mixing the benefits of his recent experiments with his older, Kuchka manner. The opening theme illustrates this well: we encounter a familiar melodic formula, bearing strong associations with the Kuchka's Russian style, a descending fourth in the melody, from scale degree 4 to the tonic (Ex.4.38). This figure was common in Russian folksong, and conveniently lent itself to a harmonization that avoided a perfect cadence; this allowed such passages to sound suitably non-Western, in conformity with Stasov's theory that plagalism ran in the blood of the Russian people (one well-known instance of this figure occurs in the opening theme of *Boris Godunov*). But in this case, Rimsky-Korsakov replaced the established Kuchka harmony with precisely the V–I which they sought to avoid; in so doing, Rimsky-Korsakov had the best of both worlds: the figure retained its Russian associations, but was also now endowed with harmonies that expressed *Sehnsucht* – a most un-Kuchka-like affect.

4.37a   Rimsky-Korsakov, *The Tale of the Invisible City of Kitezh*, Act II, Kuterma's scene with Fevroniya

4.37b   Borodin, Galitsky's song from *Prince Igor*

4.37c   Musorgsky, "Trepak" from *Songs and Dances of Death*

4.38 Rimsky-Korsakov, *The Tale of the Invisible City of Kitezh*, Fevroniya's arioso from Act I

But perhaps the most powerful subversion of the Kuchka's musical nationalism occurs at the end of the opera, where the bells of Kitezh cathedral usher us into the garden of paradise. The orchestral representation of Russian Orthodox bells had been a Kuchka trademark from *Boris Godunov* onward. Indeed, if any feature of the Kuchka style had the status of a national symbol, it was the Orthodox bells: they were quite distinct in sound from any bell-ringing traditions found in Europe, and unlike folksong, they were equally familiar to all strata of the Russian society. Yet Rimsky-Korsakov, presented in his chosen story with Orthodox bell-ringing, now abandons the Kuchka idiom that his audience would have identified with, and instead offers them the sound of Western church bells, as he had found them represented in *Sposalizio* or *Parsifal* (see Ex.4.39). And so the Cathedral of the Assumption in the old Russian city is given the sound of Western bells as filtered through the minds of Liszt and Wagner. Rimsky-Korsakov had not forgotten the sound of Orthodox bells. He had not forgotten how to represent Orthodox bells orchestrally – he was, after all, the supreme exponent of the Russian style. Rather, he had simply lost interest in maintaining the Russian style, and since this was the first opportunity to represent bells since his abandonment of nationalism, a Lisztian or Wagnerian representation offered a refreshing change, and better reflected his current musical predilections. No matter that the cathedral was Russian, no matter that the Orthodox bells were the Kuchka's most powerful symbol of Russianness for contemporary audiences: *these* were the bells that Rimsky-Korsakov wanted to hear in his opera.

For all Rimsky-Korsakov's weariness with the Russian style and his desire to depart from it, manifest in both words and actions, the Russianness of *Kitezh*

4.39a   Rimsky-Korsakov, bells pattern in *Kitezh*

4.39b   Liszt, *Sposalizio*

4.39c   Wagner, bells pattern in *Parsifal*

lacks any signs of ironic intent. The same cannot be said of Rimsky-Korsakov's last opera, *The Golden Cockerel*, where the obvious satire of the libretto was reflected by a more complex musical satire, in which the composer now firmly establishes ironic distance between himself and the Kuchka style. There were already hints of this in the fairy-tale operas which immediately preceded *Kitezh*, namely *The Tale of Tsar Saltan* (1899–1900) and *Kashchei the Immortal* (1901–02), in which Rimsky-Korsakov uses his material in a highly self-conscious manner, deliberately restricting his expressive palette to create in each opera a distinctive world, divorced from reality. Describing *Saltan* in his *Chronicle*, Rimsky-Korsakov himself remarked on his recitatives, which were "given a special character of fairy-tale naiveté", and on his use of a fanfare as a framing device. His fellow-composer, Grechaninov, was among the first to recognize this new approach:

> No one had previously managed to maintain a fairy-tale flavour consistently throughout an opera, where everything – desires, feelings, actions – is expressed as if in half-tints, where there is nothing "real".[94]

Grechaninov singled out a passage from *Saltan* in which the Tsarina Militrisa is about to be floated off to sea in a barrel:

What a temptation for a composer to write heart-rending music, yet you make her sing about the rushing waves, as if before a somewhat unpleasant sea journey.

This was not a criticism, of course – Grechaninov understood Rimsky-Korsakov's purpose. Most of Rimsky-Korsakov's listeners were less perceptive, and simply took *Saltan* to be another "Russian" opera, but by placing himself at a remove from his subject-matter, both dramatic and musical, Rimsky-Korsakov was no longer writing from within Russian nationalism, but as an outsider, taking the devices he had once used in seriousness, and now manipulating them for different needs.

Kashchei's subtitle is "*osennyaya skazochka*" – A little autumn tale; the use of a diminutive indicates that Rimsky-Korsakov did not want his audience to expect a grand nationalist elevation of a folk-inspired fairy-tale in the manner of, say, *Snegurochka*. *Kashchei* takes the Kuchka's fantastic chromaticism to a new extreme: earlier Kuchka operas had used this topic in contrast to a default diatonicism, whereas in *Kaschei* this contrast is gone, and the fantastic becomes the default. The brighter finale is insufficient to counterbalance the eeriness of the foregoing. It is based on the theme of Ivan-Korolevich's polonaise-like arietta, which neither very *bogatïrskaya*, nor even very Russian. This was no doubt deliberate, for *Kashchei* was intended as a little tale, whose little cardboard cut-out heroes, and their little feelings leave no place for a bold, triumphant finale.

The *Golden Cockerel* goes much further: the composer does not merely distance himself from the Kuchka's nationalism, but subjects it to a sustained satire. One of its most striking features is an unprecedented reversal in the opera's main conflict. Prior to the *Cockerel*, the three classic operas that had pitted Russia against an Oriental enemy had ended in a vindication of the Russian side: in *Ruslan* this was a straightforward victory; in *Prince Igor* it was Igor's heroic escape from Oriental Captivity, and a restoration of the *status quo ante*, while in *Kitezh* the victory was spiritual, to be realized only in the next world. In contrast to these precedents, the *Cockerel* hands the final victory to its two Orientals, the Astrologer and the Queen of Shemakha, while the Russians forces fail dismally and deservedly at every turn. And not only this. The Astrologer's parting words before the final curtain reveal that

Tol'ko ya lish' da tsaritsa	Only the Queen and I
Bïli zdes' zhivïye litsa.	Were living characters here,
Ostal'nïye – ten', mechta,	The rest were only a shadow, a dream,
Prizrak zhizni, pustota . . .	A ghost, a barren void . . .

The librettist, Belsky once again, no doubt inserted these words to placate the censor, reassuring him that the idiotic Russian people and their lazy, half-witted tsar were pure fantasy. But in Rimsky-Korsakov's hands, this concession becomes an essential part of the opera's structure, for a plot unfolds as a story told by the Astrologer. This means not only that the fantastic style (for the Astrologer) and the Oriental style (for the Queen of Shemakha) dominate the opera, while the Russian style representing Dodon's Kingdom is subsidiary; likewise, the two Orientals are presented as real, while the Russians belong to the realm of fantasy.

The subversion of the traditions of the Russian nationalist opera did not end there. The *Cockerel* became the first and only Russian comic opera whose humour operated largely through through self-conscious references to the Russian operatic tradition. Usually the humorous musical allusions are of two main types: in the first, the genre or style is grotesquely inappropriate to the character (in which case it is the character who is ridiculed); in the second type, the genre and style themselves become the target of ridicule for being outmoded, hackneyed, or in bad taste. Russian composers since Glinka have used allusions of the second type to express their dislike of particular genres, techniques or composers. Thus Glinka, in Farlaf's tongue-twisting Rondo from *Ruslan and Lyudmila*, mocks not only Farlaf, but also the clichés of basso buffo roles. Musorgsky, in *Rayok* (The Peepshow), similarly laughs at the old-fashioned "classicisms", Italian operatic virtuosity and the Russianisms of Serov which the Kuchka considered vulgar. And Borodin in his short-lived operetta *Bogatïri* (The Warriors) passed an ironic comment on Verstovsky and, once again, Serov through parody and direct quotation.[95] Both in Musorgsky and Borodin, a satirical musical allusion becomes so pointed a weapon that it is able to serve the purposes of musical politics: namely, the belittling of those whom the Kuchka saw as the enemies of their project. But Rimsky-Korsakov, as we shall see, turned this weapon back on the Kuchka, even though this inevitably entailed some self-inflicted wounds.

The most explicit of these satirical references in the *Cockerel* arises from the ludicrous relationship between the unworthy Tsar Dodon and his wailing, self-abasing people: here Rimsky-Korsakov selects no less a target than *Boris Godunov*. Dodon's first appearance on stage is marked by a grotesquely solemn march, followed by a contrasting, wheedling lament which is immediately contrasted by his lament, which cannot but remind us of the entrance of another unhappy tsar, Boris. The two tsars even share some vocabulary, both verbal and musical: the crown is heavy for Dodon ("*tyazhelo nosit' koronu*"), while "*tyazhelo*" and the related "*tyazhko*" are the keywords of Boris's tormented soliloquies; and we also find that the leitmotive of Dodon's torment is close to the theme of Boris's nightmare (Ex.4.40a and b). Of course, the

4.40a Rimsky-Korsakov, *The Golden Cockerel*, Dodon's "torment motif"

4.40b Musorgsky, Boris Godunov, Boris's "nightmare motif"

verbal style of the two tsars is otherwise very different, one dignified, the other absurd:

Boris	Dodon
My soul is sad.	I've gathered you here
Some sort of involuntary fear	To tell the whole kingdom
Has gripped my heart	Just how tough it is for the mighty Dodon
With a sense of evil foreboding. . . .	To wear his heavy crown. . . .

The wailing choruses of the people in the *Cockerel* present the most direct parody of Musorgsky. As Taruskin pointed out, Rimsky-Korsakov had already imitated the characteristic lamentation figures of *Boris* in his *May Night*, again for comic effect, in spite of Musorgsky's tragic intent.[96] The *May Night* parody is nevertheless quite benign in contrast with the *Cockerel*'s, where the text reads:

Our tsar is dead, our happy tsar, our carefree tsar. He was wise; he ruled us from his bed. True, when he was angry, he wanted to send everyone into exile; but when the thunder ended, he shone upon everyone like our golden sun. What will the new dawn bring us? How can we live without a tsar?

Dodon's own wailing at the sight of his two idiot sons, who managed to kill each other instead of the enemy adds insult to injury by supplying a purely musical joke, when Musorgsky's moaning figures are inverted (Ex.4.41).

4.41   Rimsky-Korsakov, *The Golden Cockerel*, Dodon's wailing

When Dodon gathers his troops for war, a similar scene is invoked, this time from *Prince Igor*, again turning dignity into absurdity:

Prince Igor	Tsar Dodon
Let us march into battle against the enemies of Russia!	Well, lads, it's war! We need your help.
People	Don't be slow now, hurry up!
God give us victory over the enemy!	Open your coffers straight away;
Prince Igor Let us march against the Polovtsian Khans!	From every household I'll need A fox's tail and beaver's coat.
People Wash away the offence with the enemy's blood!	But listen: when commanders or their officers
Prince Igor	Might want to take a little extra, don't object
We go to battle for out faith,	It's their business – so leave off!
For Russia, for the people!	*People*
	We are yours, body and soul.

Rimsky-Korsakov's targets for parody even extend beyond the Kuchka to Glinka. The musical characterization of Gvidon, Dodon's elder son, is close to that of Sobinin, Susanin's son in Glinka's *A Life for the Tsar*. Both are the Russian equivalents of the *Heldentenor*, and both sing music that is vaguely reminiscent of Russian soldiers' songs. The words they are given provide the same contrast as before:

Sobinin	Gvidon
Well! When has the valiant Russian soldier Ever returned home From the battlefield of honour Without some heartening good news! . . .	The main source of our troubles Is that our neighbour is too close Just one step over the border And our troops are at his mercy.
All were hit! And did they flee! We pursued enemy in full flight,	Let's remove our army from the borders And place it around the capital. In the capital we shall stock up

Hail, Mother Moscow!   Food and drink – beer and wine –
                            That will be a fine war!

Because of Glinka's near divine status in the rhetoric of musical nationalism, the musical likeness between these two tenors was a blasphemy for any nationalist musician holding fast to the cause.

The prime source of the Kuchka's national pride, the Russian folksong, also received its share of debasement at Rimsky-Korsakov's hands. In Act III, we encounter a parody of the customary "Glory" chorus when the people greet their tsar as he returns from battle (Ex.4.42a). In accordance with the Kuchka tradition, the chorus features a real folk melody, presented in the form of changing-background variations.

4.42a   Rimsky-Korsakov, *The Golden Cockerel*, People's chorus from Act III

4.42b   Rimsky-Korsakov, harmonization of the folksong "Krug kusta" published in his
100 Russian Folksongs

4.42c   Fragment of the folksong "Gori" from Linyova's collection

All is well so far, but now the text:

> We are your loyal serfs,
> We are glad to serve you,
> Kissing the tsar's feet,
> Amusing him with our foolishness,
> Fight with our fists on a festive day,
> Bark like dogs and crawl on our knees,
> Anything to make your hours pass more happily,
> To bring you sweet dreams.

But this is not just another jibe at the Kuchka's habits. The chosen folk
melody, "Krug kusta" (Round the bush) appears as No. 59 in Rimsky-
Korsakov's own collection of harmonized folksongs (Ex.4.42b), but the
Cockerel setting differs strikingly from the composer's earlier harmonization;
what we have here is, in fact, the composer's only preserved attempt to recreate folk polyphony after being confronted late in life with the first accu-

rate transcriptions, made with the benefit of phonographic recordings (as in Ex.4.42c).[97] The debasing text and satirical situation clearly indicate that Rimsky-Korsakov discerned no artistic potential in this new authenticity, unlike many of the young composers around him, who saw it as the true path for Russian music, revealed at last after false starts.

During the last decade and a half of his career, Rimsky-Korsakov sought to bring the era of Russian musical nationalism to a close, not merely by means of verbal argument, but also through musical example. He now disagreed with the ideology that surrounded the products of the Russian style, but this disagreement did not logically require him to condemn music which was vital and inventive; however, the arrival on stage of many epigones who treated the Russian style as a closed set of fossilized mannerisms understandably made him wish to move on. Nevertheless, on two levels the last portion of his career was not altogether successful. Firstly, the operas of these last years were not generally considered artistic triumphs. But secondly, not even the *Cockerel* could shift the nationalist epigones from their well-worn furrow, since dozens of composers continued writing in the same tired manner well into Soviet times. Instead, the most brilliant and innovative music of the years following the *Cockerel* was penned by composers who had eschewed nationalism, composers as divergent in style as Scriabin, Stanchinsky, Roslavets, Mosolov and Prokofiev. And perhaps the truth of the *Cockerel's* message is most emphatically demonstrated by Stravinsky, who started where Rimsky-Korsakov left off.[98] Those numerous Soviet critics who for many decades refused to rank Stravinsky's Russian works alongside those of the Kuchka and their followers were not only endorsing the Party line towards the émigré composer: Stravinsky's "Russian" works provided them with nothing they could recognize as the product of a sincerely-held nationalist impulse – they saw nothing but irony and mockery. Indeed, they even suspected that his intention in *Petrushka* and *Les Noces* was to mock his folk-derived material. The goal of glorifying the nation through music was now gone: there would be no more *Ruslan*s or *Prince Igor*s. The high tragedy of the nation's suffering that ennobled *Boris Godunov* was gone too. The romantic conception of beauty which animates the best pages of *The Snowmaiden* or *Kitezh* had also disappeared. Folk material was now used to represent the vulgar everyday present (as in *Petrushka*), or the archaic past to which our human link was broken (as in *Les Noces*). There was no longer a noble folk heritage to be polished up and presented to best advantage within operas and symphonies, but only a repository of material affording opportunities to amuse or even repel, as in *The Rite of Spring*. But the groundwork for Stravinsky's radical rejection of Russian nationalism had been thoroughly prepared by his teacher. Stravinsky was simply the first to create new music that had assimilated the lesson of the *Cockerel*.

CHAPTER 5

NATIONALISM AFTER THE KUCHKA

The main players of the present chapter are much more obscure than those who figured in previous chapters, and indeed they were known only to a limited circle in their own lifetimes. Few of them won any recognition as composers of concert music; instead, what little renown they once enjoyed was due to their essays, folksong collections or liturgical music. Post-Kuchka nationalism became ever more purist and restrictive, leaving little space for creativity – stimulating enough, perhaps, for the academic mind, but a stultifying environment for most composers. This late nationalist current coincided with Russia's literary "Silver Age", which drew on a fresh set of Western influences, Symbolism above all, and developed them creatively; from literature, new ideas and styles spread to the other arts, music included. The assimilation of Symbolism encouraged a less nationalist and more cosmopolitan outlook not only because it was undeniably a Western influence, but because Symbolism was based on, if anything, an opposition between the this-worldly and the other-wordly, drawing interest away from the opposition between Russia and the West (it was no coincidence that this cultural rapprochement with the West took place once large-scale Western investment in Russia's industrialization had begun). This drove nationalism towards the margins of Russian culture, although by no means into oblivion. But the late nationalist current in music provides us nevertheless with a story that is by no means devoid of interest; it is here that we can witness the most extreme manifestations of musical nationalism and its most expansive pseudo-theoretical justifications, often verging on the absurd.

Folksong after the Kuchka: authenticity and utopian dreams

What then? Where shall we direct the alto voice after this F? Yes, yes, we shall send it here – it's much juicier, much more tasty this way. What, isn't this how they do it in Petersburg? Isn't this how your textbook does it? But if instead of following the chorale-book, you do it in the way that the folk feel it, the Russian way – the Borodin way, if you like – then this little turn will sound more native.[1]

Kastalsky, as remembered by Asafyev

Critics of the Kuchka

The desire for a truly nationalist art can never be satisfied: it is always possible to seek after greater authenticity and purity, and indeed the logic of cultural nationalism demands this. For Stasov, the Kuchka had already realized the project of a national Russian music; however, the following generation of musical nationalists considered the Kuchka's achievement inadequate on several counts. The Kuchka, they said, failed to treat folksong with due respect, and never studied it in any scholarly fashion. The Kuchka also made too many concessions to Western musical style, and ultimately failed to develop a truly independent art of Russian music. As early as 1879, while the Kuchka was still flourishing, the folksong collector Yuli Melgunov passed the following harsh judgement:

> [C]ontemporary Russian composition and folksong practices are at odds with each other due [firstly] to the arrogance of some composers who thought they could invent a Russian style themselves, and to the carelessness and inattention of Russian folksong collectors.[2]

The composer Alexander Kastalsky dismissed the folksong harmonizations of Glinka and the Kuchka, saying that these were "only little pinches, or handfuls [of Russianness] which they immediately bury under heaps of European music".[3] But perhaps the severest judgement came from Sergei Taneyev:

> [W]e have no national music ... we haven't worked out [Russian] harmony. Russian music does not exist; there is only raw material – song and its mechanical mixing with foreign forms.[4]

One of the more extended and detailed critical passages is found in the writings of another folksong collector, Pyotr Sokalsky (1832–87). Instead of the Kuchka's old metaphor for folksong arrangement – placing a precious stone in a suitable setting – Sokalsky substitutes the more prosaic metaphor of translation:

Any fitting of a folksong into our notation is the beginning of its modification, or, so to speak, its translation from the old language into the general musical language of modern times; this translation can be more or less successful, depending on the talent of the translator.[5]

The principal changes to the original entailed by "translation" were listed by Sokalsky as follows: changes from non-tempered to equal-tempered tuning, the imposition of metre through bar lines on a non-metrical melody, and harmonization which is essentially at odds with the "original monody" (Sokalsky's term). It is quite astonishing that Sokalsky, writing in the late 1880s, could still imagine that Russian folksongs were only monodies, when this hoary misconception had long since been exploded (we shall discuss this issue at length a little later); nevertheless, his comments on tuning demonstrate that he was by no means a prisoner of established ideas – the Kuchka had never even considered this issue. He is scathing in his evaluation of Balakirev's and Rimsky-Korsakov's collections, which he says are nothing more than "commentaries upon folksongs" for the drawing-room. As an alternative to such "commentaries", he envisages the reconstruction on stage of as much of a song's context as possible: it would be performed in appropriate costume, as part of a "people's drama", with a similar number of performers, without harmonization; Sokalsky even hopes that the ritual within which the song functions could be recreated (this project was partially realized much later, in the Soviet Union of Brezhnev's time).

Sokalsky also challenged the artificiality of folksong harmonizations using heptatonic modes, whether the major, minor or the various church modes, with or without any leading notes. Unlike most of his contemporaries, he did not see the heptatonic modes as the solution to the problem of folksong harmonization, and denied that these modes were somehow more "natural" than the major and minor tonal systems (a notion dear to the Kuchka). He argues that strictly modal harmonizations may be fine as markers of an 'archaic' mood, but nothing else:

Why deceive yourself and others by following rules for the obligatory imitation of Western ecclesiastical modes? If this device is good for offsetting the song's own characteristics, then use it, but if your taste and talent point to other means, what rules can possibly stop you?[6]

Sokalsky also argues that the Kuchka's modal accompaniments were often spurious; for example, the first melody in Balakirev's collection (*Ne bïlo vetru*) uses only five pitches: *c, d, e, f, g*, with *d* as the initial and final note. Balakirev arbitrarily chose to harmonize this as *d* Dorian; Tchaikovsky later took the

Dorian for granted in his own harmonization, and eventually Laroche cited the song as his paradigm of Russian modality. Sokalsky, however, noted several variants of the melody among Melgunov's transcriptions; some of these used six pitches, and in each case the extra pitch was *b* flat rather than the *b* natural assumed by Balakirev, Tchaikovsky and Laroche. From this, Sokalsky argues that the melody of the song (the five-pitch version that appeared in Balakirev's collection) is not based on any of the church mode, but rather on an essential tetrachord *defg* with a decorative lower neighbour note to the *d* final (anticipating by decades the analytical strategies of Soviet-era ethnomusicologists). Sokalsky concludes that Balakirev et al. were attracted by the Dorian colouring, but that this had nothing to do with authenticity, their subsequent claims notwithstanding:

> What rules would you suggest for harmonizing this tetrachord and where did Laroche get his from, when he said the above-mentioned harmonization was "correct"? There is no rule here. We can only say that the *b* natural sounds more unusual, more archaic and harsh within a *d* mode.[7]

Sokalsky admits however, that the evolution of a progressively more authentic art of folksong arrangement is essential for the development of a national music. He is convinced that the characteristic traits of Russian folk music must be defined and then assimilated by the national art music, as with parallel movements in the visual arts and in architecture at the time. But it is striking that Sokalsky describes this as a programme for the future – there is no place for the achievement of the Kuchka (this is typical of the more radical authenticists in the post-Kuchka generation of musicians).

The search for podgoloski

We have already discussed (in Chapter 4) the occasional representation of folk hetero/polyphony – i.e. singing with *podgoloski* (undervoices) – in Russian art music from the late eighteenth century onwards. Many composers up to and including the Kuchka, recognized that there was such a thing as the choral song in peasant culture, and that it was sung in several parts, but they generally showed no desire to discover what peasants sang and how the various parts interacted. It appears that no member of the Kuchka ever attempted to transcribe choral singing, nor do we have any evidence that the nature of the *podgoloski* was discussed in the circle. There are isolated examples in Borodin and Musorgsky of quirky voice-leading owing to some indirect acquaintance with peasant practices (through the transcriptions of Melgunov), but neither cared to repeat these tentative experiments, never mind develop them further (this will be discussed in detail below). The very existence of non-unison choral singing in peasant culture was more rumour than documented fact during this century-long period. There is no mystery in this: song collectors generally did their work in the towns or cities; they would approach individual servants who had been raised as serfs or peasants, and these individuals, of course, could sing only main melody, not the *podgoloski*. The very few collectors who dared to venture into peasant communities and who managed to hear choral singing there were unable to notate what they heard. Mikhail Stakhovich is typical of these would-be pioneers in folk-music research. He compiled four volumes of Russian folksongs (published 1852–4), in which he raises the subject of choral singing, but remains extremely vague about the nature of the *podgoloski*. Here is a passage from his foreword to the second volume of the collection:

> Many Russian and foreign musicians have noticed divergent patterns in the movement of the voices in Russian choral songs; but this has also been observed in the songs of many Oriental peoples, and so the phenomenon is not as important as the essence of Russian tunes that I am discussing here.[8]

The "essence of Russian folksong", Stakhovich concluded, was its invention of distinct melodies that could be brought together in counterpoint; but this was untrue: for any given song, a solitary peasant singer would only produce one melody, while counterpoints would only be heard on the addition of further singers. The counterpoints therefore had no autonomous existence, *pace* Stakhovich. This error was, in fact, the product of wishful thinking on Stakhovich's part. He tells us that he heard the solo beginning of a choral song as the first theme, and the subsequent entry of the second voice as the beginning of a countersubject, but since he was unable to notate what he heard – even with only two voices – he chose instead to combine two melodies from *different* songs that, to his mind, made acceptable counterpoint (Ex.5.1). Stakhovich's representation of folk hetero/polyphony was therefore pure invention: a shortcoming in Stakhovich's musical abilities resulted in a makeshift solution of no scholarly value, and this in turn was projected back onto Stakhovich's account of actual peasant practices. But however dubious Stakhovich's work might be in ethnomusicological terms, his substitution of Western counterpoint for a seemingly incognizable peasant practice proved entirely satisfactory as far as composers were concerned.

The turning point in this story comes in 1879, when the folksong collector, Yuli Melgunov, published the first volume of his collection (the second followed in 1885).[9] Although Melgunov was no better able to transcribe hetero/polyphonic textures than his predecessors, his determination to

5.1   Stakhovich, an example given in the Introduction to book 3 of his collection

uncover the nature of the *podgoloski* led him to devise a method for over-
coming his limitations. He collected several versions of the same song as sung
by different singers, one at a time, and found that when he aligned these verti-
cally in score form, the result was much closer to folk hetero/polyphony than
anything hitherto notated; but having come this far, he was still unable to
check these versions by ear against an ensemble performance. When it
came to publication, Melgunov lacked the confidence to confront the public
with the transcriptions in this form; this was not so much because he was
uncertain of their accuracy, but rather because they were quite unsuitable
for domestic music-making, with a single voice accompanied by piano.
Accordingly, he commissioned a reworking that followed the normal rules of
harmonization;[10] this reworking appeared in large print, while the transcribed
lines were given below, in small print. Melgunov even shrank from presenting
these lines as polyphony, and so they appear as single staves, rather than as a
score. It is therefore hardly surprising that Melgunov, in his foreword, leaves
his public uncertain whether he intends the volume as a serious work of
ethnography or as a domestic entertainment:

The variants are presented here as raw material which requires artful
arrangement, and not as models. An experienced musician will always be
able to deal with the parallel fifths to be found in them (which can be easily
turned into ^{6} or $^6_4$ chords) and with the parallel octaves (which can be used
for doubling a voice), as well as with the seconds, which can be given a
different meaning as ninths or appoggiaturas. The frequently encountered

dominant and tonic notes which do not fit with the other notes, can be turned into higher or lower pedals. [11]

After the appearance of the first volume, Melgunov presented a paper before a body of eminent ethnographers (the Petersburg Commission of the Pedagogical Museum). The scepticism of the meeting's concluding statement beggars belief:

> The hypothesis of polyphonic folk singing [throughout Russia], presented by Mr Melgunov, is deemed insufficiently proven, the more so since Mr Melgunov certifies this phenomenon only on the basis of folk singing in one area.[12]

Melgunov had created a great stir among Russian musicians (even Rimsky-Korsakov was forced, grudgingly, to acknowledge him).[13] But in spite of this renown, and the quality of his research, Melgunov was quite unable to persuade his fellow ethnographers that Russian hetero/polyphony even existed – mainstream Russian ethnography was still conducted at several removes from the object of study. Still, the Commission was, by chance, correct in supposing that there might be significant regional variation in musical practices; Soviet-era ethnomusicologists were indeed able to confirm that those areas where rich hetero-polyphony are surrounded by much larger areas of simpler heterophony or even monody.

There may be some signs of Melgunov's influence in the music of the Kuchka, as the Soviet musicologist Yevgeny Gippius suggested.[14] In the case of Borodin, there is the chorus from *Prince Igor* (*Khor poselyan*) which we have already singled out in Chapter 4 for its enterprising imitation of *podgoloski*; Gippius speculates that this chorus resulted from a study of Melgunov. We can be certain of Musorgsky's acquaintance with Melgunov's work, since he borrowed two of its songs for use in *Khovahnshcina*, albeit the melodies only. As for his assimilation of the *podgoloski* technique, Gippius points to a group of five choral folksong arrangements which remained unpublished during Musorgsky's lifetime.[15] The first two pieces do indeed show Musorgsky attempting a new kind of choral texture (Ex.5.2), which might have been inspired by Melgunov's collection, but then again, on the evidence of the music, we might equally say that they were influenced by an earlier collection of two-part songs compiled by Prokunin.[16] Even if we grant that Melgunov was the influence here, Musorgsky's approach to folksong certainly underwent no revolutionary change: all we have is a modest step taken in an unpublished work, with no further consequences for the remainder of Musorgsky's oeuvre.

5.2   Musorgsky, chorus *Skazhi, devitsa milaya*

After Melgunov's research fell on stony ground, there was no great incentive for others to follow in his steps. The next advance came in the work of Nikolai Palchikov (1838–88), who managed to reach a much clearer understanding of *podgoloski*, thanks to the fact that was able to conduct unbroken research among peasants over three decades, during his career as a village arbitrator. His collection, published posthumously, presented 125 songs from the village where he lived. Palchikov made his transcriptions from ensemble performances, listening to each singer in turn until he arrived at an accurate transcription. Since he did not publish his work he did not have to worry about marketability; as a result, we have no harmonizations of the sort found in Melgunov's volume, indeed nothing to render the collection usable for an individual singing at the piano (at whom folksong publications were normally aimed). Although the scholarly value of the work is unimpeachable, there is one shortcoming that results from his presentation of the material: Palchikov collated extra variants of each part on the same page, so that a performance treating all the vertically-aligned parts as a single score would produce something that could never be heard in a Russian village. It is certainly possible to select among these variants in order to reconstruct a plausible version; for example, there are four different variants of a solo *zapev* (initial flourish) presented in Ex.5.3 – in a performance, three of these would have to be

5.3   Folksong "Kak u nas-to na svyatoy Rusi", No. 38 from Palchikov's collection

discarded. This is no daunting task for anyone today who has received some ethnomusicological instruction in Russian folk hetero/polyphony, but Palchikov's materials do not afford this information to the reader, and this must have been a considerable drawback for the first readers of Palchikov's volume, who would have lacked the knowledge necessary for sifting through the parts. At the most exacting level of scholarship, there is also the problem that we cannot know which variants were in fact sung together in one performance. Nevertheless, Palchikov undoubtedly made the final break-through in the understanding of *podgoloski*, even if he inadvertently obscured his findings somewhat for his readers.

But Palchikov's researches could be rejected just as easily as Melgunov's. It was only with the advent of phonographic recording in Russian ethnography that hetero/polyphony was established beyond the reach of arbitrary denials by "experts". The watershed was 1904, when Yevgeniya Linyova (1853–1919) published the first of her volumes of transcriptions from phonographic recordings (a second volume appeared in 1909). Each *podgolosok* was tran-scribed as it had occurred in a single ensemble performance (Palchikov had transcribed over repeated performances).[17] Linyova had been the director of a choir which sang Russian folksongs in popular arrangements; she tells us that in an American tour during the early 1890s, her audiences repeatedly asked whether Russian peasants harmonized the melodies in the same way. This, she said, had given her the idea of establishing the nature of the *podgoloski*, and recording technology placed the project within her grasp (without Palchikov's long years in the village).[18] Over the following years, her transcriptions won general acceptance, and nationalist musicians soon began to discuss the impli-cations for the future development of Russian music. Even the elderly Stasov wrote an admiring letter to Linyova, which is worth quoting at length:

I was deeply gratified by the news that your marvellous work is progressing so well and that in a few weeks we shall have your academic publication of the phonographic recordings of Russian folksongs. This is a superb business, and for me personally, truly appetizing – I am gorging myself on it.

In my opinion, your work signals the dawn of some mighty musical revo-lution (first of all for Russian music). Namely for choruses. Dargomïzhsky and Musorgsky had taken some great strides forward in establishing those new and uniquely-justified forms of singing and expression in opera (Russian opera). Their friends of talent and genius took this up, and boldly continued the revolutions which they had begun. But the choruses remained in the old backward and false forms of artificiality, convention-ality and complete implausibility (in spite of all the beauty and originality which can be often found in them). But now the news has come that choruses will also be subject to this operatic revolution.

And it seems that this revolution is destined for Russia, for the Russian School of music. Conventionality and implausibility should disappear, and truth and correspondence [to the folk practices] would be a feature of choruses as well. They will cease to be sung 'correctly' and conventionally; instead, they will be performed with all the truth, capriciousness, and incorrectness to be found from the mouths of the people, with all the changes in the numbers of singers: some of them enter and continue, others fall silent for a few seconds, and then enter whenever it suits them, while others again proceed through the music without any break; [choruses will be performed] also with all the changes of rhythm, movement, and even of mood that are inherent in the people – they are alive, they feel, and they create something of their own in that choir, in spite of some commanding, thinking and deliberating author.[19]

Characteristically, Stasov restricts the implications of the Linyova collection for art music to the composition of operatic choruses; the achievements of the Kuchka were for him inviolable and could not be improved upon, even with this new evidence. It was left to the younger generation of nationalists to work out the consequences of Linyova's *podgoloski*.

Among these younger nationalists was Alexander Kastalsky (1856–1926), who became the first theorist of hetero/polyphony in his *Characteristic Traits of the Russian Folk Musical System* (1923). He hoped that his work would enable and encourage composers to create a new national musical style:

If in the areas of industry, technology, agriculture we cannot manage without "good neighbours" [i.e. Europe and its technologies], in the sphere of national art and particularly music it is fully within our powers to begin from the folk foundation, which is vivid and original, and to find a new, independent and direct path . . .

As a result of the assimilation of our "good neighbours" system we have a whole galaxy of glorious creators, among whom some of genius stand out. I am sure that upon assimilating the speech patterns of folk music, a Russian school more independent and vivid than its predecessor will emerge; not only this, but the wonderful notion of unifying the people and its artists through the native art will be realized.[20]

Kastalsky begins his book with a whole series of examples, comparing the "cultured" harmonizations of folksongs in Balakirev, Musorgsky, Lyadov with the same songs harmonized "in the folk manner". To supply the "folk harmonizations", he drew from Melgunov, Palchikov, Linyova and similar sources; in some of the examples, no source is mentioned, and these must be the author's own inventions (since he made no original transcriptions). But even where a source is indicated, Kastalsky still makes various alterations: his No. 97, for example, is labelled as Melgunov's, but it contains canonic writing which is nowhere to be found in the source, and which is anything but a "characteristic trait" of Russian hetero/polyphony.

Some of the "characteristic traits" lack even a single example from a transcribed source – we can only ask how characteristic they can possibly be if Kastalsky was unable to cite a single example in his sources (remember that he was dependent on pre-existing transcriptions). One section, for example, is devoted to the whole-tone scale; Kastalsky could simply have provided this as an extension of the principles he had abstracted earlier from peasant music – something to fire the imagination of composers rather than satisfy the scholarly demands of ethnomusicologists. But instead Kastalsky attempts to persuade the reader that whole-tone sonorities are in fact a part of peasant hetero/polyphony. Kastalsky's No. 119 features a melody which was only sung as a monody (its genre, the *bïlina*, is exclusively monodic), but Kastalsky supplies it with *podgoloski* nevertheless, and the result is whole-tone harmony, justified because the *podgoloski* "use the same scale as the melody" (the melody happens to traverse an augmented 4th, sufficient for Kastalsky to discern the whole tone scale). Kastalsky's No. 120 is an imitation of bells that he devised himself, which draws from tradition inaugurated by Kuchka in which dissonant formations are used in an attempt to evoke the non-harmonic timbres of bells (here G, A, B, Eb); this has nothing to do with peasant practices, but Kastalsky, regardless, uses his example to show, supposedly, that whole-tone formations "are not foreign to the Russian ear". Kastalsky also mentions in passing that he thinks he once heard a *gusli* player experimenting with augmented triads; this is cited for the same purpose, although even if the *gusli* player's behaviour was described correctly, it offers him very little assistance in arriving at whole-tone harmony in sung hetero/polyphony (the *gusli* and hetero/polyphonic traditions do not overlap). No source is indicated for No. 121, which presents a melodic fragment that traverses an augmented 4th (B♭, C, D, E); adds a *podgolosok* designed to produce whole-tone harmony. Finally, No. 122 is a folk melody used by Rimsky-Korsakov, with two lower voices added by the composer. Again, Kastalsky is only interested in a scale segment that spans an augmented 4th – B, A, G, F – even though the scale immediately moves down to E, in a context that is clearly Phrygian.

Kastalsky's purpose was not merely to establish what peasants have done as a matter of ethnomusicological record; beyond this, he presented Russian hetero/polyphony as a technique to be acquired, a technique that he had already mastered and which he could now help others to assimilate. But Kastalsky's text, as we have seen, is far from transparent in distinguishing these two aspects of his work: the reader is not openly told that what she sees is not a series of comparisons between "cultured" and peasant harmonizations, but only comparisons between two kinds of "cultured" harmonization, namely, the Kuchka's and Kastalsky's own. Given Kastalsky's knowledge of peasant practices, some of his own arrangements might indeed fool many readers who are quite well acquainted with Russian peasant music; but Kastalsky is too often unable to resist imposing various compositional devices to produce a result that is much too neat to be mistaken for anything that would occur in peasant practice. In Ex.5.4, for example, we can see his comparison of a "cultured", chromatic harmonization, which he discounts as "decorating Russian simple-folk speech by refined German or French phrases", with his own harmonization, executed "according to the folk system"; yet Kastalsky's version contains a strikingly pretty canon, a device that is simply not characteristic of Russian folk hetero/polyphony.

In the course of the following three years, Kastalsky modified and expanded *Characteristic Traits*: the manuscript he left at the time of his death in 1926 was *Foundations of Folk Polyphony*, which was eventually published·in 1948. The new volume is at once more conventional and more ambitious: more conventional because it is more closely modelled on the structure of the traditional harmony textbook, but also more ambitious because Kastalsky now widens his remit to cover many non-Russian musical cultures (including

5.4   Kastalsky's comparison of a "cultured" harmonization (top) with a "folk-style" harmonization (bottom); the song is "Zelyonaya roshcha" taken from Melgunov's collection (figure 97 from *Characteristic Traits*)

Armenian, Georgian, Kazakh, Turkmenian, and Arabic). If we consider the institutional context in which *Foundations* was produced (conservatoire music-theory instruction), the very conventionality also witnesses to Kastalsky's ambitions: *Characteristic Traits* could easily be annexed to a traditional harmony course without demanding much time, whereas *Foundations* is presented as a complete harmony course in itself, designed to run in parallel to a traditional course. At first, the discussion is more contrapuntal than harmonic: §1 deals with typical melodic patterns, §2 with combining voices in seconds, §3 with thirds and sixths, §4 with fourths, and so on up to ninths, after which there are discussions of passing notes, then various types of voice-leading, and the addition of further voices. Eventually, however, we come round to the topic that had been the focus of *Characteristic Traits* – modes and scales; from this point onwards, Kastalsky seems to model his treatise on Rimsky-Korsakov's harmony textbook. §21 is devoted to seventh chords, but since the object of study offers none, the seventh is on each occasion a passing note seventh. The next section deals with six-four chords, then we have different cadential progressions and then, most dubiously, modulations. Kastalsky offers us examples of every kind of modulation; this might impress the innocent reader, but it is telling that Kastalsky's references to sources are now altogether absent, and we are only left with the vague "harmonized in the Russian style". Having analysed his habits in *Characteristic Traits*, we know that this means, disappointingly, that he compiled the examples of this section by selecting small fragments of folk melodies from the multi-voice collections he was using, discarding the *podgoloski* of the original transcription, and replacing these with *podgoloski* of his own devising in order to effect the desired key-change which the original had disobligingly failed to provide.

In Example 5.5 (*Foundations*, No. 574), we notice that Kastalsky wilfully imposes a semitone shift from A minor to B♭ minor on a melodic fragment that shows no signs of modulating anywhere. In Example 5.6 (*Foundations*, No. 578), there is a particularly curious distortion: a fragment that is marked "unpublished by Orlov" features an unintentional upwards shift by the singer, dutifully recorded in the transcription is quite clearly a transcription of the singer's unintentional upwards shift of pitch. Instead of explaining that this is not a normal feature of peasant practice, Kastalsky takes it at face value, not through inexperience, but because he has an ulterior motive. He uses this

5.5   Kastalsky, *Foundations of Folk Polyphony*, figure 574

5.6   Kastalsky, *Foundations of Folk Polyphony*, figure 578

chance shift in intonation in order to discuss how "folk-style" harmonizations could modulate to distant keys, using sequence for the purpose – never mind that this is all entirely alien to Russian peasant music.[21] It is hard to believe that such monstrous incongruities could be proffered by the same Kastalsky whose initial purpose was to treat folk music on its own terms.

The second new feature of the *Foundations of Folk Music* is no less bewildering: alongside his examples from Russian folk music, Kastalsky also provides examples from Armenian, Georgian, Kazakh, Turkmenian, Arabic and other musical cultures, all presented on equal terms with the Russian material. Kastalsky seems to have been little troubled by the fact that his knowledge of these other musical cultures was extremely meagre compared to his knowledge of Russian peasant music – in most cases, his acquaintance with each nation's music was limited to what he could glean from one published collection of melodies (and he had no independent means of assessing the scholarly worth of any of these). It would seem, indeed, that he was attempting to compile a composer's manual offering some kind of generalized folk manner to the student; the student could then adapt this knowledge to the specific needs of any given nationality (this is only implicit in Kastalsky's text – it is not his declared purpose). This would seem to be nothing less than the logical consequence of a practice dating back to Glinka and extended by the Kuchka: the composer produces a Russian overture, taking great pride in the distinctive Russianness of the work; the same composer then feels that this step towards peasant culture automatically enables him to produce Spanish, Serbian, Czech or Greek fantasias based on the same principles. At the same time, Kastalsky's manual anticipated the Stalinist industrial production of multiple musical nationalisms, all taking the development of Russian musical nationalism as their model (this development will be discussed in Chapter 6). It is hardly surprising, then, that *Foundations* was finally unearthed and published in the wake of the 1948 Resolution, when precisely this kind of indiscriminate, all-national "folk music" was demanded of composers. But insofar as Kastalsky's goal in publishing these two works was to found a new national style, he failed.

In the long run, attempts by Kastalsky and others to establish the study of folk hetero/polyphony as the norm for student composers all ended in failure. The first steps had already been taken in 1889, when Taneyev and Georgiy

Konyus established a course named "The Harmony of Russian Folksongs" at Moscow Conservatoire. After the Revolution, in the early 1920s, Kastalsky, now among the "Red Professors", offered his expertise to his Moscow Conservatoire students. Then under Stalinism, in 1936, Sergei Yevseyev introduced "Elements of Russian polyphony and harmony" to the Conservatoire's syllabus, and after the 1948 Resolution this course was given greater prominence. But none of these ever threatened managed to displace the sacred volume of Rimsky-Korsakov's harmony, which remains to this day the fount of harmonic wisdom for Russian students (any modifications were in the direction of Riemann, not Kastalsky).

The issue of folk intonation

Perhaps still more elusive than the *podgoloski* were the intonational patterns of peasant singing. To the extent that collectors noticed anything unusual in singers' intervals they must have dismissed them as the weaknesses of the untutored ear, since nothing of substance was published on the matter until the early years of the twentieth century. One of the first publications to discuss peasant singers' intonation came from the archive of the late Melgunov, who, many years after his collection had been published, reflected on his own transcription practices and found them wanting. Reared on Greek music theory and certain of its relevance to Russian folksong, Melgunov chose the name "enharmonic" for tones that did not seem to fit into a diatonic scale:

We should use the name of "enharmonic scale" not for a scale that consists of an unbroken row of quartertones, as in the usual definition, but for a diatonic scale in which certain degrees have been replaced by enharmonic tones. Russian songs do not contain melodies which are sung in 24 quartertones. From the studies of Westphal, Helmholtz, Gevaert and others, it is clear that the ancient peoples knew scales with enharmonic intervals. Several varieties of these scales still exist in the practice of folk singing. My ignorance of the existence of such scales led me to a misconception. In the singing of the Russian people, I took enharmonic intonation to be inaccurate intonation, as [many] musicians still imagine. As a result of this, I had to notate an enharmonic tone as either F or F# in No. 3 of my first volume (*Na zore bïlo*), thereby fitting it into our equal-tempered tuning. But with attentive listening to the intonation, it should not be difficult to notice that the normal F should be replaced with an enharmonic tone lying between F and F#. Similar examples can be found in many of the songs I transcribed.[22]

5.7   One of the variants of "Na zore bïlo", notated by Melgunov, No. 3 in his collection

The first collector who attempted to reflect unfamiliar intonational patterns in his notation, was Alexander Listopadov (see Ex.5.8).[23] Listopadov's researches had included a genre of wedding song customarily performed by the older women of peasant communities. At first he assumed that the performances he was recording suffered from random flaws in the intonation, but once he had amassed a collection of similar performances at other times and in other villages, he noticed that the "flaws" recurred consistently. He then spent much time pondering over these "extraordinary intervals", but in the end he preferred to declare that this genre must be exceptional, and that all other genres of peasant music could be reproduced on the equal-tempered piano without doing violence to the intonation of the originals; to bolster this (unsupported) conclusion, he further assumed that these wedding songs were the sole survivors from an earlier stratum of Russian peasant music.[24]

5.8   "Ishla, ishla solnushka", a wedding song transcribed from phonograph by Listopadov

Such hints were developed and systematized after the Civil War, by Arseniy Avraamov, who married ethnography with the laboratory-based experiments in tuning that were very much in vogue in the early 1920s. Since Russian nationalism was shunned at the time as "great-power chauvinism", one of Avraamov's chief concerns in his "manifesto" was the transformation of a nationalist project into a "revolutionary" one:

> For whatever reason, the dominant point of view on folk music [at present] is that it has had its day, and any attempts to revive it are treated as something deeply reactionary in social terms.
>
> Of course, a truly reactionary approach to the issue of "folk" music is possible: for example, if anyone decided to repeat Stasov today.

However, this is not a matter of the *narodnik* movement [i.e. the author is not advocating a return to *narodnik* ideology], for in musical terms folksong's formal/modal aspects contain the most revolutionary elements. The folksong thus points the way for contemporary music that is being strangled by the grip of the 12-tone temperament – it is the way to the future. A study of folksong's true modal structure provides a clue to what seemed an "insoluble" problem, namely how to bring contemporary music closer to mass perceptions without falling into "over-simplification" [*oproschhenstvo*], leading to the routinely "primitive", or to street slang.

The tuning of folksong (both Great Russian and even more so Oriental) does not fit into the European "major–minor" system; its true "restoration" demands the expansion of the melodic/intonational means of contemporary music – and not in the direction of "polytonal" or "quarter-tone" contrivances, but rather in the direction of the logical enrichment of the system by the new building blocks of these *natural* scales. Given all their novelty and originality, these scales are deeply justified in *physiological* terms and for this reason they can impress even the prejudiced listener from the first hearing.

On 19 April [1927], O. D. Tatarinova will give a concert in the Mozart Hall; she is the first singer to risk an approach to this issue in practice, and my role in the first part of the concert will be to accompany her on a naturally tuned harmonium that will reproduce precisely the original intonation of Russian songs (in this case, songs from the Don river). Of course, we inevitably had to reject all the standard harmonic devices as well, restoring not only the tuning, but also the whole system of song polyphony, operating exclusively by melodic variation and *podgoloski*. The harmonic complexes stemming from this system are striking, on the one hand for their unheard-of freshness and novelty, and on the other hand for their absolutely natural character and euphony. Such combination is unthinkable within the [currently] dominant temperament, where euphony equals routine, and novelty equals cacophony.

Of course, this is not going to be a complete "restoration", for the instrumental accompaniment only replaces the vocal ensemble of the original, yet regretfully there is no such "ensemble" around . . .[25]

In another, equally pathos-laden manifesto, Avraamov tries to dress his project up in Marxist clothing, but in the end, his real allegiance to the old nationalist discourse shows through. He begins by quoting Marx: "every phenomenon becomes its opposite by the action of its own forces"; he continues by declaring a revolution in music: "The overtu(r)ning of the existing system in music has begun"; but he closes with nothing better than nationalist cliché:

The "Wohl"-temperament [should be "equal temperament"] is destined to be overthrown by "the action of its own forces"; this two hundred-year old wedge stuck in the history of Western musical culture, will be pushed out by another wedge from the East.[26]

Here Avraamov is talking about equal-tempered instruments which, when tuned slightly lower or higher than normal can, in combination, produce a scale of 36 or 48 tones that would provide fairly close approximations of intervals found in the harmonic series. Avraamov ensured that his ideas went further than the theoretical stage, and organized concert performances with various ensembles during the 1920s. But like all other ambitious and innovative projects of this period, Avraamov's work foundered once Stalin had consolidated his power. Avraamov found it prudent to compose film soundtracks on approved subjects, and using normal tuning. Interest in the intonational patterns of peasant music disappeared until it enjoyed a brief resurgence in the New Folkloric Wave of the 1960s and early 70s.

The leading note problem

We have noted above that from Odoyevsky onwards, scholars of Russian folksong have questioned the legitimacy of the leading note (and in Russian church music, earlier, from Glinka onwards – see Chapters 3 and 4). It was generally the leading note in minor-mode melodies that was the subject of doubts, although some even disputed the leading note in the major mode. (In the discussion of the leading note that follows, all examples are minor-mode except where otherwise indicated.) During the 1860s and '70s both the Kuchka and Tchaikovsky left traces of this debate in their works: they either avoided songs with prominent leading notes, or often flattened these notes where they did occur. Tchaikovsky, for example, diatonicized the song "Na more utushka" (A little duck on the sea), having received this song from a connoisseur of Russian folksong, the dramatist Alexander Ostrovsky (he claimed that he had transcribed it himself).[27] In this diatonicized version, the song took pride of place in Tchaikovsky's first opera, *Voyevoda* (1868); Tchaikovsky must have valued it highly, because he later withdrew *Voyevoda*, but salvaged the song for a further appearance in the opera *Oprichnik* (1872). Musorgsky, as we saw in Chapter 4, once even took exception to the leading note in the major, replacing it with the sixth degree in the song "Pridanïye, udaliye" (Ex.4.13), and it was Musorgsky's version, thus altered, that appeared in Rimsky-Korsakov's folksong collection.[28]

None of them, however, went so far as to eliminate leading notes in every passage that incorporated folksong material – they preferred not to submit to such a far-reaching restriction. These compositional practices had their parallel in the folksong collections compiled by Balakirev (1866) and Rimsky-Korsakov (1876): some leading notes were altered, others left as they stood. This haphazard approach was not acceptable to the following generation of folksong collectors, whose nationalism took a more systematic bent. They did not, however, move closer to modern ethnomusicology; instead they were happy to use whatever distortions or fabrications that were grist to the nationalist mill, and they tried to build these into an internally consistent system.

Melgunov was the first to eliminate *all* leading notes from his collection, not only from his presentations of the folk melodies, but also in all the harmonizations he provides. This does not mean that the harmonizations are based upon folk hetero/polyphony; instead, he developed a theory, based entirely on his own predilections, that allowed him, supposedly, to deduce the harmonic implications of the melody (no matter that the peasant singers themselves would not have discerned these "implications"). He attempted to bolster the credibility of his theory by arguing that the harmonizations conformed to the laws of acoustics. His readings in recent German studies of Greek music theory also enabled him to use (or rather, abuse) Greek terms and ideas to justify his elimination of the leading note.[29]

Melgunov believed that Russian folksong employed two Greek modes, which he called the Dorian and the Hypophrygian. He thought that he was returning, in name and substance, to the original Greek system, rather than the Glarean or Zarlino modes known to Russian men of letters. His Hypophrygian was a white-note scale from G to G with A as "tonic", while his Dorian ran from E to E with the tonic on A. He used just-intonation ratios to define the intervals, and on this basis he found a symmetry between the two scales in question, as shown in the following figure:

5.9 Melgunov, Introduction to vol. 1 of his folksong collection

This allowed him to produce a deft inversion of the perfect cadence in the major that even had its own inverted dominant-seventh chord, while successfully avoiding the offensive leading note. "This is the true [dominant]-seventh chord of Russian minor-mode folksong", he proudly concluded.[30] Melgunov's ingenuity may distract the unwary reader from the fatal flaws in the argument that allowed him to arrive at this point. First, he assigns Greek modes to folk melodies without understanding the workings of either; this association had already become entrenched as proof, somehow, that Russia rather than the West was the true heir of the Classical world, and Melgunov, as a nationalist, would have had little desire to question this. Second, Melgunov imposes triads and cadential progressions on these supposedly Greek modes, when neither his supposed Greek sources, nor the Russian folk music he was purporting to explain justified such a move. Third, the symmetrical arrangement of ratios requires some contrivance: in effect, he has to regard the fifth degree of the minor as the tonic, i.e. the pitch assigned the value 1 for the interval ratios. Fourth, Melgunov simply ignores the fact that his sequence of ratios creates some seriously mistuned fifths. But beyond all these details, the fundamental error on Melgunov's part was to shift the boundaries of the natural too far into the realm of human practice, while largely ignoring the facts of the human practice he was supposedly examining, namely Russian peasant singing. Accordingly, a dominant-seventh chord becomes a direct consequence of acoustical laws, as does its inversion for the minor; he called the latter the "true dominant-seventh of Russian folksong", but it is, of course, to be found nowhere in that tradition.

Such are the lengths to which Russian nationalists went in order to rid themselves of the leading note. For Melgunov, it became something of an obsession. For example, he accused Palchikov of systematically omitting all seventh degrees from the majority of the songs in his collection, because he was (according to Melgunov) unable to harmonize them (presumably because he was unaware of Melgunov's symmetrical system and the inverted dominant-seventh). This criticism is entirely inappropriate, for Palchikov did not even attempt to harmonize his songs; unlike Melgunov, he presented only his transcriptions. Palchikov, moreover, was the last person who could be accused of tampering with his source material: he was, after all, the only song collector who had actually lived among the people whose music he transcribed, and he was the only collector who had sought to verify his transcriptions by singing them back to the original singers. Given the length of his time of study – three decades – he should have been well placed to shed any preconceptions that would have distorted his work in the way that Melgunov charged. If there were no leading notes in Palchikov's sources, there were no leading notes in his transcriptions; if there *were* leading notes in the songs, then his transcriptions reflected this. His scholarship was not filtered through nationalist dogmas concerning leading notes or any other musical feature.

And so various entrenched ideas of nationalism prevented the nationalists from recognizing authenticism when they saw it; for them, the authentic was whatever conformed to their theories. We shall now look at the particular problems encountered by the ethnographer Pyotr Sokalsky in his quest for authenticism. As an inhabitant of the Ukraine, Sokalsky had more opportunity to encounter the leading note in folk music than did his colleagues in Great Russia – the Ukraine had been in closer communication with the West, and had absorbed various cultural practices at an earlier stage, including melodies with leading notes. Sokalsky, we should note, was not a Ukrainian nationalist, but rather a Russian speaker who espoused Russian nationalism. Nevertheless, his case is of special interest, for instead of trying to deny the presence of leading notes (this would simply have been too blatantly absurd in the Ukraine), he chose to deny the Western origin of these leading notes. This gave him the advantage of accepting the all-too-obvious evidence, while channelling it in a direction that posed no threat to his nationalism. Even though it was generally accepted in the Ukraine that the frequent occurrence of leading notes in peasant music was due to Western influences, Sokalsky asserted that the origins were in fact Eastern without adducing a shred of evidence. Indeed, his speculations run well beyond what was necessary for his thesis, even claiming that leading notes in Western music were also an Eastern import.

> If even for Europe the leading note was an import from the Asian East, due, as seems most probable, to Europe's contacts with the East during the era of the Crusades, then what of the South of Russia? For this had always been much closer to that same East than Western Europe ever was.[31]

The substitution of Eastern for Western origins was a considerable improvement as far as Russian nationalists of the period were concerned, since they were generally happy to accept an Asian component in their ethnic and cultural identity, as we noted earlier (see Chapter 1). Sokalsky's motives are laid bare in the following words from one of his polemical essays:

> ... Russian folk music was created without any influence from the Hellenic-Roman civilization that laid the foundation for elite West-European culture. [Our folk music] is an independent stem grown from a common root: this is the Asian cradle of humanity, whose other stem led to Southern Europe (Greece and Rome).[32]

Sokalsky also attempted to provide theoretical support for his ideas on the leading note. He started out from a melody he had found in Gulak-Artemovsky's collection (*A v nedilyu rano*), reproduced here in Example 5.10. Sokalsky's argument is confused and contains various errors in the detail, but with careful reading, we can extract a kernel that makes sense: A would seem the main modal centre; we note that its lower neighbour is G natural rather than G#. But the listener prejudiced by Western music theory might prefer to argue that D is the true modal centre here, since it has C# as its lower neighbour. But Sokalsky pointed out that the C# often moves down to A, rather than directly up to D; Sokalsky then tried to argue that this C# was sung as a just major third in relation to the A, which would make it flatter than any true melodic leading note to D. The C#, tuned in this way, is therefore unable to function as a leading note to D. Sokalsky's argument, charitably paraphrased in this way, is logically consistent, but whether it is true is quite another matter, since Sokalsky's conclusion on the tuning of the C# was speculative – he had no empirical means of proving his contention. But our purpose here is not so much to dismiss or endorse Sokalsky, but rather to show how Russian discourse around the leading note had advanced in complexity and sophistication over the decades, even if it was still an exercise in fitting the evidence to the desired conclusion, rather than a genuine ethnomusicological project.

We can see that the issue of the leading note became a playing-field for nationalists of different persuasion. Melgunov chose the myth of Russian culture as true heir of Ancient Greece, while Sokalsky preferred the myth of its Asiatic provenance independent of Europe. Although it does not seem that Sokalsky and Melgunov could possibly agree, their chosen myths in fact had a common root. Mathieu (Matthew) Guthrie, whose *Dissertations sur les antiquités de Russie* (1795) was published in Russia, was the first to draw parallels between Russian folksong and the music of ancient Greece. But for Guthrie, this meant that Russia and Greece descended independently from the root culture of ancient Persia. This point was further elaborated in the work of Rudolph Westphal, another foreigner eagerly read and reread by

5.10 "A v nedilyu rano" from Sokalsky's collection

Russian nationalists and perpetually quoted by them. For Westphal too, Russian culture was no mere offshoot of European culture, but he also argued that Russian culture was superior. He favoured the Slavs among all the Aryan tribes that supposedly migrated from Eastern Iranian origins, but of all the Slavs, he finds the Russians most perfect in their culture:

> In our times, the most important representative of the Slavs is undoubtedly the Russian nation, which also differs from all the other Slavs because it managed to preserve the ancient Aryan foundation best, both in its language and customs. The Russian people, moreover, preserved this foundation with such integrity and authenticity that in the eyes of science it takes first place in this respect among all contemporary Aryan nations.[33]

But Westphal came no closer to empirical methods (such as archaeology) than Guthrie or the Russian nationalists. He drew up comparisons between Russian culture and the cultures of ancient Greece and Rome. For example, Westphal was evidently delighted when judicial practices in Russian villages reminded him of the Roman judicial system; he even asserts that the systems of the Russian *starosta* (village elder) and the Roman *curia* are one and the same thing. But Greek literature was Westphal's special strength, so here we find a much more thoroughly worked-out Greek example:

> In the canon compiled by Greek rhetoricians on the basis of their poetic and rhetorical literature, one can hardly find a single trope that is not also to be found in Russian folk song. In this we see the obvious proof that the Russian people are endowed with a high poetic gift. The philosophy of history has every right to draw from this the brightest conclusions regarding the future course of Russian history.[34]

This means that the same methods and evidence that had been used to prove Russian culture's Hellenic provenance were equally good for proving its Persian provenance. For this reason, it need not be so surprising that Melgunov considered himself an ardent follower of Westphal, rather than his opponent. Westphal reciprocated, basing some of his own conclusions on the first volume of Melgunov's collection. This connection allows us to put the work of Melgunov and other authenticists into their political context, for Westphal's "proof" of Russia's greatness did not emerge from a vacuum of pure, scholarly disinterest. Westphal spent ten years (1876–86) teaching in the Lyceum, an institution founded by Mikhail Katkov, an influential journalist whose name became synonymous with chauvinism and reaction. As a matter of course, then, Westphal published his articles in Katkov's own journal, *Russkiy vestnik* (The Russian Messenger). Placed in this context, Westphal's talk of Russian superiority is perfectly comprehensible, and also acquires darker undertones; the rhetoric of the passage just quoted is a reflection of his employer's rhetoric. Katkov was already a significant influence on Russia's domestic and foreign policy, and after the ascension of the reactionary Alexander III, he became still more entrenched in the Russian establishment, becoming one of the prime movers in the infamous Russification campaign. In general, Russian cultural nationalism was never at odds with state policy for too long, and this time it aligned itself with a particularly vicious strain.

Should it surprise us that Linyova, that paragon of scientific method, also happily subscribed to Westphal's pronouncements? (He is quoted approvingly in the foreword to Linyova's Volume I.) Although she appeared to be a champion of empirical research, she was just as much in thrall to nationalist myths as Melgunov and Sokalsky. She unreservedly adopted Melgunov's exegesis of the Greek modes and believed just as doggedly in the strict diatonicism of Russian song. She had at her disposal a corpus of 170 recorded songs, of which she rejected around 30 as not worth transcribing, and of the rest, she only presented 22 for publication. She was therefore able to eliminate any songs which did not meet her requirements, including the "modern", or "modish" songs she so disdained, above all for their use of leading notes. But even when it came to the old *protyazhnïye* from the "purest" regions, untouched by urban influence, she still encountered the problem of what she called "chromatically altered degrees". There was only one answer: diatonicize. This dark secret was only uncovered decades later, when the Soviet musicologist Gippius decided to check Linyova's transcriptions against her recordings. Here is one of the examples demonstrating how Gippius corrected Linyova:

5.11   Comparison of Linyova and Gippius's transcriptions of "Kak po Kame, po reke"

In Linyova's collection of Ukrainian folksongs (published in 1905),[35] her desire to impose strict diatonicism is equally apparent. In her introduction, she reveals her bias thus:

> I was extremely interested in true Ukrainian song. Up to that moment [i.e. the time of the expedition], I had known only the "Europeanized" version of Little-Russian [i.e. Ukrainian] song; I thirsted to hear it in its pure form . . .[36]

And so she looked for the same type of songs she had favoured in her Russian collection: mainly *protyazhnïye* with rich hetero/polyphony and without leading notes (most of these she found in the Cossack regions). Nevertheless, she did admit a very few songs with leading notes, demanding some editorial comment. Two of these songs she summarily dismisses as "nothing original: modern D-minor with the leading note". But song No. 2 ("Stoyala Marinka", Ex. 5.12), which also contained leading notes, was sung as part of the calendar ritual and thus had to belong to what she had called the "pure" songs in her introduction. She could not admit that the song had A as its modal centre, with G# leading notes. Instead, she tortuously argued that the modal centre was instead E, with E- F#–G#–A as the main tetrachord used in the melody, even though F# did not appear. Through this implausible contrivance, she transformed G# into a harmless third degree of the scale, instead of a leading note.

5.12   "Stoyala Marinka" in Linyova's transcription

The pleasures of folksong arrangement

Despite the persistent myth-making and the incompetent theorizing, the last third of the nineteenth century saw a substantial advance in Russian folksong research. But, as we have seen, the understanding of folksong was generally a happy by-product; the real goal was to find an "authentic" basis for a new national style to supersede the Kuchka's legacy. Since years of work at folksong had still not generated this new Russian style, many advanced to a half-way stage between research proper and fresh artistic creation – namely the folksong arrangement. We have already seen how Kastalsky set about this task, although he usually equivocated over what was compositional work and what was strict transcription. But Kastalsky was only one of many engaged in folk-song arrangement. We can distinguish three approaches current at the time. First, the systematic approach, which proceeds in accordance with a particular theory. Second, the authenticist approach, which follows peasant practice (or rather, what was believed to be peasant practice). And third, the artistic approach, which meets the needs of a particular composer. Whatever the claims made in their commentaries, arrangers tended to shift freely from one approach to another. But we shall look now at the minority which stuck deter-minedly to a theoretical system, leading them to the most bizarre and absurd dead-ends of cultural nationalism.

The foremost representative of the systematic approach was Yuri Arnold (1811–98), who published a number of music-theoretical works between the 1860s and '80s. Arnold followed Odoyevsky in believing that folksong harmonization was a scientific problem with only one possible solution. He presented his views in an essay, "On the issue of the harmonization of one Russian song", written in 1873 and unpublished during his lifetime. It was later found in Melgunov's archive and eventually published by the Ethnographic Commission in 1906;[37] although the editors claimed to have reservations over "certain points", the very fact of the essay's publication tells us that it was still considered to be of some relevance. In the essay in ques-tion, Arnold takes issue with one of Odoyevsky's folksong harmonizations (its source remains unknown), and offers his own version, whose authority was wholly derived from Arnold's own system. Since Odoyevsky's version had also been written to correct an earlier harmonization in the Lvov–Prach collection, which he said had "totally disfigured" (izurodovana) the song, we shall examine all three side by side in Ex. 5.13. We shall not discuss here the changes that Odoyevsky made (his method was discussed at the beginning of Chapter 4), but shall proceed straight to the reasons for Arnold's dissatisfac-tion with it. He writes of Odoyevsky's harmonization: "In spite of its origi-nality, it seems to me that it does not reveal the true prototype of Russian folk music."[38] It is not quite clear what Arnold means by "prototype", whether he sincerely thinks peasants performed the song this way at the time of writing, or whether he thought they must have sung it thus in some distant, more perfect past, or whether he entertained the notion of a Platonic type for each Russian folksong.

Whatever the nature of Arnold's "prototype", it is clear that he is seeking an authentic version, and that this authenticity can only be uncovered by means of his own "scientific" method. Arnold's method is not original in its outlines, since, like Odoyevsky's, it marries modal theory (a confused amalgam of Greek and Renaissance theorizing) with some elements of acoustics. In Arnold's hands, three hypotheses, which Odoyevsky had

5.13a "A mï proso seyali" from the Lvov-Prach collection

5.13b Odoyevsky's harmonization of the same song

5.13c Arnold's harmonization of the same song

expressed tentatively, now become axiomatic. First, Arnold takes the "Greek" modal system to be the same as the modal systems both of Russian folksong and of the Russian Orthodox church (the *os'moglasiye*). Second, he states that only common triads are admissible in harmonization, "since ancient music knew no other chords". Finally, unlike Odoyevsky, he stipulates that the bass can move only from one chord root to another, because this was the case "in ancient music, and therefore in church and folk singing as well" – Arnold's "therefore" is particularly self-indulgent here. Arnold also introduces tuning considerations which rule out the use of certain triads even thought their notes are all contained within the mode. He contends that the triad G–B–D in the last bar of Odoyevsky's harmonization will be mistuned, given the context of the Aeolian mode, or "the scale of the second *glas*" as Arnold styles it.

The framework within which Arnold couches his argument is spurious, but within this framework it is possible to make some sense of what he says. He argues specifically that the fifth G–D cannot be tuned correctly in this context; what he must mean is that when G is tuned to a just minor third above E (required because of the E-minor triads in the harmonization), and D is tuned as a true perfect fourth above A, then G and D, thus tuned, will not form a true perfect fifth, since the D will be a comma sharp (Arnold means a syntonic comma). This is to assist Arnold somewhat, since he fails to realize that his argument will only work because of the presence of E-minor triads. On these grounds, he rules Odoyevsky's harmonization inadmissible. The framework of the argument is wrong-headed because Arnold treats a choir as if it is a keyboard, with no flexibility in pitch – there is nothing to prevent a singer from producing slightly differently tuned Gs, or compromising slightly in their tuning; even to remain within Arnold's doctrinaire approach, he never considers the possibility of the A final itself being allowed to fall by a comma, since this would remove the difficulty (to be fair to Arnold, this muddle over just intonation has a distinguished pedigree going back to Zarlino in the sixteenth century). Arnold then offers a harmonization of his own that respects the terms of his argument. He makes matters simple for himself by resorting to two expedients that remove the offending G: where a cadence is required, he uses an E–B dyad, omitting the third of the chord; and where this is not possible, as in the final bar, he uses a plagal cadence. Although Arnold, as we have seen, held that his system would generate the single, definitive harmonization for any folk melody, he admits that his harmonization was guided by taste and a sense of balance; he sees no contradiction here, since these aesthetic faculties, as he says, are the common property of all humanity. The harmonization, "revealing the true prototype", is now complete.

Comparing the three harmonizations in front of us, we may find Prach's unadventurous, while Odoyevsky's is more varied in sonority, although rather artificial; Arnold's, however, is more akin to a student's first attempt at chorale harmonization. Prach's aim was simply to provide the song with a simple and palatable accompaniment in order to make his collection more attractive to the buying public. Odoyevsky instead offered an approach to harmonization which, he believed, better reflected the folksong's genesis and which "corresponded well to the kind of harmony that can be heard in the folk choral performances".[39] Arnold, however, believed he could uncover the unique solution for each folksong harmonization. No empirical test was of interest to him; the validity of his harmonizations depended only on the coherence of his theoretical system. And since he thought this system was founded on general laws equally applicable to "ancient, church and folk" music, he could not imagine how he could possibly be in error.

Leaving aside the absurdity of Arnold's theorizing and his oddly incompetent-looking harmonizations, it is clear that folksong harmonization was becoming a philosopher's stone, ready to consume whole careers of misguided speculation. The solution, once found, would have the farthest-ranging consequences: it would bind together music ancient and modern, folk and art, Russian and European. Remember too that Arnold's essay had been published in 1906, even though Linyova's work was by then well underway; and it was published not as an historical curiosity to raise scholarly eyebrows, but as a serious contribution to contemporary folksong discourse.

Our next example of a systematic approach to folksong arrangement is the musical utopia of the youthful Sergei Taneyev. Taneyev had studied under Tchaikovsky and, in common with the bulk of the "Moscow School", he did not accept that the Kuchka had succeeded in creating a Russian national music. But this was not because he rejected any such project as nonsensical. In 1879, after he had considered at length how a genuine national music might be created, he wrote out a bold manifesto in his notebook. This document is worth quoting at length:

Russian musicians learn[ing] Western music immediately encounter ready-made forms. They either compose in a European style or try to squeeze Russian song into European forms, ignoring the fact that these forms grew out of elements foreign to us, that Russian [song] is something external in relation to them, that it is not organically connected to them. ... The Russian musician is like an architect who, seeing wooden huts, begins to fashion something similar out of stone, trying to position the stones in such a way as to recreate all the depressions and curves that came from the shape of the logs. He would soon feel that there was no point in continuing.

European forms are foreign to us, and we have none of our own. We have no national music. Tchaikovsky, our best composer, writes a harmony textbook, but what harmony? – European harmony. We haven't worked out any [Russian] harmony. Russian music does not exist. There is only raw material – song and its mechanical mixing with foreign forms, but nothing else. Every Russian musician's task is to help in the creation of a national music. The history of Western music answers the question "how do we achieve this?": we have to apply to Russian song the same thought processes that had been applied to the song of the Western peoples; then we will have a national music. We have to begin with simple contrapuntal forms, then move on to more complex forms, working out a Russian fugal form, and then there will be just one step left to arrive at complex instrumental forms. Europeans needed several hundred years to achieve this, but for us this time will be shortened. We know the way, we know the goal, and we can easily use the experience the Europeans accumulated during several centuries ... Let us assimilate the experience of the old contrapuntists and take this difficult but glorious task upon ourselves. Who knows, maybe we shall bequeath new forms, new music to the next generation. Who knows, perhaps at the beginning of the next century, Russian forms will emerge. It does not matter when, but they must emerge.[40]

This was not empty bluster. Taneyev took up the arduous "glorious task" himself and churned out contrapuntal exercises in their hundreds, composed countless fugues and even tried his hand at an early seventeenth-century style "Dutch Fantasia" based on Russian folksongs from Balakirev's and Prokunin's collections. However, the scathing dismissal he received from Tchaikovsky must have dampened his enthusiasm.[41] 1880 saw Taneyev's First String Quartet, which was graced with any number of contrapuntal combinations, but by the composer's own admission, there was "unfortunately nothing Russian in it".[42] This was a sign of things to come: Taneyev's later works witness to his perpetual quest for contrapuntal perfection, but they contain hardly any Russian raw material; perhaps Russian melodies jarred on his sensibilities the more he assimilated European contrapuntal styles.[43] But this does not mean that Taneyev simply abandoned his early utopian dream. He still saw history as a sequence of inevitable stages, and this idea continued to direct his artistic path. Although he had renounced the idea that Russian culture could develop organically, purely from its own resources, he nevertheless devoted his life to filling in the gaps (as he saw them) in Russia's cultural history. Specifically, the missing stages in Russia's musical development were all provided by Taneyev. For example, his quartets, as many have observed, are Mozartean, while his final monumental work, the cantata *Upon Reading a Psalm*, provides Russia with its own Handelian oratorio.[44] He even tried to create a Greek musical tragedy for Russia, in his opera *Oresteia*.[45] In spite of the lack of Russian material, and in spite of his careful assimilation of historic Western styles and techniques, his music is nevertheless unthinkable without the motivation of the nationalist project he hatched in his youth.

Let us move on now to the authenticist approach in folksong arrangement. Strictly speaking, this is a contradiction in terms, since authenticity requires the transcription of peasant performances, not the creation of yet more arrangements. But we shall use the term here for arrangements which were constrained principally by knowledge (however incomplete) of peasant performance practices, any theoretical or artistic considerations being subordinate to this. We have already discussed the case of Kastalsky, who set out from an authenticist position, but allowed himself ever greater liberties as he began to feel he had assimilated a style in which he could now compose freely. A similar transition from an authenticist to an artistic approach takes place before our eyes in a paper presented by Alexander Nikolsky in 1908 (he refers to himself in the third person throughout):

> The existing folksong arrangements are in most cases no more than piano accompaniments, which, in their typically pianistic textures, cannot be considered characteristic for Russian folksong. An idiomatic arrangement should represent the natural manner of singing with its various *podgoloski*. The existing arrangements are also clumsy for performance, for they are given in two or three strophes, so each time one needs to fit [different] words to the same melody, and this is sometimes difficult. The arrangements that Nikolsky offers as examples attempt to build a more complex form on the basis of a song, without repetitions of the same melodic variant. His methods of arrangement are as follows: the melody, having been made familiar to the ear, is then varied, and diverges from its first statement while retaining the same spontaneous counterpoint in the *podgoloski*. In Nikolsky's opinion, folksong demands a great variety of forms, and so all earlier arrangements are incorrect, since they fix [in a single version] melodies that are open to variation. On this basis, Nikolsky allows: 1) transposition of melodies; 2) a change of mode from minor to major, and 3) modulation – in order to avoid monotony.[46]

Thus, Nikolsky started his paper with authenticist fervour, rejecting the standard harmonizations and their strophic structures; but as the continuation of the passage and his own arrangements witness, he ends up treating a folksong like any other melody in the hands of a composer, subjecting it to Glinka-style variations, or even to pre-Glinka devices such as a contrasting *minore* or *maggiore* variation.

While some, like Kastalsky and Nikolsky, were led away from authenticity by their composerly bent, others compromised authenticity for the sake of traditional voice-leading rules. Even the song collectors took such rules into account. Melgunov's collection presented piano arrangements that were made to approximate familiar chorale textures, by means of octave transposition and other adjustments. The collection of Lopatin and Prokunin (1889), suffers from the same insecurities, even though it probably contains the best examples of *podgoloski* textures before Linyova. They had to forewarn the users of their collection that "the issue of how to harmonize Russian folksongs has not been solved, and everything that is done in that direction should be considered only an experiment".[47] Since only a few of their songs were transcribed from a group of singers, only these represent their authenticist intentions. Many of the other songs, which were transcribed only as a melody from a solo singer, were supplied with *podgoloski* invented by the collectors. The difference between the fully transcribed songs and the melodies with composed accompaniment is immediately obvious: in the latter category, the second voice usually joins the first much earlier and in a more-or-less imitative fashion – something that never happens in the field (Ex.5.14). Worse still, Lopatin admitted that

> As far as possible, I tried to reconcile the practice of peasant singing with music theory, thus avoiding forbidden progressions where I could. Still, without damaging the character of the song, it was very often impossible to

5.14   Folksong "Tï vzoydi-ka, krasno solnïshko", No. 32 from Prokunin's collection avoid movement in octaves or concealed octaves, or the conjunct motion of two parts into the unison – hardly any song choral performance by the people can avoid this.[48]

The practice of combining clean voice-leading with a whiff of authenticity was, at this time, often considered a worthy and tasteful compromise. For this reason, much praise was lavished on Anatoly Lyadov, Rimsky-Korsakov's star pupil. Lyadov readily acknowledged the discovery of *podgoloski* in his commentary, but he still took great care that the rules of the harmony text-books were upheld. Proceeding in this way, he produced the only series of arrangements that left the parlour and entered the realm of public art music: his *Eight Russian Folksongs for Orchestra*. This cycle represents a new stage in the aestheticization of Russian folksong, in its total separation from the reality of Russian village. Even one admirer of Lyadov's method, Yevseyev, had to admit that "Lyadov favoured only a few moods: a reserved epic tone, tender contemplation, slight excitement, the cunning smile, and good-humoured irony . . .".[49] Many critics at the time and much later, in the Soviet Union, admired this "true" image of Russian peasantry which proved to be so palatable and even beautiful. It contained no hint of the violence that was once so disturbingly depicted by Musorgsky in the Kromï scene (*Boris Godunov*); it was much more cosily reminiscent of pre-*narodnik* representations of peasant life. If Lyadov had ever heard peasants sing, he certainly does not make this evident in these or any other arrangements.

Lyadov had hit on the correct recipe for public approval at the time: a folk melody with an accompaniment largely the result of free composition, but with heavy hints that the final product was somehow authentic. Very few were prepared to argue openly for a free, artistic approach to folk material. The most prominent of these was Sokalsky, whom we have already seen unravelling the pretences of authenticism; he always stated flatly that he was arranging folksongs just as he pleased. It may seem strange that he claimed to be continuing in the line of Balakirev, but this makes sense when we remember that before the authenticism cult introduced its distortions, Balakirev's arrangements were seen, accurately enough, as Schumannesque miniatures that happened to be based on folk melodies. In Ex 5.15, we can see how Sokalsky constructed this kind of miniature from a Ukrainian song.

The efforts of the numerous collectors and composers who churned out folksong arrangements at this time never brought about the desired qualitative leap: they never made the passage from arrangement to the creation of a new national style, organically Russian in a way that the Kuchka had never been. There is one example of a composer assimilating techniques learnt from

5.15   Sokalsky's *Duma*, an arrangement of the folksong "Sivïy konyu"

the folksong movement, and applying them to a larger form, but this bizarre piece is symbolic of the failure of the whole project. The composer was Alexander Olenin, a student of Balakirev, and his folk-inspired work the opera *Kudeyar* (1911). Olenin had contributed to the critique of the Kuchka for their lack of authenticity, and he proved very responsive to new fashions in folksong arrangement. His opera project was the only significant attempt to realize the utopian world that many of his contemporaries only dreamed of. It reflected Olenin's penchant for authenticity, his grand artistic ambition, and his readiness to sacrifice both from time to time, for the sake of a system of self-imposed rules. Olenin described the opera thus:

> It is like a Russian song taken to extremes, for no device characteristic of the West is employed in the music; it is based, rather, upon Russian two-part textures with their peculiar voice-leading features.[50]

In fact the composer maintained a largely three-part texture, in which two parts often proceed in parallel thirds or sixths (Ex.5.16a). Olenin also generally restricts his harmonic palette to seven-note modes free of additional leading notes. The metre changes freely throughout, parallel fifths and octaves are permitted, and there are no transitions between keys or modal centres. But his ascetic rigour sometimes dissolves when the temptations are too great: when dramatic tension is required, he slips back into operatic clichés that bring with them full four-part harmony and a more conventional use of tonality (Ex.5.16b). Olenin's *Kudeyar* demonstrates all too well how nationalist doctrines of authenticity cannot turn lead into gold, no matter how faithfully

5.16a Olenin, *Kudeyar*, orchestral prelude to Act I

[I love you, I love you, my beauty!
I love you even more than ever!
But I also love my freedom!]

5.16b Olenin, *Kudeyar*, scene with Kudeyar and Natasha from Act IV

the artist adheres to them; without the support of considerable talent, skill and taste, the result can totter on the brink of absurdity.

Pesennost' equals Russianness

To end this story of the nationalist quest and its frustrations, let us turn to a reawakening of that impulse decades later. While the October Revolution seemed to have consigned such cultural nationalist projects to the dustbin of history, Stalin steadily re-introduced nationalist rhetoric during the 1930s (since it suited his political purposes). The Nazi invasion in 1941 gave a further boost to this nationalism and it was during the war that Asafyev, the most distinguished Soviet musicologist (and sometime composer), returned to the quest in a series of essays on Russian music. Given the power and originality of Asafyev's earlier writings from the 1920s, it is difficult to see how the same mind could have produced a string of nationalist clichés, or how he could have brought his impressive erudition to bear on such a spurious issue. But we cannot simply say that he was writing in a spirit of grim detachment, fulfilling the demands of the authorities and nothing more. The horrors of war had their effect on all aspects of life, and Asafyev had seen his share during the siege of Leningrad, where some of the essays were written. The wartime issues of *Sovetskaya muzïka* displayed a certain ascetic patriotism which Asafyev's essays fitted well. But after the war, the essays were not forgotten, and they proved useful as ammunition against Shostakovich and others after the 1948 Resolution condemning the "formalism" that was supposedly rife in Soviet musical life. After the dust had settled, Asafyev was promoted to head the Union of Composers (very shortly before his death). But whatever interpretation we attach to Asafyev's behaviour, for our purposes these essays reveal the link between the thinking of late nineteenth/early twentieth century nationalism and the culture of high Stalinism.

Under Socialist Realism, it was held that the gap between high and folk art was too large, and that both sides should make steps towards each other. Asafyev, in these essays, puts it much more strongly: high and folk art should fuse to become one. He laments that a number of obstacles presently bar the way to this utopia: the study of folk music has become a mere positivist science, which cannot inspire composers to learn from folk examples, let alone provide any answer to their most burning question, "how to compose?"[51] Composers, he says, still fail to assimilate folk *intonatsia* "logically", rather than "by chance". What this means soon becomes apparent when Asafyev complains that composers are unable to compose in *podgoloski* textures: "logical" assimilation would be assimilation along the lines of Kastalsky's manuals. Armed thus with a "logical" understanding of folk creativity, they would be able to develop their musical material organically like the people, not working things out cerebrally, but "singing" [*raspet'*]. Out of this, a new national style can be born:

> We should not exaggerate. A monumental work forged from these skills, in which the old rift between folk art and individualistic art is closed through the mastery of each in a conscious unification, a unity still more complete than anything in the practice of the classical geniuses – such a work does not as yet exist. But the sturdy prerequisites for such a unification doubtless exist, and the sensitive ear detects them everywhere.[52]

For Asafyev, the kind of music Soviet composers should aim for will be impossible without a reliance on the traditions of Russian music; the new music will have to share in the essential character of Russian music (we shall soon see that Asafyev does not want to commit himself on the issue of whether that essence belongs to culture or nature). In a series of essays grouped together as *The Music of My Motherland*, Asafyev discusses this essential character of Russian music; here, his ever-expanding concept of *pesennost'* [songfulness] and its synonyms *napevnost'* and *raspevnost'* feature very prominently:

> How can we explain that constant, profound attraction to *pesennost'* which is always felt by every Russian musician . . . ? The deeper and the more "rooted" the song melodies of the people are, and the purer they are in the sense of the authenticity of their *intonatsiya* (i.e. the tone in which the essence of the nation, the openness and broadness of expression is heard) – the stronger the attraction.[53]

> The heart of Russian music is folk *pesennost'* (not song in the narrow sense of genre or type of musical form) and the rhythm of human breathing, which dominate everywhere in Russian music, both vocal and instrumental, over the bars and patterns of the periodic formal architecture. Should we say that this quality of *raspevnost'* is a tradition or, better, the nature of a man who has lived in the steppes and fields, on the edge of the great rivers and severe forests of our Motherland? It is still hard to say what the genesis of this quality is, but it is perhaps the most viable strand of Russian culture. . . .
>
> In the *raspevs* of our music, we are too used to hearing the merit of talent alone, rather than *the will of the nation*, which through song and the intonations of folk poetry has expressed its anxieties for the life of Motherland, and which has rooted itself in the sensitive ear of great musicians who are voices for the masses.[54]

In these quotations we see how Asafyev has come to use his celebrated "into-national theory" in the most promiscuous way in order to maintain his successful career in Stalin's Soviet Union. He allows the theory to degenerate until it becomes a mere fig leaf for the old banalities of Romantic nationalism. Asafyev even writes an ode to the *protyazhnaya* that could have come from Gogol's pen, aside from a nod toward the more active outlook encouraged by Socialist Realism.

But where in Russian music does Asafyev find his proof that *pesennost'* equals Russianness? *A Life for the Tsar* is of course mentioned, together with *Eugene Onegin*, Asafyev's two examples of the "songful" opera. The Kuchka is only mentioned in passing, with the occasional example, usually from Musorgsky or Borodin. Compared to the scant coverage given to these acknowledged "geniuses" of Russian music, the attention lavished on Lyadov, Taneyev and especially Kastalsky might seem out of proportion to their importance; the editors in 1948 seemed to think so too, since they removed this section altogether. Nevertheless, the omitted section is very useful for our purposes, since it allows us to trace the probable source of Asafyev's insistence on *pesennost'*. The young Asafyev's formative years overlapped with the waning of the post-Kuchka folksong movement; he was taught by Lyadov and was at one time close to Kastalsky. He showed great enthusiasm for Kastalsky's ideas, and even claimed that that it was under his prompting that Kastalsky wrote his first hetero/polyphony manual. This fascination is still evident in the obituary he wrote on Kastalsky's death in 1927.[55] In the 1940s, when Lyadov, Taneyev and Kastalsky attracted very little interest, Asafyev used them to substantiate his concept of Russian *pesennost'*, and it is in this part of his discussion that he argues most passionately and persuasively. However, in order to give expression to one youthful fascination, he betrays another: the trinity of Lyadov–Taneyev–Kastalsky, united by the "idea of Russian song-based voice-leading", is treated by Asafyev as the chief safeguard against the assault of "Western mechanized instrumentalism". This refers to Futurism, whose Russian incarnation in the post-Revolutionary decade was cheered on by the young Asafyev, who devoted many an essay to it. But now he can only deplore what had once delighted him; perhaps it was so hateful to him in later life precisely because his youthful enthusiasm for it could at any moment be recalled by his superiors if they ever tired of him.

And so, heralded by Asafyev, the 1948 Resolution ushered in a revival of the post-Kuchka folksong movement. But the revival was short-lived. Asafyev died the following year, but ultimately, the prospects of a folksong utopia were defeated by Stalin's death. For as the post-Stalin state relaxed its grip on culture, composers drifted away from this imposition – clearly they had regarded Asafyev's vision as an imposition, not a shared goal.

The curse of the leading note: nationalism and the "New Trend" in church music

I see the violation of the true faith by the heretics and by you, traitors; I see the destruction of the holy churches of God and I can no longer bear to hear Latin sung in Moscow.

Patriarch Hermogen, during the Time of Troubles

Russian chant, like folksong, flows as a broad, free stream from the people's breast, and the freer it is, the more it speaks to the heart. We share our chants with the Greeks, but the Russian people sings them in a different way, because it put its soul in it.

Pobedonostsev

The prehistory

In the 1880s, a new quest for authenticity came into the public eye, namely the attempt to retrieve the pre-Petrine purity of the Russian Orthodox sung liturgy. These concerns had occupied church musicians from early in the century, but the debate was confined for decades to a handful of specialists; even when the Kuchka sought Russian roots for their musical enterprises, church music was overlooked, owing to Stasov's determined secularism. But as powerful as Stasov's influence was, he cannot shoulder the full responsibility for the marginalization of Russian Orthodox music during a period when one might have expected it become a focus of nationalist interest: after all, the retrieval of information about Pre-Petrine liturgies called only for normal scholarly work in archives, whereas the serious investigation of folk music required scholars to gain expertise in transcribing the sounds of an unfamiliar musical tradition and to live for long periods in rough and squalid conditions among peasants. We shall begin by seeing what other factors kept a scholarly interest in liturgical music at the margins of nationalist or musical discourse in Russia.

A series of rulings within the church effectively restricted liturgical composition to a small, self-selecting elite. The first of these rulings, pronounced in 1816, gave the Court Cappella exclusive and comprehensive powers to determine what liturgical music could be published and performed; all composers of liturgical music were required to submit their work to the Cappella for approval, and over the following decades favour was granted to an ever diminishing number (by 1878, the were only eight composers whose works could be performed, and most of these were, unsurprisingly, directors, past and present, of the Cappella).[56] In 1825, the liturgical use of choral concertos was banned; the ruling followed swiftly upon the death of the long-serving Cappella director and composer Bortnyansky (installed 1796), whose principal contribution to liturgical music as a composer lay precisely in the genre of the choral concerto – his demise must have been eagerly anticipated by the opponents of liturgical concertos. In order to ensure the strict observation of the 1816 ruling, the Holy Synod later prohibited the use of handwritten scores or parts on church premises. The Synod also had ambitions beyond the institution it presided over, and eventually succeeded in banning the concert performance of any Orthodox liturgical music, thereby removing all other outlets for would-be composers of church music. These rulings removed church music from the mainstream of Russian music-making; while a lively public discourse had developed around folk music, any parallel discussion of church music during this period would have been futile, since the influence of musicians or scholars outside the Cappella was nil.

It was not until 1878 that any serious challenge to the Cappella's powers was mounted. In that year, Tchaikovsky composed his Liturgy of St John Chrysostom and submitted it to the publisher Jurgenson; Tchaikovsky had not sought the Cappella's authorization for the work, which was in any case unlikely to win their approval, but we cannot assume that he intended to act in defiance of the Cappella, since Jurgenson was entirely at liberty to publish the work abroad. Instead, Jurgenson decided to provoke a confrontation with the Cappella by publishing and distributing the work in Russia. In the subsequent scandal, the police were instructed to search the publisher's premises and confiscate all copies of the score, and with the evidence in hand, the Cappella sought legal redress in the case Jurgenson vs Bakhmetev (the director of the Cappella at the time).[57] The court surprisingly found in favour of Jurgenson, immediately breaking the power of the Cappella over church music; in the ensuing years, there was a massive increase in the number of composers who turned to the liturgy, and a large repertoire of new liturgical music soon developed. The decision against the Cappella also encouraged nationalist thinkers to annex Russian Orthodox music as legitimate subject-matter for their ruminations; the polemical scholarship of Stepan Smolensky was particularly influential, and his ideas were embodied in liturgical works by Kastalsky, Chesnokov, Rakhmaninov and many others.

The church-music nationalists had soon devised an historical narrative that served to justify their efforts; this narrative runs a parallel course to the nationalist account of folksong history we have examined in the previous chapters. Both accounts are entirely consonant with the Slavophile meta-narrative: the original pristine Russianness of folksong/chant is contaminated by the importation of Western ideas and practices in the seventeenth and eighteenth centuries, but since it is not part of Russia's destiny to be assimilated to the West, men emerge to serve the nation by restoring Russian music to its original purity, thereby providing the foundation for a cultural rebirth. To sketch in the details of the church-music narrative, we begin with a purely Russian form of liturgical chant, which was strictly monodic and diatonic; knowledge of the melodies was preserved through the use of an indigenous Russian system of neumes (*kryuki*, or *znamena*). At this point the accounts diverge: some writers prefer to skate over the Byzantine origins of the music and notation in order to present the tradition as a spontaneous emanation of the Russian soul, while others, on the contrary, were only too pleased to dwell on this because the connection to the Classical world via Byzantium provided Russian culture with a suitably noble foundation, to be cited against any who might be inclined to dismiss Russia as a nation of brutish barbarians prior to contact with the West in the early modern era. This spontaneous Russian, or noble Byzantine tradition was maintained until the late seventeenth century, when the state of blissful innocence was destroyed by the importation of Western liturgical music via Poland and the Ukraine; under this baneful influence, the Russian liturgy began to acquire rhymed verses, regular metres, harmony, and the leading note. While all accounts broadly agree on this part of the narrative, writers suggest a number of different watershed dates. In 1666, an ecumenical council granted permission for Polish-style *partesnoye* singing to be incorporated into Orthodox services; Antonin Preobrazhensky thought that this was the decisive event.[58] About twenty years later, the tsar's deacon Vasiliy Titov produced musical settings for Simeon Polotsky's psalter in rhymed verse, which was merely a translation of a standard Polish psalter into Church Slavonic; Vasily Metallov sees the fall of Russian church music in the dissemination of the Polotsky/Titov psalter. The original *znamenniy* chant melodies were not abandoned at first, but instead many were projected through the distorting prism of harmonization, Metallov complains:

> The first to harmonize the *znamenniy* chant melodies were either students of Polish choral directors or of music theorists who had fallen under the influence of foreign Catholic and Protestant music . . .[59]

The irregular structure of the *znamenniy* melodies impeded their assimilation into the new, Western style of liturgical music, and they were gradually supplanted by the more regular-structured melodies of the Kievan and so-called "Greek" chant traditions. Peter the Great and Catherine the Great characteristically accelerated the pace of Westernization in church music, and Galuppi and Sarti, the Italian operatic composers of the Imperial Court, were given free rein to compose fresh liturgical music in their customary style.

Bortnyansky and Berezovsky, the two most eminent "Russian" composers of church music at this time, offered no resistance to the encroachments of the operatic style; both were of Ukrainian extraction (as many of the nationalist accounts emphasize), and both studied composition in Italy, where they gained fluency in the genre of the choral concerto. This elaborate Italianate music contrasted starkly with the *znamenniy* and other chant-based parts of the liturgy, which survived into the nineteenth century, both as monody, and in the form of the now antiquated harmonizations that had constituted the first stage of Westernization. The prolific Bortnyansky, mocked by Glinka as "Mr Sugar MacHoney-Treacle" (*Sakhar Medovich Patokin*), became a symbol of secularization and Westernization for the church-music nationalists at the close of the century.

While Bortnyansky's reputation as a composer suffered at the hands of the church-music nationalists, the publication in 1878 of a document found among the composer's papers established him, ironically, as an important precursor of the church-music renaissance. The document's editors, who belonged to the Association of Lovers of Ancient Literature, entitled the text "a project ascribed to Bortnyansky", and the contents made it clear that the author had anticipated the church-music renaissance – by more than half a century if we can assume the author was indeed Bortnyansky: he passionately advocated the publication of the old *znamenniy* chant books in their original notation, in conjunction with a primer for reading the neumes.[60] The author's hopes were not fulfilled until 1888, when one of the leaders of the church-music renaissance, Stepan Smolensky, finally published such a primer. In Smolensky's foreword, much of Bortnyansky's paper was reproduced, such as the following extracts:

[The publication of *znamenniy* chant books] should bring a stop to the clumsy and arbitrary modifications which have distorted the melodies and changed the solemn pace of church singing. Then we will be able to make a comprehensive and reliable translation of chants, setting them out in measured form; this would provide the firmest foundation for an indigenous contrapuntal technique.

[The publication of a primer for reading] neumatic [*kryukovaya*] notation would become the foundation for a comprehensive and detailed guide to all aspects of church singing; this would offer the best means of understanding the character of the diatonic mode in church singing, so different from the modern musical system.

The old chant repertoire would then become an inexhaustible source for modern chant, and thus act as a counterpart of the Old Slavonic language, which gave birth to its own harmonious poetry; likewise the old chants would revive the native genius that had been overgrown by brambles, and this revival an independent [i.e. non-Western] musical world will emerge . . .[61]

If these words were indeed Bortnyansky's, he was effectively advocating a departure from his own earlier practice, for the chant melodies in his arrangements were usually trimmed to fit standard harmonic progressions; these were arrangements designed to suit contemporary musical sensibilities, not a scholarly attempt to retrieve authentic versions of the chants. His arrangements followed the conventions observed in many provincial churches and monasteries: the old chant melody formed the middle voice of a three-part homophonic texture (similar to *kant*) in which the top line doubled the chant in thirds, and the bottom line was written to form common triads, as we saw in Ex.4.16 [*Pomoshchnik i pokrovitel'* (Helper and protector)]. Such singing became known as the "old", "monastic", or "tender" (*umilitel'nïy*) style, and some later writers acknowledged that Bortnyansky followed (and helped to preserve) a living tradition of chant harmonization which owed nothing to any textbook rules.[62]

Although the "Bortnyansky project" was not realized until the end of the nineteenth century, Fyodor Lvov, Bortnyansky's successor at the Cappella, made a first, faltering step towards the re-establishment of the old chant repertoire in everyday liturgical use.[63] Lvov and his colleague Pyotr Turchaninov (1779–1856) compiled what they took to be a complete collection of *znammenïy* chant melodies for the church year; the task of harmonizing the chants was undertaken by Turchaninov alone, although Lvov continued to oversee the project. The collection was published in 1830 under the title *The Cycle of Simple Church Chants used at the Highest Court from Time Immemorial*, and two years later it was distributed to parishes throughout Russia with the instruction that it should supersede any manuscript parts still in use (and so the new collection helped to advance the Cappella on its path towards complete control over church music). The distributed version, however, contained only the chant melodies (sung as the alto line) and their basses; no doubt this was desirable as an economy, but the addition of suitable tenor and soprano lines was often beyond the abilities of provincial choirs, resulting in disorderly improvisations which Lvov might well have found worse than the music-making he had replaced.[64] The goal of absolute uniformity might have proved unreachable at this stage, but Turchaninov's arrangements nevertheless became very popular – Metallov in 1912 claimed that

Turchaninov "had become everyone's favourite church composer, and still is even today".[65] A certain cleric Lisitsïn even called him the "one and only Russian national composer".[66] But nationalists with a more purist streak (Laroche among them) considered him no better than his predecessors: Lvov wrote Italian-style Orthodox music, while Turchaninov was thought to be under German influence. But while Turchaninov's harmonies seem only slightly more adventurous than Lvov's (compare their versions of the sticheron on the Birth of Christ, Examples 5.17a and 5.17b), he took much greater care in preserving the older forms of chant melodies. Turchaninov, as an enthusiastic autodidact, apparently fell in love with the old chants in his youth, as he listened to the singing in the Kievo-Pecherskaya Lavra: "I understood then, that . . . in order to preserve all the beauty and magnificence of our

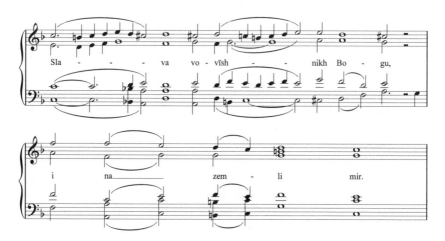

5.17a   Lvov, sticheron on the Birth of Christ (transposed)

5.17b   Turchaninov, sticheron on the Birth of Christ

old music, the melody should be retained in its entirety."[67] It was the Kievan versions of chant melodies that he later chose to harmonize. Smolensky in 1909 acknowledged Turchaninov's contribution to the development of the nationalist project in these terms:

> At the time, Turchaninov's arrangements were an enormous step ahead, of great importance, and sobering to think of, for this was a step ahead for the Land of Russia itself, so to speak. It was only after Turchaninov that the governing classes were able to recognize the necessity of returning to the former times of our native culture, that is, the necessity of taking our old chants as the foundation of our church singing.[68]

A further step in the same direction was taken by Aleksei Lvov (1798–1870), who succeeded his father, Fyodor, as director of the Cappella (he occupied the post from 1837 to 1861). Lvov began his reforms by removing his father's chant collection from use; between 1846 and '49, he prepared a more comprehensive replacement collection in collaboration with Lomakin and Vorotnikov. In association with the new collection, he provided an essay "O svobodnom ili nesimmetrichnom ritme" (On free, or non-symmetrical rhythm),[69] in which he explained his deviations from regular metre, and why Russian chant melodies required such treatment. Interestingly, he published the essay in 1858, a few years before Balakirev published his folksong arrangements with changing metres; not only was Lvov the pioneer in this respect, but he also went further than Balakirev, almost dispensing with bar-lines. This lack of barring is the most significant difference between the harmonizations of Lvov and Turchaninov; otherwise, their versions of the chant melodies and their principles of harmonization are much the same (as we have seen in Examples 5.16 and 5.17). Lvov's essay reflects his concerns for authenticity, but his aesthetic preferences are equally in evidence. It was authenticism that caused him, as he explains, to abandon bar lines. Authenticism likewise led him to add an appendix in which he showed how the same chant melody was written in the neumatic notation of the sixteenth and seventeenth centuries, in the modern five-line notation of the eighteenth, and finally, in his own harmonization (this does not mean, however, that he managed to check every melody against its neumatic version).

Returning to one of the chapter's central issues – the leading note and its supposed non-Russianness – we must note that Lvov's collection showed no tendency to flatten the seventh degree or to avoid it; evidently, Lvov saw no conflict between leading notes and his chant material. But the same unconcern about leading notes was also shown by Turchaninov in his collection and equally by Bakhmetev, whose collection superseded Lvov's (Bakhmetev was

Lvov's successor at the Cappella, and its least distinguished director). When a hostility towards the leading note did eventually emerge, it was only because of the strength of nationalist tendencies outside the Cappella walls. In Chapter 3 we have already discussed Glinka's striking anticipation of the nationalist movement in church music: at the end of his career, Glinka had hoped to revitalize Russian Orthodox church music by becoming a Russian Palestrina, and for this purpose he undertook a study of Western "medieval modes". In connection with this, we also discussed his suspicions towards the use of leading note in church music. But since Glinka's new project was cut short by his premature death before any substantial results could emerge, it had only the most limited influence on the next generation of musicians. The only tangible result of his late studies in Russian Orthodox music was the vocal trio, *Da ispravitsya molitva moya* (Let my prayer be answered), which is strictly heptatonic, in the minor but free of leading notes (Ex.3.27). But even this very slight piece was not published until 1878 (again, by Jurgenson), and was therefore unable to influence Cappella directors before then. But Glinka's final ruminations were much strengthened when they received a posthumous theoretical justification (however erroneous) through the work of Odoyevsky.

Odoyevsky, with his predilection for purely abstract theorizing, put forward several crucial ideas that proved highly influential among generations of nationalist musicians. First, he stated that all Russian folksongs could properly be categorized as belonging to one of eight *glasï* (modes); since these were effectively the same as the *glasï* of Russian Orthodox music, Odoyevsky had for the first time established a common basis for Russian church and folk music (that is, according to his claims, but not in truth). Second, he equated the 8 *glasï* of Russian church music with "Kirchen-Tonarten, toni ecclesiastici, tons d'eglise", and as a corollary, he rejected all the current practices of harmonizing chants in the major and minor. Third, he suggested that harmony, both in chant arrangements and in independent sacred works, should be chiefly heptatonic, and that chromaticism could be allowed "only in the accompanying voices, as an exception, to the extent that is required by dramatic movement".[70] Later he withdrew even this concession, advising composers:

> If you do not want the chant melody to perish under the weight of your arrangement, limit your counterpoints to the pitches supplied by the melody's mode. [71]

Odoyevsky's teaching soon found its followers, but still outside of the Cappella. Perhaps his most important advocate was Dmitry Razumovsky, a pioneering historian of Russian church music.[72] Razumovsky, in turn, passed Odoyevsky's ideas on to his student Sergei Taneyev, the composer, theorist and pedagogue, whose nationalist project we shall discuss later in the chapter. A few enthusiasts tried to put these ideas into practice. Nikolai Potulov (1810–73) went as far as harmonizing the complete circle of chants in a strict and rather unadventurous reading of Odoyevsky's method (Ex.5.18); he compiled four volumes all published posthumously. Gavriil Lomakin (1812–85) showed more imagination: he accepted unquestioningly Odoyevsky's equation of *glasï* with the Western modes, but in his harmonization he treated the chant melodies with some freedom, "searching for chords . . . guessing instinctively".[73]

5.18 An example of Potulov's harmonization

An unusual gloss on Odoyevsky's theory was provided by Yuri Arnold, in a treatise ambitiously titled: *Harmonization of old Russian chant according to Hellenic and Byzantine theory as well as acoustic analysis* (1886). In truth, Arnold's scholarship was largely window dressing for a syncretism of modal theory with modern harmony and tonality. Arnold proposed various arbitrary justifications for retaining leading notes and modulatory dominant-seventh chords while continuing to claim that his harmonizations were modal. For example, descending white-note scales from *e* to *e* (Arnold's hypomixolydian) and from *a* to *a* (his mixolydian) are harmonized in the following way:

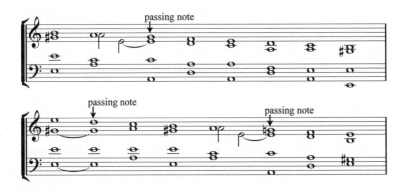

5.19a Arnold's "mixolydian" (above) and "hypomixolydian" (below)

Anyone else would regard these as straightforward A-minor harmonizations, but for Arnold they were correct harmonizations that followed two Greek modes while at the same time meeting "the essential needs of our aesthetic feelings" (i.e. the leading note and the expectation it creates). With similar ease, Arnold allows dominant-seventh chords back into Odoyevsky-style harmonization (which had allowed nothing beyond common triads) by claiming that they are based on something he called the "paraphonia of the tritone". Arnold defines "paraphonia" as a common tritone between two modes (Ex.5.19b), so had he followed his own definition, he could remain locally within Odoyevsky's strict heptatonicism, while departing from it on the larger scale using pivot chords incorporating these tritones.

5.19b Arnold's illustration of his "paraphonia of the tritone"

But even this concession wrung from spurious theorizing proves insufficient for Arnold, and in practice he simply used dominant-seventh chords as he saw fit. Here is an example of Arnold's "modal" harmonization:

5.19c An example of Arnold's "modal" harmonization

And so, while some scholars amassed arguments against the leading note, the others expended even more energy to justify the retention of leading notes. There was little to choose between the two sides, since they both relied on highly dubious theorizing.

By the beginning of the 1880s, concerns about the propriety of the leading note in church music had trickled all they way down to the bottom rung of the musicians' ladder, as the following story will attest. A certain Markell Lavrovsky, headmaster of a remote provincial grammar school (located in present-day Poland), decided to produce his own chant harmonizations, and burning with nationalist fervour, sent the results to the very top, to the director general of the Most Holy Synod, the infamous Konstantin Pobedonostsev. Upon receiving these harmonizations, Pobedonostsev forwarded them to Balakirev, who was now director of the Cappella; Balakirev, true to form, looked through the manuscript and corrected a few errors (parallel fifths and octaves); the corrected copy was conveyed back to Lavrovsky. The latter, unfortunately, was not suitably flattered by Balakirev's efforts, and he sent off another letter to Pobedonostsev; Balakirev, now no doubt weary of the matter, filed the letter away unanswered.[74] Lavrovsky's second letter, which is preserved in Balakirev's archive, speaks of its author's unease over the small number of changes that Balakirev had called for; it seems he was fishing for further-reaching improvements, and he urged Pobedonostsev to prod Balakirev:

> If only Mr Balakirev or some other musical celebrity expert in ecclesiastical chant would compile some specimen harmonizations of *znamennïy* chant – at least one for every mode [*glas*] – then I myself, after learning the rules of this harmonization, would undertake the arrangement of the Kholmsk Heirmologion . . . However, this task seems to me very difficult. Being far from expert in music, and therefore unable to go into details, I shall limit myself to the most general considerations, namely, that modern music theory took root in the West, while Orthodox singing originates in the East, and in particular from the scale of [Byzantine] Orthodox chant. This can be seen even from the fact that the major scale of the Heirmologion lacks [the degree] a major seventh [from the tonic], and the minor scale raises neither the sixth nor seventh degrees in ascending (the raised seventh in the arrangements of Lvov and Turchaninov was an arbitrary decision justifiable only by the requirements of modern music theory). We would not be mistaken, therefore, if we were to conclude that the harmonization of Orthodox chant must have, to some extent at least, its own special rules. . . . Orthodox church music, particularly the harmonization of *znammenïy* chant, is still awaiting its lawgiver, its Bach . . .[75]

It seems quite remarkable that an obscure provincial headmaster now expressed the same concern that was once uniquely entertained by Glinka. Even so, Balakirev, for all his nationalism in relation to folk music, remained unmoved by the Lavrovsky's appeal. In spite of his directorship of the Cappella, he showed little interest in composing liturgical music, and the few pieces he did produce display no nationalist intent. The grander task of composing music for the *Obikhod* he passed on to his assistant, Rimsky-Korsakov (the *Obikhod* required music not only for the equivalent of Western mass ordinaries, but also for many, but not all propers). As he sweated over this task during the summer of 1883, Rimsky-Korsakov wrote:

> I am sitting at the dacha and compiling the *Obikhod*, surrounded by all kinds of Potulovs, Razumovskys and editions of the Holy Synod. At the moment the entire All-Night Vigil is ready in monodic form and will now be harmonized. ... Doing nothing else musically – I've become a complete deacon. I am afraid only that Mily Alekseyevich [Balakirev] would confuse things a lot, for some confusion has already begun: first he told me that I should compile the most complete *Obikhod*, but when the Vespers was already done, he said that it would be better to exclude most of the *znammeniy* melodies, that it would be better to publish them separately at a later stage, and that for now it would be better to publish the Kievan and Greek chant melodies that are used more often; now that the entire All-Night Vigil was ready, he says that there was little point in compiling the monodic version and that a harmonized version should be written directly ... And when I start harmonizing, I am afraid there will be a lot more trouble.[76]

This letter shows that Balakirev had only a very hazy idea of the new *Obikhod* he wanted Rimsky-Korsakov to produce, and far from *znamenniy* chant being a pressing nationalist concern, on the contrary he is so indifferent that he encourages Rimsky-Korsakov to abandon most of it. But the new setting does provide us with a chance to discover Rimsky-Korsakov's position on chant harmonization, especially since he didn't treat the task as mere hack work, but published several of his arrangements in 1884. One of them (Ex.5.20), Heirmoi of the Canon at Matins on the Easter Saturday, clearly demonstrates that the composer had no system of rules to guide him, and freely followed his artistic intuition. He chose two principal, contrasting types of harmonization: one is austere in texture (almost exclusively thirds and fifths from the bass) with octave doubling, consistently heptatonic and modal (Ex.5.20a); the other is a more traditional three- or four-part homophonic texture, tonal with only slight modal colouring, and with unrestricted use of leading notes (Ex.5.20b). The first style invokes images of the archaic, and in the case of the present example is prompted by the visions of ancient terror related by the text; the second style is more modern and tender, as if inviting the laity to relate to the

5.20a   Rimsky-Korsakov, Heirmoi, I

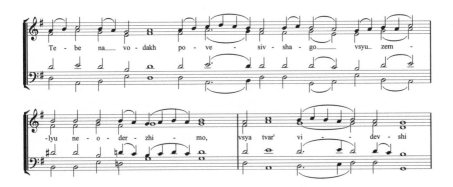

5.20b   Rimsky-Korsakov, Heirmoi, III

emotional side of the liturgy. Starkly contrasted at the beginning, the two styles tend to merge more often as the text progresses.

Although Rimsky-Korsakov's chant arrangements and other sacred pieces fell into complete obscurity for many decades (they were missing from otherwise reliable lists of his works), they made a noticeable impact when they were published. In early Soviet times, the music historian Preobrazhensky assessed them as ground-breaking:

> In none of the earlier literature can we find any example of a harmonizer who dared to set aside [the Western conventions of] harmony, even for a brief moment, in order to present the authentic melody, with octave doublings, in a two- or three-part texture, using thirds and sixths only – in other words, as in church practice, when the chant melody is sung by clerics only. . . . In none of the earlier literature, moreover, can we find any

arrangements of melodies or independent works that would use such characteristically folk-style devices as empty fifths, endings on the unison, or
chords without thirds.[77]

Tchaikovsky was another "musical celebrity" who could perhaps have
suggested an answer to the headmaster's appeal. The unexpected fame of his
Liturgy (which does not yet show any nationalist intent) placed him at the
centre of the church music debate; in turn, he himself was following the
debate closely, as the following remark demonstrates:

> We need a messiah, who will destroy the old with a single blow and stride
> out on a new path; this new path will mean a return to grey antiquity – the
> old chants, that is, will be presented with suitable harmonies. Just how these
> old chants should be harmonized, no one has yet determined, but there are
> those like Razumovsky, Rimsky-Korsakov, Azeyev [Rimsky-Korsakov's
> collaborator from the Cappella] who know and understand what Russian
> music needs.[78]

Around the time when Rimsky-Korsakov's arrangements were published, and
perhaps prompted by them, Tchaikovsky wrote his *Three Cherubic Songs*,
which, though not based on chant, show how the new nationalist ideas
affected him. His "Cherubic Song No. 3", for example, is strictly heptatonic –
Tchaikovsky unexpectedly proved himself a greater purist than Rimsky-
Korsakov on this occasion. For the most part, though, Tchaikovsky's harmony
does not venture too far from familiar tonic–dominant progressions, merely
flattening the leading note in the minor-key pieces (Ex.5.21). But the

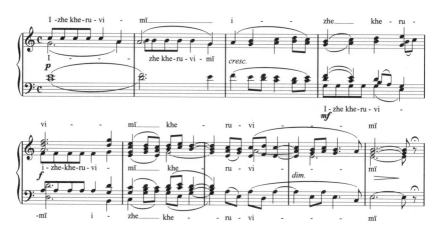

5.21   Tchaikovsky, Cherubic Song No. 3

composer took most pride in the fact that he had incorporated the priests' recitations into the score (these were always omitted from the notated part of the liturgy at the time), somewhat in the manner of the instrumental recitations the slow movement of his Third String Quartet. Balakirev, to whom Tchaikovsky sent his work for perusal, did not approve of this novelty, since he managed to perceive the recitations as exhibiting inappropriate "dance rhythms", no doubt against Tchaikovsky's intentions.[79]

But neither Rimsky-Korsakov nor Tchaikovsky wished to make further substantial contributions to the church music "renaissance", and they left the field again to the church musicians. Among their contemporaries, the only distinguished composer of concert music who had ambitions to reform church music was Taneyev. Indeed Tchaikovsky had sought Taneyev's advice on what would be possible stylistically in chant arrangements; in reply, Taneyev laid out a comprehensive nationalist project, complete with a quasi-philosophical justification:

Both Catholic and Protestant music are complete, closed phenomena. By looking closer at what their composers did and how they developed a musical style through to its final stage, we could learn what we should do in our own church music. The foundation of Catholic church music is Gregorian chant, the foundation of Protestant music the chorale. On these foundations the Catholic and Protestant churches have built magnificent edifices, while we have built nothing on our church melodies. What did Western composers do with their chants and in what forms can a church melody be presented? The most elementary form of arrangement would be the harmonization of a melody. . . . Examples of such a form are psalmody in the strict style [late sixteenth century], or the harmonized chorales of Protestant music . . . We already have such elementary arrangements in Bortnyansky, Turchaninov, and Potulov. This is, so to speak, the first stage of art (from a musical rather than historical point of view), but it does not leave any space for artistic creation, it does not present any musical interest; nevertheless, we cannot do without it. In every case, when the text of a prayer is long (and this happens very often with us), we must use this form. Only in those cases where the chant text is short can we turn to another kind of arrangement, which is the starting point of true art, with its richness and infinite variety of form. This is the field of the contrapuntal arrangement of melodies. . . . By entering this field, our music will be able to reach the highest stage of development and work out its own future style, just as European music has done.[80]

Nevertheless, Tchaikovsky could not have been entirely surprised by his young friend's response, for a year earlier Taneyev had sent him a description of a similar project: how composers should grow "the tree of Russian music" from native folksong, also through contrapuntal development – both these projects were effectively an extension of Glinka's late ideas. At that stage, Tchaikovsky had gently mocked Taneyev, calling him "a Slavophile Don Quixote"; now he once again tried to persuade Taneyev that such abstract prophesies were of no value. Taneyev may have hoped to realize these projects, but in neither case did he succeed. In the area of religious music, Taneyev provided two substantial cantatas, his early *Ioann Damaskin* (John of Damascus), and at the end of his career *Po prochtenii psalma* (Upon reading a psalm); although both were worthy contributions, they were certainly not sufficient to change the course of Russian church music. This was still much better than his achievements with folksong, which began and ended with a series of often elaborate contrapuntal exercises based on folk melodies (one of these was in no less than twelve parts).

The nationalist "renaissance" begins

In the end, the crucial role in launching the church music renaissance was performed by a scholar rather than a composer. This was Stepan Smolensky, whose research, teaching and propagandizing moved the centre of church music composition from St Petersburg to Moscow and laid the foundations for a whole school of church-music composers. The activities of this school soon became known as the New Trend. Smolensky's career began inauspiciously in Kazan, where he gave courses on church singing in various institutions. Throughout the 1870s and '80s, he undertook research in old chant, not only from the study of neumatic manuscripts, but also through listening to Old Believer congregations. His first significant work was the publication in Kazan of the important seventeenth-century source, *A Primer of Znamenniy Chant by the elder Alexander Mezenets* (1888). In the following year, Smolensky moved to Moscow to take up an appointment as director of the Moscow Synodal College; in Moscow he was also hired to take over the course on church singing at the Moscow Conservatoire. Smolensky succeeded in raising the performing level and public prestige of the Synodal Choir, and many Moscow composers – including Taneyev, Kalinnikov, Chesnokov – began to write sacred works specifically for it. In addition to acting as catalyst for the creation of new Russian repertoire, Smolensky was also the first Director to introduce the Choir to the riches of Western sacred music, from Palestrina to Schumann – at first, rehearsals had to be conducted in secrecy for fear of arousing the displeasure of the church hierarchy. Although the Holy

Synod's ban on concert performance of church music was never officially revoked (that is, until the end of the Synod itself in 1918), by the mid-1890s the political climate was relaxed enough for the ban to be safely ignored. Thus in 1895 the Synodal Choir gave a Historical Concerts series in Moscow, after which concert performances of church music were a staple part of Moscow's musical life and even became a fashionable entertainment. In 1899 the Synodal Choir undertook its first trip abroad, to Vienna, but it was in 1911 (after Smolensky's death) that the Choir's European tour finally sparked an international interest in Russian Orthodox sacred music.

The scholarship that fed into the "New Trend" never followed any single, coherent ideology, and indeed contained various conflicting tendencies, a state of affairs traceable back to Smolensky himself. On the one hand, Smolensky's direct knowledge of old manuscript sources encouraged high-level scholarship among his associates, and the Synodal College attracted a strong group of researchers, such as Preobrazhensky and Metallov. On the other hand, Smolensky's deep-seated nationalism often prevailed over his scholarly rigour, and both he and his followers tended to create new nationalist myths in the place of those they had debunked. The following passage gives us a telling glimpse of the heady nationalism that could sweep all before it in Smolensky's circle. Kastalsky, whom we shall discuss at length below, is boasting to Smolensky how he inserted nationalist fantasies into one of his scholarly commentaries:

> In the notes . . . I daringly state (relying on your views on the age of Russian church singing) that [church singing] could have existed in Russia from the second or third century as a result of the sermon Andrey the First-Called delivered to "those obedient, pacific, song-loving people!"[81]

Thus Kastalsky saw fit to place the beginnings of Russian church singing no less than eight centuries before Russia's adoption of Christianity, and he clearly judged that Smolensky would approve the publication of such an absurdity.

One idea which did, however, occupy a central place in Smolensky's teaching was the supposed kinship of old Russian chant and Russian folksong; but this idea was born of pure conjecture, although it no doubt borrowed some credibility from Smolensky's genuine scholarship in chant manuscripts. While the roots of the idea can be traced back to Odoyevsky, Smolenky drew more immediately from a declaration issued in the early 1880s by the Society for Lovers of Church Singing; a concise summary of the contents appeared in a subsequent announcement of a competition for composers of liturgical music, which made the following recommendations to entrants:

[In chant arrangements, the composers should] move closer to the natural harmonic singing of chants that undoubtedly existed in antiquity, but which was not written down, and which disappeared from practice for a number of reasons. . . . Faint remnants of such natural harmonic singing can be heard in the choral singing of old deacons and monks who have not been put through the new school of singing; it can be heard in the singing of peasants alongside their village deacons; and also in the singing of the Old Believers, when they sing without music and thus do not adhere strictly to their intended unison. The fact that these are only faint remnants is obvious when we compare them to the rich polyphony of folksongs and *dukhovnïye stikhi* ["spiritual verses", i.e. folksongs on sacred texts]. . . . The harmony of the chant arrangements should agree with the harmony of Russian folksongs, and the accompanying voices should be given movement in the spirit of chant and folk melodies.[82]

These highly tendentious pronouncements certainly owe something to Melgunov, whose folksong collection we examined earlier in the present chapter. But Melgunov was at least dealing with a tradition of folk hetero/polyphony that incontrovertibly existed, whereas the Society was urging composers to imitate "faint remnants" of a tradition that is at best shrouded in uncertainty and at worst non-existent. The examples that they give are of widely diverging kind: "the singing of old deacons and monks" probably refers to a "monastic" style of harmonization which we saw exemplified in Bortnyansky (Ex.4.15); the "peasants singing alongside their village deacon" could apply to anything from an untutored imitation of official church music to a spontaneous transferal of secular folk practices to church singing; and the supposed polyphony of Old Believers is merely wishful thinking – the Old Believers' practice is monophonic, and the occasional error does not constitute polyphony, "unintentional" or otherwise. Melgunov's "discovery" of folk hetero/polyphony clearly led the Society to desire a parallel tradition in the church, and that desire led to bold assertions that such a tradition existed. The Society even contacted Melgunov, inviting him to research the singing in Moscow's Cathedral of the Assumption, since this was a case of a local tradition being transmitted orally for several generations after the skill of reading neumatic notation had been lost. But if the Society had commissioned Melgunov solely in the hope that he would unearth some polyphony, they must have been sorely disappointed: when Melgunov's transcriptions were published in 1883 (by the Society), there was nothing but monophony to be seen.

For Smolensky and his followers, the imagined kinship between chant and folksong had practical consequences: old chant melodies should be treated with the same respect that folksong was already accorded, and the approach to their harmonization should be similar; monophony, of course, had far better claims to authenticity, but this held little attraction for the New Trend school: monophonic chant would have left nothing for composers to do, and so Smolensky and the Synodal Choir would have lost their route to celebrity. Here, for example, is the appeal of Alexander Nikolsky, one of Smolensky's loyal disciples; Nikolsky first draws his readers' attention to the (supposed) fact that folksongs are no longer harmonized according to textbook traditions, but authentically, according to the peasant practice of *podgoloski*. Now he turns to church music:

> [W]e must go the same way in the sphere of church melodies. Bringing [folk]song and ancient chant together should not be considered contrived or shocking, for it is doubtless true that the same national spirit and basic foundations of musical thinking manifest themselves in both these varieties of Russian music.[83]

Establishing a unity of principle in chant and folksong harmonization became the driving force behind the work of Alexander Kastalsky, who for many years worked as with the Synodal Choir as Smolensky's assistant (he deserves separate treatment which we shall undertake later in the chapter). Many lesser figures also followed this new approach to chant harmonization, which completely supplanted the trend of imitating Renaissance homophony. The same Nikolsky wrote thus:

> The use of harmonies, even if they are in the pure, or "strict" style, bestow on a piece the character of a Protestant chorale; therefore they will impose on a sacred musical work a colouring that may indeed be ecclesiastical, but which is foreign to the spirit of our Orthodoxy. The "modes" too, if understood in the spirit of Western counterpoint, are just as unsuitable here, and for the same reasons. It remains for us to wait for the appearance and establishment of completely new devices in the harmonization of our old chants that will give them an ecclesiastical character that is Russian. The originality of these devices, if they are worked out ably and tastefully, should be cultivated as a striving towards the expression of the chant melodies' Russian nature, and taken as a sign of the best way to understand their spirit.[84]

Smolensky, it has to be said, chose to disregard the part of Odoyevsky's theory that equated *glasï* with Western modes and recommended strict-style settings (i.e. in the manner, roughly, of Palestrina's homophonic passages).

Moreover, in 1900 one of the scholars in Smolensky's circle, Vasiliy Metallov, proposed a ground-breaking alternative theory of *glasï*: they were not to be regarded in terms of scales or modes, but were instead collections of melodic formulae (*popevki*).[85] This alternative theory was based on honest and careful research, and remains the foundation of all scholarship in the field up to the present day. The myth of Russian chant's Hellenic origins now lost all serious adherents, but the nationalist myth-making machine was not stopped so easily. Metallov's findings were accepted, only to be absorbed into a new myth of folksong-chant kinship. Nikolay Kompaneysky, another New Trend scholar, hit on the fact that "popevki", Metallov's term for chant formulae, was already used in the field of folksong research. This observation led him to search for a body of short melodic figures that could be regarded as the common core of chant and folksong. He settled upon four-note cells, and when he had (inevitably) found a few shared by both traditions, he proudly termed these "the primal words of Russian musical speech".[86]

The theory of the folksong-chant kinship became very widespread in pre-revolutionary Russia, in spite of the irritation this caused the church hierarchy, and, of course, in spite of a complete absence of empirical support. Among the New Trend scholars, only Preobrazhensky was intellectually ruthless enough to cut through nationalist wishful thinking. He took the practice of the New Trend for what it was: an attempt to associate chant in the public mind with various musical devices that were already perceived as "Russian", rather than a discovery of any mysterious kinship with folksong:

> [W]e can consider "Russian" only those features, which had crystallized as such within Russian folk music. Only through comparison with those features can we assess whether a piece of music is national or not; our history has not developed any other criteria, and our church singing in itself does not contain any Russian national features. The reason for bringing church chant closer to folk song should be as follows: church chant melodies only became Russian and national, in the same sense as Orthodox churches, icons, chasubles, stoles and the whole liturgy became "Russian" and "national" – through their long-term use and assimilation by tradition. Their essence, however, still remains borrowed and unchanged. [87]

These sceptical words were however soon forgotten, when the hypothesis of folksong-chant kinship was resurrected in the Stalin era. At least in part, its endorsement could have been a defensive tactic on behalf of church music scholars, a ploy to present their subject as a kind of folk culture and thus secure a permission to continue with their research.

The New Trend: invention as reconstruction

As touched on already, the conflict between scholarship and nationalist ideology had a practical correlate: the tension between the authenticist practices and the need to maintain or expand the audience for the Synodal Choir and New Trend music. Authenticism tended to push the composers towards monophony and heptatonicism, but the new possibilities (aesthetic and pecuniary) offered by concert performance of sacred music led them in the opposite direction, towards richer harmonies and more inventive choral textures. While they needed to pay at least occasional lip-service to the former tendency for the sake of the music's cachet, the latter tendency was stronger, and pushed them towards the aesthetics of secular concert music: prominent solos and such novelties as the imitation of bells were introduced into a cappella singing, and there were even calls for the introduction of organ or even orchestral accompaniment (still banned by Russian Orthodoxy where sacred music was concerned).[88]

Whether prompted by nationalism, authenticity, or artistic ambition, the stylistic innovations of the New Trend composers were received with hostility by the church hierarchy, which was all too aware of the secularizing tendency of the new repertoire. This tendency, moreover, was dividing the church music experienced by Moscow and St Petersburg elites from the traditional music still heard by the rest of the populace since only a handful of city choirs could assimilate new repertoire of this complexity. Nor did the church welcome the phenomenon of lay people hurrying from one service to another in order to sample the finest compositions and performances on offer. Yet the New Trend eventually won the battle, and in 1913 its victory became institutionalized: the Fourth Congress of Precentors declared os'moglasiye (the body of ancient chants used by the New Trend), to be the foundation of church singing and decided that chant arrangements should agree with the "spirit and style of the chant itself" rather than with European music theory – in effect, this was an endorsement of New Trend claims.[89] It seems likely that the declaration only ratified what was already underway – there had been rumours circulating for some time that precentors were being dismissed on grounds of musical conservatism.[90]

Let us now look at some of the New Trend composers in more detail. Smolensky himself composed only a small body of modest pieces, largely individual liturgical numbers of a purely functional nature. They offer no evidence in themselves that their author was the great reformer of church music (as we saw, his reforms were not dependent on his activities as a composer). Since the Synodal Choir sang daily services in the Cathedral of the Assumpion at the Kremlin, it had a need for more run-of-the-mill liturgical music; Smolensky was accordingly perfectly happy to commission very conventional harmonizations of the old chants melodies he had unearthed. He also encouraged the injection of "Russian inflections", which in practice meant some musical references to urban popular-song styles – this was the same music the Kuchka had disdained in favour of peasant song. Smolensky's right hand at the College, Kastalsky (we have already encountered him in the first part of the chapter), was much more prolific and influential as a composer of church music. He was a competent rather than a brilliant musician, but he was able to flourish under Smolensky – the latter gave him constant encouragement, and Kastalsky had the advantage of hearing his works performed immaculately by the Synodal Choir, which doubtless allowed him to develop the keen sense for effective choral textures that has enabled him to remain in the repertoires of both church and secular choirs in Russia.

Kastalsky's works are in many ways a practical realization of his mentor's ideas. For example, *Milost' mira* (The mercy of peace, Ex.5.22) is strictly heptatonic but with much greater freedom in dissonance treatment than anything to be found in the almost exclusively triadic harmony of Palestrinian colleagues such as Potulov. Kastalsky avoids the leading note in the minor in two ways. The first is the expedient of flattening of the third in dominant

5.22   Kastalsky, *Milost' mira* (The Mercy of Peace)

chords, which makes the familiar church-style progression sound strange, cold, and, for many, wrong – this is why Kastalsky chose to enforce the accurate performance of his music by inserting naturals before the seventh degree wherever the singers were likely to treat it as a leading note. The second, more enterprising option was the use of the II$^6_5$–I cadence, the first chord being Melgunov's "Russian dominant seventh". This progression was would already have been familiar to the habitués of the concert hall among Kastalsky's audience, since it had frequently been used by the Kuchka in their folk manner, and so it came ready-made with "Russian" associations. Kastalsky thus followed Smolensky's advice that "Russian inflections" should be incorporated, only substituting concert music for the popular songs Smolensky had in mind.

In *Blagoslovi dushe moya, Gospoda* (the first number of the All-Night Vigil in the synodal *Obikhod*), Kastalsky goes much further, both in the defamiliarization of church-style features, and in the insertion of folk-style devices. The former is exemplified by Kastalsky's fragmentation of the chant melody: successive phrases flit from one voice to another, as shown in Ex.5.23. When Kastalsky showed such arrangements to the bearers of the tradition – the singers of the Assumption Cathedral – they did not recognize the familiar chant melodies in their new garb (a phenomenon often encountered by folksong collectors/arrangers).[91] But these singers were more intimately acquainted with the chant melodies than anyone else, so if they failed to recognize the melodies, there was no chance at all that the laity would recognize

5.23   Kastalsky, *Blagoslovi dushe moya, Gospoda* (Bless the Lord, O my soul)

them. Fortunately, Russian Orthodoxy never demanded such recognition of the laity, so Kastalsky was able to proceed with the device. Kastalsky's use of folk devices could compensate for the defamiliarization; witness the introduction of *podgoloski*, for example, at the end of the first system of Ex.5.23: the top voice is given a more prominent melodic phrase, which is related to the main melody exactly in the manner of the uppermost *podgolosok* in peasant singing. Each melismatic passage is treated in a similar way. Even if Kastalsky's Moscow audiences were not sufficiently familiar to identify this device with folk singing, they certainly would have recognized the convergences on a unison as a marker of the folk-style, since this had entered art music even before Glinka. Kastalsky's folk-style innovations, arbitrary as they were, pleased and convinced many critics; even the usually sober-minded Preobrazhensky wrote that Kastalsky's arrangements "proved, in practice, the influence of folksong on the formation and development of *znamennïy* chant" – this was the same scholar we earlier saw blithely cutting through the pretensions of nationalism. [92]

While the two previous examples demonstrated only minor modifications of the traditional four-part harmonic texture (doubling of the descants by the tenors in *Milost' mira*, or a few unisons in *Blagoslovi*), the next example is far more radical and is representative of Kastalsky's authenticist streak. It is taken from Kastalsky's *Peshchnoye deystvo*, presented by the composer as a reconstruction of a fifteenth-century liturgical drama (Ex.5.24).[93] However, only the text and a small body of chant melodies had survived from this extinct tradition in the annals of the Assumption Cathedral, so Kastalsky's harmonizations and structure owe nothing to scholarship and everything to his imagination. To resurrect the spirit of antiquity, he abandoned four-part harmony altogether in preference for three- and austere two-part textures, applying modal colouring more generously than usual. Once again, Kastalsky managed to convince himself and others that his work was somehow an authentic reconstruction rather than an experiment in "historical" colour. The relative success of the *Peshchnoye deystvo*, which enjoyed several performances in 1907, led Kastalsky to probe further:

> I probably had a little of the restorer in me from birth, because soon after finishing this work I started another – similar, but from more remote times and lands. I dug deeper, wishing to prove, contrary to historians, that non-unison music had existed in the world from ancient times and that it tended to be expressive, pictorial, etc. The public, it appears, was in time convinced of my abilities in restoring music, and I was dubbed a "musical pasticheur".[94]

5.24   Kastalsky, Two fragments from *Peshchnoye deystvo*

The work in question is a cycle of piano pieces *Iz minuvshikh vekov* (From bygone times), divided into four books: Book I is set in China, India and Egypt, Book II in Judaea, Greece and "the birthplace of Islam", Book III features different parts of Christendom, from Ethiopia to Georgia, while Book IV is devoted to Russia. The material taken from Fétis, Gevaert, Naumann and other universal music histories was presented in large note-heads, while the composer's additions are in smaller notes, to enhance the collections scholarly claims (see Ex.5.25 for Kastalsky's rendering of Pindar's Ode). Only in Book IV, the Russian section, is everything is in large print, as if to imply that here, at last, fully authentic reconstruction is achievable.

Kastalsky resumed his musical globe-trotting during the World War I, when he began work on a kind of Russian requiem (drawing from the Latin requiem mass) which was to include music from each nation of the Entente. This was

5.25   Kastalsky, *From Past Ages*, beginning of Pindar's Ode

not so difficult when musical allusions to France, Britain, Italy and Serbia were to sit alongside Russian chant arrangements, but as more states joined the war on the Entente side, the work became increasingly outlandish. He now included American and Japanese melodies, and as he noticed that colonial soldiers were being coerced into the conflict, he even hoped to use "the songs of savages" from New Zealand. The last version of the work was drafted in 1917 (prior to the October Revolution), under the title *Bratskoye pomi-noveniye* (Fraternal commemoration). Kastalsky now thought that music alone was insufficient for his grandiose purposes, and he called for staged activities to include an English Archbishop, a Greek priest, Italian and Romanian nurses, Russian peasant women, various Serbs and Montenegrans, Hindu warriors and priests, a whole Japanese religious procession, and so on. It is scarcely necessary to mention that the performance of such an extrava-ganza, unlikely at any time, was out of the question amidst the turmoil of 1917.[95]

Kastalsky's war-time flights of fancy may seem remote from our account of the New Trend, but an expansion beyond the ideological boundaries of nationalism and the musical boundaries of Orthodox liturgical music was a general tendency in the later years of the movement. Grechaninov, for example, began to expand the harmonic palette of his church music in ways that owed much more to Wagner than Russian nationalism, particularly in his non-chant-based works, such as *Strastnaya sed'mitsa* (The Passion Week, 1911). From 1912 onwards, Grechaninov began to incorporate instrumental parts in his sacred works, which automatically disqualified them from litur-gical use; as a result, he eventually turned to the Latin mass, since this allowed him to participate in an existing tradition of sacred composition for voices and instruments. Rebikov indulged his modernist inclinations in the All-Night Vigil, which includes numbers based exclusively on the parallel movement of a chosen chord (a device also to be found in his experimental piano pieces). The less extravagant followers of the New Trend continued to exploit a fairly small set of trademark devices, such as austere unisons and two-part textures, folk-style heterophony, the use of parallel octaves or fifths, occasional colourful key changes, pedal notes. Kastalsky's invention, the choral imitation of Russian bells, was worn to death, as one cleric complained in 1911.[96] Some devices came from theoretical strands in Russian musical nationalism: the use folk heterophony, for example, was dependent on theorizing that held Russian church and folk music to have common roots, while the use of pedal notes supposedly harked back to the Byzantine roots of Russian church music (although the Kuchka's ubiquitous pedal notes were undoubtedly an unacknowledged influence here). Other devices, such as the key changes, were simply incorporated because composers found them attractive for the variety they offered. Where formerly the New Trend sought a consistent authenticity as defined by one or other strand of nationalist theorizing, this imperative was evidently forgotten once these composers found themselves able to gain a substantial and enthusiastic audience. Their motley collection of devices soon congealed into a new style that was no longer dependent on authenticist justifications.

Emblematic of this lack of concern for authenticism is the inconsistent application of the prohibition on leading notes. While the "austere" avoidance of the leading note was generally considered a New-Trend trademark, all the principal composers of the Trend compromised, and the avoidance of leading notes became a stylistic option rather than a universal rule. This was not simply because of the artistic limitations this self-imposed rule entailed; far more significant was the fact that the return to a supposed original purity ran aground on the contradiction inherent within nationalist authenticism: it threatened to destroy precisely the established traditions that enabled the church to maintain the idea of a single Russia under God, uniting peasant and landowner, worker and factory owner. The return to the medieval corpus of chants, now presented with strictly heptatonic harmonizations, served only to render the new music of the liturgy alien to the faithful (and in any case, harmonization, heptatonic or otherwise, was no part of the medieval practice). Pervasive dominant–tonic progressions in the liturgy were of course considered Russian by the church-going millions: there had been a two-hundred year tradition of singing in this way, and the laity of all classes associated the style with the most important moments in their lives, with their most cherished hopes, with tearful repentance, with consolation. These progressions, according to the self-defeating nationalism of the New Trend, were to be replaced with the deluded recreation of a largely imaginary past that no one but the *cognoscenti* recognized as Russian. Complaints were voiced by priests, singers and laity alike, but more importantly, criticism also came from the menacing and omnipotent Director General of the Most Holy Synod, Pobedonostsev, even though he had been a patron of the New Trend.

The paradoxes of Russianness

It will be useful to examine the interventions of Pobedonostsev in greater detail, especially since the contradictions of New Trend nationalist authenticism can then be set in their proper context of a much wider contradictory tendency. Pobedonostsev had served as tutor to the heir, and when Alexander III ascended to the throne he remained the Tsar's closest confidant, and was the real author of Alexander's promulgations. As the *eminence grise* behind Alexander's reactionary policies, he rightly became associated with the Jewish pogroms, the executions of political prisoners, and the forced Russification of the Baltic lands. His first act in power set the scene for all that followed: he advised the tsar to reject the proposals, modest as they were, for Russia's first constitution (the Loris–Melikov constitution, 1881); thereafter, he steadfastly opposed religious freedom, trial by jury, freedom of the press, secular state education and many other proposed reforms. Unsurprisingly, his name came to be reviled across the empire. But for our present purposes, it is his influence upon Russian Orthodoxy that we must examine. As director of the Synod, Pobedonostsev was the bureaucrat in charge of church policy; predictably enough, his policies in this area were both ultra-conservative and ultra-nationalist. But because Pobedonostsev's ideas were not mere contributions to the debate on church music, but had to be implemented as state policy, the contradictions inherent in the ideas were forced out into the open. As a nationalist (his intellectual roots lay in the Moscow Slavophile circles), Pobedonostsev welcomed and supported the ideas of Smolensky and the practices of the Synodal Choir under his direction. Pobedonostsev's policy on the revival of *znamenniy* chant melodies was of a piece with his defence of Church Slavonic, under attack at the time from those who sought to make the liturgy comprehensible to the laity by translating it into modern Russian. For Pobedonostsev, the chant revival, the construction of grand new churches, and the establishment of new monasteries, were all designed to impress the public with the idea that Russian Orthodoxy was being regenerated, sweeping aside the scepticism, atheism and religious alternatives that had emerged in the 1860s. The magnificent edifice of Orthodoxy, thus renovated, was now supposedly fit to support the crumbling autocracy for centuries to come. The changes wrought by this enormous project were certainly impressive, but they brought Pobedonostsev face-to-face with the contradictory nature of his vision for the church: unlike the reforms of Peter the Great, Pobedonostsev's reforms were carried out in the service of conservatism. But conservatism, in Pobedonostsev's own words, depended upon "the natural force of inertia", whereas Russian Orthodoxy, at his hands, had just experienced quite the opposite. And so Pobedonostsev was left unhappy with the results of his own reforms.

Pobedonostsev was chiefly concerned about the effect on the public of his conservative-nationalist reforms. But he himself was not simply a detached manipulator of other people's thoughts and emotions. His reforms also eventually jarred with the habits and preferences shaped by his own upbringing within a devout family. His religious nostalgia manifests itself in a series of short essays on church festivals that sometimes exhibit a certain lyricism, but often degenerate into a cloying sentimentality. He lovingly depicts traditional Orthodox music and its effects on the believer – traditional in the sense of what had already existed before his reforms:

Something solemn is about to happen – and the Orthodox believer waits for the moment after the Vespers when the moving [*umilitel'nïye*] songs of the great Canon flow and the quiet magnificence of the heirmos melodies are heard . . .[97]

Tired out by six days of bustle and care, man thirsts for Saturday evening, and here again the sacred poem of Saturday opens before him in the All-Night Vigil: the solemn beginning of the Vespers, with the voices of nature calling upon us to glorify the Lord, then the *os'moglasiye* of the Sunday stichera, and the evening song at the sunset; then, in the darkness and silence, the prayers and the elevated images of the Psalms of David; then in the sunshine the loud solemn songs of Resurrection . . . and in the Canon the marvellous heirmos chants in eight *glasï*, each one more harmonious and solemn than the last, all of them long familiar to the ear, all of them invariably moving [*umilyayushchiye*] the soul . . .[98]

But in another series of essays, *The Moscow Collection*, Pobedonostsev implicitly concedes that his own reforms have made such moving experiences harder to come by:

Russian chant, like folksong, flows as a broad, free stream from the people's breast, and the freer it is, the more it speaks to the heart. We share our chants with the Greeks, but the Russian people sings them in a different way, because it put its soul in it. Those who want to hear this soul should not go where the celebrated choruses and cappellas flaunt their voices, where the music of new composers is performed and where the *Obikhod* is sung from the new official arrangements. [Instead,] they must listen to singing in a well-appointed monastery or in one of those parish churches where choral singing has been established in a good way; there they will hear how a festive heirmos pours out of the Russian breast like a broad, free-flowing stream . . .[99]

Smolensky's memoirs give us another indication of Pobedonostsev's disappointment with his own reforms. Smolensky was himself a protégé of Pobedonostsev, and so he presents his mentor's (self-)criticism as benign fatherly grumbling:

Ah, these neumes! Ah, this *znamennÿ* chant! They would begin their ou-u-u-u-u and it goes on forever, then they would say one more word, and it's ou-u-u-u again! . . .What is this like? Take Turchaninov or Lvov's heirmos of the 5th *glas* – this I can understand; it moves me, I've heard it since childhood and am used to praying with it . . . No, don't sing [*znamennÿ* chant] when I am around . . . [100]

Pobedonostsev wanted a people who clung to a blind faith in the God of Orthodoxy and his anointed tsar; this was sufficient, Pobedonostsev believed, to guarantee the stability of the Russian autocracy. But he had bombarded believers with what were inevitably perceived as innovations, even though they were supposed to be a return to earlier practices. Nevertheless, one of his innovations could help to minimize the thought and questioning he had unintentionally stimulated: this was the new system of parish schools. Pobedonostsev had placed all existing local schools under the authority of the church – ultimately under his own authority. He now sought to use them to ensure that educational levels among the peasantry would remain very low (he was a firm believer in child labour where the peasant and working classes were concerned). He did not even wish them to instil them with an understanding of the Orthodox liturgy: peasants were only to be moved, viscerally, by familiar rituals and chants.

The adjectives *umilitel'nÿ*, *umilyayushchiy* and the noun *umileniye* are often found in Pobedonostsev's writings; other writers of the time also often use these words to pick out the most desirable quality in church singing. There is no single English equivalent, and translations must vary according to context, but the expressions "simplicity of heart", "warmth", "humility", "meekness" can serve as a starting point. *Bogomater' Umileniye* (Mother-of-God of Tenderness) is the name given to the most popular type of Russian icon, which features Mary and the Christ Child, the boy's humanity and vulnerability being emphasized as he clings to his mother (in contrast, the other main icon type emphasizes the boy's divinity, and he sits on Mary's lap like a king upon a throne). In this context, the Russian word *umileniye* would seem to be a long-standing mistranslation of the Greek *eleisa* (the merciful), which is the word used for the same type of icon in Byzantine Orthodoxy. When applied to church singing, the word should probably be rendered simply as "moving", although the English word does not carry all the connotations of *umilitel'nïy*. A stronger emotional response is signified when the word occurs in the standard Russian translation of the Bible at Acts 2:37: *I oni umililis' serdtsem* ("and their heart was pierced"), where the crowd is deeply affected by the preaching of Peter, immediately after the Holy Spirit has descended upon him. Such then, was the emotional response that the Russian liturgy was supposed to draw from the faithful. By Pobedonostsev's time, the pre-New Trend chant harmonizations, with their leading-notes, were universally thought to exhibit *umileniye* (as we have mentioned earlier, a certain type of harmonization was even termed *umilitel'noye peniye*. But such associations require time to accrue, and the new heptatonic harmonizations were perceived to be at best emotionally neutral, and at worst austere and distant. Removing the leading-note from standard progressions effectively removed the *umileniye* from the liturgy as far as many believers were concerned; while pleasing some connoisseurs, the New Trend threatened to alienate the majority and therefore shatter Pobedonostsev's ideal of "praying together with the people, in one church assembly, feeling the same heartbeat as the people".

The composers of the New Trend duly noted the murmurs of discontent and soon began to dilute their musical doctrines at least in practice; Pobedonostsev was therefore never placed in the embarrassing position of issuing an edict against his New Trend protégés. The music which resulted was not simply a return to the *status quo ante*: instead, the heptatonic manner became a stylistic option, co-existing with a harmonically more relaxed style that included leading-notes, dominants and secondary dominants and sometimes a little chromaticism. For ease of reference, I shall refer to the second style as "non-heptatonic". The term "style" is a little problematic here, for sometimes an otherwise heptatonic phrase can take a sudden non-heptatonic turn as it cadences. But just as often, the New Trend composers would maintain the distinction in their music, using one or the other style exclusively for a substantial section, or for a whole number, as we shall see in the examples that follow.

As a clear example of the mixed approach, Ex.5.26, from the second number of Grechaninov's first *Liturgy of St John Chrystostom* (1898), presents a long phrase harmonized consistently in G Aeolian until the moment of the

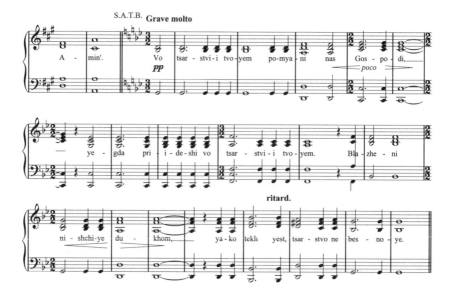

5.26 Grechaninov, fragment of "Antiphones" from his *Liturgy of St John Chrysostom*

final cadence, when a standard dominant chord is used. On paper, this seems quite unremarkable, but in the hands of Grechaninov, one of the most accomplished New Trend composers, the result is very striking: the suddenness of the F#'s entrance after such a long heptatonic stretch is enhanced by the chromatic voice-leading (F–F#–G) in the alto. The other sections in the number proceed likewise, but from the combination of these sections, something more colourful emerges. Grechaninov opens the piece with what would seem to be A Dorian, although we might say that the repeated G triads look ahead to the eventual emergence of G major as the final tonic. En route, we pass through a myriad of keys: not only G minor and B minor, but also F# major/minor and G# minor. The G-minor triad at the beginning of Ex.5.26 was immediately preceded by an A-major triad. By such means, it was possible for the more enterprising New Trend composers to incorporate heptatonicism within a much richer tonal palette.

In the works of Pavel Chesnokov, we find heptatonic and non-heptatonic styles in equal measure, but they are not generally mixed within a single number. To take an example from each style, Ex.5.27a is heptatonic while Ex.5.27b is clearly non-heptatonic; both are from Chesnokov's cycle of Sunday troparia, op.19. But something of deeper significance emerges here, for Chesnokov labels his heptatonic piece "6th *glas*" and the non-heptatonic piece "8th *glas*"; the latter would be absurd if Chesnokov took "*glas*" to mean "mode". In fact Chesnokov is quite correctly following Metallov's scholarship

5.27a   Chesnokov, *Bog Gospod'* in the 6th *glas* from his Sunday Troparia, op. 19

5.27b   Chesnokov, *Bog Gospod'* in the 8th *glas* from op. 19

on the matter: as discussed earlier, each *glas* was most accurately understood as a collection of melodic formulae rather than a mode. But Chesnokov, in applying this knowledge, takes a further step: he sees that Metallov effectively demolishes the established New Trend doctrine on heptatonicism: if a *glas* is not a mode, then heptatonic chant harmonizations have no more claim to authenticism than non-heptatonic harmonizations. Chesnokov feels free to retain the heptatonic approach in some of his pieces, but purely as a stylistic option, detached from its roots in nationalist authenticism.

But perhaps the most interesting examples are to be found in Rakhmaninov's All-NightVigil (1915), which undoubtedly constitutes the pinnacle of the New Trend. Continuing with the tendency already described, Rakhmaninov freely uses the characteristic devices of the New Trend, and with equal freedom forsakes them. The Vigil is sometimes heptatonic, sometimes not; some pieces are based on *znamennïy* chants, others are not. Where Rakhmaninov uses a chant melody, he often shapes it to suit his purposes, and he happily writes his own chant-style melodies when the need arises. From the very beginning of the first number, *Priidite, poklonimsya* (O come, let us worship), we hear that Rakhmaninov has no intention of banishing the leading note; indeed, the leading note and dominant triads play an integral role in creating the mood for this ardent call to worship. The flattened 7th degree only surfaces in a later, more subdued passage on the words "and fall down before the Lord." Thereafter, the opposition between these two moods is maintained not least through the contrast between leading note and flat 7. Attractive as this idea may be, it is not used each time a similar textual opposition appears in subsequent numbers – clearly, Rakhmaninov had no desire to elevate this device into a general principle.

In *Blagoslovi, dushe moya, Gospodi* (Bless the Lord, O my soul) we find a single isolated non-heptatonic progression in the course of a lengthy piece (Ex.5.28). At this point, Rakhmaninov returns a portion of the chant melody for the fourth time. This stretch of melody had been re-harmonized on each appearance, the preceding statement being particularly strong, with a progression utilizing parallel fifths; by the fourth appearance, Rakhmaninov probably felt that he had already exhausted the resources of heptatonicism. And so Rakhmaninov momentarily lifts his stylistic restriction, with a progression that would sound ordinary enough in isolation, but as an island in a sea of heptatonicism, it immediately catches the listener's attention.

5.28   Rakhmaninov, All-Night Vigil, No. 2

Even more curious is another example, *Blagosloven yesi, Gospodi* (Blessed art thou, O Lord), No. 9 in the Vigil. The V–i progression plays an important role in the D-minor sections, but until a single instance shortly before the end, the dominant chord always lacks the leading note; sometimes the chord is simply the root and the fifth, quite often with a seventh added and sometimes with the minor third. The later episodes, contrasting in key/mode, tempo and local tonic, make repeated use of leading notes, dominants and applied dominants. On the evidence of No. 1, *Priidite, poklonimsya*, which we have already discussed, we might look to the text to explain this pattern. The first appearance of a leading note occurs, promisingly, in a passage of mourning for the crucified Jesus, but later occurrences prevent any correlation between the use of the leading note and textual *umileniye*. In the final, climactic section of the piece, we find all three versions of the dominant chord side by side (Ex.5.29), as if purely for variety's sake. It is interesting to observe that this passage, for Rakhmaninov, is by no means a stylistic by-road; although the bulk of his oeuvre is for instrumental forces rather than chorus, these bars, with their different versions of the dominant, are entirely characteristic of the composer in his maturity; indeed the *Symphonic Dances* close with a reminiscence of this passage.

5.29   Rakhmaninov, All-Night Vigil, No. 3

Before the Vigil was written, New Trend harmony was already an influence upon Rakhmaninov. Rakhmaninov, in return, raised New Trend music to a higher artistic level in his Vigil. The work was composed as a fund-raiser and morale-booster for the Russian war effort. Rakhmaninov could hardly have guessed that the war would set in train a series of events that (among more important things) would ensure his Vigil was also the terminus for the New Trend, or for any elaborate Orthodox liturgical music. Those New Trend composers who left Russia (such as Grechaninov in 1925) found themselves without a public and generally without performers for Orthodox music and they had to turn their hand to music better suited to their new environment. Those who remained in Russia (such as Kastalsky), although under no compulsion for the first decade, were generally eager to shed their former habits and take up new tasks that would demonstrate their commitment to the Revolution (as in the West, musicians employed by the church were not necessarily devoted believers themselves).

As for Pobedonostsev, he died a decade before the Revolution. But he lived long enough to see his life's work begin to crumble in the events of 1905–07. When peasants laboured under impossible debts ("compensation" for their former feudal masters) and workers' demonstrations were answered with bullets and sabres, no amount of religious window-dressing would have sufficed to preserve the status quo, and pogroms served to distract dwindling numbers from the real source of their problems. Pobedonostsev, undaunted, advised the tsar to make no concessions. He was confronted by the consequences later in the year, if only for a few minutes, and with no real danger to his person. A demonstration of hundreds of thousands demanding an amnesty for political prisoners had set out from St Petersburg's Kazan cathedral; the route, by chance, took the march past Pobedonostsev's residence. A commentator sympathetic to Pobedonostsev pictured the scene inside the chambers of the Director of the Synod:

> But he is engrossed in prayer and scholarly work. The revolutionary song of the street is drowned in those ancient Russian church chants that fill his soul . . .[101]

However, among those present in the street below was Leon Trotsky, recently elected head of the Petrograd Workers' Council, who recalled:

> Below, a human ocean was seething. Red banners waved upon it like sails of the revolution. . . . [T]hey bare their heads; here the procession is joined by the ghosts of the victims of January 9. The crowd sings "Eternal Memory" and "You Have Fallen Victim". Red banners outside Pobedonostsev's house. Whistling, curses. Does the old vulture hear them? Let him look out of the window without fear; they will not touch him at this hour. Let him gaze with his old, guilty eyes at the revolutionary masses, masters of the streets of Petersburg. Forward![102]

Within a fortnight, the imperial court decided that it would be wise to retire Pobedonostsev from his post as director of the Synod. The composers of the New Trend continued for a few years, unlatched from Pobedonostsev's now unwelcome patronage; another dozen years, and the same composers would unlatch themselves either from the church or from Russia.

CHAPTER 6

MUSICAL NATIONALISM IN STALIN'S SOVIET UNION

The development of cultures that are national in form and socialist in content is necessary for the purpose of their ultimate fusion into one General Culture, socialist both as to form and content, and expressed in one general language.

Stalin[1]

Comrades, we want – we passionately wish – to have our own Mighty Handful.

Zhdanov[2]

Let us create Mighty Handfuls across the whole of our multinational Motherland, so that we would have not just one Mighty Handful in Moscow, but sixteen in our national republics.

M. Leviyev[3]

The main focus of this chapter is the return of various nationalist ideas in Stalin's Soviet Union, all strangely transformed to fit their new environment. Where Lenin, towards the end of his life, had seen the persistence of "Great Russian chauvinism" as the most serious of all the obstacles to the potential emergence of a socialist society, Stalin, during the 1930s, took great strides towards the revival of Russian nationalism, as an important ideological force intended to bind Russians to the system he had created. At the same time, Stalin also encouraged various projects that would foster nation-building among the other officially recognized nationalities of the Soviet Union – but always on a purely cultural level, so that no threat was posed to Stalin's interests in maintaining his control over the entire Union. All the arts, including music, were enlisted for this purpose, and established Russian artists were sent out to collaborate with local artists in the outlying Republics. The project of musical nation-building in the republics was gigantic in scale: there was hardly a composer in the Soviet Union who failed to make a contribution, and dozens made a career out of "national" music, often moving from one "nation" to another, following Moscow's shifts in demand. In the years immediately following the collapse of the Soviet Union, some of the former republics decided to reject Soviet cultural developments, and accordingly closed down opera houses, and left musicians trained in the Western classical tradition jobless, all for the purpose of building their cultural nationalism afresh. But others have tried to preserve the Soviet "national" heritage and use it as a base for fostering new connections with the West, now without the mediation of Moscow. Whatever the outcome in each case, the cultural institutions and musical works that resulted from Soviet national policy are at the very least of great historical interest.

The twists of Soviet national policy

Well before the October Revolution of 1917, the Bolsheviks understood that the task of making a revolution in Russia was greatly complicated by the existence of the multinational empire that had developed over the previous three centuries. They realized that the national self-consciousness that was a by-product of Russian domination would not easily fade away, and nor would their understandable suspicions towards anything emanating from Russia. Seeking a programme that would decrease or overcome these problems in a post-revolutionary situation, Lenin in 1916 charted a path towards federalism, regarding it as a long-term, if not permanent solution:

> Having transformed capitalism into socialism, the proletariat will create an *opportunity* for the total elimination of national oppression; this opportunity will become a *reality* "only" – "only!" – after a total democratization of all spheres, including the establishment of state borders according to the "sympathies" of the population, and including complete freedom of secession. This, in turn, will lead *in practice* to a total abolition of all national tensions and all national distrust, to an accelerated drawing together and merger of nations that will result in the *withering away* of the state.[4]

The argument behind this statement was as follows: the exploited classes in oppressed nations would always tend to unite with their own national exploiting class against the external oppressor. Revolutionary Russia would only be seen as a potential liberator by these exploited classes once they had seen two things for themselves: first, that their own national ruling class could only serve as the agents of imperialist powers (and there were indeed many examples of this during the Civil War);[5] and second, that their former Russian oppressor had no further imperial ambitions, which required that all vestiges of Great Russian chauvinism must be stamped out.[6] Initially, not everyone in the party supported Lenin on the matters of national policy: some of his opponents (among then Bukharin and Dzerzhinsky) accused him of paying too much attention to nationality rather than class and thus compromising Marxist theory.[7] But Lenin held that Marxism was a practice, and not merely a body of theory, and that the oppressed of other nations had to be engaged with at their present level of consciousness. In any case, the benefits of such tactics soon became evident: even the Chechens, with their impressive record of resistance to imperial Russia, now sided with the Reds, while those parts of the empire that had initially taken the other side, repelled by the actions of the Whites, eventually drifted into the Red camp (as the only alternative during the Civil War).[8] In 1922, the Union of the Soviet Socialist Republics was formed out of four constituents: the Russian Federation, Ukraine, Belorussia and Transcaucasia. In 1923, however, there emerged a new opposition to Lenin's policies on nationalism: Stalin argued that the independent republics should simply be absorbed into the Russian Federation, because the indulgence of the nationalities was supposedly endangering the new revolutionary state. As a result of this, and in particular Stalin's overbearing treatment of Georgian Bolsheviks, Lenin famously accused Stalin of acting as "a vulgar Great Russian bully", his Georgian origins notwithstanding (perhaps it was precisely because Stalin was not Russian that he had been given the task of writing up the Party's national policy back in 1913).[9]

Between 1922 and 1936, another five national republics entered the USSR (Kazakhstan, Uzbekistan, Turkmenistan, Tajikistan and Kirghizstan). The principle of federalism was also in force inside these larger units, which were subdivided into autonomous regions, districts, soviets etc. Until 1930, there were practically no obstacles to the endless proliferation of ethnic-based units. Once a given ethnic minority was found (language was usually the defining criterion), local government organizations, schools and newspapers were created, all using the local language. If the language was regarded as under-developed for the purposes of modern society, it was codified and often given a new Roman alphabetic scheme (no doubt partly in response to Atatürk's adoption of the Roman alphabet for Turkish, but also because Cyrillic must have seemed less outward-looking and internationalist). By 1928, books were being published in 66 languages, and 205 non-Russian newspapers were circu-lating in 47 languages.[10] Official support and funding for this multitude of national languages and cultures was intended to win the confidence of the peoples so that they would "join in the universal culture, revolution and communism sooner".[11] An elaborate system of quotas ensured that being a *natsional* (a non-Russian) opened doors to Party and government organizations, both local and central; this was deemed necessary in order to erode the dominance of Russians in local administration and industrial management inherited from the tsarist state.

The Russian nationality was, of course, excluded from all these projects, since the encouragement of national cultures was not an end in itself – the exercise was to remove Russian dominance and prove that revolutionary Russia would not behave in the same way as its predecessor states. This was reversed by Stalin, particularly after 1936. It might have seemed that the reversal was far from complete, since there were still some vestiges of the original design left untouched, such as the Russian republic's lack of its own Communist Party or Academy of Sciences – institutions possessed by all the other republics. However, Stalin could well afford to leave these matters unchanged, since the central institutions of the Union, which were all housed on Russian soil, could easily be used to enforce Russian dominance.

The advent of Stalinism seemed, on a superficial level, to allow national policy of the '20s to continue. While classes had officially disappeared thanks to the completion of the First Five-Year Plan, nations were held to be much more persistent. In 1930, Stalin had even apparently moved over to Lenin's position on a continuing national plurality:

> The theory of the fusion of all nations of . . . the USSR into one common Great Russian nation with one common Great Russian language is a nationalist-chauvinist and anti-Leninist theory that contradicts the main thesis of Leninism, according to which national differences cannot disappear in the near future but will remain in existence for a long time, even after the victory of the proletarian revolution on a world scale.[12]

Consistent with this statement, local nation-building projects further proliferated for a while; by 1938, for example, state funding was provided for 2188 non-Russian periodicals in 66 languages.[13] Behind all these activities, however, Stalin always ensured that local leaders could never win any real autonomy in their respective domains. Accordingly, there were frequent dismissals and occasional wide-ranging purges of local parties, above all in the Ukraine, in order to show that the centre remained in control. The official justification was that such disciplinary action was required to prevent the development of "bourgeois nationalism" within the republics.

In order to wield power effectively over the rather chaotic collection of ethno-territorial units left over from the '20s, Stalin rationalized the system, creating a tidy hierarchy, established in the new Constitution of the USSR (ratified 5 December 1936). At the top was the Soviet Union itself, with its various all-Union institutions; immediately below this stood the national republics; within some of the national republics, there were up to three further levels, which were, in descending order of status and scale, the autonomous republics, autonomous regions and national districts. Some of the units were only brought into being with the ratification of the Constitution. Elaborate as this scheme was, however, it still left various smaller peoples, overlapping groups or enclaves unaccounted for. But this was not a problem for Stalin: the new hierarchical system was not intended as a description, but as a ruling. Those who did not fit into the scheme were expected to assimilate into the titular nationality of the unit in which they lived. The scheme did undergo some changes after 1936, but these were wrought by Stalin for his own purposes, and certainly not at the behest of groups who wanted recognition or improved status. The most substantial changes resulted from the various mass deportations that occurred during the war, as peoples and groups such as the Chechens, Crimean Tatars and Volga Germans were taken far from the reach of the German invasion forces (with whom Stalin believed they might collaborate).

After the ratification of the new Constitution, however, it became increasingly clear, even at a superficial level, that there were strong tendencies running counter to the inherited policy on the nations. The promotion of the nations only made sense in the context of a determined undermining of Russian nationalism. But Stalin now promoted Russia as a great nation, going so far as to suggest that Russia's imperial conquests under the tsars might be admired rather than deplored – the change was soon evident even in school history texts. This move was blatantly incompatible with the original aims of Bolshevik policy on the nations, and now approximated more to "the white man's burden", Tajik newspapers and Kirghiz operas notwithstanding. Beginning in 1937, the Roman script that had been introduced in the '20s for many languages in the Union now had to be abandoned in favour of Cyrillic, regardless of the disruptions this would cause in education and in all printed communication, from newspapers to street signs – another symbol of Stalin's desire to establish the Russian nation as master. This task was largely completed within a mere two years. There was never any need for an overt Russification policy across the Union, since Stalin was creating the conditions that would lead to this outcome in any case. After the war, there were further steps in this direction. There had, of course been the deportations of various groups, and these were no longer officially recognized. But beyond these cases, it was insinuated that many of the nations had played a less-than-heroic role in the war – where they had not actually collaborated with the Nazis, they would have collaborated given the chance, or would at least have shown little resistance. Only the Russian nation supposedly emerged with its reputation entirely spotless, a heroic beacon, and a lesson to the other nations. These sentiments were implicit in Stalin's 1945 toast to the Russian people, which was broadcast to the whole Union:

> I would like to raise a toast to the health of our Soviet people and, first and foremost, to the Russian people.
>
> I am drinking to the Russian people first, because in this war it earned everyone's recognition as the leading force among all the peoples of the Soviet Union.
>
> I am proposing a toast to the Russian people not only because it is a leading people [leader among the peoples], but also because it possesses a clear mind, a steadfast character, and patience [persistence, a spirit of endurance].
>
> Our government had made many mistakes, and we had found ourselves in a desperate situation, when our country retreated because . . . there was no other way out. Some other nations might have said to the government: you have not fulfilled our expectations, go away, we will install another government which will make peace with Germany and give us calm. But the Russian people did not do so, for it believed in the rightness of the policy of its government and chose to make sacrifices to ensure that Germany was defeated. It was this trust of the Russian people in the Soviet government that proved to be the decisive force ensuring the historic victory over the enemy of humanity – over fascism.
>
> We thank the Russian people for this trust.
>
> To the health of the Russian people![14]

The glorification of tsarist Russia's imperial expansion now reached its most blatant level. Russia's annexation of the Caucasus and Transcaucasus, for example, was now to be regarded as "the salvation of the national existence" of the peoples native to these regions.[15] Similarly, the annexation of the territories now comprising Kazakhstan was "of profoundly progressive significance", with the Kazakhs as the main beneficiary, having "comprehended the advantages of life in the mighty state of Russia"; they had "wisely chosen" the patronage of Russia over British colonization.[16] What in the revolutionary years had been Russia's shame was now, in the late Stalin era, Russia's glory, to be celebrated by all Russians, and eagerly acknowledged by the other nations.

The Kuchka's lowest point

For at least a decade before the October Revolution, nationalism had persisted only as a minority current within Russian music, and was now largely backward-looking. Russia's heavy defeat at the hands of Japan – an Asiatic power – had severely dented the credibility of nationalist rhetoric, and the revolutionary period of 1905–07, although ending in an uneasy re-establishment of the old order, had set many leading artists and writers on new paths. After another few years, the epigones of the Kuchka were soon outnumbered by the epigones of Scriabin. With the October Revolution and the defeat of the Whites in the Civil War that followed, it must have seemed that Russian nationalism was finally dead in all its manifestations, musical and otherwise. In the '20s, neither of the two main organizing forces on the Soviet music scene had any interest in keeping the music of the Kuchka alive. RAPM, the Russian Association of Proletarian Musicians, thought only Musorgsky worthy of attention, as a creator of "dramas of the people"; the rest of the Kuchka was regarded as the irrelevant product of its aristocratic or bourgeois roots. The rival organization, ASM, the Association for Contemporary Music, contained a lively modernist and internationalist component that looked towards Hindemith, Krenek and Les Six; for them, casting aside the Kuchka seemed a necessary step towards solving the problem of Russian musical provincialism. Boris Asafyev, the leading advocate of the ASM modernists, warned in the mid-1920s against Kuchka epigonism of the sort that Grechaninov had recently displayed in his opera *Dobrïnya Nikitich*; he argued that "the task set by Rimsky-Korsakov has been fulfilled" and that the time for such things was therefore past.[17] Warming to his subject, he even criticized Russian musical culture of the past for its "thinness":

> In Germany, the appeal "back to Handel" will always be fruitful, but for us [in Russia] any appeal to look back will sound ridiculous. On no account can we look back to Glinka – his work can be admired and his mastery revered, but he cannot serve as any foundation.[18]

And it was not only the composers, of whatever stripe, who dismissed the Kuchka. The '20s also witnessed the debunking of the various Kuchka myths at the hand of music historians. They argued that the Kuchka's treatment of folksong was pure stylization, owing nothing to genuine peasant performance practices. The Kuchka's exoticism, moreover, was a regrettable product of great-power chauvinism and colonialism. Again, Musorgsky was considered exempt from these charges, whether for his "democratic" or his "modernist" qualities.

But dismissing the Kuchka as a compositional model, and exposing the pretensions behind their representation of peasant music was only the negative aspect of a larger task. What should a democratic music sound like? Should it simply try to assimilate peasant music while avoiding the delusions of the Kuchka? Or should it look elsewhere for a proper basis? It seemed that the answer to the last question was a simple "yes". In the Revolution and Civil War, after all, the Bolsheviks had argued that only the working class was in a position to lead the struggle; the peasant, for understandable economic reasons, found it difficult to see beyond the plot of land he had now received. Russian workers, they argued, could look towards unity with fellow workers of other countries, on the basis of a common interest in seeing the defeat of their exploiters, whereas the peasant's interest was now only to work his land – his horizon was local rather than international. With this as a background, it seemed obvious enough that a new democratic music should look first towards the workers and their urban culture, while peasant culture should be assigned a subordinate position.

But whenever musicians, whether proletarianist or modernist, turned to scrutinize the musical tastes of the urban workers they found little to praise and much to condemn: workers, it seemed to them, had been corrupted by the influence of the bourgeois light music. Workers listened to sentimental and cynical romances, salon waltzes, pre-Revolutionary marching songs, and cabaret cancans. Yes, it was conceded, this low music was often fitted out with fresh texts about the Revolution and Civil War, but this was scant comfort to anyone looking here for the basis of a whole new musical culture appropriate to a post-revolutionary people. Neither the proletarianists nor the modernists thought any concessions should be made to such tastes, but RAPM in particular set itself the task of replace this depraved repertoire with something altogether more worthy. Much ink was spilt on the subject, and there was many a heated debate, but in the end, the few who actually got round to composing any of this new proletarian music, such as RAPM's leading figure, Dmitriy Vasilyev-Buglay, found themselves turning to something that bore a remarkable resemblance to the old Kuchka-style arrangements and stylizations of folksong.[19]

ASM could not let this contradiction pass unnoticed. Irritated by the constant jibes from RAPM, in its game of ideological one-upmanship, ASM now grasped this opportunity to reciprocate. The anti-folksong polemic that resulted perhaps received its most extreme statement in an article by Nikolai Roslavets, one of ASM's leading modernist composers, who was as fluent as RAPM in the construction of pseudo-Marxist arguments to suit the agenda of the day:

Allow us to ask: why is it that the folksong, which was created in the prehistoric era of the agrarian economy, should contain riches of melody, harmony, and rhythm sufficient to answer the needs of both a proletariat that has sampled urban capitalist culture, and the composer, who is refined by the achievements of a centuries-old musical culture? A peasant is close to nature, he is naturally a contemplative individualist – he does not hear and cannot hear any other sounds but the most primitive; he does not feel any need for the complex combination of sounds, nor does he search for laws governing these combinations. And so we find harmonic poverty – a natural scale of the most frugal range, only slightly expanded by artificial constructions under the influence of the ancient Greek church modes); melodic uniformity, which is clear from the ease with which the folksong style can be faked; and a simplicity or, more precisely, a primitivism of form, coupled with a customary anarchy in its construction.[20] . . .

On no account can we support the false and harmful view that the future music of the country that has seen victorious proletariat will grow out of folksong. Such an assertion is not just an artistic heresy, but a sociological heresy too, since it clearly stems from the long-buried *narodnik* doctrine that socialism would develop directly out of the agrarian community . . . Now that even the epigones of Russian musical nationalism have died out, the further artificial cultivation of folksong as a model for "proletarian art" would only be so much reactionary nonsense.[21]

RAPM soon mustered two arguments in its defence. Firstly, the ideology of a "working peasantry" to some degree approximated the ideology of the working class, and therefore composers who based their art on rural folksong were already halfway towards their destination. Secondly, the starting point for RAPM composers was Musorgsky in particular, and not the Kuchka as a whole, and even then they focused only on Musorgsky's "realist" method.[22] But whatever the RAPM window-dressing, at the end of the '20s there was a definite return to Kuchka-style folksiness. This tendency displaced two options that had been explored earlier in the decade: first, there was the ethnographically based performance and recreation of unadulterated folksong (which RAPM considered reactionary); and secondly there was the possibility of approaching folksong from a modernist perspective, as advocated by Avraamov (see Chapter 5).

At the end of the decade, ASM was heavily engaged in a struggle against the rise of Kuchka epigonism, but it was soon to be removed altogether from the cultural battlefield through the actions of RAPM.[23] The 1930 manifesto of VOSM (the All-Union Society for Contemporary Music, which ASM now called itself), contained perhaps the last anti-Kuchka invective:

"Infecting" the listener with certain emotions, contemporary music simultaneously – and this is very important – sets in motion a whole chain of
conditional reflexes revolving around modernity. The social-qualitative
character of these reflexes, their purposefulness, is determined by the whole
aggregate of the class self-consciousness of the listener, which is pre-
existing. Here is a rough example: when listening to *Pacific* [*231*], a progressive worker imagines Western transport workers on strike, thinks about the
significance of transport in the industrialization of the USSR etc., while the
former shareholder of the Nicholas Railway will be reminded by this music
about the present dictatorship of the proletariat. Both listeners' wills will be
charged respectively. On the contrary, the strong *narodnik* tendency of the
music of the Mighty Handful and its epigones, which is now cultivated
here, awakens conditional and unconditional reflexes of yesterday – for
instance, a worker who has not yet been boiled in the factory pot for long
enough is drawn back under the influence of narrow-minded ideas and
limited images of rural culture, or of the "cretinism of village life", as Karl
Marx put it.[24]

But perhaps the author of the manifesto was too hasty in lumping RAPM
together with Kuchka epigonism: their merger was by no means complete in
1930. This is clear from the paper that a RAPM member Viktor Belïy gave at the
First Conference on National Music (1931), where he exposed the "reactionary
and bureaucratic great-power faction" of conservative Russian composers
who were, according to him, fostering a pernicious Kuchka exoticism in
some of the Soviet Republics:

> The faction I have mentioned directs the development of the cadres of
> national composers along the course of Russification, a course that is acad-
> emicist and which produces epigones. Everyone knows the creative face of
> this faction's representatives: it can be described as an impoverished edition
> of the Mighty Handful . . .

> This faction . . . has created an Oriental style. . . . This is an emasculated
> Orient, ridden with rickets, which [is reduced to] the notorious interval of
> the augmented second . . .[25]

> The worst thing is when some specimens of "monumental", but clichéd and
> reactionary operatic "culture" from the centre are taken as a model [in the
> Republics]. [26]

To provide a positive finale to his paper, Belïy quotes one of Stalin's recent slogans, exhorting Soviet culture workers to strive for a culture that would be "national in form, proletarian in content". Belïy presents this as the antidote to the pernicious developments he has exposed, a glorious new hope for the national musical cultures of the Republics. The quote from Stalin was no doubt an astute move (the leadership cult was beginning to take off), but it would be of little benefit to Belïy since just a few years later, the objects of his contempt, those monumental Oriental operas in the Kuchka style, were officially designated as the true musical embodiment of Stalin's idea.

"National in form, socialist in content"

During the 1920s, the various musical organizations in Russia paid little attention to the musical culture of the non-Russian nationalities; nor did central government have any effect, since it refrained, as a matter of principle, from actively shaping the course of the arts even in Russia. In the 1930s, on the contrary, the deliberate and systematic development of the national cultures was placed at the heart of Stalin's cultural policy and, as we shall argue, this to a great extent defined the musical face of Socialist Realism.

The new directive was made public at the beginning of 1934 as "The development of cultures national in form and socialist in content";[27] Stalin's slogan was given pride of place in every newspaper and journal, including, of course, *Sovetskaya Muzïka*, the new official serious music journal (the only one permitted at this stage).[28] The slogan itself was not new: its first appearance was in a speech of Stalin's from as far back as 1925, although with "proletarian" in place of "socialist" (Belïy's RAPM speech quoted it in this version). On that occasion, Stalin had elaborated the meaning of "proletarian" culture for the national minorities in his characteristically repetitive manner:

We are building proletarian culture. This is absolutely right. But proletarian culture, which is socialist in its content, takes on different forms and means of expression with the different peoples who have been drawn into socialist construction, depending on differences of language, lifestyle, etc. Proletarian in content and national in form, this is the pan-human culture that socialism is moving towards. Proletarian culture does not cancel out national culture, but provides it with content. And vice versa: national culture does not cancel out proletarian culture, but provides it with form. The slogan of national culture was a bourgeois slogan when the bourgeoisie was in power and the consolidation of a nation took place under the aegis of the bourgeois way of life. But now that the proletariat has come to power, the slogan of bourgeois culture has become a proletarian slogan, and the consolidation of a nation is taking place under the aegis of the Soviet power. [29]

This statement remained authoritative for the remainder of Stalin's rule. The change from "proletarian" to "socialist" was only intended as an acknowledgement of changed circumstances: the collectivization of agriculture had brought an end to private property holding among the peasants, turning them into agricultural workers, thereby dissolving the proletarian/peasant class distinction. The following passage from the Communist Manifesto is interesting in connection with Stalin's slogan:

> Though not in content, yet in form, the struggle of the proletariat is at first a national struggle.[30]

It would seem that Stalin simply slotted "culture" in place of "struggle" in order to provide himself with a resonant phrase with a familiar and respectable aura – no matter that the original had no bearing on Stalin's subject-matter. Where Marx and Engels urgently desired to persuade their readership with arguments and facts, Stalin can afford simply to play with words – at this stage he could usually impose his will without any need to persuade.

At the same time, the term "Socialist Realism" had come into circulation, beginning in the literary sphere and then spreading to the other arts. Against all the innovations in poetry, the novel and theatre of the '20s, there was to be a return to what Soviet modernists would once have decried as nineteenth-century bourgeois realism (they now knew they should keep their mouths shut). This was the "realism" in "Socialist Realism" – it was certainly not to be taken as an exhortation to hold a mirror up to the world that Stalin had created. Good Socialist Realist artists were to depict the world as it was seen through *partiynost'* (Party consciousness), with a view to the "glorious future". The "socialism" was simply whatever served to glorify Stalin and his works; at some times this meant blatant Stalin worship, decked out with religious imagery, while at other times the devices were more subtle and indirect. Both parts of the formula could be transferred without much trouble to painting, sculpture and film. But music posed a problem. With purely instrumental music, and with much non-dramatic texted music, it made little sense to ask what realism would be, let alone socialist realism. Opera was somewhat less problematic – there was the "realist" tradition of Musorgsky – but even here the very notion of people singing where in reality they would not caused problems: the idea of a singing Stalin on stage was altogether unacceptable (whereas actors could portray Stalin in films).

But in conjunction with the slogan "national in form, socialist in content" the problem was eventually overcome. Since Socialist Realism was effectively "realist in form, socialist in content", composers were able to substitute nationalism for realism without adding anything extraneous to Stalin's instructions. Once it was established that realist music implied folk music, composers were able to work with the same speed and confidence as other artists. Russian and native composers in the non-Russian republics were able to take advantage of this understanding first, but as Russian nationalism gathered apace, composers working in Russia were also able to turn towards folk-music – as filtered through the Kuchka's nationalism, of course. Since the peasants had been transformed into workers, folk music was now above suspicion. There were other, classicizing devices available to composers under Socialist Realism, and the Beethovenian narrative of victory won through struggle was still *de rigueur* for large-scale works, but the use of folk music was the single most prominent strand of musical Socialist Realism (one could hardly deduce this from Shostakovich's music, but Shostakovich was exceptional in this respect).

But the creation of music that was national in form, socialist in content could not be left to the ad hoc activities of individual composers. The construction of musical repertoires for the non-Russian nations was organized in accordance with the administrative status of each national territory within the Union. National republics were set the target of building a national opera house (where this did not already exist) and creating a repertoire for it – certainly several operas with spoken dialogue, but also at least one all-sung, large-scale opera. This was to be achieved by the end of the '30s. This applied equally to all the national republics, whether Georgia, which had an opera house and concert halls of several decades standing, or the Central Asian republics, where these institutions were previously unknown. Autonomous republics were expected to produce a full compendium of their folksong repertoire; beyond this, they might receive an overture or two from Russian composers. And so the task was reduced in scope at each lower rung; the bureaucrats and composers only admitted defeat in the case of some purely nomadic peoples in far-flung districts.

Here are some of the results for various republics (extracted from the *Muzïkal'naya entsiklopediya*, 1973–82), allowing us to see how determinedly they were kept abreast of each other, in spite of very different cultural histories:

Azerbaijan: presentation of national operas at the 1938 *Dekada* (a 10-day festival) of national art in Moscow;[31] in the same year the Azerbaijani Opera was awarded the Order or Lenin and was provided with a newly-refurbished theatre seating 1281.

Armenia: presentation of national operas at the 1939 *Dekada*; in the same year the Armenian Opera was awarded the Order of Lenin, and in 1940 it was provided with a new theatre seating 1130.

Belorussia: presentation of national operas at the 1940 *Dekada*; in the same year the Belorussian Opera was awarded the Order of Lenin, while in 1938 it had already received a new theatre seating 1200.

Georgia: presentation of national operas at the 1937 *Dekada*; in the same year the Georgian Opera was awarded the Order of Lenin (no new theatre was provided, since Tbilisi already possessed a fine opera house dating from 1894).

Kirghizstan: presentation of national operas at the 1939 *Dekada*; in the same year the Kirghiz Opera was awarded the Order of Lenin, but only in 1955 was it provided with a new theatre seating 941 (this was because the Kirghiz Studio for Music and Drama had only been founded in 1937, and a fully-fledged opera company only emerged in 1942).

Kazakhstan: presentation of a national opera already at the first ever *Dekada*, in 1936 (after only three years of operatic experience); the Kazakh Opera was awarded the Order of Lenin only in 1958, after its second *Dekada* appearance (this was because the long established Ukrainian Opera also appeared at the 1936 *Dekada*, and won the Order of Lenin that year); the company was provided with a new theatre in 1941.

Where Western musical traditions and institutions were weak or non-existent, as was the case in the Central Asian Republics, Russians were sent out to oversee the task, or even to carry it out themselves. Not only were opera houses and conservatoires built to Russian specifications, but members of the Composers' Unions of Moscow and Leningrad had to write numerous pieces themselves, including entire operas. Architects, instrumental and vocal teachers, composers, librettists, and so on, were sent out, their activities closely coordinated by Moscow, in much the same way that teams of Russian experts and workers would be sent out to construct a hydro-electric power station in a Central Asian Republic. And like the power station, the resulting national musical culture was supposed to be something that would be of general benefit to the Soviet Union – it was supported by the "unanimous Soviet public opinion on musical matters" (as *Sovetskaya Muzïka* put it).[32]

The results were sometimes bizarre beyond any expectation: a team of three composers, two Russians and a Kirghiz, jointly wrote six operas, as well as several ballets and symphonic works styling themselves with their combined surnames "Vlasov-Fere-Maldïbayev". Another composer, Balasanyan, was of Armenian descent, but was born in Turkmenistan; yet he took up neither of these nationalities and instead became the leading Tajik national composer. Reinhold Glière, after collecting every available award for composing the first Azerbaijani national opera, moved on to Uzbekistan, where Moscow thought his experience and talents were most urgently needed. Almost every Soviet composer was soon to become involved in this campaign; it was not merely the preserve of opportunistic mediocrities. By way of illustration, consider the careers of Mosolov and Roslavets, who had been leading Soviet modernists during the '20s. Roslavets, constantly harried by RAPM, eventually had to seek work outside of Moscow; as a result he spent the years 1931–3 in Tashkent, contributing to some of the earliest examples of Uzbek music theatre. Roslavets busied himself harmonizing folksongs for these productions, and composed the Uzbek ballet *Pakhta* (Cotton); he also produced a string quartet on themes from neighbouring Turkmenistan during this period. Mosolov's engagement with the Central Asian republics is more complicated, since he had developed a spontaneous interest in Turkmen folk music in the mid-1920s, when RAPM had little or no power to obstruct his career. The finale of his Fifth Piano Sonata (1926) is a rendering of two folk songs, one Turkmen, one Russian, without in any way compromising his robustly modernist style; two years later, in a similar vein, he composed the piano suite *Turkmenian Nights* in 1928. A decade later, he was still using such musical material, as in his Turkmen and Uzbek suites of 1936, but the results were very different. In the '20s examples, he was acting as a free agent, in a manner comparable to Bartók, while in the mid-'30s he was responding to Stalin's call for national music in the republics. In the two suites, he had clearly tried to purge himself of his modernist predilections, but for all his efforts the authorities were still not satisfied. It is only from the late '30s onwards that we find his style settling irreversibly into a thoroughly anonymous Socialist Realist manner. His experiences in a labour camp had in all probability broken his will to maintain any artistic individuality (even though the charge was not connected to his music). The remainder of Mosolov's catalogue of works consists largely of patriotic cantatas and further (but much blander) national suites based on the folk songs from many regions of the USSR, resulting from his many "business trips" *(komandirovki)* and "folklore expeditions".

The case of Shostakovich is of special interest: in 1936, after the publication of denunciatory articles in *Pravda*, Shostakovich went to see Platon Kerzhentsev, chairman of the Committee for Artistic Affairs, who had quite possibly been the instigator of the denunciations.[33] Among other things, Kerzhentsev advised him to follow "the example of Rimsky-Korsakov", and "travel around villages of the Soviet Union transcribing the folksongs of Russia, Ukraine, Belorussia and Georgia; then to choose some and to harmonize the hundred best" (never mind that in reality Rimsky-Korsakov never ventured out into the field).³⁴ Although Shostakovich was anxious to restore his standing within the Soviet Union, he did not follow this particular course. Yet he did not manage to avoid the trend completely: in 1963, he wrote an overture on Russian and Kirghiz themes, dedicated to the "friendship" of the two nations. There was also the much more embarrassing Suite on Finnish Folk Themes of 1939, which was commissioned to celebrate the Soviet invasion of Finland; Shostakovich later managed to conceal the existence of this work, which was only rediscovered in 2000.³⁵ Much better known, however, is the song cycle *From Jewish Folk Poetry* (1948), although its inclusion in the category of the officially encouraged "national" work is contended. On the one hand, it is possible that Shostakovich deliberately chose his Jewish subject matter in order to display solidarity with Soviet Jewry; at the time, Jews in the higher echelons of Soviet society suspected they were facing a covert policy of discrimination (the overt campaign against "cosmopolitanism" only emerged several months later, when the work was promptly withdrawn). On the other hand, the relatively light character of the cycle and the presence of some official propaganda verses suggest that Shostakovich intended the work as an example of the officially encouraged genre. Indeed, the Jewish cycle is very close in character, form and scoring to the earlier Finnish Suite.

Folk material, for most other composers, provided a much-needed degree of safety. Without folk material, composers knew that there was only the narrowest stretch of dry land between "formalism" on the one side, and banality on the other. Both faults were equally open to condemnation, the former because it ignored the (supposed) needs of the people, the latter because it patronized and underestimated the people. But the use of folk material greatly decreased the likelihood that a composer would suffer either of these criticisms. At the end of the '30s, one critic even suggested, in effect, that art music should always draw upon folk music if it was to have any legitimacy:

> All great masters, all great composers of the past (of all peoples, without exception!) started out from [folk music]. And, on the contrary, those who were locked in a narrow world of shallow, subjective feelings, and who tried to "create [music] out of their own selves" – eventually found they had departed from the culture of the people. Their false creations were rejected by the people, because the people will never tolerate a fraud.³⁶

Similar pronouncements began to appear in the press with threatening regularity, each time persuading more composers that it was in their interests to write music that was national in form, socialist in content.

There were also many positive inducements: composers who devoted themselves to the music of the republics found that the commissions never dried up, and awards were much easier to come by. They could embark on frequent expenses-paid "business trips" to a chosen republic or region, with VIP status on arrival and gifts from local government officials. Those who chose to stay longer became local celebrities, with a lifestyle to match. These privileges sometimes led to corruption: in one case brought to the attention of the Composers' Union, a composer Rechmensky had been invited to one of the republics to act as judge in a national music competition; Rechmensky decided to submit his own works for consideration, and duly became the proud recipient of no less than four awards.[37]

The political importance attached to national works ensured that several featured in each year's list of candidates for the Stalin Prizes in music. Examining the prizewinners during this period, it seems quite clear that national works were not measured by the same standards as other music. Here, for example, is Solomon Mikhoels speaking as an advocate for Shteynberg's Symphony-Rhapsody on Uzbek Themes at a plenary session of the Stalin Prize Committee in 1943 (the Committee drew members from all the arts) – note the rather backhanded or apologetic terms of praise:

> The history of this Symphony-Rhapsody is interesting. The secretary of the Uzbek Central Committee Yusupov called Shteynberg and offered him to write a symphonic work based on Uzbek folk tunes, so that not a single note be changed in them and that every Uzbek could recognize these tunes, so that the tunes are not developed too far, but some symphonic devices are used all the same. And he set him a shockworker's deadline. If we take all of this into account, the work turned out wonderfully. Of course, it is not a [truly] symphonic work, it is a rhapsody, a parade of many tunes ... Very imposing. With the use of a great number of national instruments. After the hearing it made such an effect that Cmrd. Yusupov invited the intelligentsia who were present to speak out, and then climbed the stage himself, hugged and kissed the composer. It was a celebration in full sense of the word. There is a fierce debate going on there at the moment between their local "Slavophiles" [i.e. their defenders of traditional values] and Westernizers [i.e. followers of the Moscow line]. And here, in this sense, it was a fight: how to inculcate European mastery [in Uzbeks] so that it would be accessible to Uzbek listeners. Yusupov says this: if an Uzbek is listening to music and does not sway, then the music did not make an effect. He himself also sways while listening.[38]

Mikhoels seems in little doubt that Shteynberg's piece lacked various qualities that would otherwise have been expected of a symphonic work nominated for a Stalin Prize; but this is not the point – it is being judged by the criteria appropriate to national music, hence the great emphasis on the positive reactions of Uzbek listeners. In this particular case, the composer of the national work was highly proficient in all technical areas (Shteynberg had been a favoured pupil of Rimsky-Korsakov, and also became his mentor's son-in-law). But in many other cases, the technical adequacy of nominated works, and even of prize-winners, was doubtful. There was a tendency to use the prize as an encouragement to indigenous composers of the republics; in the case of the central Asian republics, it would have taken a decade or more before polished conservatoire composers could have been produced, but the Committee preferred to reward ambition and effort at an earlier stage.

At this point, we shall explore the case of Uzbekistan in more detail; the development of Uzbek opera usefully serves to illustrate the predicament of the Central Asian republics. *Sovetskaya Muzïka*, in 1934, discussed the progress made so far: in the new theatre, Uzbek musicians involved in the opera project had put together a repertoire of spoken plays interspersed with monodic songs, accompanied by Uzbek instruments.[39] Now they were faced with the much more daunting task of creating continuously-sung operas out of the plays.

Due to the maturing expectations of the Uzbek audience, the further matter of harmonizing opera arises, since the most cultured among the Uzbeks can no longer be satisfied with unison music. This issue appears ever more frequently on our agenda. It is mentioned in the resolution on Comrade Ikramov's paper at the 5th Session of the Uzbek Communist Party Central Committee. Some steps are being taken in that direction: European instruments are being added to the orchestra, and the harmonization of several numbers is underway. A piano accompaniment is being introduced, sometimes composed for the whole piece [i.e. for all the songs] (e.g. Roslavets, *Uttan Parchalyar*).

In 1933–34 the work on harmonization took on the character of a mass-production process. Comrade Mironov, who was invited to do this job, is filling the operas *Arshin mal alan*, *Purtana* and others with harmonized numbers.

The next step to which [the listener previously unfamiliar with Western music] will ascend is the ability to take in harmonic music. But for the further evolution of Uzbek opera, harmonization alone will not suffice. The spectator will not be satisfied by emotional empathy alone: he will demand the reconstruction of the very musical forms constituting the opera – arias, choruses, finales. At present there still is absolutely no recitative, which remains unassimilated by Uzbek singers: immediately after singing, their characters switch back to spoken dialogue.[40]

By 1937, for the second of the *Dekadï* festivals, Uzbekistan was ready to present its achievements in Moscow. There was now a repertoire of ten plays with music, all billed as operas, although some merited the label better than others. The earliest piece in their repertoire was merely an adaptation of Hajibeyov's Azerbaijani operetta *Arshin mal alan*. A later, entirely original addition, *Farkhad and Shirin*, was the work of several hands: first the Russian ethnomusicologist Uspensky notated three thousand bars of folk music, which guest composers Mushel and Tsveifel then harmonized and orchestrated – such procedures were quite common. With each new work added to the repertoire, the amount of spoken dialogue was reduced, and there was a clear trend away from the original reliance on the traditional song repertoire and traditional instruments. One of the most recent, Glière's *Gyul'sara* was written for large symphony orchestra and began with an imposing overture. Nevertheless, the items in this variegated repertoire were placed on an equal footing when they were performed in Moscow, and seemed to enjoy a uniformly warm reception. In a review of the Uzbek festival, the critic Georgy Khubov (a model of Party orthodoxy) bestowed high praise on the art of Uzbek opera, which even in its infancy compared favourably with "the operatic inventions of the consumptive art of Western formalists".[41] Khubov then deftly applied one of Stalin's favourite similes to his subject: "Like Antheus, revitalized by Mother Earth herself, Uzbek art gains strength from the juices of the native soil."

Thanks to the rebuilding of Russian nationalism, the heyday of the itinerant "guest composer" was already past by the late 1930s; but while the majority turned their attentions towards "Russian" music, some decided to take up permanent residence in their adoptive republics. For example, Yevgeny Brusilovsky, who had founded Kazakh national opera, continued his work in Kazakhstan through to the 1950s, by which time the first generation of native composers had graduated from conservatoire. In the post-Stalin years, some of the republics preferred to forget about their Russian "guest-composers": in Azerbaijan, this even meant the complete exclusion of the once-celebrated Glière from their music-history texts. Nevertheless, the lasting influence of these "guests" on indigenous composers was undeniable. Over the years, although the initial impetus and overall control lay with Moscow, the growing intelligentsia in the national republics, and eventually the population at large accepted these national cultures as their own. This should not be so very surprising – the "national cultures" that developed around the world during the nineteenth and twentieth centuries were generally marked both by a high degree of artifice, and strenuous efforts to obscure this artifice. It was only in the late '80s, when many of the national republics began to strain against Moscow's control that the national cultures were re-examined. Even then, there could be no turning the clocks back to pre-Stalin times, since what had been large peasant or even nomadic societies were now modern industrialized states.

Whose nationalism?

The development of national musical cultures in the republics was soon expected to follow the model of nineteenth-century Russian nationalist music. According to the narrative provided by Stasov and the Kuchka, and now revived in Stalin's Soviet Union, Russian nationalist music began with Glinka's two operas; accordingly, the national republics should all produce their own national operas. But the task did not end here, for these operas were also expected to fit one or other of the two genres the Kuchka had derived from Glinka: namely, the heroic drama of the people, and the national epic. *A Life for the Tsar*, now re-worked as *Ivan Susanin* (1939), provided the archetype for the first genre, and here an element of class struggle was particularly encouraged; *Ruslan and Lyudmila* provided the archetype for the latter genre. As soon as the operatic projects of the national republics had passed the experimental stage, each new work was measured against the yardstick of the Russian classics: for example, the Azerbaijani national opera *Keroglu* by Uzeir Hajibeyov was officially acknowledged as a successful embodiment of the national-epic type;[42] if there was any flaw, it was the lack of a monumental overture in the manner of *Prince Igor*.[43]

The Central Asian republics, of course, stood at one extreme, while the Western republics of Ukraine and Belorussia stood at the other. In the middle, both in geographical and developmental terms, were the three Caucasian republics, which all possessed major cities that had seen industrialization in the late tsarist period. The industrialization was accompanied by an influx of Russians: not only workers, but also a substantial middle class of engineers, managers and civil servants, who brought Western cultural practices with them. And so the Georgians had their first national opera by 1908, and the Armenians by 1918; the composers, respectively Paliashvili and Spendiarov, had both completed their education St Petersburg. The Azeris, however, were not cultivated in the same way by tsarist governments, which had found the Christian Georgians and Armenians more congenial subjects. But the discovery of oil in the Caspian transformed Baku into an oil port of major economic importance. It is particularly interesting to look at the cultural policies of the '20s administration in Baku, since it provides evidence that Russification could sometimes take place in the absence of Russian pressure. Firstly, the Bolshevik administration in post-Civil War Baku was not dominated by ethnic Russians – as mentioned above, Lenin sought to avoid any reproduction of the "Great Russian chauvinism" of the late tsarist era.

Secondly, Moscow during the pre-Stalinist period had no particular interest in the details of the republics' arts policies (as opposed to such broad matters as progress towards universal literacy). Given these circumstances, it is remarkable that the ethnically Azeri Minister of Education in Baku, Mustafa Kuliyev, introduced musical reforms in the mid-'20s which closely prefigured those imposed by Stalin a decade later.

In the years prior to Kuliyev, there were already some rudimentary attempts to shoehorn Azeri music into the framework of opera. The solo improvisations of the *mugamat* tradition were strung together within a narrative and performed on stage, and the result was labeled "*mugam* opera". There were some harmonized sections, but the results did little more than to highlight the incongruity of two very different musical traditions. In 1924, Kuliyev initiated a long-running discussion on the state of opera in the press. He disparaged *mugam* opera for what he saw as its artistic and technical shortcomings, and called for a thorough modernization of opera in Azerbaijan. Another feature of his campaign which anticipated later practices under Stalin was the appearance of "spontaneous" support in the letters pages of the newspapers from oil and railway workers, who had suddenly discovered an urgent need for "real opera": "We need new Azerbaijani operas", "Cultured modern opera or nothing", "Ban the old *mugam* opera", and "Türk opera must go, along with the Arabic alphabet and the yashmak!"[44]

Again anticipating Stalin's national-culture project of the following decade, Kuliyev imported composers to speed up the process of Westernization. This is why the first of the Soviet national operas Glière's *Shahsenem*, graced the Baku opera season of 1927, at a time when opera could hardly have been further from Stalin's mind (he was preoccupied with foreign trade relations and the crushing of the Opposition at the time). Glière's career up to this point was a combination of some quite disparate strands: he had been a nationalist follower of the Kuchka, a Wagnerian (the Third Symphony), and more recently the composer of *The Red Poppy*, a celebrated Soviet ballet in a very light, popular style. None of this prepared him for Kuliyev's commission, but he set about the task conscientiously, studying the various folk sources made available to him, and provided Kuliyev with a solid foundation for his project.

Kuliyev argued tirelessly for the need to abandon the legacy of Persian cultural dominion, and for its replacement by the radical Westernization of musical culture along Russian lines. But unlike the Stalin of the '30s, Kuliyev could not simply rule by fiat, and he had to contend with the arguments of various opponents. One of the principal contentions against Kuliyev's project was that the Azeri scales, with their characteristic tuning system, constituted an insurmountable obstacle to the Westernization of their music. But Kuliyev was undaunted:

Some of our musicians are forever repeating that Türk songs cannot be transcribed within the European system. But Russian or German songs cannot be fitted into the European twelve-note temperament either. . . . And yet this never prevented Russian music from adopting the foundations and techniques of European music wholesale, or from developing them to such heights as we find in Glinka.[45]

The argument of Kuliyev's opponents was quite correct within its own terms, but failed to address Kuliyev's position. His opponents, he says, could not make a special case for Azeri music without implying that the concert and operatic traditions of Europe and Russia were to an equal extent distortions of their respective folk music traditions. One could challenge this where European music is concerned, since its dependence on folk traditions, as Kuliyev supposes, is far from clear. But it is only Russia that is of real importance for Kuliyev, and here he has a stronger case, since the Kuchka insisted that Russian national music was of necessity rooted in Russian folk music. The Kuchka and their followers had never acknowledged any discrepancy between the songs they heard sung by peasants and the transcribed versions of those songs, and their rendition on the equal-tempered piano, and yet where some of the Russian traditions were concerned, this discrepancy was no less glaring than in the case of Azeri music. But it was quite irrelevant for Kuliyev that the Kuchka's folk roots were only a central plank of their mythology – Russia had led the way, whether it was in political revolution or in music, and there Azerbaijan should follow.

In the 1930s, Moscow therefore had no need to impose its Russian model on the development of Azerbaijani music, since Kuliyev and his supporters had already embraced it. News of the Azerbaijani project soon passed beyond the bounds of the Soviet Union: the new Turkey of Atatürk noted the success of Glière's *Shahsenem* in Baku. Atatürk was sufficiently impressed to invite Glière to Turkey, with the hope that a Turkish *Shahsenem* would result. In the end, Glière never came, but Turkey managed to enlist the services of two prestigious modernists, Bartók and Hindemith. A group of Turkish nationalist composers, styling themselves as the Kuchka of their nation, now expressed the "Turkish soul" in the manner of Hindemith and Bartók;[46] there can be little doubt that they would have been equally ready to adopt the manner of Glière had he taken up Atatürk's commission.

The attractions of Russian musical nationalism as a model are not hard to see. The Russian project was unique in many respects. It embraced composers of several generations, with a significant degree of continuity and common purpose. It set itself ambitious goals in creating a national musical language, and this was acknowledged at home and abroad as a success. And, not least, it produced rich and diverse artistic results. Much as the Kuchka imagined that emulating Glinka guaranteed the authentic Russianness of their works, so in the following century nationalist composers elsewhere assumed that the Russian model would enable them to arrive at equally authentic results. Not only did they base their nationalist projects on the same romantic premise – the primacy of folk music – but they were also prepared to borrow the techniques used by Russians to assimilate their folk material, and they even employed some of the very same stylistic devices that Russian composers had supposedly derived from Russian folksong (but which were more likely to have come from Schumann or Liszt).

As an example, let us take one of the founding fathers of Armenian national music, Alexander Spendiarov. His family was Armenian, but Spendiarov himself was born in the Crimea, and his musical education was European/ Russian, with Rimsky-Korsakov as his most distinguished teacher. Although he lacked a background in Armenian music, and even though he never troubled himself to learn the language of his forebears, in the 1910s he devoted himself to the study of Armenian folk music, with a view to creating a national music for Armenia. His efforts culminated in the opera *Almast* (1918), which was later treated as a worthy precursor to the national operas produced under Stalin's cultural policies, although the density of Spendiarov's style was subjected to some mild criticism.[47] In the mid-1920s, Spendiarov published the following nationalist appeal (note that at this stage Georgia, Armenia and Azerbaijan were still incorporated within a Transcaucasian federal republic):

European music is already too refined; it has offered us everything it can. It has nothing more to say and, to compensate for a lack of anything new, it has to resort to various musical tricks. In order to introduce something fresh, Western musicians turn to the East, and rightly so.

I cannot understand why so many of our musicians sitting in Baku, Tbilisi, and Yerevan conduct their search while facing in the wrong direction. To arouse any interest in Europe [at present], an Armenian, Azerbaijani or Georgian composer must display a talent at least the equal of Scriabin's. Nevertheless, a moderately gifted musician, if he were to move in the right [i.e. nationalist] direction, would achieve results sufficient to arouse interest in Europe.[48]

It is amusing to encounter familiar rhetorical strategies in a new context: the nineteenth-century Russian nationalist opposition between old Europe and young Russia is now, in the hands of this professional Armenian, generalized into the opposition old West/young East. Spendiarov also evidently imagined that if Europeans enjoyed the music of Russian Orientalism, then they would enjoy the true music of the Orient even better. This last point was, of course, no longer relevant in the '30s or '40s, when most Soviet composers could no longer entertain any hope of reaching an audience beyond the borders of the USSR.

There are indeed many such parallels to be found in the literature of musical nationalism in the Republics, sometimes created quite deliberately, at other times unconscious. The Russian nationalists, to take another example, left a large and entirely spurious discourse arguing that the modes of Russian folksong had their origins in the modes of Ancient Greece. And so the national composers and musicologists of the Republics did likewise; even in a very late Soviet-era book on Turkmen music, F. Abukova stated that the "synthesis of Turkmen modes with the major–minor system" was easily achieved owing to the closeness of the Turkmen modes to those of the Greeks, and she labelled the resulting hybrids "Phrygian" and "Locrian".[49] Or to take a further example, the fact that Russian nationalist composers and writers had assumed (wrongly) that Russian folksong was monodic meant that the problems of harmonizing such material had already been explored at length, again providing a Russian model for the national composers of the Republics as they attempted to assimilate what was often genuinely monodic material. Harmonization was, of course, a non-negotiable, defining element of the national music projects, just as it had been the defining element of the original Russian nationalist project. Here is the advice of the Azerbaijani national composer Hajibeyov on the subject of harmonization:

> The unskilled harmonization of an Azerbaijani melody may change its character, neutralize its modality and even vulgarize it. But this does not mean that Azerbaijani music should forever remain monodic. . . . Polyphony should be based not on correct chord progressions or harmonic cadences that require changes in modal structure, but rather on the combination of logically constructed independent melodies.[50]

In the accompanying example that Hajibeyov provided (Ex.6.1), the same melody is harmonized first in what Hajibeyov considers the wrong manner (albeit correct by conservatoire standards), and then second in a manner that Hajibeyov considers appropriate for the melody. But on what grounds does he make this judgement? While his prose suggests that he favoured a more contrapuntal approach, the two examples vary little in this respect. Instead, his guiding principle is the studied avoidance of anything that he felt would render the harmonization too obviously Western in style. He achieves this by three principal means: he treats fourths as consonances; he allows a subordinate line to merge with the melody in places; and he replaces the characteristic

6.1 Hajibeyov, two harmonizations of an Azerbaijani melody

harmonies of the minor mode with the flattened 7th and natural 6th of the Dorian mode. Hajibeyov was thereby following a distinguished precedent, namely the *via negativa* of Russian nationalist music, first expressed by Odoyevsky, and cultivated to brilliant effect by the Kuchka. This was the principle used to distinguish between the earlier, supposedly artificial folksong harmonizations of the Lvov–Prach collection, and the supposedly natural or authentic harmonizations of Balakirev's collection. The same phenomenon recurred in the republics during the 1930s; in the case of Spendiarov's Armenia, the *via negativa* was behind the denigration of the earlier Kara–Murza collection, to the benefit of the later Komitas collection. Of course the principle itself was rarely spelt out, since this would have given the game away; it was more normal, both in the nineteenth- and twentieth-century cases, to bury the principle behind rhetoric claiming that somehow a given repertoire of folk melodies contained certain harmonic implications which could be deduced by musicians whose sensibilities were sufficiently rooted in the nation's soil. In each case, the application of the *via negativa* principle eventually led to the emergence of various positive devices which composers could freely use to create further authentic national music.

Many of these parallels arose from the assumptions of the Moscow and Leningrad composers, as they worked out how they could provide the required "fraternal assistance" to their colleagues in the Republics. Take, for example, the group of composers Vlasov-Fere-Maldïbayev who worked on the national-music project of the Kirghiz Republic. For their first full-blown opera, *Ai-churek*, the Kirghiz member of the collective, Maldïbayev, had provided transcriptions of original folk material, and had also composed some melodies in a similar style. But Maldïbayev's role was only to furnish his Muscovite colleagues with raw material which they could refine and shape into the required opera. In order to devise a Kirghiz style true to the monodies Maldïbayev had given them, they turned to the old Kuchka strategy that

Rimsky-Korsakov had revealed in the candour of his later years: namely, the consistent avoidance of anything that pointed too obviously to Western traditions – whatever positive devices replaced them was then an arbitrary matter.[51] Vlasov and Fere accordingly purged themselves of a great many ingrained compositional techniques, and instead adopted devices such as doubling the given melody in fourths, and their composed bass-line in fifths. This owed nothing to Kirghiz music, but it successfully distanced their music from the characteristic sounds of Western harmony.[52] The result of this approach can be seen in Ex.6.2.

6.2   Vlasov-Fere-Maldïbayev, *Ai-churek*, Act II: orchestral introduction to Ai-churek's tale

Although the negative way was thus passed on from the Russian nationalists to the national composers of the Republics, the peculiarities of the Russian nationalist style were to be treated as somehow neutral. Consistency with the Kuchka's principle (which admittedly were far from watertight) would have required the avoidance of Russian styles just as much as any other European styles, but the political circumstances were hardly conducive to such scruples. Glinka was even depicted as the father of all musical nationalism, and so anything that stemmed from him, or by extension from the Kuchka, was above suspicion. The consistent use of ♭6 within the major, the use of chromatic counterpoint to accompany diatonic melodies, and, above all, the changing-background variation technique – these Russian nationalist devices all found a home in the national operas of the Republics. In the Caucasus, they featured *inter alia* in Paliashvili's *Abesalom y Eteri* and *Daisi* (Georgia), Spendiarov's *Almast* (Armenia), and Glière's *Shahsenem* (Azerbaijan); in Central Asia they can be heard in Brusilovsky's *Zhalbïr* (Kazakhstan) and *Gyul'sara* (Uzbekistan), and *Ai-churek* (Kirghizstan). Another characteristic feature is the adoption of Rimsky-Korsakovian means for evoking the mysterious or fantastic: in *Ai-churek*, for example, the appearance of the dervishes is signalled by the contrary chromatic motion and parallel thirds of Example 6.3. Sometimes, surprisingly, we are reminded not of the Kuchka directly, but of the Kuchka's lesser epigones. In Chapter 5, we saw how Olenin, a student of Balakirev's, followed the negative principle with austere rigour, except at moments of greatest dramatic tension, when he inexplicably lapsed into conventional Western four-part harmony with dominant sevenths. Likewise, to the detriment of *Ai-churek*, we find the same device re-appearing: at first, the opera's eponymous heroine sings a Kirghiz-style melody with "appropriate" harmonization, but when she "joyfully embraces her friends", we are given the characteristic textures and progressions of Western harmony (Ex.6.4).

6.3   Vlasov-Fere-Maldïbayev, *Ai-churek*, Act II: Kalïyman and other girls drive away the witch and dervishes

Orientalism

The artificial environment and the forced pace took their toll on the musical results: the national operas of the republics rarely rise beyond the level of the Kuchka's more pedestrian writing, and often fall well below this. But they filled the immediate purpose eminently well – they played their role in the larger project of absorbing the nationalist aspirations of each republic's intelligentsia, thereby minimizing any resistance to Stalin's rule from this quarter (it was only during the period of economic crisis and relative freedom of the late 1980s that the intelligentsias of the republics decisively turned away from Moscow). Nationalism among the colonized peoples of an empire is normally an expression of opposition to the imperial power, a desire for economic and political independence, which in turn generates the various aspects of nationalist culture; Stalin effectively offered the republics nationalist culture while closing the door on these economic and political aspirations (Moscow was, of course, developing the republics industrially, but only as integral parts of the Soviet economy).

6.4 Vlasov-Fere-Maldïbayev, *Ai-churek*, Act II: Ai-churek joyfully embraces Kalïyman and the girls

The culture of Russian nationalism, on the other hand, arose in a very different context. During the nineteenth century, although the Russian intelligentsia certainly sensed the backwardness of Russia in relation to the Western European powers, Russia was itself an empire still in the process of expansion. Nationalism within an imperial power displays itself in the cultural domain (since such a power already has its economic and political autonomy). In this context, nationalist culture not only exalts the nation in which it arises, but also patronizes or demonizes the peoples within its imperial reach (depending, respectively, on whether those peoples are acquiescing or resisting at a given moment). The concept of Orientalism, as formulated by Edward Said, deals with precisely this phenomenon.[53] The colonized peoples, if they have largely acquiesced, are represented through exotic fantasies, most often with stereotypes of femininity, and erotic associations. The fact that the republics' cultural nationalism was largely initiated and controlled by the imperial power is reflected in the otherwise puzzling retention of Russian Orientalism in the national music of the republics.

The "nationalism" of the republics therefore mixes aspects of both the normal manifestations of nationalism – unsurprisingly, since we have already seen that the imperial power in this case directed the national cultures of its dependents along safe channels. Those indigenous artists who helped to create their national culture were also in part products of the imperial power's education system, they shared many of its values, and remained aware that their careers and positions remained dependent on Moscow's approval. A further complication lies in the fact that the relationship between Russia and the national republics changed significantly between the end of the Civil War and the Constitution of 1936; Stalin, moreover, carefully employed his official rhetoric (the Lenin cult, "fraternal help", etc.) to mask these and other changes, so that the real direction of his policies was often only discernible in retrospect (outside government circles). This is why we should be careful to separate a figure such as Kuliyev in the 1920s from the local officials administering Stalin's national-culture policies in the following decades – however similar the musical results, the context and motivations were very different.

Westerners approaching the Stalin-era music of the republics should also take care to remember a further twist in the history of Russian Orientalism, namely that Western reception of Russian music, from Diaghilev onwards, failed to see the distinction between the "Russian" and the "Oriental" styles. This was partly because Western audiences lacked the experience of their Russian counterparts – they were unable to trace any Russian elements back to Glinka, and they had never been able to build up a repertoire of associations through operas that unmistakably presented the opposition between the Russian and the Oriental on stage. Nevertheless, the first misleading impressions could have been overcome with time, if it were not for the fact that Western audiences received Russian music itself as something exotic – as a product of the Orient. Western listeners, to the extent that they lack the knowledge or desire to overcome this tradition of misinterpretation, are therefore twice removed from the perceptions of the young composers of the republics when they were confronted by Russian Orientalism during their conservatoire training in Moscow or Leningrad. These composers were able to see on the operatic stage the lurid fantasy worlds, and hear the associated musical idioms that were supposed to represent their homelands. Many – most prominently Khachaturian – were apparently content to accept the entire package of Russian Orientalism (although even Khachaturian showed that he was uneasy with his public role).[54] Others, as we have seen, fought a rearguard action, within the confines of permitted discourse, to have more control over the representation of their nation's music, and to find a more authentic musical language that would still fulfil the demands of the task that Moscow had set them. This reflects the tensions within the indigenous intelligentsias of the republics. Should Russian culture be absorbed wholeheartedly as a progressive, Westernizing step, much as Russian engineering or petrochemistry was being absorbed? Or should indigenous culture be developed so far as possible along separate lines? The answers to these questions depended on whether Russian/Western technology and culture were seen to be interlinked or independent. We shall now examine how these tensions were played out in the music and musicological writings that emerged in several of the republics.

The most prominent of the national operas *avant la lettre* was Glière's *Shahsenem* (1927, rev. 1934), which set a precedent for complacent Orientalism in the genre. Glière had displayed mastery of various styles, from the epic Wagnerianism of his Third Symphony to the light, popular style of his early Soviet ballet, *The Red Poppy*. But he was also able to play the role of a consummate and polished Kuchka epigone when he wished, and in *Shahsenem* he demonstrated that he was capable of the steamiest post-Kuchka Orientalism. This may seem puzzling, since Glière was able to hear the genuine music of the Azeris for himself, and the opera was to be premièred in Azerbaijan, with an audience that included Azeris as well as Russians. And yet it is difficult to see how Glière's music would have been altered if the opera had been a pre-Revolutionary work designed to pander to the fantasies of Russian noblemen about the conquered peoples of the empire. The passage in Ex.6.5 shows Glière's key to the treasures of the Orient: the flattened sixth degree in a major-mode context. On the melodic level, he uses this scale-step to form an augmented second with the leading note; on the harmonic level he uses it as the root of the minor subdominant chord. Both these devices were time-worn elements of Russian Orientalism dating back to the Kuchka. But *Shahsenem* was not accepted with uncritical gratitude: Uzeir Hajibeyov, the first native Azerbaijani composer of significance, ventured to fault Glière:

6.5   Glière, *Shahsenem*, Kerib's aria from Act I

Augmented seconds in music, images of the nightingale and rose in poetry, flower-bud ornaments in the visual arts, multi-coloured costumes and ceremonious bows in the theatre: all this pseudo-Eastern style can only jar on an Eastern people and violate their spirit and tastes.[55]

Such arguments were later echoed by Russian critics writing in *Sovetskaya Muzïka*, who condemned "conventional external exoticism" and "old and dead Orientalist traditions"; but unlike Hajibeyov, they tended to see these problems in works of the past, especially from the tsarist era. In 1939, one such critic, Iosif Rïzhkin, outlined three main differences between pre-Revolutionary Russian Orientalism and the new Soviet national music of the republics. First, before the Revolution the colonizer's art represented the colonized, while the latter were not given a voice; but in Stalin's Soviet Union, representation worked in both directions: Russians depicted the East (Vasilenko, Glière, Shekhter, and Brusilovsky), but the East also represented

Russia (Khachaturyan, Hajibeyov, and Ashrafi). Second, before the Revolution only a handful of Russians became acquainted with the music of the conquered peoples of the empire; now the majority of Soviet Russian composers worked with this material: "Soon the melodic richness of the East will become the common property of Soviet music, and Soviet culture will incorporate not single streams, but the full waters of Eastern music".[56] Thus far, we can concede that Rïzhkin is dealing in partial truth rather than outright falsehood. But his third point amounts to a defence of Russian Orientalism: Rïzhkin says that criticism of Orientalist dramatic and musical conventions had gone much too far. To the extent that they were true to the music of the Caucasian and Central Asian Soviet peoples, he argues, these conventions were a legitimate part of the Soviet composer's language. Rïzhkin is only prepared to concede that there was an element of distortion in the past when these conventions were presented as the whole picture; but Soviet artists, he says, would broaden their focus and supplement the existing conventions. But what Lenin had once condemned as Great Russian chauvinism was now fully revived by Stalin, and behind the rhetoric of fraternal equality, the non-Russian nationalities were subordinate to Russia. Accordingly, it was easy for a Russian critic to consign the problems of Orientalism to the past, since he was simply able to disregard the complaints of Hajibeyov and others in the republics.

Returning to Azerbaijan, we shall now examine Hajibeyov's attempts to counter this persistent Orientalism, which included not only polemical and scholarly articles but also a reply in kind to the Glière's *Shahsenem*, namely, Hajibeyov's own opera *Keroglu*. Hajibeyov began his project, as one might expect, with a careful study of Azeri folk music, and on the basis of this study he abstracted a set of melodic modes which he held to be basic to the construction of this music.[57] His scholarly activities proceeded smoothly, but problems emerged as soon as he tried to apply his theories to composition, as he began work on his opera. Hajibeyov was, in effect, a victim of his own superior knowledge: he was now so immersed in Azeri folk music that every step in assimilating it to the very different world of opera seemed like a gross distortion: how was he to match such different tuning systems, and how was he to translate Azeri vocal idioms into bel canto? The Kuchka had never encountered such problems in their time, thanks to their ignorance of Russian folk music as it was actually performed in the villages. Harmonization, of course, was also a source of vexation. But Hajibeyov could not maintain his scruples for long, since he had to satisfy a state commission; the authorities would not have been amused if he had abandoned the opera and handed them instead a set of essays on the errors of official cultural policy. The score of *Keroglu* is therefore a record of necessary compromise, rather than the embodiment of Hajibeyov's earlier statements on the future development of Azerbaijani national music.

With regard to tuning, Hajibeyov soon accepted that Azerbaijani composers would have to settle for twelve-note equal temperament; the matter had already been decided by Kuliyev, the Minister of Education, and composers would have found it difficult to mount a serious challenge. Nevertheless, Hajibeyov initially set out the problems very clearly. First, he explains that on the traditional *tar*, there could be 12, 13, 17 or 19 pitches within the octave. He then shows how the piano would seriously distort a particular Azeri melody that had a "tonic" on, say, E: there would be another scale degree passably close to the piano's Eb/D#, but a further, functionally distinct scale step was required between these two piano notes. The piano would force a composer to assimilate this last note to either the E or the Eb, thereby making a nonsense of the melody in places (to the ear of anyone acquainted with Azeri music, that is).[58] But by 1939 Hajibeyov was renowned as a composer across the Soviet Union, and the change in status appears to have coloured his judgements considerably:

> I myself ignore the groundless claims of some musicologists that the international musical alphabet is not sufficient for the representation of the characteristics of Azerbaijani music. This opinion is wrong, since the chromatic scale satisfies us completely.[59]

Accordingly, he now claimed that Azeri music possessed no intervals smaller than the semitone; indeed, he goes still further, saying "our semitone, in fact, is wider".[60] He also reported approvingly that players of the *tar* had now begun to adjust their movable frets in order to approximate 12-note equal temperament.[61] This *volte face* cannot even be characterized as political pragmatism, since Hajibeyov had never yoked his earlier views to a rejection of equal temperament. It seems unlikely that Hajibeyov had sincerely changed his mind: on the one side was carefully researched opinion, on the other some throwaway comments that failed even to make sense (if one semitone is wider than on the piano, there must logically be another which is narrower). It seems more plausible that his new-found celebrity and life of relative ease encouraged him to make a virtue of a necessity.

Turning to harmonization/polyphony, since this was a defining feature of the music required by Soviet cultural policies, there was again nothing to be gained by arguing that its imposition fundamentally distorted Azeri music. The problems were there to be overcome, not used as reasons for rejecting polyphony. The most Hajibeyov could do was to advise against the wholesale adoption of a four-part harmonic style, and recommend sparser contrapuntal textures instead. In spite of this, Hajibeyov's own compositions suggest that once polyphony was accepted, it was difficult to avoid drawing from the general harmonic resources of Western music.[62]

But surrender in these areas still left Hajibeyov with some leeway where modal or tonal organization was concerned. He theorized, initially, that it would be possible to reconcile the melodic modes he had found in Azeri traditional music with some manner of tonal harmony. And after *Keroglu* had enjoyed great success in Azerbaijan, he conjectured that this was largely due to his "purely national" modal writing:

> It is suggested that if Azerbaijani music, which is monodic by nature, were to be supplied with harmony, then all its modal characteristics would be reduced to naught ... Now the unskilful attachment of harmony to an Azerbaijani melody can change its character, neutralize its vivid modal traits, and even vulgarize it. But this does not mean that Azerbaijani music must forever remain monodic.[63]

> While working on the opera *Keroglu*, I allowed myself to deviate occasionally from the strict framework of the folk style; that is, I composed it in a freer manner. As the outcome has demonstrated, the opera succeeded, on the whole, to gain access to a wide stratum of listeners because the modal system was the starting point of its musical text and of my creative fantasy.[64]

But these words provide us with a highly misleading idea of *Keroglu*'s music. Western tonal idioms are employed more crudely than Hajibeyov suggests, and this tends to obliterate the modes employed in the melodic writing. What we find in Ex.6.6a is the minor subdominant in a major key, fully in line with the Orientalism of Glinka or Glière, together with the alternation of tonic major and minor triads, another Orientalist cliché. *Keroglu* is comparable to *A Life for the Tsar*: it was the first major opera in the native language by a native composer, celebrating events from national history. To the extent that Azerbaijani's have identified with *Keroglu*, this is surely the reason, rather than the authenticism that Hajibeyov tried to claim for himself. Russian nationalism had already shown that tonal harmony has a strong tendency to dominate and suppress the modality of a melody, and Hajibeyov made no substantial advances in assimilating tonal harmony to the modal character of a given folk melody.

The issue of modality also brings us back to the controversy over the augmented second: was it a mere Orientalist fiction, or was it a genuine feature of at least some music in the Caucasian and Central Asian republics? The latter, according to Armenian and Uzbek composers, who tried to avoid the interval

6.6a Hajibeyov, Keroglu's aria

because they saw it as a melodic feature specific to Azeri music. But were they correct in their supposition? At the height of his early anti-Orientalist polemics, Hajibeyov vehemently rejected any such notion:

> The "Oriental" style is a convention, a cliché that frees a composer from all responsibilities. It is represented largely by an abundance of chromaticism, by the augmented second, and by certain melodic idiosyncrasies. Azerbaijani music has no chromaticism – on the contrary, we have the strictest diatonicism.[65]

Later, however, Hajibeyov had to concede that two of the eight traditional modes of Azeri music did indeed contain tetrachords with augmented seconds; still worse for the anti-Orientalist, these two modes were associated with texts expressing passionate yearnings and the pains of love. By the time he composed *Keroglu*, he had already accepted the use of augmented seconds as legitimate in Azerbaijani national music, but the result seems suspiciously similar to the unashamed return of that most shop-worn of Orientalist clichés (note the emphasis on the augmented second in the conventional final cadence of Keroglu's Aria, shown in Ex.6.6b).

Turning now to vocal style, we find Hajibeyov in two minds once again. He expresses discomfort, on the one hand, at the prospect of introducing a bel canto standard into Azerbaijani national opera:

> European singing is, to our ears, still something strange and unpleasant; sometimes it is found to be such an irritant that people would prefer to leave the opera house.[66]

But Hajibeyov can also be found denying the very existence of any characteristic folk manner that would conflict with bel canto.[67] While Hajibeyov's theorizing was still in a state of flux, one of his compatriots was boldly attempting to forge a practice that would combine the bel canto with the Azeri folk manner. The musician in question was Byul-Byul Mamedov, who had mastered bel canto during a period of study in Italy, emerging as a very polished operatic tenor. The school of Azeri singing that he created can be

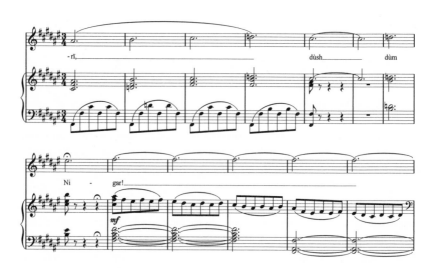

6.6b Hajibeyov, Keroglu's aria

dated back to 1932; Mamedov and his protégés mixed bel canto with traits of Azeri *ashug* singing such as a particular manner of virtuosic delivery in the high register, and the cultivation of long endurance – accomplished *ashug* singers could continue performing for hours. The recordings of his perform- ances that come down to us on vinyl disc (in music by Hajibeyov, for example) are striking for their microtonal ornamentation and "neutral" thirds.[68]

In 1937, *Keroglu* was performed in Moscow, as an important event in the Festival of Azerbaijani Art. Interestingly, Glière's *Shahsenem* was performed in the same festival, allowing critics to draw comparisons. When the reviews appeared, it emerged that the critics had failed to detect any opposition between the Hajibeyov and Glière operas; they even saw fit to praise *Keroglu* by comparing it to Borodin's *Prince Igor*, a touchstone of Russian Orientalism. In the following decades, *Keroglu* was often singled out as proof of Soviet opera's high achievements, and it was also judged a resounding success by the criterion of "national in form, socialist in substance". But as an anti- Orientalist gesture, *Keroglu* must be declared a failure. Since it does not sound significantly different from Russian Orientalist operas, the comparisons are legitimate, but here *Keroglu* fares badly, due to the rudimentary nature of Hajibeyov's technique. In a superficial sense, Hajibeyov's treatment of the Western musical component in *Keroglu* is an unintended reversal of Orientalism: Western music is treated as a collection of desiccated conven- tions, such as *da capo* form, middle-section sequences and final *ritardandi* (in a superficial sense because Orientalism contains a vital historical component of national oppression which is not under consideration here).

Given the requirements of the task, the composers of the republics eventu- ally had to settle for a combination of Orientalist conventions, together with some new conventions of their own, all overlaid upon already distorted versions of their own traditional melodies, adapted for Western instruments. Some Orientalist conventions were even found acceptable as reasonable approximations. The Armenian composer, Nicogaios Tigranyan (1856–1951), for example, used ornamental semitone figures to represent the peculiarities of Armenian singing, but the result came very close to the characteristic melodic decorations of Russian Orientalism. Similarly, Hajibeyov admitted that the cor anglais so favoured by the Orientalists was indeed close in timbre to the traditional zurna. Beyond this, the new devices created as an alternative to the Orientalist conventions, such as clusters and melodic doubling in fourths, eventually became nothing more than an extension of the Orientalist palette.

Of all the Soviet composers to emerge from the nationalist project, only Aram Khachaturian attained world renown, and his music does not even begin to challenge the Russian Orientalist style. He never dissociated himself from the traditions of Russian music, and came to be regarded in Moscow as a mouthpiece of the whole Soviet Orient, sweeping up all the diverse traditions into a grand generalization once more. His music permits us to believe that the following quotation is more than a mere demonstration of loyalty to humour the authorities:

> [Russian Oriental music] showed me not only the possibility, but also the necessity of a rapprochement between, and mutual enrichment of Eastern and Western cultures, of Transcaucasian music and Russian music . . . the Oriental elements in Glinka's *Ruslan*, and in Balakirev's *Tamara* and *Islamey*, were striking models for me, and provided a strong impulse for a new creative quest in this direction.[69]

It is hardly surprising that Khachaturyan's most popular number, the Sabre Dance, was parodied mercilessly by Nino Rota in the satirical Orientalist episode from Fellini's *Amarcord*. Insofar as any non-Western music is poured into the moulds of Western institutions (whether opera houses, orchestras, harmony or equal temperament), it will have great trouble escaping the Orientalist legacy, whether the impulse is indigenous (as in the cases of Turkey and pre-'30s Azerbaijan) or external (as in the Stalin-era Caucasian and central Asian republics). The arbiters of Socialist Realism were shrewd enough to see that Bartók's and Stravinsky's approaches to folk music would subvert the national-music project, but this greatly narrowed the scope of legitimate artistic endeavour for the national composers of the republics. They were left with the Russian Orientalist classics, but long after that tradition had grown stale, and worse, they generally lacked the technical expertise of Russian Kuchka epigones such as Glière. Their knowledge of local musical traditions sometimes led them to conduct valuable ethnomusicological work, but this knowledge usually went to waste because it was not assimilable to the required Western framework.

The "Russian style" returns to Russia

During the early Stalinist period, Russia itself remained untouched by nationalist rhetoric. Russian artists were encouraged to work with the epics of any people other than the Russians themselves. Signs of change began to appear from the beginning of 1936; the *Pravda* editorial of 1 February 1936, for example, introduced the notion that the Russian people was "first among equals" within the Soviet Union, supposedly because of their leading role in the Revolution and in "socialist construction".[70] While it is well for us to note the emergence of such rhetoric with hindsight, the signals were not so obvious at the time to many, and even those in high positions were not necessarily acquainted with the full implications of the shift, as is demonstrated by the mistake Bukharin made in March of that year. Bukharin was at this time editor of *Izvestiya*, the daily newspaper second only to Pravda in prestige, and he remarked that Russia had been "a nation of Oblomovs" prior to the Revolution. While this would hitherto have been considered an unexceptionable journalistic *aperçu*, it now brought public censure upon Bukharin's head.[71] For anyone paying close attention, this incident would have demonstrated that the new doctrine held Russia's greatness to be an essential part of the nation's character, and not merely an accident thrown up by the Revolution.

At the close of 1936, however, the Politburo chose to underline the change in a more forthright and unmistakable manner. Suddenly, Demyan Bedny's *The Warriors* (*Bogatïri*) was banned – this stage work was an adaptation of Borodin's operatic farce, which poked fun at Russian epic tales (*bïlinï*). Bedny, an opportunist of meagre talents, had previously been a darling of the authorities, and *The Warriors* had even received official approval from the Committee for Artistic Affairs. If the Politburo had selected a less-favoured artist or a work that had not yet been granted approval, the message would not have been so strong and unambiguous. The ban made it clear to artists that it was henceforth unacceptable to treat Russian epic warriors as comic figures, since these now represented "the heroic traits of the Russian people" (as the ban stated); the tenth-century baptism of Russia was also to be treated seriously, since it was a "positive step in the history of the Russian nation".[72] Stalin was able to monitor the reaction of Soviet artistic circles to the resolution through informers (this was now a customary practice). The informers' reports, which have only recently been made available, are as useful now to historians as they once were to Stalin. In the case of the Bedny ban, they show us two different kinds of reaction. Many welcomed the ban on the grounds that *The Warriors* was indeed weak, and that Bedny had done little to merit his previous success; the director, Tairov, was also resented, being regarded by many as pretentious and opportunistic. But others were more concerned with the wider import of the ban: some were disturbed by the reversal of the old Bolshevik policy on nationalism, but others welcomed it:

Trauberg, film director (*The Counterplan*):
The Soviet state is becoming ever more nationalistic and even chauvinistic. Because of this, some of the most surprising things gain the support of the party officials.[73]

Vsevolod Vishnevsky, playwright:
This is a history lesson: "hands off our guys". History will be useful for us, and very soon too. An opera *Minin and Pozharsky, Deliverance from the Invaders* is already being prepared. [74]

Grigory Sannikov, poet:
. . . I welcome the resolution . . . It's good – not just about Demyan but about the general approach to Russian history. For a long time the C[entral] C[ommittee] hadn't any time for this. But now they've taken the matter seriously and corrected it. It's high time they stamped out this vulgarization of history.[75]

In the last example from the informers' reports, we find both resentment of Bedny and Tairov in particular, together with a general enthusiasm for the return of Russian nationalism, with its attendant prejudices (note the contemptuous reference to one of the Siberian minority peoples, and the casual anti-Semitism):

S. Klïchkov, writer:
The great Russian people numbers a hundred million, and of course it has a right to art that is more significant than the things you see on powder boxes and kiosks *à la russe*. Perhaps one day they will dare to call me a Russian writer as well. The Vogul epic cannot be allowed to trample down Russian art.

Who was allowed to profane the Russian epics? The Jew Tairov and the weakling Bedny. But now some intelligent and subtle fellow is taking them by the backside and shaking loose the excess stink. . . .

This resolution rehabilitates Russian history. . . [76]

A month after the *Warriors* affair, the Politbureau passed a resolution on the commemoration of the 100th anniversary of Pushkin's death which fell during the coming year. The planned festivities for 1937 were on an unprecedented scale. There was an All-Union Pushkin Exhibition in Moscow; in order not to diminish the scale of the exhibition and to retain central control over the shaping of Pushkin's image, the various local Pushkin museums were not allowed to organize their own exhibitions without special permission. There was the publication of the Pushkin Complete Works and also several volumes of selections; if critical and biographical works are included, the anniversary saw the printing and distribution of over 13 million books. An impressive range of translations was commissioned: Pushkin was to be rendered in the languages of the Soviet National Republics, as well as English, French and German. Pushkin sites were restored and new Pushkin museums opened.

Monuments were erected, including the landmark statues of Moscow and Leningrad. Plaques were placed on any building connected with the poet.[77]

With the Pushkin celebrations as a precedent and model, festivities were held for a succession of Russian cultural figures. Glinka was honoured in 1939, even though there was no anniversary to mark – the prestigious première of *Ivan Susanin* (refashioned from *A Life for the Tsar*) provided sufficient justification. The centenary of Tchaikovsky's birth was marked in 1940, while the following year saw the centenary of Lermontov's death. At the same time, various Russian military commanders and even tsars were glorified on the cinema screen: *Peter the Great,* Part I (1937) and Part II (1939); *Alexander Nevsky* (1938), a personal favourite of Stalin's; *Suvorov* (1940), with screenplay and script co-written by Stalin himself. The film release, in each case, was accompanied by nationalist rhetoric to drive the message home; here, for example, is Eisenstein's exhortation marking the release of his *Alexander Nevsky* (*Battleship Potemkin* was only filmed a dozen years earlier, but it now seems a world away):

[I]f the might of our national soul was able to punish the enemy in this way, [thus, at a time] when the country lay exhausted in the grip of [under] the Tatar yoke, then nothing will be strong enough to destroy this country which has broken the last chains of its oppression; a country which has become a socialist motherland; a country which is being led to unprecedented victories by the greatest strategist in world history – Stalin.[78]

It is clear from this that the country was preparing itself for the coming war; interestingly, "the might of our national soul" implies that the country in question was not the supra-national Soviet Union, but simply Russia (no official statement was likely to make this slip, but it was certainly in keeping with the prevailing mood).

Even before the *Warriors* ban and the Pushkin celebrations, some artists had begun to respond to earlier, more subtle signs of the change. An interesting case in point is provided by Prokofiev's Russian Overture, which was premièred on 21 October 1936, just before the *Warriors* ban. But while the idea was timely in principle, its manner of execution was criticized. It was not so much the presence of comic elements (although there certainly is comedy in the Overture); it was chiefly the particular Russian style that Prokofiev had adopted, which veered much too close to Stravinsky's *Petrushka* manner. Stravinsky, as an émigré hostile to the Soviet Union (and a public admirer of Mussolini) was not rehabilitated until the end of the '50s, and he was certainly not acceptable in the mid-'30s even as an implicit or partial model. The critics tactfully pointed out this error of judgement somewhat obliquely, without referring to Stravinsky by name – a frank condemnation would have damaged Prokofiev's career. Israel Nestyev, for example, compared the Overture to the brilliant, multi-hued canvases of Filipp Malyavin (better known in the West as Philippe Maliavine), a member of the "Mir iskusstva" school; this implied, in a relatively benign way, that the work's Russianness was of the pre-Revolutionary, Diaghilev–Stravinsky variety. Nest'yev also took exception to the brass clusters in Ex. 6.7 (the Overture's most harshly modernist feature):

> The thunderous roaring of the brass that breaks through this elemental dance movement several times – this seems an unnecessary and out-of date illustration of the stereotypical Russian *shirokaya natura* [rakish, heart-on-sleeve nature] but the composer was forgiven this strange eccentric detail thanks to the joyful and energetic onslaught of the dance themes and the wonderful songfulness of the second subject.[79]

6.7   Prokofiev, Russian Overture (piano reduction)

Here Nestyev seems to be referring to the *ukhar'-kuptsï* [dashing, rakish merchants] from *Petrushka*; Stravinsky had used drunkenly exaggerated *glissandi* figures in portraying these characters, and Prokofiev took this feature to still further extremes in the Overture. The word "out-of-date" and the comments that follow imply that Prokofiev failed to acknowledge how Russia had changed: where Stravinsky's merchants lived dissolutely, as if they might face ruin tomorrow, in the official portrayals of life in Stalin's Soviet Union there was no such drunken revelry. According to such portrayals, the well-rewarded and economically secure collective farmers celebrated their steady successes in an appropriately restrained manner. But again, Nestyev chose not to state this directly.

There is much truth in Nestyev's hints at Stravinsky. The Russian Overture employs many of the devices Stravinsky used in his assimilation of folk or folk-style material, although Prokofiev was careful enough to use a much more classical structural and tonal framework than anything to be found in *Petrushka*. On the Stravinskian side, there is the metrical play of folk-style motives (Ex. 6.8, first subject), the montage-like interpolations of themes (like the *Poco piu sostenuto* that always arrives as a surprise), and the combination of diatonic folk-like tunes with a densely chromatic background – these are all modernist devices originating in Stravinsky, and in *Petrushka* in particular. The melodic material of the Overture, where it is not distinctly Prokofievian, is much closer to urban popular song than peasant song, another feature pointing to *Petrushka*, which had once struck Russian nationalist musicians as highly vulgar. On the classicizing side, the Overture is plainly enough in sonata form, and its tonality is for the most part made clear through the use of functional harmony, albeit with piquant and characteristically Prokofievian dissonances. These had rarely been absent from Prokofiev's work, in spite of the variety of styles his career had embraced; in order to make his music conform with the demands of Socialist Realism, he could simply bring these elements to the fore – a radical transformation was unnecessary.

6.8   Prokofiev, Russian Overture

Most importantly for the acceptance of the Overture, there is a closing apotheosis based on a cantabile theme: this begins in the manner of a chant, continues like a popular song and ends as a grandiose hymn – an overtly nationalistic procedure, endowing the simple music of the people with weight and ceremony. This Romantic device was also a standard feature of large-scale Socialist Realist works, and Prokofiev was well-advised to adopt it. Stravinsky, on the other hand, had arrived at *Petrushka*'s tongue-in-cheek treatment of the folk style precisely by abandoning all vestiges of nationalist glorification, even though this was a prominent feature of his own first great success: *The Firebird*. Now Prokofiev threw together both the Romantic nationalist and the modernist portrayals of Russianness, in the hope that he would be allowed a foot in both camps. But if this was his hope, it was misplaced. He clearly understood the criticisms of the Overture, because his next nationalist project, the music for *Alexander Nevsky*, minimizes the Stravinskian influence and greatly boosts the references to the Romantic nationalism of Borodin and others. This was a prudent move: two years later Shcherbachov's *Izhorskaya* Symphony was heavily criticized for its Stravinskian character.[80] A few years later, Prokofiev had airbrushed the mistake out of his career: in criticizing the Stravinskian second movement of Popov's Second Symphony, Prokofiev adopts the tone of one superior in wisdom and experience, and uses the criticisms that had once been levelled against him. Of Popov's movement, he said that "To imitate [*Petrushka*] 33 years later and to call this imitation a "Symphony of the Motherland" is not proper" (Popov, although younger, had spent his entire career in the Soviet Union, unlike Prokofiev).[81]

In the years following the *Warriors* ban, there was a shift in emphasis for Russian composers: where they had previously used the folk music of other nations they now increasingly used Russian folk music. This was heightened after the German invasion in the summer of 1941, when Russian nationalism dominated the rhetoric surrounding the war effort. Vissarion Shebalin, for example, had written a well-received Overture on Mari Themes back in 1936 (the Mari were a Siberian people). But in 1939 and 1940, he was at work on a set of orchestral variations on the "classic" Russian folksong "Uzh tï, pole" ("Ah you, my field"). Then, with the beginning of the war, there is a succession of Russian works: in 1941, the Russian Overture and a Russian March, followed by his Slavonic Quartet (No. 5) in 1942. The latter invokes the Pan-Slavist phase of nineteenth-century Russian Nationalism, which was revived during the War. Shebalin's Quartet also has the specific musical precedent of Glazunov's Slavonic Quartet of 1888, and the two works are not dissimilar, despite the gap of over half a century. Shebalin was able to pose as a highly competent Kuchka epigone when the demand arose: the Quartet contains sorrowful songs and merry dances, changing-background variation technique, and much melodic motion from $\hat{4}$ to $\hat{1}$ (the so-called "Russian plagalism"). Shebalin evidently knew what he was doing, since this backward-looking nationalist concoction was awarded a Stalin prize of the first degree in 1943.

The Slavonic Quartet was only one particularly well-crafted example from a whole industry of second-generation epigonism (the first-generation epigones had matured during Shebalin's childhood). This was what the state encouraged, and composers responded accordingly. But before the War stilled all voices of complaint, there had been some evidence of a rear-guard action against the trend. Viktor Tsukkerman, a distinguished music analyst, had written thus in 1940:

> The question of how folk music is employed is posed differently for Russian folksong on the one hand, and, on the other, for the music of those peoples

who only set foot on this broad road after the Great October Socialist Revolution. In the latter case, both the use of folk material and the composers' imitation of it are fully justified. Russian folksong, on the contrary, in its best-known types, has already been used to such an extent that here the listener cannot be satisfied by the "nth + 1" version of a song. There are still some strata of Russian songs that are lying spare, and indeed there are many of these; to this day composers do not dare to touch the riches of those Russian songs that are highly organized both modally and polyphonically; instead, they limit themselves to the simplest types.[82]

Tsukkerman's thoughts were shared by many other composers and critics, but they went unheeded. Shebalin himself must have understood the issue perfectly well: he was not, after all, a newcomer capable of nothing more than rehashing the Kuchka, but on the contrary an experienced and highly respected composer who had been developing a distinctive style of his own since the late '20s. Composers who responded to the appeals for "Russian" works knew by this stage what was expected of them. What Tsukkerman regarded as "highly organized modally and polyphonically" might simply have been viewed as "formalism" by the authorities. Perhaps Tsukkerman had thought in 1940 that that there was still some leeway available, and that composers were conceding more than was necessary, but other "Russian" works of the period showed that in practice composers disagreed with Tsukkerman. Even the old Balakirev and Rimsky-Korsakov folksong collections were re-established as the sources of folk material; the fact that they had long been discredited by ethnographical research was now an irrelevance. If they were good enough for the Kuchka, they were good enough for the composers of wartime "Russian" works.

Anyone who knows Soviet music largely or exclusively through the works of Prokofiev and Shostakovich might find all of this rather puzzling; after all, Russian folksong and Kuchka pastiche does not even constitute a minor strand in the oeuvre of either composer. But this does not mean that Soviet critics withheld the descriptions "Russian" or "national" from their music: on the contrary, they were used liberally, as if the terms themselves would be enhanced by their association with the music of Prokofiev and Shostakovich. Prokofiev's score for Eisenstein's *Alexander Nevsky* was taken by the critics as firm proof that his musical language was "*pochvennïy*" ("rooted", literally "of the soil"); this effectively provided him with credit to cover works such as the Fifth Symphony or Seventh Sonata, which were also greeted by the critics as "national" music, even though they contain little or nothing that would normally be termed "Russian". The critics did not even require the equivalent of an *Alexander Nevsky* from Shostakovich, since the officials (and hence the critics too) were supportive of him after the Fifth Symphony (Shostakovich only felt compelled to write "Russian" works after the 1948 Resolution). Gorodinsky, the Leningrad party official in charge of culture, made a statement at a meeting of composers which illustrates well the latitude available to Shostakovich:

> Recently I have been working much in the field of what we call "national" music. . . . But what does not belong to "national" music? Russian music? But Russian music *is* national. If they say to me: what about a work of such great significance as Shostakovich's Fifth Symphony? Is it national music? Of course it is national – this is Russian music.[83]

Note also how this statement marks the later stages of a transition: where "national music" had applied only to the music of the republics during much of the 1930s, it was now (in 1941) to be applied additionally – or even especially – to Russian music. A year or so later, people like Gorodinsky no longer had to spell this out.

The Seventh Symphony gained automatic official and critical acceptance; it was to be regarded as "Russian first and foremost", to use the words of the contemporary critic Ivan Martïnov.[84] At one level, this was hardly surprising, since the work was being used as a vital means of boosting morale during the siege of Leningrad, and it also helped to broaden support in the USA for the Soviet war effort. The officials' ploy was therefore to treat "Russianness" as a functional rather than a descriptive concept whenever it suited them. But Shostakovich's less fortunate fellow composers were not satisfied – their own works, after all, never seemed to benefit from this semantic sleight of hand. The grumbling at this perceived double standard persisted; in a composers' meeting of 1944, V. Belyayev said

> The issue of *narodnost'* in Shostakovich's work deeply troubles Soviet composers and Soviet musical public.[85]

(The invocation of the public can be ignored, since it was a standard device in Soviet polemic.) But after the Seventh, Shostakovich failed to deliver another such prestigious "civic-minded" work (let alone a work displaying any recognizable Russian traits), and so the *narodnost'* and nationality of his music were called into question ever more insistently. Another official, Vladimir Surin, while granting that "*narodnost'*" need not simply mean the inclusion of folksong, reprimanded Shostakovich for the abstract language of his Eighth Symphony: he "could not feel those life-giving features of *narodnost'*, which are always so close and precious to us . . . [this was] the most vulnerable spot in Shostakovich's work."[86] Some eminent musicologists from the Shostakovich camp rushed to his defence: Lev Mazel, for example, made an implausible attempt to how the unfolding of the first movement of the Eighth reflected the principles of the *protyazhnaya*.[87] The Ninth Symphony provoked an escalation: a grand civic work marking victory in the Great Patriotic War was expected, but instead Shostakovich provided a short work that never attempts to rise to such expectations, and which closes with a particularly irreverent finale. The criticism was now couched in graver terms: the musicologist G. Bernandt, for example, claimed that "Shostakovich's path is separate from the paths of Russian artistic culture." Bernandt leavened this with the jibe that in Shostakovich's Four Romances on verses by Pushkin (op. 46) "the gap between the poet and the composer proved to be incredibly great". Since the time of the Pushkin centenary, in 1937, a lack of sympathy for Pushkin was a lack of Russianness.

The 1948 Resolution against "formalism" not only delivered a broadside against modernism, but reinforced musical nationalism. Since all the most eminent Soviet composers, including Prokofiev and Shostakovich, were pulled down from their pedestals, the Russian nineteenth-century classics for a time became the only possible compositional model, and the only appropriate subject for musicological research. Even the ranks of the classics underwent a purge: not only Scriabin, but also Rakhmaninov and even Lyadov were removed for their modernist tendencies. New attacks were made on "folkloristic modernism", represented now not only by the familiar culprits Stravinsky, Bartók and Szymanowski, but also by Prokofiev in his Kabardin–Balkar Quartet (Quartet No. 2), and even Khachaturian in his "Poem about Stalin". Musicologists now had to avoid all mention of Western influences on Russian music, resulting in such bizarre statements as "If we start thinking that the major–minor system is a product of Western classicism, this would undermine the national originality of Russian music".[88] This desperate period was summed up by the contemporary quip, "*Rossiya–rodina slonov*" (Russia – native land of the elephant).

At the close of 1950, the Moscow Composers' Union organized a special discussion on "*narodnost'*" in Soviet music". Stalin's public campaign against "rootless cosmopolitanism" had now been running for a year, and this gave a boost to its opposite – "Russian patriotism". This Composer's Union meeting was only one of several held by the various culture workers' Unions, effectively as a part of the cosmopolitanism campaign. The proceedings witness to the forced and artificial nature of the task. Many of the musicologists were themselves anxious to stave off the charge of cosmopolitanism, a threat which hung over substantial numbers of artists and writers during this period, the majority (but not all of them) Jews. The task of defining and illustrating "socialist *narodnost*" after a decade of bleeding Kuchka epigonism dry was trivial and futile, but fear motivated several contributors to use their ingenuity in constructing arguments that sounded as plausible and earnest as was possible in the circumstances.

Lev Mazel, for example, attempted to connect the issue of *narodnost'* in music with Stalin's recent theoretical polemic on the state of Soviet linguistics. Mazel quoted the following passage from Stalin's polemic:

> a) Language, as a means of intercourse, always was and still remains the single language of a society, common to all its members; b) The existence of dialects and jargons does not negate this, but rather confirms the existence of a language common to a given people in its entirety, of which they are offshoots and to which they are subordinate . . .

Before we see how Mazel applied these rather bland remarks to folk music, it is worth pausing to consider the source, since this is also germane to developments in nationalism during this period. The quoted remarks are only bland when taken out of context. Stalin's essay on linguistics was in fact a polemic against the bizarre theories of the late Nikolai Marr, by far the most influential Soviet linguist. With full state support, Marr had founded the Institute of Language and Thought, which, through the '30s and '40s had not only propagated and developed the theories of its founder (who died in 1934), but had also vigorously persecuted dissenting scholars (one had even been executed as a result). Although its theories offended the fundamentals of orthodox linguistics and Marxism in equal measures, this had never bothered Stalin until 1950. Now he decided the Institute must be closed down, accompanied by a public demolition of Marr's theories. This explains the blandness of the quoted lines: Marr's waywardness began at such a fundamental level that any argument against him will sound like an assemblage of truisms.

But another issue was at work here: Marrism had finally subdued all dissenting linguists in 1949, and only at this stage was it brought to Stalin's attention that this doctrine ran entirely counter to Stalin's policies on nations and nationalism. Marr had held, among other things, that language was split most profoundly along class lines, and not according to the divisions of orthodox linguistics (Marr in his later writings even denied the existence of language families); as a corollary of this, language could undergo revolutionary change when a new class took power, and Marr predicted that the Soviet Union, on these grounds, should soon converge on a single "socialist" language. Stalin pointed out that the grammar and core lexis of a language changes very slowly, and that major economic or political change does not bring about equally radical linguistic change. Language, Stalin argues, spans the class divide within a given nation in all but superficial aspects; it is not to be confused with culture, which can vary according to class, and which may indeed undergo abrupt changes at a time of political revolution. It is plain to see that the ideas of Marr and his Institute did not fit Stalin's projects for the Soviet Republics, or his revival of Russian nationalism (its unscientific character was not necessarily a problem – witness Stalin's promotion of Lysenko). Why, then, had Stalin not taken action against the Institute long before? We cannot be certain, but the answer is most probably that Stalin simply had more important matters to attend to. Stalin had once awarded Marr the Order of Lenin, but this was back in 1934, when Stalin's national policies had not coalesced.

Returning to the narrower issue of how the quoted lines were used at the Union of Composers meeting, Mazel turned Stalin's arguments against the practice of ethnomusicologists in Russia. Although there was nothing necessarily Marrist about their endeavours, ethnomusicologists had, in Mazel's words "concentrated only on local, regional traditions of Russian folksong, its 'territorial dialects'". Now this was simply because Soviet ethnomusicologists, like their Western counterparts, spent much of their time carrying out empirical fieldwork, and the music of Russian-speaking peasants was indeed highly variegated, as one would expect of a population spread over such a large geographical area for many generations. But Mazel argued instead that ethnomusicologists provided such a fragmented picture of Russian folk music because they were "afraid to generalize the essential characteristic of Russian national [musical] language as a whole". The denial of a unitary Russian musical language was, of course, at odds with Stalin's aims in promoting Russian nationalism in the arts. The idea of a single, unified national folksong tradition had been overturned by the painstaking fieldwork of Soviet ethnomusicologists, but it was the myth that Stalin wanted, not the science. Composers had learnt to treat Russian folk music as a monolith over a decade earlier, and ethnomusicologists were out of step. In effect, they were in the same position as the Marrist linguists, albeit for very different reasons – but it did not suit Mazel's purposes to discuss the differences. Mazel even singles out Asafyev as the exception, although Asafyev writings on this subject were of negligible scholarly value (as discussed at the end of Chapter 5).[89]

Mazel, to strengthen his case, does not limit himself to the notion of a "national musical language" in the abstract, but also provides several examples of true socialist *narodnost'*, the most prominent being Shostakovich's *Song of the Forests*, a cantata about Stalin's post-war reforestation plan, which, like the Fifth Symphony, was "a composer's response to just criticism" (the two works do not bear comparison in any other respect). It was only the second denunciation, in 1948, which led Shostakovich to adopt the Russian style at the

expense of his individual style, thereby catching up with colleagues such as
Shebalin, who had set out on this path nearly a decade earlier. Because the new
cantata so clearly signalled the composer's submission, it was showered with
praise. Mazel illustrates his point with examples of folk-style *peremennost'* and
modality from the Cantata (see Ex.6.9). Although these may seem to us no
more than a cursory nod in the direction of the Kuchka, they were accepted in
the circumstances as sufficient evidence that Shostakovich was at last speaking
the national musical language. The additional presence of so-called "intonations of appeal" – lively march rhythms and ascending melodic gestures –
connected Shostakovich's Russianness with the Soviet present. Shostakovich
had therefore achieved the elusive socialist *narodnost'*.

6.9   Shostakovich, *Song of the Forests*

In this assessment of both ethnomusicology and Shostakovich, Mazel is
joined by Nadezhda Bryusova, a musicologist with a very different background
– she had been a member of RAPM. Bryusova recalls one of Kastalsky's activities in the 1920s: he aired his own arrangements of folksongs in various
workers' circles, but was generally met with a cool reception. If Kastalsky had
expected his arrangements to strike a chord with Russian workers due to their
peasant backgrounds, it is not difficult to see why he was mistaken. As
discussed in Chapter 5, Kastalsky had painstakingly attempted to reproduce

certain local traditions of rural hetero/polyphony, but it was statistically unlikely that he would have found former peasants from the same localities; they would either have been completely unfamiliar with a given song, or would only have known it in a very different version. In fact Kastalsky had failed precisely because his experiment lacked the regional particularism that had governed his fieldwork and arrangements. But this is the last thing Bryusova would say in 1950. In order to avoid this obvious explanation, she muddies the waters, stating that "this was not folksong in its immediacy; Kastalsky apparently failed to breathe new life into the music he composed". Everything is contained in the word "immediacy": if only Kastalsky had imbued his work with this undefined quality, his work would have been recognizable to the whole nation. But where Kastalsky failed, Shostakovich has succeeded, according to Bryusova: avoiding Kastalsky's mistakes, he followed the folksong examples more directly and also filled them with the spirit of the socialist present:

> The prototype for the main theme of Dmitry Shostakovich's *Song of the Forests* [it is fair to label this the "Stalin theme"] is the melody of a beautiful *khorovod* folksong "So v'yunom ya khozhu" [I walk with a wreath]. In the folksong, every phrase ends calmly and smoothly. In Shostakovich, the melody is interrupted every time by a new ascending gesture in the voice. The composer's melody may lack the breadth of the folksong melody, but in the repeated ascending gestures of his melody he reflects some new traits typical of our time, such as a striving for action, and wilful impulses that are insistent and tireless. . . .
>
> This language, new for [Dmitry Shostakovich and Gavriil Popov], changed their creative work, and gave a new, finer, and more perfect expression to the images embodied in their works. At the same time it is clear that this truly was their native language, which they turned to in order to liberate themselves from earlier creative errors – errors which had hindered the truthful expression of their thoughts.[90]

The discussion of *narodnost'* in 1950, as we can see with hindsight, marked a further stage in Stalin's policies on nations and nationalism. From the original Bolshevik policy of eradicating Russian chauvinism, Stalin by this stage had rebuilt it in its entirety, with its old strains of anti-Semitism and contempt for non-Russian peoples. Now nation-building in the republics was at best relegated to the background, and sometimes even denounced. There were attacks in the press on various works that displayed a non-Russian nationalism, among them the Ukrainian opera *Bogdan Khmel'nitskiy*, by Konstantin Dan'kevich, which supposedly failed to "show the joy of the liberated people that found its happiness in the union with Russia".[91] The denunciation of Muradeli's *The Great Friendship* in 1947 had anticipated this trend: the libretto had been faulted for misrepresenting "the great friendship" between the Russian and the Georgian peoples:

> This opera contains serious political errors. The agents of the progressive, the bright, and the revolutionary are the peoples of the North Caucasus (Lezghins and Ossetians), and the music is packed with Oriental motives almost throughout. As for the Russian people, they are shown only as incidental participants in the events; the only positive character, the Russian Bolshevik Mikhail, is limited to two or three recitatives. The negative [Russian] characters in the opera proved to be much more vivid (the Cossacks); the music is almost entirely lacking in Russian intonations.[92]

The thinly-veiled anti-semitism of the cosmopolitanism campaign also shaped various otherwise inexplicable directives in the field of the Soviet mass song. Composers of mass songs were told most emphatically that the genre could not be considered in any way international or supranational (even though this was a strong feature of the genre from its origins in the Civil War years). The mass song was now declared a peculiarly Russian phenomenon. One highly regarded and popular mass-song composer, Mark Bernes, was now held up as an example of all that must be avoided; it is difficult to find any basis for this in the music or lyrics – that fact that Bernes was Jewish seems to have been sufficient. Non-Jewish Russians were held up as models: Vladimir Zakharov, head of the celebrated Pyatnitsky folk choir, and Vasilyev-Buglay, who was once a leading light of RAPM. Even those mainstays of the genre, Dunayevsky and Blanter, were not above suspicion – it was insinuated that they had been responsible for some of the Jewish characteristics that had crept into the mass song.

By 1951, therefore, composers of Soviet Russia had to write music that celebrated its Russianness. They could no longer think of complaining that nothing more could be drained from the Kuchka or its approach to Russian folksong. Appeals made in the past by Tsukkerman and even Asafyev that composers should seek out hitherto unused varieties of Russian folksong were heard no longer. And any innovative folksong treatments, however modest, were roundly criticized; the Kuchka, or at most, their first-generation epigones had settled these matters once and for all. The standard accusation of formalism was levelled at Prokofiev's folksong arrangements and Kabalevsky's folksong-based Preludes op.38 because both composers treated folksong melodies freely, as if they were their own. Popov's *Bïlina about Lenin*, which failed to filter the epic song genre through the Kuchka, was accused of "savouring the archaic", that is, preferring the past to the present (the Kuchka *was* the present). Any slight departure from the Kuchka was only possible if marked strongly with "intonations of appeal", as they were called, namely lively march rhythms and ascending melodic gestures – trademarks of a now highly depleted Socialist Realism.[93]

That this was a new aesthetic nadir was obvious enough to all participants. Shostakovich desperately tried to withdraw his *Song of the Forests* from the Stalin Prize list, repeating insistently that he "had done nothing new" in this work; the Stalin Prize committee initially accepted this, judging the music to be "commonplace", but pressure from above forced them to reverse their decision and grant Shostakovich the prize.[94] But we should not even suppose that this was the kind of music Stalin and his ministers wished to hear, since by all accounts they much preferred Russian (and Western) classics – the original rather than the imitation. On the grand and small stages of the Soviet Union, *Ivan Susanin, Ruslan* and *Prince Igor* were performed endlessly, signalling that these works conveyed the nationalist and imperial message more effectively than their pale Socialist-Realist counterparts. The singers found them more satisfying, and the public, at least in the Russian republic, displayed a marked preference for the original Kuchka, regardless of how much "*narodnost'*" was to be found in their Socialist Realist epigones.

After a period of uncertainty after Stalin's death, the Khrushchev "Thaw" finally brought an end to Kuchka epigonism as official music policy. Performances of Stravinsky's works were now permitted, and the composer himself was even received back in his homeland as a VIP guest of the Kremlin. Now there were various choices open to Soviet composers. There was modernism: not merely Prokofiev's and Shostakovich's "formalism", but everything from the West up to and including Boulez and Stockhausen. But this was only the pursuit of a significant minority, and at the genuinely avant-garde end there was no state funding or approval (although performances were possible nevertheless). The mainstream of Soviet music preferred a new "Russian style" that favoured Stravinskian devices, and made free use of humour and irreverence. Rodion Shchedrin enjoyed great success with *Ozornïye chastushki* (Naughty ditties), a work that celebrated the "low" stratum of folk/popular music in the manner of *Petrushka*. Georgiy Sviridov fascinated Soviet audiences with his *Kursk songs*, which employed strangely non-diatonic folk melodies and rich harmonies that sounded very distant from the Kuchka, but much closer to *Les Noces* (which was as yet unknown to Sviridov's Soviet audience). The discourse of "*narodnost'*" and the affirmation of the primacy of Russian classics lingered on, however, in the writings of critics and musicologists, and continued to leave its mark in the repertoire of the opera houses and concert halls. While this discourse never recovered its late Stalinist peak, it was never relegated to the background, and if anything it has become much stronger in the last few years, as Russian nationalism has been promoted more assiduously by Russia's post-Soviet rulers.

* * *

What has become of the national music heritage of the former republics in the post-Soviet period? Although in the early '90s they may have seemed unanimous in their celebration of independence, they have since gone in very different directions, according to the depth of economic problems, the presence of war in some cases, and the way in which the transition was managed at the top. The range of outcomes is especially astonishing in Central Asia.[95] In Turkmenistan, a closed, highly authoritarian state, almost all traces of Soviet/European culture have been wiped out (although the state receives support from the USA). The capital Ashgabat was rebuilt and has acquired an "Asian" architectural face, university education was drastically narrowed, the conservatoire and opera house closed down, and the symphony orchestras disbanded. The father of the nation, Turkmen-Bashi, published his own version of the history and culture of the country, and there are even bookshops that sell only this one book. Further east, in Tajikistan, the musical institutions inherited from Soviet times were also shut down, but in this case not for ideological reasons, but due to the dire economic situation and civil war. Yet also in central Asia, we find the other extreme exemplified by Kazakhstan, whose leaders have embraced the West without Moscow as its intermediary, and which is relatively prosperous owing to its natural resources. Accordingly, we find Western foundations sponsoring concerts and festivals, and for any hopeful student violinist from the neighbouring Central Asian republics (an increasingly rare breed), a scholarship to Almatï Conservatoire is very welcome (Moscow Conservatoire is now out of reach for most). Kirghizstan falls somewhere in the middle: it lacks the wealth to keep its Soviet-era cultural institutions at the Kazakh level, but it displays not merely tolerance, but a degree of pride in trying to maintain them. The initial post-Soviet wave of Kirghiz nationalism led to the curious reappearance of Soviet-era national operas such as *Ai-churek*. But whatever national feeling they were supposed to instil, the audience remained resolutely small, and even the enlistment of school pupils could not save the enterprise. Admitting defeat, the government turned instead to a production of *The Magic Flute*, with a Swiss conductor brought in for the purpose; the event was turned into a major celebration of

European culture, and the president even delivered a speech to this effect. Interestingly, all music lessons in the European tradition are still held in Russian – no one would think of using Kirghiz for the purpose.

Thus, the grand Stalinist design for the flowering of national culture in the Republics, even though it was guided by ulterior motives, and even though it often resulted in some grotesquely misshapen hybrid artefacts, left behind a legacy that outlasted both Stalin and the Soviet Union.

NOTES

Chapter 1 Constructing the Russian national character: literature and music

1. A brilliant investigation of this topic can be found in Liah Greenfeld, *Nationalism: Five Roads to Modernity* (Cambridge, MA: Harvard University Press, 1992), 189–274.
2. *Rassuzhdeniye o starom i novom sloge rossiyskogo yazïka*, 1803. Alexander Semyonovich Shishkov (1754–1841) was a man of letters who occupied various high offices (government minister, Chairman of the Russian Academy of Sciences, etc.). A detailed examination of his "Dissertation . . ." can be found in Mark Altshuller, *Predtechi slavyanofil'stva v russkoy literature* (Ann Arbor: Ardis, 1984).
3. It should be noted here that the common use of the term "nobility" as a translation of *dvoryanstvo* can be misleading; due to the lack of any primogeniture restriction on the transmission of titles from generation to generation, the ranks of the "nobility" included a substantial proportion of the population, and therefore I adopt "gentry" as the nearest equivalent for Anglophone readers. In the early nineteenth century, moreover, university graduates automatically acquired a personal, non-hereditary title, until personal titles accounted for 45 per cent of the *dvoryanstvo*. After 1814, however, all such *dvoryane* were officially barred from setting themselves up as feudal lords. To acquire an hereditary title through academic means, the holder of a personal title had to reach professorial rank. As for the size of the two "nations", in 1811 in Russia there were 440 000 people belonging to the *dvoryanstvo* and the priesthood, and 17.5 million peasants (out of which 10.5 million were serfs). A detailed account of these matters can be found in V.V. Poznanskiy, *Ocherk formirovaniya russkoy natsional'noy kul'turï* (Moscow: Mïsl', 1975).
4. F. M. Dostoyevskiy, *Dnevnik pisatelya za 1873 god* (Berlin, 1922), 114. The word *poskonnïy* comes from *poskon'* (hemp) and was associated with peasant clothing.
5. Rostopchin (in Tolstoy's text Rastopchin) is portrayed ironically; it seems that the text chosen here specially irritated Tolstoy, since he quotes it at length in the third part of the novel. See L. N. Tolstoy, *Polnoye sobraniye sochineniy* (Moscow–Leningrad: Gosudarstvennoye izdatel'stvo khudozhestvennoy literaturï, 1932), vol. 11, 174.
6. This and the following extracts are taken from *Rostopchinskiye afishi 1812 goda* (St Petersburg: Suvorin, 1889), 19–21.
7. An ordinary and slightly comic name.
8. *Meshchanin* – member of the urban lower middle class: a small trader, or craftsman, or junior official.
9. One of Moscow's squares.
10. Presumably the double-headed eagle from Russia's coat of arms.
11. Fur cap with ear-flaps.
12. Cloth worn inside boots to retain heat.
13. Cabbage soup.
14. January was supposed to be especially severe around Epiphany.

15. A small entrance-hall in the *izba*.
16. The upper part of the stove is the warmest place to sleep in the *izba*.
17. Citizen Minin and Prince Pozharsky famously gathered peasants for the "people's war" during the 1612 Polish invasion. A. S. Pushkin, "Roslavlyov", *Sobraniye sochineniy v 10 tomakh*, vol. 5 (Moscow: Khudozhestvennaya literatura, 1975), 117–27 (121).
18. Pyotr Chaadayev, "Pervoye filosoficheskoye pis'mo", first publ. in *Teleskop* (1836), no. 15, repr. in Chaadaev, *Stat'yi i pis'ma* (Moscow, 1989), 40–55. English translation can be found in *The Main Works of Peter Chaadaev*, transl. and ed. by Raymond T. McNally (Notre Dame-London: University of Notre Dame Press, 1969), 23–51 (34).
19. *The Main Works of Peter Chaadaev*, 35.
20. Ibid., 38.
21. Ibid., 39.
22. Ibid., 40.
23. Ibid., 46.
24. The phrase "Orthodoxy, Autocracy, Nationality" was coined in 1833 by S. Uvarov, the Minister of Education under Nicholas I, who had initiated the policy of Official Nationalism (as its critics called it). It was widely disseminated by two professors of Moscow University, M. Pogodin and S. Shevïryov, and by several journalists including F. Bulgarin, N. Grech, and O. Senkovsky. Among the literary partisans of Official Nationalism were the popular writers N. Kukolnik (a friend of Glinka) and S. Zagoskin, but the doctrine was supported by many others such as Gogol and Tyutchev. The ideology of Official Nationalism will be touched upon in Chapter 2, but for a comprehensive account see Nicholas V. Riasanovsky, *Nicholas I and Official Nationality in Russia, 1825–1855* (Berkeley and Los Angeles: University of California, 1959).
25. Pyotr Chaadayev, "The Apologia of a Madman", English translation in *The Main Works of Peter Chaadaev*, 205.
26. Ibid., 199–218 (210).
27. Ibid., 199–200.
28. Ibid., 207.
29. Ibid., 215.
30. I. S. Turgenev, "Dïm", *Sochineniya*, vol. 9 (Moscow–Leningrad: Nauka, 1965), 173.
31. Quoted in K. Kasyanova, *O russkom natsional'nom kharaktere* (Moscow, 1994), 36–7.
32. N. V. Gogol', "Myortvïye dushi", *Sobraniye sochineniy v 6 tomakh*, vol. 5 (Moscow: Gosudarstvennoye izdatel'stvo khudozhestvennoy literaturï, 1953), 233.
33. This phenomenon of "transvaluation" is given special attention in Liah Greenfeld, *Nationalism: Five Roads to Modernity*.
34. F. M. Dostoyevskiy, *Dnevnik pisatelya za 1873 god* (St Petersburg: Suvorin, 1883), 104–5.
35. This and the following quotations are taken from "Otvet Khomyakovu", written in 1839, repr. in I.V. Kireevskiy, *Kritika i estetika* (Moscow: Iskusstvo, 1979), 143–53.
36. Ibid., 148.
37. N. A. Berdyayev, " 'Russkaya ideya': Osnovnïye problemï russkoy mïsli XIX i nachala XX vekov", in *O Rossii i russkoy filosofskoy kul'ture: Filosofï russkogo posleoktyabr'skogo zarubezh'ya* (Moscow: Nauka, 1990), 78.
38. Aleksey Khomyakov, quoted in Nikolai Zernov, *Tri russkikh proroka: Khomyakov, Dostoyevskiy, Solovyov* (Moscow: Moskovskiy rabochiy, 1995), 86–7.
39. Ivan Kireyevskiy, "Nechto o kharaktere poezii Pushkina" (On the nature of Pushkin's poetry), originally publ. in *Moskovskiy vestnik*, 8 (1828), 6, under the pseudonym "9.11". Transl. by Paul Debreczeny and Jesse Zeldin, publ. in *Literature and National Identity: Nineteenth-century Russian Critical Essays*, transl. and ed. by Paul Debreczeny and Jesse Zeldin (Lincoln, 1970), 3–16 (12).
40. V.F. Odoyevskiy, *Russkiye nochi* (Leningrad: Nauka, 1975), 148 and 182.
41. Kireyevskiy, as in note 39.
42. A. Gertsen, "O razvitii revolyutsionnïkh idey v Rossii", *Sobraniye sochineniy*, vol. 7 (Moscow, 1956), 137–53.
43. Shestov (1866–1938) was the creator of a post-theistic "philosophy of despair".

44. Lev Shestov, quoted in B. N. Bessonov, *Sud'ba Rossii: vzglyad russkikh mïsliteley* (Moscow, 1992), 192–3.
45. Ivan Andreyevich Il'yin, quoted in Bessonov, 212–13.
46. F. M. Dostoyevskiy, "Igrok", *Polnoye sobraniye sochineniy v 30 tomakh*, vol. 5, (Leningrad: Nauka, 1973), 225.
47. F. M. Dostoyevskiy, *Dnevnik pisatelya za 1873 god*, 39–40.
48. Andrei Belïy, *Peterburg* (Moscow: Nauka), 594.
49. Vladimir Solovyov, the first of three discourses in memory of Dostoyevsky, "Tri rechi v pamyat' Dostoyevskogo" (1881–3), originally publ. in the collected edition: V. S. Solovyov, *Sobraniye sochineniy* (St Petersburg, 1901–7), vol. 3. Transl. by Paul Debreczeny and Jesse Zeldin in *Literature and National Identity*, 169–79 (172).
50. Apollon Grigor'yev, in *Literature and National Identity*, 100.
51. Ibid., 118.
52. Ibid., 104.
53. Ibid., 107–8.
54. N. A. Dobrolyubov, "Chto takoye Oblomovshchina?", first publ. in *Otechestvennïye zapiski* (1859), no. 1–4, repr. in *Sobraniye sochineniy v 9 tomakh*, vol. 4 (Moscow–Leningrad: Gosudarstvennoye izdatel'stvo khudozhestvennoy literaturï, 1962), 307–43 (338).
55. *Literature and National Identity*, 166.
56. Ibid., 149–50.
57. Leo Tolstoy, *War and Peace*, transl. by Aylmer Maude (New York–London: W. W. Norton, 1996), 859.
58. Ibid., 861.
59. Commentary to A. P. Chekhov, *Sochineniya*, vol. 12 (Moscow: Nauka, 1986).
60. Ibid., 312.
61. Quoted in Bessonov, 268.
62. N. A. Berdyayev, *Sud'ba Rossii* (Moscow: Sovetskiy pisatel', 1990).
63. Institut Russkogo Yazïka imeni A. S. Pushkina, Kafedra stranovedeniya Rossii, *Russkiy narod: istoki, etnograficheskiye svedeniya, natsional'nïy kharakter*, (Moscow: Russkaya ideya, 1994), 34.
64. Ibid., 35.
65. *A Collection of Russian Folk Songs by Nikolai Lvov and Ivan Prach* (ed. M. H. Brown, introduction and appendixes by M. Mazo) (Ann Arbor: UMI Research Press, 1987), Facsimile 12. Lvov's diagnosis of an essential melancholy in Russian folksong is apparently based on musical impressions. He goes on to identify other moods and characters in the texts of the *protyazhnïye*, such as "military valor".
66. Richard Taruskin explored this special status of the *protyazhnaya* in his essay "The Little Star: An Etude in the Folk Style", see R. Taruskin, *Musorgsky: Eight Essays and an Epilogue* (Princeton: Princeton University Press, 1993), 38–70.
67. I. S. Turgenev, "Pevtsï" [The Singers], *Sochineniya*, vol. 3, (Moscow, 1979), 208–25 (222).
68. These facts are related in the commentary to one of the collected editions, see I. S. Turgenev, *Sochineniya*, vol. 4 (Moscow–Leningrad: Izdatel'stvo Akademii Nauk SSSR, 1963), 583.
69. Ibid.
70. A. S. Pushkin, "Domik v Kolomne", *Polnoe sobraniye sochineniy v desyati tomakh*, vol. 4 (Leningrad: Nauka, 1977), 237, XV.
71. N. V. Gogol', "Vïbrannïye mesta iz perepiskis druz'yami", *Sobraniye sochineniy v devyati tomakh*, vol. 6 (Moscow: Russkaya kniga, 1994), 79.
72. N. V. Gogol', "Myortvïye dushi", *Sobraniye sochineniy v 6 tomakh*, vol. 4 (Moscow: Gosudarstvennoye izdatel'stvo khudozhestvennoy literaturï, 1953), 258–9.
73. Ibid., 230.
74. N. V. Gogol', "Vïbrannïye mesta iz perepiski s druz'yami", *Sobraniye sochineniy v devyati tomakh*, vol. 6, 74.
75. N. A. Berdyayev, "'Russkaya ideya': Osnovnïye problemï russkoy mïsli XIX i nachala XX vekov", in *O Rossii i russkoy filosofskoy kul'ture: Filosofï russkogo posleoktyabr'skogo zarubezh'ya* (Moscow: Nauka, 1990), 63.
76. Ibid., 66.

77. A. N. Radishchev, *Puteshestviye iz Peterburga v Moskvu* [A Journey from Petersburg to Moscow] (Moscow, 1979), 48–9.

78. Ivan Kireyevskiy, "Nechto o kharaktere poezii Pushkina" [On the nature of Pushkin's poetry], first publ. under the pseudonym "9.11" in *Moskovskiy vestnik*, part 8, no. 6 (1828), 171–96. English version in *Literature and National Identity*, 3–16.

79. N.V. Gogol', "Vïbrannïye mesta iz perepiskis druz'yami", *Sobraniye sochineniy v devyati tomakh*, vol. 6, 147

80. Ibid., 184.

81. O. I. Bodyanskiy, *O narodnoy poezii slavyanskikh plemyon* (Moscow, 1837); quoted in F. Russo, "Kratkiy istoricheskiy ocherk razvitiya muzïki v Rossii", *Muzykal'nïy mir*, 6 (1882), 4.

82. F. Russo, ibid.

83. Quoted in A. A. Gozenpud, *Russkiy opernïy teatr XIX-go veka, 1836–1856* (Leningrad: Muzïka, 1969), 405–6.

84. On the critical reception of Glinka's operas in Russia see Richard Taruskin "Glinka's Ambiguous Legacy and the Birth Pangs of Russian Opera", *Nineteenth-Century Music*, vol. I/2 (1977), 142–62.

85. Richard Taruskin, *Musorgsky*, 54.

86. V. V. Stasov, "Nasha muzïka za posledniye 25 let", first published in *Vestnik Yevropï*, no. 10 (1883), 561–623, repr. in *Stat'yi o musïke*, vol. 3 (Moscow: Musïka, 1977), 143–97 (188–9).

87. V. V. Stasov, "Muzïka" (from *Iskusstvo XIX veka*), first publ. in *XIX vek: Illyustrirovannïy obzor minuvshego stoletiya* (St Petersburg, 1901), 299–328, repr. in, *Stat'yi o muzïke*, vol. 5b (Moscow: Muzïka, 1980), 9–105 (95).

88. Hugo Riemann, *Kleines Handbuch der Musikgeschichte mit Periodisierung nach Stilprinzipe und Formen* (Leipzig: Breitkopf & Härtel, 1908), 259.

89. See Ts. A. Kyui, *Izbrannïye stat'yi* (Leningrad: Gosudarstvennoye musikal'noye izdatel'stvo, 1952), 37; M. A. Balakirev and V. V. Stasov, *Perepiska*, 2 vols (Moscow: Gosudarstvennoye muzïkal'noye izdatel'stvo, Muzïka, 1970–71), 1:122; V. F. Odoyevskiy, *Muzïkal'no-literaturnoye naslediye* (Moscow: Gosudarstvennoye musikal'noye izdatel'stvo, 1956), 119.

90. Letter to Stasov of 23 July 1873, see M. P. Musorgskiy, *Pis'ma* (Moscow: Muzïka, 1984), 155.

91. Letter to Kruglikov of 18 April 1890, see N. A. Rimskiy-Korsakov, *Polnoye sobraniye sochineniy: Literaturnïye proizvedeniya i perepiska*, vol. 8a (Moscow: Muzïka, 1978), 178.

92. Letter of 18 Nov. 1904, publ. in N. A. Rimskiy-Korsakov, *Polnoye sobraniye sochineniy: Literaturnïye proizvedeniya i perepiska*, vol. 8b (Moscow: Muzïka, 1982), 153.

93. I. S. Zil'bershteyn and V. A. Samkov (eds), *Sergey Dyagilev i russkoye iskusstvo*, vol. 1 (Moscow: Izobrazitel'noye iskusstvo, 1982), 421.

94. Ibid., 467.

95. Ibid., 420.

96. Interview with Alexander Sanin, NN, "Boris Godunov v Parizhe", *Teatr* (1908), no. 214, 26 Mar, 11–12. Quoted in *Sergey Dyagilev i russkoye iskusstvo*, vol.1, 415.

97. *Sergey Dyagilev i russkoye iskusstvo*, vol.1, 420. Shaliapin's acting, especially in the scene of Boris Godunov's death, was a clear exception here, because of its dramatic depth, but even this was perversely interpreted as barbaric naturalism so that it conformed to the desired stereotype.

98. Ibid., 420.

99. A. A. Blok, "Skifi", *Polnoye sobraniye sochineniy i pisem v 20 tomakh*, vol. 5 (Moscow: Nauka, 1999), 77–80 (77).

100. Ibid., 79.

Chapter 2   The Pushkin and Glinka mythologies

1. Quoted in B. S. Shteynpress, "'Dnevnik' Kukol'nika kak istochnik biografii Glinki", *M. I. Glinka: Issledovaniya i materialï*, ed. by A. V. Ossovskiy (Moscow–Leningrad: Gosudarstvennoye muzïkal'noye izdatel'stvo, 1950), 88–119. The status of Kukolnik's diary has been placed under some doubt; scholars now accept it as a memoir rather

than a diary in the strict sense, so this prophetic phrase could conceivably have been written much later.

2. V. F. Odoyevskiy, "Pis'mo k lyubitelyu muzïki ob opere g. Glinki 'Zhizn' za tsarya'" (Letter to a music lover on the subject of Glinka's opera *A Life for the Tsar*), first publ. in *Severnaya pchela*, 7 Dec. 1836, no. 280, transl. by Stuart Campbell in *Russians on Russian Music, 1830–1880: an Anthology* (Cambridge: Cambridge University Press, 1994), 1–3.

3. I. V. Kireyevskiy, "Nechto o kharaktere poezii Pushkina", first publ. in *Moskovskiy vestnik*, part 8, no. 6 (1828), 171–96; repr. in I. V. Kireyevsky, *Kritika i estetika* (Moscow: Iskusstvo, 1979), 43–55 (53).

4. N. V. Gogol', "Neskol'ko slov o Pushkine", from "Arabeski", first publ. in 1835, repr. in *Sobraniye sochineniy v 6-ti tomakh*, vol. 6 (Moscow: Gosudarstvennoye izdatel'stvo khudozhestvennoy literaturï, 1953), 33.

5. Ibid.

6. A. N. Maykov, quoted in O. S. Murav'yova's essay "Obraz Pushkina: istoricheskiye meta-morfozï" in *Legendï i mifi o Pushkine*, ed. by M. N. Virolainen (St Petersburg: Akademichekiy proekt, 1994).

7. F. M. Dostoyevskiy, *Pushkin* (St Petersburg, 1899), 15–16.

8. Even an incomplete list of probable sources for Pushkin's *Ruslan* is quite impressive: Ariosto, Parny, Wieland, Hamilton, Voltaire, La Fontaine, in addition to Russian works, such as Karamzin's *Ilya Muromets*, Radishchev's warrior poems, Zhukovsky's *Dvenadtsat' spyashchikh dev*, the *bïlinï* from Kirsha Danilov's collection, and Russia folk tales reworked by Tchulkov (such as the story of Yeruslan Lazarevich). The sources for Glinka's *Ruslan* were no less international: commentators mention Mozart, Cherubini, Beethoven, Weber, Rossini, Auber as well as composers from Russian opera and ballet traditions.

9. S. S. Trubachov, *Pushkin v russkoy kritike* (St Petersburg, 1889), 267. Bayan was a semi-mythological Russian epic bard. The same image of Pushkin as epic singer occurs in Bayan's second song from *Ruslan*.

10. Marcus C. Levitt, "Pushkin in 1899", in *Cultural Mythologies of Russian Modernism: From the Golden Age to the Silver Age*, ed. by Boris Gasparov, Robert P. Hughes, Irina Paperno (Berkeley: University of California Press, 1992), 183–203 (185).

11. Ibid., 192.

12. D. I. Pisarev, "Pushkin i Belinskiy", first publ. in *Russkoye slovo*, 1865, books 4 and 6; repr. in D. I. Pisarev, *Sochineniya v 4-kh tomakh*, vol. 3 (Moscow: Gosudarstvennoye izdatel'stvo khudozhestvennoy literaturï, 1956), 306–417.

13. "Koleblemïy trenozhnik", quoted in Brian Horowitz, *The Myth of A. S. Pushkin in Russia's Silver Age: M. O. Gershenzon, Pushkinist* (Evanston, Illinois: Northwestern University Press, 1996), 78.

14. *Pushkinskiy kalendar': K 100-letiyu so dnya gibeli Pushkina* (Moscow: Ogiz-Sotsekgiz, 1937), 4.

15. *Vlast' i Khudozhestvennaya intelligentsiya: dokumentï Tsk RKP(b)–VKP(b), VChK–OGPU–NKVD o kul'turnoy politike, 1917–1953* (Moscow: Mezhdunarodnïy fond "Demokratiya", 1999), 345.

16. *Alexander Pushkin: A Celebration of Russia's Best-Loved Writer*, ed. by A. D. P. Briggs (London: Hazar Publishing, 1999).

17. This was the date of the St Petersburg première; the Moscow première was held on 9 Dec. 1836.

18. To realize the importance of this step, we may recall the race between Spohr and Weber to complete the first German sung-through opera in 1823 (*Jessonda* and *Euryanthe* respectively). Weber was obviously not satisfied with the form of German opera as defined by his own *Freischütz* in spite of its great popular success. He considered "grand opera" (i.e. opera that was all sung) to be the higher genre and had great hopes for his *Euryanthe*; in the end, however, it was Spohr's turn to win the acclaim of critics and public alike: his *Jessonda* quickly became a favourite repertoire item both in Germany and abroad.

19. *Russkiy invalid* (1836), no. 307, quoted in A. A. Gozenpud, *Russkiy opernïy teatr XIX-go veka, 1836–1856* (Leningrad: Muzïka, 1969), 37.

20. Ya. M. Neverov, "Novaya opera g. Glinki 'Zhizn' za tsarya': Pis'mo iz Sankt-Peterburga"[Mr Glinka's new opera "A Life for the Tsar" – a letter from St Petersburg to the *Moscow Observer*], first publ. in *Moskovskiy nablyudatel'*, 10 Dec. 1836, book 1, 374–84 (my translation).

21. Odoyevskiy, "Pis'mo", transl. Campbell, 1–3.

22. Ya. M. Neverov, "Novaya opera g. Glinki 'Zhizn' za tsarya': Pis'mo iz Sankt-Peterburga"[Mr Glinka's new opera "A Life for the Tsar" – a letter from St Petersburg to the *Moscow Observer*], first publ. in *Moskovskiy nablyudatel'*, 10 Dec. 1836, book 1, 374–84, transl. in Campbell, 4–8.

23. Stasov's letter to Balakirev, 21 March 1861; see M. A. Balakirev and V. V. Stasov, *Perepiska*, vol. 1 (Moscow: Muzïka, 1970), 130. More on the critical responses to *A Life for the Tsar* in Richard Taruskin, "Glinka's Ambiguous Legacy and the Birth Pangs of Russian Opera", *Nineteenth-Century Music*, vol. I/2 (1977), 142–62.

24. A. S. Khomyakov, "Opera Glinki 'Zhizn' za tsarya'", *Moskvityanin*, no. 5, part 3 (1844) 98–130, quoted in A.V. Ossovsky, "Dramaturgiya operï M. I. Glinki 'Ivan Susanin'", *M. I. Glinka: Issledovaniya i materialï*, 7–71 (34).

25. Sadko, "Pered operno-baletnïm sezonom", *Zhizn' iskusstva*, no. 28 (14 July. 1925), 3.

26. "Omolozheniye operï i baleta", *Zhizn' iskusstva*, no. 6 (9 Feb. 1926), 8–9.

27. Viktor Belyayev, "GABT – v preddverii sezona", *Zhizn' iskusstva*, no. 41 (11 Oct. 1927), 9–10 (10).

28. Ye. Vilkovir, "M. I. Glinka: k 70–letiyu so dnya smerti", *Muzika i revolyutsiya*, no. 2 (1927), 3–8 (6).

29. V. Gorodinskiy, "O muzïkal'nom teatre", *Zhizn' iskusstva*, no. 27 (7 July 1929), 6–7.

30. See L. Kaltat and D. Rabinovich, "U istokov russkoy narodnoy muzïkal'noy shkolï", *Sovetskaya muzïka*, 3 (1934), 27–47. The Soviet authorities insisted on neutralizing Tchaikovsky's *1812 Overture*, replacing the tsarist national anthem wherever it occurred with the tune of *Slav'sya*, which was the second national song in the same period. Ironically, *Slav'sya* was itself an item from the finale of *A Life for the Tsar*. Evidently, the authorities could dissociate the *Slav'sya* melody from its words more easily than they could in the case of the tsarist national anthem.

31. S. M. Gorodetskiy, B. A. Mordvinov, "Why and how we are producing *Ivan Susanin*", typescript held in RGALI (Russian State Archive for Literature and Art), fund 1220 (S. Gorodetskiy), list 1, folder 31.

32. The rough chronology of the period is as follows: the Poles occupied Moscow in 1610, and the treacherous boyars pledged loyalty to Wladyslaw, son of the Polish King, Sigismund. Sigismund, however, preferred to procrastinate, since he was wary of sending his son to Moscow so soon after the previous two claimants had met with violent death (the original libretto refers to this in Act II). In the autumn of 1611, Minin began to draw together an army in Nizhny Novgorod (this is referred to in Act I of the Soviet libretto), and under the leadership of Prince Pozharsky the army fought a series of battles in 1612 leading to the liberation of Moscow in October of that year (again mentioned in Act I of the Soviet libretto). Sigismund tried to retake Moscow in December 1612, but without success (it is the Russian triumph on this occasion which is referred to as a victory in the original Act I). In early 1613, the Electoral Assembly (*Zemskiy sobor*) gathered in Russia to elect the new tsar. After lengthy discussions, a preliminary decision to elect 16-year-old Mikhail Romanov was made on 7 February, but the proclamation was postponed for two weeks – this is why in the original Act I, Sobinin can only present the news as a rumour. The coronation of Mikhail eventually took place in April 1613.

33. I owe this observation to Professor Yevgeniy Levashev.

34. RGALI , fund 1220 (S. Gorodetskiy), list 1, folder 31.

35. S. Gorodetskiy, "Libretto 'Ivana Susanina'", *Sovetskoye iskusstvo*, no. 41 (5 Sep. 1937), 3.

36. These can be found in RGALI, Fund 1220 (S. Gorodetskiy), List 1, Folder 28; the following examples are also taken from this source.

37. *Mikhail Ivanovich Glinka: Kalendar' k stopyadesyatiletiyu so dnya rozhdeniya* (Leningrad, 1954), 83.

38. It appears that Stalin wanted to be seen on horseback as he reviewed parades, but his equestrian skills fell short of his ambitions. The closest he came was in 1945, when he fell off his

horse while rehearsing his entry. As a result, the parade was greeted by two Marshals, Zhukov on a white horse and Rokossovsky on a black one. Stalin, of course, was always able to ensure that he had the last laugh: Zhukov was demoted for "immodest behaviour", while Rokossovsky was later arrested and tortured.

39. Ye. S. Bulgakova, *Dnevnik Yeleni Bulgakovoy* (Moscow, Knizhnaya palata, 1990), 100. English translation quoted from Anatoly Smelyansky, *Is Comrade Bulgakov Dead? Mikhail Bulgakov at the Moscow Art Theatre*, trans. Arch Tait (London: Methuen, 1993), 304–5.

40. M. I. Glinka, "Zapiski", *Polnoye sobraniye sochineniy (literaturnïye proizvedeniya i perepiska)*, vol. 1 (Moscow: Muzïka, 1973), 211–350 (229).

41. A comprehensive overview of Glinka's treatment by Soviet musicologists can be found in Albrecht Gaub, "Mikhail Glinka as preached and practiced in the Soviet Union Before and After 1937", *Journal of Musicological Research*, vol. 22 (2003), 101–34.

42. V. Vasina-Grossman, "Glinka i liricheskaya poeziya Pushkina", in *M. I. Glinka: Sbornik materialov i statey*, ed. by T. Livanova (Moscow-Leningrad: Gosudarstvennoye muzïkal'noye izdatel'stvo, 1950), 93–113 (95–6).

43. A.V. Ossovskiy, "Dramaturgiya operï M.I. Glinki 'Ivan Susanin'", *M. I. Glinka: Issledovaniya i materialï*, 7–71.

44. Ibid., 23.

45. An example of such interpretation can be found in N. Tumanina, "Otechestvennaya geroiko-tragicheskaya opera Glinki 'Ivan Susanin'", *M. I. Glinka: Sbornik materialov i statey* (Moscow–Leningrad: Gosudarstvennoye muzïkal'noye izdatel'stvo, 1950), 162–214.

46. Ye. Kann-Novikova, *M. I. Glinka: Novïye materialï i dokumentï* (Moscow–Leningrad: Muzgiz, 1950), 119.

47. G. B. Maryamov, *Kremlevskiy tsenzor: Stalin smotrit kino* (Moscow: Konfederatsiya Soyuzov Kinematografistov "Kinotsentr", 1992), 87.

48. V. V. Poznanskiy, *Ocherk formirovaniya russkoy natsional'noy kul'turï* (Moscow, Mïsl', 1975), 161–2.

49. Yu. Kremlyov, *Natsional'nïye chertï russkoy muzïki* (Leningrad: Muzïka, 1968), 31.

50. V. G. Belinskiy, "Konyok-Gorbunok", *Sobraniye sochineniy*, vol. 1 (Moscow: Khudozhestvennaya literatura, 1976), 366–7.

51. Kremlyov, 31.

Chapter 3: Glinka's three attempts at Russianness

1. V. F. Odoyevskiy, "Vtoroye pis'mo k lyubitel'yu muzïki ob opere g. Glinki 'Zhizn' za tsarya'" [Second letter to a music lover on the subject of Glinka's opera *"A Life* for the Tsar"], first publ. in *Severnaya pchela*, 15 Dec. 1836, no. 287 and 16 Dec. 1836, no. 288. Transl. by Stuart Campbell in *Russians on Russian Music, 1830–1880: an Anthology* (Cambridge: Cambridge University Press, 1994), 9–13.

2. Ya. M. Neverov, "Novaya opera g. Glinki 'Zhizn' za tsarya': Pis'mo iz Sankt-Peterburga" [Mr Glinka's new opera "A Life for the Tsar" – a letter from St Petersburg to the *Moscow Observer*], first publ. in *Moskovskiy nablyudatel'*, 10 Dec. 1836, book 1, 374–84, transl. in Campbell, 4–8(8).

3. First publ. in *Russkiy vestnik* in 1808, quoted in A. A. Gozenpud, *Muzïkal'nïy teatr v Rossii: ot istokov do Glinki* (Leningrad: Gosudarstvennoye muzïkal'noye izdatel'stvo, 1959), 135.

4. First publ in *Vestnik Yevropï*, 1810, quoted in Gozenpud, 276. "White-stone Moscow" probably refers to Moscow prior to the building of the present-day Kremlin (construction began in the fifteenth century); the earlier building was made of white stone.

5. V. I. Morkov, *Istoricheskiy ocherk russkoy operï s samogo eyo nachala po 1862 god* (St Petersburg, 1862). Quoted in *Istoriya russkoy muzïki v 10-ti tomakh*, vol. 4 (Moscow: Muzïka, 1986), 141.

6. Quoted in M. M. Ivanov, *Istoriya muzïkal'nogo razvitiya Rossii* in 2 vols (St Petersburg: Suvorin, 1910–12), vol. 1, 275.

7. See V. F. Odoyevskiy, "Pis'mo k lyubitelyu muzïki ob opere g. Glinki 'Zhizn' za tsarya'" (Letter to a music lover on the subject of Glinka's opera *A Life for the Tsar*), first publ. in

Severnaya pchela, 7 Dec. 1836, no. 280, transl. by Stuart Campbell in *Russians on Russian Music, 1830–1880: an Anthology* (Cambridge: Cambridge University Press, 1994), 1–3; Ya.M. Neverov, transl. in Campbell, 4–8; Nikolai Melgunov's "Glinka i yego muzïkal'nïye sochineniya" ["Glinka and his Musical Compositions"] was written in 1836 and circulated widely; reprinted in T. Livanova, V. Protopopov, *Glinka*, vol. 2 (Moscow: Gosudarstvennoye muzïkal'noye izdatel'stvo, 1955), 202–9.

8. Neverov, transl. in Campbell, 6.
9. Mel'gunov, quoted in V. V. Stasov, "Mikhail Ivanovich Glinka", *Stat'yi o muzïke*, vol. 1 (Moscow: Muzïka, 1974), 175–351 (233).
10. Odoyevskiy, "Pis'mo", transl. in Campbell, 3.
11. Odoyevskiy, "Vtoroye pis'mo", transl. in Campbell, 12.
12. Neverov, transl. in Campbell, 7.
13. Ibid., 8.
14. Ibid., 7.
15. The first of the quotations is found in Susanin's first utterance and comes from a coachman's song that Glinka had himself transcribed. The second quotation, from a popular song "Down the Mother Volga" would have passed unnoticed by many listeners, since it is hidden in the accompaniment to one of Susanin's arioso passages in Act IV.
16. David Brown, *Mikhail Glinka: A Biographical and Critical Study* (London and New York, Oxford University Press, 1974), 118, 129–30.
17. Richard Taruskin, *Defining Russia Musically* (Princeton: Princeton University Press, 1997), 30.
18. The facsimile of the 1806 edition was published in *A Collection of Russian Folk Songs by Nikolai Lvov and Ivan Prach* (ed. M. H. Brown, introduction and appendixes by M. Mazo) (Ann Arbor: UMI Research Press, 1987).
19. Ivanov, vol. 1, 287.
20. In Kashin, the Italianate operatic virtuosity is confined to the clarinet part, otherwise the work would have been too difficult for amateur singers to attempt. Since Glinka's cavatina was written for performance in the opera house, rather than the drawing room, there was no need for such a restriction, so clarinet and voice are treated in a similar manner.
21. This was a standard assimilated form within art music of what was, strictly speaking, an upward portamento with no determined ending pitch.
22. This observation was made in a lecture by Levashev as heard by the present author in 1988.
23. See M. I. Glinka, "Zapiski", *Polnoye sobraniye sochineniy: Literaturnïye proizvedeniya i perepiska* (hereafter *LPP*), vol. 1 (Moscow: Muzïka, 1973), 211–350 (275).
24. Mel'gunov, "Glinka i yego muzïkal'nïye sochineniya", in Livanova and Protopopov, vol. 2, 202–9.
25. Stasov's modal interpretation of *Slav'sya* is discussed in both Brown, 133–5, and Taruskin, *Defining Russia Musically*, 44–6.
26. Odoyevskiy, transl. in Campbell, 11.
27. Neverov, transl. in Campbell, 8.
28. *A Life for the Tsar*'s Milan production in 1876 did not bring the opera European fame.
29. Taruskin, *Defining Russia Musically*, 36.
30. Both the expressive and symphonic possibilities of the mazurka were of course explored by Chopin, but it is not clear whether Glinka knew any of the Chopin mazurkas by that stage. The first reference to them in his Memoirs is in the year 1842, when he heard some of them played by Liszt.
31. Neverov, transl. in Campbell, 7.
32. In Glinka's draft manuscripts for his two operas, we find one instance of the label "recitative (*chantant*)", and one instance of the label "characteristic singing *non motivé*". The two would appear to be synonymous: the former appears in the original plan of *Ivan Susanin* (before it was renamed *A Life for the Tsar*) in connection with Susanin's replies to the Poles in Act III; the latter is found in the plan for *Ruslan and Lyudmila* and refers to a passage of Ruslan's recitativo arioso (a passage, it happens, that was dropped before the final draft). Both plans are published in Glinka, *LPP*, vol. 1, 29–33 (32) and 95–108 (99). For present purposes, I use the term "recitative *chantant*" consistently.

33. There were, of course, accompanied recitative passages of a more melodic character to be found in Italian opera, for example in Rossini's seria operas. But these passages were mixed with normal recitative still preponderant, whereas Glinka's completely avoided the latter.

34. Even a sympathetic Western commentator, David Brown, works under the same assumption; his praise for the chorus is laced with condescension.

35. Glinka, *LPP*. vol. 1, 29–30. He also refers to it here as the "the chorus *en fugue*".

36. When cuts are made to productions of *A Life*, this is one number which usually disappears; it is not essential to the drama, and the intricacy of the music is perhaps too much for the stage; indeed, were the vocal parts to be removed, it would stand as a self-sufficient orchestral piece.

37. Ivanov, vol. 1, 292.

38. Serov, "Opïtï tekhnicheskoy kritiki nad muzïkoyu M. I. Glinki: Rol' odnogo motiva v tseloy opere 'Zhizn' za tsarya'", first publ. in *Teatral'nïy i muzïkal'nïy vestnik*, no. 49, 13 Dec. 1859, repr. in A. N. Serov, *Stat'yi o muzïke*, vol. 4 (Moscow: Muzïka, 1988), 186–92.

39. It is perhaps notable that Beethoven and Glinka had a shared passion for Cherubini whose operas consistently employ musical reminiscences.

40. Another likely prototype is Amina's reminiscence from Bellini's *La Sonnambula*, as persuasively suggested by Rutgers Helmers, in *Mikhail Glinka and His Debt to Italian Opera* (MA thesis, University of Utrecht, 2007).

41. On the other hand, Glinka wrote down his list of personae with particular singers in mind, and was later ready to indulge Petrova-Vorobyova by significantly extending the part of Vanya.

42. O***, "'Ruslan i Lyudmila, opera M. I.Glinki'", *Mayak*, vol. 9, book 17 (May 1843), 30–32.

43. G. A. Larosh, "Glinka i yego znacheniye v istorii muzïki"(1867–68), repr. in *Izbrannïye stat'yi*, vol.1 (Leningrad, 1974), 33–156 (53).

44. M. P. Musorgsky, *Pis'ma* (Moscow: Muzïka, 1984), 156 (letter to Stasov of 23 July 1873). The Russian word is "obyevropeivshiysya", which carries associations with "obyevshiysya" (having overeaten).

45. Larosh, 55–6.

46. V. F. Odoyevsky, *Muzïkal'no-literaturnoye naslediye* (Moscow: Gosudarstvennoye muzïkal'noye izdatel'stvo, 1956), 276–85, 318–30, 371–80.

47. V. V. Stasov "O nekotorïkh formakh nïneshney muzïki"), *Stat'yi o muzïke*, vol. 1, (Moscow: Muzïka, 1974), 362–83. First published as "Über einige neue Form der heutigen Musik", *Neue Zeitschrift für Musik*, Bd. 49, Nos 1–4.

48. V. V. Stasov, "Mikhail Ivanovich Glinka", *Stat'yi o muzïke*, vol. 1, 175–351.

49. M. A Balakirev and V.V. Stasov *Perepiska*, vol. 1, (Moscow: Muzïka, 1970), 114–15.

50. Ibid., 116.

51. Larosh, 62.

52. This example has become a part of Russian musicological "oral culture", passing from lectures to exam answers without necessarily seeing print.

53. While it can be instructive to compare individual examples of passages displaying a tendency towards the subdominant with certain folk patterns, as does David Brown (*Glinka*, 116–17), the attempt to generalize from these instances is a treacherous game. Examples of the latter kind can be found in Brown's Tchaikovsky biography: "Nor does the tune leave any doubt about its creator's nationality. . . . [This] with its latent plagalism and especially its end, is Russian to the core . . ." (*Tchaikovsky: A Biographical and Critical Study*, vol.1, London, 1978, 103). "This is a fresh, airy tune, especially Russian in its high content of fourths and its repetitive behaviour . . ." (110). Michael Russ also takes up this false generalization when he refers to "the plagal cadences and melodic cadential formulas of Russian folk music" (*Musorgsky: Pictures at an Exhibition,* Cambridge: Cambridge University Press, 1992, 53).

54. B. V. Asaf'yev, "Glinka", written 1940–42, first publ. 1947, repr. in *Izbrannïye trudï*, vol. 1 (Moscow: Izdatel'stvo Akademii Nauk SSSR, 1952), 58–278 (154).

55. Larosh, 61.

56. O.Ye. Levasheva, *M. I. Glinka*, vol. 2 (Moscow: Muzïka, 1988), 124.

57. An attempt to explain some *Ruslan*'s harmonic procedures by referring to *non-Russian* folk modes was made by Ruth Halle Rowen in "Glinka's Tour of Folk Modes on the Wheel of Harmony", *Russian and Soviet Music: Essays for Boris Schwarz*, ed. M. H. Brown (Ann Arbor: UMI Research Press, 1984), 35–54. While the supposed source of Glinka's modality is different, Rowen's argument runs a parallel course to the traditional Russian exaggerations and inventions, with some quite bizarre derivations.

58. The chorus "*Lel' tainstvennïy*" from Act I, Finn's Ballad and The Head's Tale from Act II, Persian Chorus from Act IV, chorus "*Akh tï, svet Lyudmila*" in Act V.

59. A clear example of this from a reputable theorist can be seen in V. Berkov, '*Ruslan i Lyudmila*' *M. I. Glinki* (Moscow–Leningrad: Gosudarstvennoye muzïkal'noye izdatel'stvo, 1949), 23.

60. Levasheva, 113.

61. Brown, *Tchaikovsky*, vol. 1, 189.

62. Stasov's letter to Balakirev, 29 June 1861, Balakirev and Stasov, vol.1, 145.

63. Larosh, 139.

64. B. V. Asaf'yev, " 'Yevgeniy Onegin': liricheskiye stsenï P.I. Chaikovskogo", *Izbrannïye trudï*, vol. 2 (Moscow, Izdatel'stvo AN SSSR, 1954), 96–8.

65. Berkov, 13.

66. Larosh, 119.

67. G. A. Larosh, "Po povodu vïkhoda v svet orkestrovoy partiturï 'Ruslana i Luidmilï' Glinki za granitsey", *Izbrannïye stat'yi*, vol. 1, 184.

68. L. Grossman, *Pushkin v teatral'nïkh kreslakh* (Brokgauz i Yefron, 1926), 123.

69. See N. El'yash, *Pushkin i baletnïy teatr* (Moscow: Iskusstvo, 1970), 58. The performances took place in Moscow, during December 1821; the ballet-master was Glushkovsky, and the music composed by Scholz.

70. The issue of the authorship of this article remains controversial: Gozenpud (A. Gozenpud, *Russkiy opernïy teatr XIX veka*, Leningrad: Muzïka, 1969, 173–7) sees in it Odoyevsky's hand, while Protopopov (cf. 32) rejects Odoyevsky's candidature without proposing his own.

71. O***, 31–2.

72. Quoted in: A. N. Serov, *Stat'yi o muzyke*, vol. 4, 344.

73. It was reintroduced into currency by Vladimir Protopopov, the main points first published in T. N. Livanova, V. V. Protopopov, *Opernaya kritika v Rossii*, vol. 1 (Moscow: Muzïka, 1966), 279.

74. Martin Cooper in his little illustrated book *Russian Opera* (London, 1951), 23, mentions that Dostoyevsky views *Ruslan* as a political fable: western Slavs are represented by Lyudmila, the Orthodox Empire of Russia by her rescuer Ruslan, Turkey by the oppressor-magician Chernomor, and Austria by the comic coward Farlaf. I cannot locate this passage anywhere in Dostoyevsky, though it sounds very much in the style of his "Writer's Diary", where the author dedicated a lot of space to Russia's defence of Western Slavs; he could easily have chosen there to appropriate the plot of *Ruslan* in his reflection on contemporary situation.

75. L. Kaltat, D. Rabinovich, "U istokov russkoy narodnoy muzïkal'noy shkolï", *Sovetskaya Muzyka*, 3 (1934), 44.

76. Igor' Glebov [B.V. Asafyev], "Slavyanskaya liturgiya Erosu", *Simfonicheskiye etyudï* (Petrograd: Gosudarstvennaya filamoniya, 1922), 20–21.

77. Larosh, 127.

78. The Danilov collection was first published in 1807 with texts only; a new version complete with melodies appeared in 1818.

79. We can accept this as Glinka's train of thought since we would otherwise have to accept that he sought out a Finnish folksong which would match the arbitrary melodic feature he had already chosen as an epic marker; but this seems most unlikely, given his lack of interest in discovering anything about *bïlinas* – surely he would not have made such an effort to achieve authenticity in the music for a Finnish character when he was so little concerned about authentic music for the Russian characters. The only other possibility is that the "epic" melodic feature is only coincidentally present in Finn's Ballad, which also seems unlikely given the extent of Glinka's highly conscious artifice in creating various markers for epic and other features of this opera.

80. As in David Brown: "The whole-tone scale, which is always associated with Chernomor, is the one really clear Leitmotif in *Ruslan and Lyudmila*, but since it occurs only three times during the opera, it has no all-pervasive importance." Brown, *Glinka*, 202.
81. B.V. Asafyev, "Glinka", *Izbrannïye trudï*, vol. 1, 254–65.
82. Glinka's letter to N. V. Kukol'nik of 19 Jan. 1855, see Glinka, *LPP*, vol. 2b, 49.
83. Glinka's letter to V. P. Engelgardt of 29 Nov. 1855, Glinka, *LPP*, vol. 2b, 102.
84. *Znamennïy* chant gradually dropped out of liturgical practice after the schism provoked by Petrine reforms in the late seventeenth century. By the early nineteenth century, *znamennïy* chant was only to be heard among the communities of Old Believers and in a few remote monasteries. The church choirs sang a circumscribed corpus of officially approved and specially composed music which adopted Western styles; provincial churches only differed by simplifying the Western-style music in order to accommodate a lower level of musical expertise.
85. Glinka's letter to V. P. Engelgardt, Berlin 29 June 1856, see Glinka, *LPP*, vol. 2b, 142–3.
86. Glinka's letter to L. I. Shestakova, Berlin 16 May 1856(?), see Glinka, *LPP*, vol. 2b, 129.
87. Glinka's letter to D. V. Stasov, 18 Sept. 1856, see Glinka, *LPP*, vol. 2b, 171.
88. Glinka's letter to L. I. Shestakova, Berlin 15 July 1856, see Glinka, *LPP*, vol. 2b, 153.
89. Glinka's letter to K. A. Bulgakov, Berlin, 3 Nov. 1856, see Glinka, *LPP*, vol. 2b, 180.
90. Bortnyansky and Lvov are discussed in Chapter 5.
91. Levasheva, vol. 2, 302.
92. This early eighteenth-century manuscript, known as "Odoyevsky's *troyestrochnik*", is now in the Russian National Library (210, no. 24). It was published in N. D. Uspenskiy, *Drevnerusskoye pevcheskoye iskusstvo* (Moscow: Sovetskiy kompozitor, 1971), 268–70.
93. Quoted in Uspenskiy, 266.

Chapter 4: The beginning and the end of the "Russian style"

1. A. N. Serov, "Spektakli ital'yan'koy i russkoy opernïkh trupp (Galevi, Dyutsh)", first publ. in *Iskusstva*, no. 6 (1860), 33–6, repr. in A.N. Serov, *Stat'yi o muzïke*, vol. 5 (Moscow: Muzïka, 1989), 141–8 (141).
2. Pan-Slavist doctrines sometimes induced critics, mainly during the 1850s and '60s, to expand the Russian school into a Slav school, which gave them the happy opportunity of enlisting Chopin posthumously to the ever-growing band. See for example A. N. Serov, "Rusalka, opera A. S. Dargomïzhskogo", first publ. in *Muzïkalïnïy i teatralïnïy vestnik* (20 May 1856), repr. in A. N. Serov, *Stat'yi o muzïke*, vol. 2b, (Moscow: Muzïka, 1986), 42–136. By the 1870s this vogue had receded among the music critics; Stasov and Balakirev even began to speak of the Kuchka as the "New Russian School", without, of course, troubling to explain what the implied Old Russian School might have been.
3. Gerald Abraham, "Evolution of Russian Harmony", *On Russian Music* (London, 1939), 265.
4. Richard Taruskin, "'Entoiling the falconet': Russian Musical Orientalism in Context", *The Cambridge Opera Journal*, vol. 4 (1992), 253–80, revised version reprinted in *Defining Russia Musically*, 152–85 (all further quotations are taken from the latter version).
5. Taruskin's definition of his "essential *nega* undulation" is simply "a chromatic pass between 5 and 6"; this is a little wider than my definition of the KP definition, but the difference does not substantially affect the present discussion.
6. Taruskin, *Defining Russia Musically*, 168.
7. Ibid., 176.
8. V. I. Dal', *Tolkovïy slovar' zhivogo velikorusskogo yazïka*, first publ. 1863–6.
9. Taruskin, *Defining Russia Musically*, 159.
10. Ibid., 168.
11. Ibid., 176.
12. Note, however, that Taruskin's purpose was to examine possible Orientalist tropes and not the KP *per se*.

13. Note also that within the Oriental scenes, we find that #5/♭6 chromaticism is by no means specific to the languorous, feminine East of *nega*, as Taruskin suggests, for we find it (in ascending and the descending form) in the Lezghinka, which is the most macho of the Oriental dances. We should not forget that the image of savage masculine power that is so compelling in the *Polovtsian Dances* originates in this same Lezghinka from *Ruslan*, nor should we forget that the Caucasus, Russia's Orient, held not only literary dangers from beautiful maidens, but also dangers literary *and* real from ruthless warriors.

14. See Stasov's letter to Balakirev of 29 June 1861 and Balakirev's reply of 14–15 July 1861, M. A. Balakirev and V. V. Stasov, *Perepiska*, 2 vols (Moscow: Muzïka, 1970–71), vol. 1, 143–53.

15. In fact, it is strict heptatonicism, rather than chromaticism, which is exceptional in *Ruslan*, but even this is not obviously a marked feature, for we find it both in Russian scenes (the first statement of the chorus "Mysterious Lel"'), and Oriental scenes (the Turkish dance in Act IV).

16. Laroche lists Ratmir's waltz among "the excerpts of little significance" which "carry traces of Italian of French influence" in his "Glinka i yego znacheniye v istorii muzïki", G. A. Larosh, *Izbrannïye stat'yi*, vol. 1 (Leningrad: Muzïka, 1974), 55. Cui is unequivocal in defining the fast section of Ratmir's aria as "brilliant salon waltz", see Ts. A. Kyui, *Izbrannïye stat'yi*, (Leningrad: Gosudarstvennoye muzïkal'noye izdatel'stvo, 1952), 40.

17. Stuart Campbell, *Russians on Russian Music, 1830–1880: an Anthology* (Cambridge: Cambridge University Press, 1994), 20.

18. Entry for 30 Nov. 1901, *N. A. Rimskiy-Korsakov: Vospominaniya V.V. Yastrebtseva* in 2 volumes (Leningrad: Gosudarstvennoye muzïkal'noye izdatel'stvo, 1959–60) (hereafter Yastrebtsev), vol. 2, 215.

19. Even the Czech Overture contains a passage displaying a number of these Oriental conventions. This work will be discussed later.

20. We can see evidence of this in Balakirev's letter to Stasov of 20 June 1861, see Balakirev and Stasov, vol. 1, 139.

21. V. V. Stasov, "Proiskhozhdeniye russkikh bïlin", first publ. in 1868, repr. in *Sobraniye sochineniy*, vol. 3 (St Petersburg: Skorokhodov, 1894), 947–1200.

22. Ibid., 950.

23. Ibid., 1250.

24. Taruskin, in a footnote to his essay, insightfully comments that "[oriental coloration] was simultaneously and ambiguously a self-constructing and other-constructing trait". See *Defining Russia Musically*, 158, fn 8.

25. See Balakirev's letter to Boleslaw Kamenski of 30 June 1906, quoted in I. Belza (ed.), *Iz istorii russko-cheshskikh muzïkal'nïkh svyazey* (Moscow: Muzgiz, 1955), 46–7; also E. Frid, "Simfonicheskoye tvorchestvo", in *M. A. Balakirev: Issledovaniya i stat'yi*, 153.

26. Balakirev's letter to Stasov of 3 June 1863, see Balakirev and Stasov, vol. 1, 211.

27. 10 April 1897, Yastrebtsev, vol.1, 453. The reference to the queen being carried out on her litter comes from Rimsky-Korsakov's original programme, which he scrapped before publication.

28. See Tchaikovsky's letter to Balakirev of 2 Oct. 1869, publ. in *Miliy Alekseyevich Balakirev: Vospominaniya i pis'ma* (Leningrad: Gosudarstvennoye muzïkal'noye izdatel'stvo, 1962), 135.

29. In its earlier stages, the impact of *Tamara* on Rimsky-Korsakov was so overwhelming that he ignored its Oriental associations. In his orchestral fantasy *Sadko* (1867) the influence of *Tamara* (and of Liszt's *Mephisto Waltz*) is heard when the sounds of Sadko's *gusli* cause the whole Underwater Kingdom to enter into an orgiastic dance. Under the influence of *Tamara*, what was supposed to be a Russian dance is invested with arabesque-like chromatic lines (this music was transferred without significant alteration to the opera *Sadko*, of 1895).

30. A. P. Borodin, "Kontsertï Russkogo Muzïkal'nogo Obshchestva (1-y, 2-y)", first publ. in *Sankt-Peterburgskiye vedomosti*, no. 339 (11 Dec. 1868), repr. in *Muzïkal'no-kriticheskiye stat'yi* (Moscow–Leningrad: Muzgiz, 1951), 17–29 (27).

31. Taruskin, *Defining Russia Musically*, 185.

32. According to Nataliya Firsova (St Petersburg Institute of Art, Theatre, Music and Cinematography), Balakirev even copied out his protégés' works: for example, a two-piano reduction in MS of Borodin's First Symphony (1st movement, Manuscript Department of the St Petersburg State Conservatoire, no. 2527) is written in ink in Balakirev's hand with pencil corrections by Borodin. See more on that in N. F. Firsova, "Borodin i Balakirev – uchenik i uchitel: k istorii sozdaniya Pervoy simfonii", *Peterburgskiy muzïkal'nïy arkhiv*, vol. 2 (St Petersburg: Kanon, 1998), 100–6. Nor did Balakirev alter his habits later in life: for example, in the 1890s, he made copies of several works by his new disciple and admirer Sergei Lyapunov, changing the orchestration and even the harmony as he saw fit (see letters to Lyapunov quoted in *Miliy Alekseevich Balakirev: Issledovaniya i statyi* (Leningrad: Gosudarstvennoye muzïkal'noye izdatel'stvo, 1961), 392.

33. Entry for 28 Feb. 1895, Yastrebtsev, vol. 1, 269.

34. Collective authorship was only declared openly in the case of the abortive *Mlada* opera project, in which each participating composer took on responsibility for a single act. But the tacit practice of the 1860s did not allow authorial responsibility to be disentangled so easily.

35. Yastrebtsev, entry for 21 April 1894, vol.1, 173.

36. Yastrebtsev, entry for 23 Aug. 1904, vol. 2, 313.

37. As, for example, in Percy Scholes' entry on Rimsky-Korsakov: "Like others of the Russian nationalists (Glinka, Balakirev, Musorgsky) he was of 'gentle' birth and was reared in the country, so enjoying the early advantages of a soaking in folk-song", *The New Oxford Companion to Music*, ed. by D. Arnold (Oxford and New York: Oxford University Press, 1983), vol. 2, 1570. There are at least two blatant mistakes here: Balakirev was not of gentle birth, and Rimsky-Korsakov was not reared in the country – the myth of "folksong soaking", which Scholes endorsed, simply implied these facts, obviating the need for any empirical confirmation.

38. N. A. Rimskiy-Korsakov, *Letopis' moyey muzïkal'noy zhizni* (Moscow: Muzïka, 1982), 56.

39. V. F. Odoyevskiy, "Starinnaya pesnya", first published in *Russkiy arkhiv* in 1863, repr. in V. F. Odoyevskiy, *Muzïkal'no-literaturnoye naslediye* (Moscow: Gosudarstvennoye muzïkal'noye izdatel'stvo, 1956), 252–4 (253).

40. A discussion of such Westernization can be found in Chapter 1 of Richard Taruskin's *Defining Russia Musically*.

41. Ibid., 253.

42. Ibid., 253–4.

43. Yastrebtsev, entry for 9 April 1895, vol.1, 281.

44. Yastrebtsev, entry for 4 April 1894, vol. 1,166.

45. Ibid.

46. Rimskiy-Korsakov, *Letopis'*, 189.

47. Prach was Lvov's partner in the compilation of the earliest, and most influential collection of Russian songs; Lvov transcribed the melodies, and Prach arranged them.

48. See G. Golovinsky, *Musorgsky i fol'klor* (Moscow: Muzïka, 1994), 46–8.

49. This view persists to the present day, as in the case of the Russian scholar Yuliya Kondakova, who presented a paper at the 1998 Rimsky-Korsakov Conference (Goldsmiths College, University of London) that upheld this myth.

50. Quoted from M. P. Rakhmanova, in *Russkaya khudozhestvennaya kul'tura vtoroy polovinï XIX veka* (Moscow: Nauka, 1991), 69.

51. Fragments from Glinka's notebooks were published in the Complete Edition, vol. 17, p.112.

52. Stasov was too busy mining "Slav'sya" for modality and plagalism to comment on stylistic matters. Then in the Soviet era, Asafyev chose to highlight another possible source of "Slav'sya", the *kant* (Russian part-song of the early eighteenth century); by this stage, "Slav'sya" had almost the status of a second national anthem, and to discuss its origins in Orthodox liturgical music would not have served Asafyev's career well, to say the least. This is not to say that Asafyev was wrong, for the connection with the "celebratory" *kant* (*khvalebnïy kant* – usually celebrating military victories) is present in the very genre of "Slav'sya". The use of parallel octaves and thirds was also a feature of the *kant* tradition, as Asafyev says; indeed, we can regard it simply as a general feature of

eighteenth-century Russian polyphony. However, the connection between "Slav'sya" and the liturgical style would certainly have been more readily picked up by Glinka's listeners, who would have been less familiar with the tradition of *kant* singing, which was dying out by this time.

53. In the Ukraine, for example, wandering singers often accompanied themselves on a *kolyosnaya lira* (a kind of hurdy-gurdy), which provided a continuous pedal note. The pedal in Musorgsky's chorus may be a representation of this tradition.

54. See more on this in Vladimir Morosan, "Musorgsky's Choral Style", in *Musorgsky: In Memoriam, 1881–1981*, ed. by Malcolm Hamrick Brown (Ann Arbor, Michigan: UMI Research Press, 1982), 95–134.

55. V. F. Odoyevskiy, "Russkaya i tak nazïvaemaya obshchaya muzïka", first publ. in *Russkiy* (24 April 1867), repr. in *Muzykal'no-literaturnoye naslediye*, 318–30.

56. Yastrebtsev, entry for 30 Jan. 1908, vol. 2, 470.

57. See *Miliy Alekseyevich Balakirev: Issledovaniya i statyi*, 180. The *Molokane* are a sect that split from the mainstream Russian Orthodox Church in the eighteenth century under the influence of English Protestant ideas.

58. Readers unfamiliar with Russian Orthodox bell-ringing should note that it differs from its Western counterpart in two respects: short ropes are always used, so that higher bell-towers require a platform for the ringers, and more importantly, the ropes are connected to the clappers rather than the bells themselves. These differences allow the ringers to maintain fast rhythmic patterns accurately in the higher bells, over a slower pattern in the lower bells; this gives Russian bell-ringing a very distinctive sound, quite unlike its Western counterpart.

59. Richard Taruskin, *Musorgsky: Eight Essays and an Epilogue* (Princeton: Princeton University Press, 1993), 106–7.

60. Yastrebtsev, entry for 8 April 1893, vol.1, 93.

61. Schumann was also of some importance here, but the Kuchka's debt to him lay chiefly in other areas; see M. V. Frolova, *Simfonii Shumana v istoricheskoy perspektive* (PhD diss., Moscow, 1994).

62. Ts. A. Kyui, " 'Pskovityanka', opera Rimskogo-Korsakova", first publ. in *Sankt-Peterburgskiye vedomosti*, 9 Jan. 1873, signed ***, repr. in *Izbrannïye stat'yi*, 215–24 (219).

63. Familiar devices such as pedal notes, however, are often used in a way which departs from the Western *locus classicus*. This is especially prominent in the Kuchka's symphonic works, where a superficial deference to sonata form leads the listener to expect that Germanic norms will prevail; the frustration of these expectations have lead Western commentators to describe Russian symphonic forms as "decorative", as opposed to "organic" German forms. We shall touch upon these issues in the next chapter, during our discussion of Schumann's influence.

64. Yastrebtsev, entry for14 May 1895, vol. 1, 119.

65. An exhaustive discussion of the Kuchka's use of whole-tone harmonies and octatonicism, as well as of their Western precedents, can be found in Richard Taruskin, "Chernomor to Kashchei: Harmonic Sorcery; or, Stravinsky's Angle", *Journal of the American Musicological Society*, vol. 38/1 (Spring 1985), 72–142.

66. Yastrebtsev, entry for 12 Jan. 1892, vol. 1, 46.

67. Yastrebtsev, entry for 20 April 1893, vol. 1, 100.

68. Liszt's symphonic poems also provided the Kuchka with a wealth of alternatives to the cadential V–I: at the end of *Hunnenschlacht*, for example, III^6 and IV^6 alternate with the tonic, in place of V–I alternations; at the end of *Orpheus*, the final cadence is approached via a non-diatonic chain of triads; and the beginning of *Les Préludes* offered them examples of the "plagal" and "Mixolydian" cadences.

69. Yastrebtsev, entry for 16 Oct. 1901, vol. 2, 207.

70. Rimskiy-Korsakov, *Letopis'*, 227.

71. Similarly, when Rimsky-Korsakov revised his First Symphony in the 1880s, he transposed it from E-flat minor to E minor; he no longer saw any virtue in his original choice of key, which had caused much discomfort for the players.

72. Ibid., 30.

73. Yastrebtsev, entry for 19 Nov. 1900, vol. 2, 150.
74. Rimsky-Korsakov's letter to his wife of 21 Aug. 1891, quoted in *Stranitsï zhizni N. A. Rimskogo-Korsakova: Letopis' zhizni i tvorchestva* in 4 vols (hereafter *Stranitsï*), vol. 2 (Leningrad: Muzïka, 1969–73[1971]), 326.
75. Letter to Kruglikov of 9–10 May 1890, see N. A. Rimskiy-Korsakov, *Polnoye sobraniye sochineniy: Literaturnïye proizvedeniya i perepiska* (hereafter *LPP*), vol. 8a (Moscow: Muzïka, 1981), 184.
76. Letter to Kruglikov of 24 June 1903, see *LPP*, vol. 8b, 117.
77. Balakirev's letter to Tchaikovsky of 1 Dec. 1869, publ. in *Miliy Alekseyevich Balakirev: Vospominaniya i pis'ma*, 146.
78. The epithet was bestowed by Rimsky-Korsakov's friend Kruglikov, much to the composer's disgust, in Kruglikov's letter to Rimsky-Korsakov of 30 Sept. 1897, see *LPP*, vol. 8b, 20.
79. Yastrebtsev, 15 May 1900, 2/135.
80. This was in addition to her prejudice against the opera – she suspected that the charms of the principal singer, Nadezhda Zabela, were the true inspiration for the opera's lyricism.
81. Rimsky-Korsakov's letter to his son Andrey of 28 Oct. 1901, *Stranitsï*, vol. 3 (Leningrad: Muzïka, 1972), 263.
82. Yastrebtsev, 9 May and 14 Sept. 1900, vol. 2, 133, 141–2 .
83. V.V. Stasov, "Iskusstvo XIX veka" ("Art of the Nineteenth Century"), first publ. in 1901, in a special edition of *Niva*, "XIX vek"; the section on music repr. in *Stat'yi o muzïke*, vol. 5b (Moscow: Muzïka, 1980), 9–105 (84).
84. P. Karasyov, "Rimskiy-Korsakov, Vrubel' i Zabela-Vrubel'", written in 1944, publ. in *Nikolay Andreyevich Rimskiy-Korsakov*, ed. by A. Kandinskiy (Moscow: Moskovskaya konservatoriya, 2000), 146–68. An earlier version of this passage can be found in P.A. Karasyov, "Besedï s Nikolayem Andreyevichem Rimskim-Korsakovïm", *Russkaya muzïkal'naya gazeta*, 15, no. 49 (7 Dec. 1908).
85. V. F. Odoyevskiy, "Russkaya i tak nazïvayemaya obshchaya muzïka", *Muzïkal'no-literaturnoye naslediye*, 318–30.
86. Rimsky-Korsakov was not only motivated by a desire to distance himself from the Kuchka aesthetic, since he had already based operas on two of Mey's three dramas (*The Maid of Pskov* and *The Tsar's Bride*) leaving *Servilia* as the third and last of the set.
87. N. A. Rimskiy-Korsakov, *Letopis'*, 275.
88. Ibid.
89. The 1898 St Petersburg tour of the Mamontov Private Opera was crucial to the spread of Rimsky-Korsakov's renown: four of his operas were produced in one season (*Sadko, The Maid of Pskov, May Night* and *The Snowmaiden*) and drew large audiences even though the German Opera's Wagner cycle was playing at the same time.
90. See Yastrebtsev, entry for 6 Aug. 1901, vol. 2, 203.
91. *Die Walküre* was produced by the Mariinsky company in the season of 1900/01, *Siegfried* in 1901/02, *Götterdämmerung* in 1902/03 and *Das Rheingold* in 1905/06; for several years beginning in 1907, the whole *Ring* was performed. While these were the first performances by a Russian company, the Russian première had been given by a German company, under Karl Muck, in St Petersburg, during the 1888–89 season.
92. Another Wagnerian project was a trilogy based on Russian epic poems, *Ilya Muromets*, for which Tyumenev (librettist of *The Tsar's Bride* and *Pan Voyevoda*) prepared a complete libretto; this plan, however, was set aside when Rimsky-Korsakov became interested in *Kitezh*.
93. Belsky had previously collaborated with Rimsky-Korsakov on the libretto of *Sadko*, and later provided the two Pushkin-based libretti, *The Tale of Tsar Saltan* and *The Golden Cockerel*.
94. Grechaninov's letter to Rimsky-Korsakov of 21 Oct. 1902, quoted in *Stranitsï*, vol. 3 (Leningrad: Muzïka, 1972), 292.
95. See the description of this work and musical extracts from it in Richard Taruskin, *Opera and Drama in Russia* (Ann Arbor: UMI Research Press, 1981), 121–4, 450–90.
96. Taruskin, *Musorgsky*, 258–60.

97. It is not completely clear what Rimsky-Korsakov thought about these transcriptions; he was clearly irritated on discovering that Russian folksongs proved to be very different from what he had always imagined, although he no longer tried to brush the evidence aside as he had when confronted with Melgunov's collection. In Yastrebtsev, however, it appears that Rimsky-Korsakov eventually reconciled himself to the facts; in 1902, he comments thus on Lyadov's 35 Russian Folksongs: "They are wonderfully crafted . . . but too refined. They are all like the 9th or 10th variation on a folksong, rather than ethnographic transcriptions. Actually, Balakirev's collection and both of mine have the same shortcomings. . . . If I were to transcribe folksongs now, I would harmonize them in a very different manner." (Yastrebtsev, 5 Feb 1902, vol. 2, 234).

98. As Richard Taruskin has demonstrated, Stravinsky sincerely adhered to certain nationalist beliefs; these were most clearly manifest after he had left Russia, during the period when he associated himself with the "Eurasianist" group of Russian nationalist émigrés. Although these views exerted a direct influence on Stravinsky's artistic development, above all in *Svadebka*, non-émigré Russians never accepted that any sincerely held nationalism could be expressed in such a "grotesque" style (as they perceived it); on the contrary, they heard nothing but mockery directed towards Stravinsky's folk sources.

Chapter 5: Nationalism after the Kuchka

1. B. Asaf'yev, "O Kastal'skom", radio sketch of 1948, first published in *Sovetskaya muzïka*, no. 1 (Jan. 1951), repr. in *A. D Kastalskiy: Stat'yi, vospominaniya, materialï*, ed. by D. Zhitomirskiy (Moscow: Gosudarstvennoye muzïkal'noye izdatel'stvo, 1960), 17–18.
2. Yu. N. Mel'gunov, *Russkiye pesni neposredstvenno s golosov naroda zapisannïye i s obyasneniyami izdannïye*, vol. 1 (Moscow: Messner and Roman, 1879), IV.
3. Quoted in V. Paskhalov, "Vstrechi i vospominaniya", *A. D Kastalsky: Stat'yi, vospominaniya, materialï*, 22.
4. *Sergey Ivanovich Taneyev: Lichnost', tvorchestvo i dokumentï yego zhizni* (Moscow–Leningrad: Muzsektor, 1925), 74.
5. P. P. Sokal'skiy, *Russkaya narodnaya muzïka velikorusskaya i malorusskaya v eyo stroyenii melodicheskom i ritmicheskom i otlichiya eyo ot osnov sovremennoy garmonicheskoy muzïki* (Kharkov: Darre, 1888), 198.
6. Sokal'skiy, 208.
7. Sokal'skiy, 202.
8. Mikhail Stakhovich, Foreword to the second volume of *Russkiye narodnïye pesni* (Moscow, 1964), 15–16.
9. A few years before Melgunov, Vasily Prokunin (1848–1910) published a collection of folksongs, three of which contained a pair of transcribed voices, but this contribution passed almost unnoticed. See nos 32, 37 and 65 in *Russkiye narodnïye pesni dlya odnogo golosa s soprovozhdeniyem fortepiano*, collected and arranged by Prokunin, ed. by Tchaikovsky (Moscow: Jurgenson, 1873).
10. This work was done not by Melgunov himself, but by N. S. Klenovsky (vol. 1) and P. I. Blaramberg (vol. 2).
11. Mel'gunov, 395.
12. "O ritme i garmonii russkikh pesen: iz posmertnïkh bumag Yu.N. Mel'gunova", *Trudï muzïkal'no-etnograficheskoy komissii*, vol. 1 (Moscow: Levenson, 1906), 361–99 (391).
13. For Rimsky-Korsakov's grudging reaction, see Chapter 4, 170–2.
14. Ye.V. Gippius, "O russkoy narodnoy podgolosochnoy polifonii v kontse XVIII – nachale XIX veka", *Sovetskaya etnografiya*, no. 2 (1948), 86–104 (103).
15. Five choral arrangements of Russian folksongs written for the vocal classes of Darya Leonova. See vol. 5/10 of the Musorgsky *Complete Edition*, ed. Pavel Lamm.
16. V. Prokunin, *Russkiye narodnïye pesni dlya odnogo golosa s soprovozhdeniyem fortepiano*, ed. by Tchaikovsky (Moscow, 1872–3).
17. Ye. Linyova, *Velikorusskiye pesni v narodnoy garmonizatsii* (St Petersburg: Imperatorskaya Akademiya Nauk, 1904–09), in 2 vols.

18. There were in fact several inaccuracies in Linyova's transcriptions. In the years following the publication of her collection, only her colleague Listopadov suggested that there might be any problems, commenting on the limitations of the technology at the time (he had also transcribed from phonograph recordings). Some decades later, Soviet musicologists checked Linyova's rolls against the transcriptions and were able to confirm the presence of discrepancies. Indeed, she did not notate everything she heard, and omitted or modified the *podgoloski* that seemed wrong to her (presumably according to a folk standard that she had tacitly adopted, rather than wrong by any textbook criteria). See Ye. Kann-Novikova, *Sobiratel'nitsa russkikh narodnïkh pesen Yevgeniya Linyova* (Moscow: Gosudarstvennoye muzïkal'noye izdatel'stvo, 1952), 14–15.

19. Stasov's letter to Linyova on receipt of the first volume of her collection, quoted in Ye. Linyova, "Mïsli V.V. Stasova o narodnosti v muzïke", Izvestiya Imperatorskogo Obshchestva Lyubiteley Yestestvoznaniya, Antropologii i Etnografii", vol. 114, Trudï etnograficheskogo otdela, vol. 16, *Trudï Muzïkal'no-Etnograficheskoy komissii*, vol. 2 (Moscow: Levenson, 1911), 384–5.

20. A. D. Kastal'skiy, *Osobennosti narodno-russkoy muzïkal'noy sistemï* (Moscow: Muzgiz, 1961), 19.

21. A. D. Kastal'skiy, *Osnovï narodnogo mnogogolosiya* (Moscow–Leningrad, 1948), 323.

22. "O ritme i garmonii russkikh pesen: iz posmertnïkh bumag Yu.N. Mel'gunova", *Trudï muzïkal'no-etnograficheskoy komissii*, vol. 1 (1906), 361–99 (377).

23. Linyova stated in her preface that "the people sing in natural intervals", but she evidently did not feel it necessary to modify the standard notation she used for her transcriptions. See Ye. Linyova, *Velikorusskiye pesni v narodnoy garmonizatsii*, vol. 1, XLVI.

24. A. M. Listopadov, "K voprosu o zapisyakh narodnïkh pesen", *Muzïka i zhizn'*, no. 1 (1909), 5–6.

25. Arseniy Avraamov, "Fol'klor i sovremennost'", *Sovremennaya muzïka*, no. 2 (April 1927), 286–7.

26. Arseniy Avraamov, "Klin – klinom . . .", *Muzïkal'naya kul'tura*, no. 1 (1924), 42–4 (42).

27. Tchaikovsky's letter to Rimsky-Korsakov of 7 Sept. 1876, see P. I. Chaykovskiy, *Literaturnïye proizvedeniya i perepiska*, vol. 6 (Moscow: Gosudarstvennoye muzïkal'noye izdatel'stvo, 1961), 67–9 (67).

28. This example is discussed in G. Golovinskiy, *Musorgskiy i fol'klor* (Moscow: Muzïka, 1994) 47.

29. Melgunov gives references to the following works: Westphal, *Metrik der Griechen* (2nd ed. 1867); Fortlage, *Das musikalische System die Griechen in seiner Urgestalt* (Lepzig, 1847); Kraushaar, *Der accordliche Gegensatz und die Begründung der Scala* (Cassel, 1852); Hauptmann, *Die Natur der Harmonik und Metrik* (Leipzig, 1873); Arthur von Oettingen, *Harmoniesystem in dualer Entwickelung* (Dorpat, 1866). It was Oettingen's work that suggested to Melgunov the idea of a mirror symmetry between major and minor; the same idea also found its way into the works of Hugo Riemann.

30. Mel'gunov, vol. 1, XI.

31. Sokal'skiy, 177.

32. Sokal'skiy, 366.

33. R. G. Vestfal', "O russkoy narodnoy pesne", *Russkiy vestnik*, vol. 143, no. 9 (September 1879), 111–54 (112).

34. Vestfal', 127.

35. Ye. Linyova, *Opït zapisi fonografom ukrainskikh narodnïkh pesen*, first publ. in Moscow in 1905, repr. (Kiev, Muzïchna Ukraina, 1991).

36. Ibid., 17.

37. Yu. K. Arnol'd, "Po povodu garmonizatsii odnoy russkoy pesni", *Trudï muzïkal'no-etnograficheskoy komissii*, vol. 1 (1906), 437–40.

38. Ibid., 437.

39. V. F. Odoyevskiy, "Starinnaya pesnya", first published in *Russkiy arkhiv* in 1863, repr. in V. F. Odoyevskiy, *Muzïkal'no-literaturnoye naslediye* (Moscow: Gosudarstvennoye muzïkal'noye izdatel'stvo, 1956), 253–4.

40. *Sergey Ivanovich Taneyev: Lichnost', tvorchestvo i dokumentï yego zhizni*, 74.

41. P. I. Chaykovskiy, S. I. Taneyev, *Pis'ma* (Moscow: Goskul'tprosvetizdat, 1951), 56–61.

42. Taneyev's letter to Tchaikovsky of 18 Aug. 1880, ibid., 58–60.

43. The only clear instance of a Russian theme in his mature works is to be found in the Overture on a Russian Theme in C major.

44. P. Kovalyov, "Tvorchestvo S. I. Taneyeva", *Sergey Ivanovich Taneyev: lichnost', tvorchestvo i dokumentï yego zhizni*, 14–48 (14–15).

45. The first production of *Oresteia*, in 1895, passed almost unnoticed. A posthumous revival in 1915 fared much better, since it latched on to the current fashion for Greek subjects in poetry and painting.

46. "Doklad A.V. Nikol'skogo o garmonizatsii russkikh narodnïkh pesen", in Protokolï zasedaniy muzïkal'no-etnograficheskoy komissii 1906–1910, *Trudï muzïkal'no-etnograficheskoy komissii*, vol. 2 (1911), LVII–LVIII.

47. N. M. Lopatin, V. P. Prokunin, *Sbornik russkikh narodnïkh liricheskikh pesen* (Moscow, 1889), foreword to Part 2.

48. Ibid.

49. S. Yevseyev, *Russkiye narodnïye pesni v obrabotke A. Lyadova* (Moscow: Muzïka, 1965), 89.

50. Quoted in *Miliy Alekseyevich Balakirev: Vospominaniya i pis'ma* (Leningrad: Godudarstvennoye muzïkal'noye izdatel'stvo, 1962), 344.

51. B. V. Asaf'yev, "O russkom muzïkal'nom fol'klore kak narodnom muzïkal'nom tvorchestve v muzïkal'noy kul'ture nashey deystvitel'nosti", first publ. in *Sovetskaya muzïka*, no. 1 (1943), repr. in Asaf'yev, *Izbrannïye trudï (hereafter IT)*, vol. 4 (Moscow: Izdatel'stvo Akademii Nauk SSSR, 1955), 22–4.

52. B. V. Asaf'yev, "Kompozitor – imya yemu narod", written in 1942, first publ. in *Sovetskaya muzïka*, no. 2 (1949), repr. in *IT*, vol. 4, 17–21.

53. B. V. Asaf'yev, "O russkoy pesennosti" from the series of essays "Muzika moey Rodinï". The essay was written in 1944, first publ. in an abridged and sanitized version (e.g. with passages about Stravinsky and *Lady Macbeth* removed) in *Sovetskaya muzïka* no. 3 (1948), repr. in *IT*, vol. 4, 75–84 (77). Another version of the manuscript (shortened for different reasons) was published in *Sovetskaya muzïka*, no. 4–5 (1984).

54. B. V. Asaf'yev, "Velikiye traditsii russkoy muzïki", written in 1945, first publ. in *Sovetskaya muzïka*, no. 3 (1952), repr. in *IT*, vol. 4, 66–153 (66–7).

55. Igor' Glebov [B. V. Asafyev], "Kastal'skiy: vmesto nekrologa", *Sovremennaya muzïka*, no. 19 (Feb. 1927), 233–5.

56. Ye. Levashev, "Traditsionnïye zhanrï drevnerusskogo pevcheskogo iskusstva ot Glinki do Rakhmaninova", *Traditsionnïye zhanrï russkoy dukhovnoy muzïki i sovremennost'* (ed. Yu. Paisov), vol. 1 (Moscow: Kompozitor, 1999), 6–41 (17).

57. For more colourful details, see S.V. Smolensky, "O 'Liturgii' op. 41 Chaykovskogo: iz literaturno-yuridicheskikh vospominaniy", *Russkaya muzïkal'naya gazeta*, no. 42–3 (1903), cols 992–8, 1009–23.

58. Antonin Preobrazhensky, "Iz pervïkh let partesnogo penya v Moskve", *Muzïkal'nïy sovremennik*, no. 3 (1915), 33–41 (38).

59. V. Metallov, *O natsionalizme i tserkovnosti v russkoy dukhovnoy muzïke* (Moscow: Russkaya Pechatnya, 1912), 10.

60. On the controversy over the attribution of this project see Carolyn Dunlop, *The Russian Court Chapel Choir, 1796–1917* (Amsterdam: Harwood Academic Publishers, 2000), 65–6.

61. S. Smolenskiy, foreword to *Azbuka znamennogo peniya startsa Aleksandra Mezentsa* (Kazan: Tipografiya Imperatorskogo Universiteta and Tipo-Litografiya N. Danilova, 1888), 26.

62. See A. V. Preobrazhensky, *Kul'tovaya muzïka v Rossii* (Leningrad: Academia, 1924), 81.

63. Fyodor Lvov (1766–1836), cousin of the folksong collector Nikolai Lvov, was director of the Cappella from 1826 to 1836.

64. A. F. L'vov, Foreword to *Obikhod notnogo tserkovnogo peniya* (St Petersburg, 1848), 11.

65. Metallov, *O natsionalizme i tserkovnosti v russkoy dukhovnoy muzïke*, 13.

66. Prot. M. Lisitsïn, "Epokha Bortnyanskogo, Turchaninova i L'vova i znacheniye nazvannïkh kompozitorov v istorii russkoy kul'turï", *Pamyati dukhovnïkh kompozitorov Bortnyanskogo,*

Turchaninova i L'vova (St Petersburg: Vremennïy komitet po uvekovecheniyu pamyati nazvannïkh kompozitorov, 1908), 43.

67. Quoted in Preobrazhenskiy, *Kul'tovaya muzïka v Rossii*, 84.

68. Stepan Smolenskiy, "O pamyatnike Bortnyanskomu, Turchaninovu i Lvovu v Sankt-Peterburge", *Khorovoye i regentskoye delo*, no. 3 (1909), 65–70 (68).

69. A. L'vov, *O svobodnom ili nesimmetrichnom ritme* (St Petersburg: Bauman, 1858).

70. V. F. Odoyevskiy, "Russkaya i tak nazïvayemaya obshchaya muzïka", first publ. in *Russkiy* (24 April 1867), 170–7, repr. in Odoyevskiy, *Muzïkal'no-literaturnoye naslediye*, 318–30.

71. Quoted from K. A. Yanchuk, "Knyaz' V. F. Odoyevskiy i yego znacheniye v istorii russkoy narodnoy i tserkovnoy muzïki", *Trudï muzïkal'no-etnograficheskoy komissii*, vol. 1, 409–27 (424).

72. D. V. Razumovskiy, *Tserkovnoye peniye v Rossii: opït istoriko-tekhnicheskogo izlozheniya* (Moscow, 1867–9).

73. Quoted in Ye. Levashev, "Traditsionnïye zhanrï drevnerusskogo pevcheskogo iskusstva ot Glinki do Rakhmaninova", *Traditsionnïye zhanrï russkoy dukhovnoy muzïki i sovremennost'*, vol. 1, 6–41 (21). Fragments from Lomakin's "Autobiographical notes" were published by Yu. Goryaynov in *Sovetskaya muzïka*, no. 11 (1991), 47–9. Lomakin's All-Night Vigil of the Znamennïy Chant was published in 1884.

74. Russkaya Natsional'naya Biblioteka (Russian National Library), fund 41 (Balakirev), No. 332.

75. Ibid.

76. Rimsky-Korsakov's letter to Kruglikov of 5 July 1883, see. N. A. Rimskiy-Korsakov, *Polnoye sobraniye sochineniy: Literaturnïye proizvedeniya i perepiska*, vol. 8a (Moscow: Muzïka, 1978), 116.

77. Preobrazhenskiy, *Kul'tovaya muzïka v Rossii*, 109.

78. Quoted in Metallov, *O natsionalizme i tserkovnosti v russkoy dukhovnoy muzïke*, 14.

79. See Balakirev's letter to Tchaikovsky of 18 Dec. 1884, quoted in *Khorovoye i regentskoye delo* (Feb. 1913), 26–7.

80. Taneyev's letter to Tchaikovsky of 10 Aug. 1881, see P. I. Tchaikovsky, S. I. Taneyev, *Pis'ma*, 74–6.

81. Quoted in S. Zvereva, *Aleksandr Kastalskiy* (Moscow: Vuzovskaya kniga, 1999), 93.

82. Quoted in M. P. Rakhmanova, "Obshchestvo lyubiteley tserkovnogo peniya", in *Russkaya dukhovnaya muzïka v dokumentakh i materialakh*, vol. 3 (Moscow: Yazïki slavyanskoy kul'turï, 2002), 205.

83. A. Nikolskiy, "S.V. Smolenskiy i ego rol' v novom napravlenii russkoy tserkovnoy muzïki", *Khorovoye i regentskoye delo* (Oct. 1913), 151–6.

84. A. Nikolskiy, "O 'tserkovnosti' dukhovnoy muzïki", *Khorovoye i regentskoye delo*, no. 11 (1909), 263–9 (267).

85. V. Metallov, *Osmoglasiye znamenogo rospeva: opït rukovodstva k izucheniyu osmoglasiya znamenogo rospeva po glasovïm popevkam* (Moscow: Sinodal'naya tipografiya, 1899).

86. N. Kompaneyskiy, "Kharakternïye chertï russkikh pesen tserkovnïkh i mirskikh", *Muzïka i zhizn'* (1909), no. 5, 6–9 and no. 6, 4–14.

87. Preobrazhenskiy, *Kul'tovaya muzïka v Rossii*, 116.

88. Yu. I., "Novïye zadachi pravoslavnoy tserkovnoy muzïki v Rossii", *Khorovoye i regentskoye delo*, no. 5, (May–June 1913), 80.

89. "Rezolyutsii IV-go regentskogo syezda", *Khorovoye i regentskoye delo* (July–Aug 1913), 114–15.

90. F. Vladimirskiy, " 'Staroye' i 'novoye' v tserkovnoy muzïke", *Muzïka i zhizn'*, no. 1–2 (Jan.–Feb. 1911), 17–19.

91. A. D. Kastalskiy, "O moyey muzïkal'noy kar'yere i moi mïsli o tserkovnoy muzïke", *Muzïkal'nïy sovremennik*, 2 (Oct. 1915), 31–7 (36–7).

92. A. Preobrazhenskiy, "A. D. Kastalskiy: materialï k biografii", *A. D Kastalskiy: Stat'yi, vospominaniia, materialï*, 30–1.

93. The *Peshchnoye deystvo* is based on a story from the book of Prophet Daniel about three youths Ananiy, Azariy and Misail, who refused to serve the golden idol. To punish them, King Nebuchadnezzar ordered to put them into a burning stove, but they were miraculously rescued by an angel.

94. Quoted in A. Preobrazhenskiy, "A. D. Kastalskiy: materialï k biografii", *A. D. Kastalskiy: Stat'yi, vospominaniia, materialï*, 34.
95. See Zvereva, 150–60.
96. F. Vladimirskiy, "'Staroye' i 'novoye' v tserkovnoy muzïke", *Muzïka i zhizn'*, no. 1–2 (Jan.–Feb. 1911), 17–19.
97. K. P. Pobedonostsev, "Prazdniki Gospodni", first publ. in 1893, repr. in Sochineniya (St Petersburg: Nauka, 1996), 218–63 (219). The "heirmos melodies" Pobedonostsev refers to were probably ancient in provenance but non-*znamennïye*; Pobedonostsev would have heard such melodies in modern harmonized arrangements by Lvov, Turchaninov and others.
98. K. P. Pobedonostsev, "Prazdniki Gospodni", first publ. in 1893, repr. in *Sochineniya*, 220.
99. K. P. Pobedonostsev, "Moskovskiy sbornik", first publ. in 1896, repr. In *K. P. Pobedonostsev: Pro et Contra (Lichnost', obshchestvenno-politicheskaya deyatelnost' i mirovozzrenie Konstantina Pobedonostseva v otsenke russkikh mysliteley i issledovateley: antologiya)* (Moscow, Izdatel'stvo Russkogo Khristianskogo gumanitarnogo instituta, 1996), 80–275 (221). For an explanation of "heirmos", see note 97.
100. Quoted in Zvereva, 57.
101. B. B. Glinskiy, "Konstantin Petrovich Pobedonostsev", first publ. 1907, repr. In *K. P. Pobedonostsev: Pro et Contra*, 387–415 (388).
102. Leon Trotsky, *1905* (New York: Random House, 1971), 82–3.

Chapter 6: Musical nationalism in Stalin's Soviet Union

1. I. V. Stalin, *Marksizm i natsional'no-kolonial'nïy vopros* (Moscow: Partizdat, 1934), 195.
2. Zhdanov's introductory speech at the meeting of Soviet musicians in the Central Committee of the Communist Party, see "Vïstupleniye tov. A.A. Zhdanova na soveshchanii deyateley sovestkoy muzïki v TsK VKP(b) ", *Sovetskaya muzïka*, no. 1 (Jan.–Feb. 1948), 14–26 (26).
3. "Pervïy vsesoyuznïy syezd sovestkikh kompozitorov"; *Sovetskaya muzïka*, no. 2 (March 1948), 23–75 (73).
4. V. I. Lenin, "Itogi diskussii o samoopredelenii" (1916), in *Voprosï natsional'noy politiki i proletarskogo internatsionalizma* (Moscow: Politizdat, 1965), 129.
5. For example, until the Germans were defeated in the West, they had control of Ukraine through their puppet ruler Skoropadsky, and later the French were the controlling power in the Ukraine. Similarly, the Georgian Menshevik government provided its territory and resources first to the Germans, and later of the British and White Russian forces of General Wrangel. In the circumstances of the Civil War, "the choice was not between dependence and independence, but dependence on Moscow or dependence on the bourgeois governments of the capitalist world", as E. H. Carr put it in *The Bolshevik Revolution, 1917–23* (London, 1966), vol. 1, 273.
6. These arguments are set out in greatest detail in Lenin, "The Right of Nations to Self-Determination", V. I. Lenin, *Collected Works* (Moscow, 1972), vol. 20, 393–454. They were frequently reiterated in Lenin's writings up to the end of his life (see note 9 below).
7. Bukharin declared his opposition at the 8th Bolshevik Congress, characterizing the right to self-determination as a "right to foolishness"; see D. Gluckstein, *The Tragedy of Bukharin* (London: Pluto Press, 1994), 52–6. Dzerzhinsky, himself a Pole, did not see a distinction between the nationalism of an imperial power (Russia), and the nationalism of an oppressed nation (such as Poland); see *Sed'maia (Aprel'skaia) Vserossiiskaia Konferentsia RSDRP (Bol'shevikov): Protokolï* (Moscow, 1958), 224.
8. For a discussion of how the White General Denikin turned actual and potential allies into enemies, whether peasants of South Russia, Kuban Cossacks, Ukrainians, Dagestanis, Georgians or Azerbaijanis, see W. H. Chamberlin, *The Russian Revolution, 1917–1921* (London: Macmillan, 1935), vol. 2, 255–61. Even Poland's military leader, Marshal Pilsudski, who was openly hostile to the Bolsheviks, refused to intervene in favour of Denikin, preferring to launch his own attack on Russia (with the encouragement of the

French government) only after the Whites were defeated – he was convinced that a White victory would be worse for Poland; see Chamberlin, ibid., 259–60.

9. Lenin's letter of 31 Dec. 1922 to the impending Congress of Soviets (part of his so-called "Last Testament"), was suppressed by the "troika" of Stalin, Zinoviev and Kamenev (the "Testament" also called for the removal of Stalin from the Central Committee). "The Question of Nationalities or 'Autonomization', V.I. Lenin, *Collected Works*, (Moscow, 1972), vol. 36, 593–611.

10. Yuri Slezkine, "The USSR as a Communal Apartment, or How a Socialist State Promoted Ethnic Particularism", *Slavic Review* 53, no. 2 (Summer 1994), 414–52 (431–2).

11. S. Dimanshtein, "Sovetskaya vlast' i mel'kie natsional'nosti", *Zhizn' natsional'nostey* 26 (54) (7 Dec. 1919), quoted in Slezkine, 420.

12. Stalin's speech at the 16th Party Congress, quoted in Slezkine, 437–8.

13. Slezkine, 439.

14. Quoted in Arkadiy Vaksberg, *Stalin protiv yevreev: sekreti strashnoy epokhi* (New York: Liberty Publishing House, 1995), 210.

15. *Far Eastern Economic Review*, 1952, quoted in Tony Cliff, *State Capitalism in Russia* (London, Chicago, Sydney: Bookmarks, 1996), 257–8.

16. *Literaturnaya gazeta*, 1952, quoted in Cliff, 258–9.

17. Igor' Glebov, "Gryadushchaya era russkoy muziki", *K novim beregam*, no. 1 (1923), 5–13 (12).

18. Igor' Glebov, "Krizis muziki", *Muzikal'naya kul'tura*, no. 2 (1924), 99–120 (102).

19. Trotsky, as it happened, had already argued at length that no working class was capable of producing cultural traditions that could remotely rival those produced by the artists who had served the feudal or capitalist ruling classes in the past; the working class was granted an education that only sufficed for its tasks within capitalist society, and little energy was left after the working week for any great cultural achievements to be undertaken in the scant leisure time available. By the time such deficiencies could be rectified in a post-revolutionary society, Trotsky had argued, there would be no working class (or any other class) left. But Trotsky was already being pushed to the political margins at the time he was publishing these arguments (1924), and before long a persistent attachment to anything associated with Trotsky was bad for one's career, to say the least. In any case, too many composers and critics, especially in RAPM, had hitched their careers to causes that would have been undermined if Trotsky's arguments were accepted. See Leon Trotsky, *Literature and Revolution* (London: RedWords, 1991), 213–42.

20. Dialektik [N. A. Roslavets], "O reaktsionnom i progressivnom v muzike", *Muzikal'naya kul'tura*, no. 1 (1924), 45–51 (45–6).

21. Ibid., 48.

22. Yuriy Keldish, "Problema proletarskogo muzikal'nogo tvorchestva i poputnichestvo", *Proletarskiy muzikant*, no. 1 (1929), 12–21 (15).

23. During the First Five-Year Plan, RAPM was tacitly supported by the Party and managed to displace its opponents from their administrative posts. As a consequence, ASM effectively ceased to exist around 1929, although it was officially disbanded only in April 1932, when the state abolished independent artistic organizations (including RAPM).

24. Derzhanovsky's letter to Asafyev of 18 Jan. 1930, housed in RGALI (Russian State Archive for Literature and Art), fund 2658 (Asaf'yev), list 2, folder 45. The manifesto survives in the form of this draft.

25. V. Beliy, "Printsipial'niye voprosi razvitiya natsional'nikh muzikal'nikh kul'tur", *Proletarskiy muzikant*, no. 6 (1931), 1–13 (3).

26. Ibid., 12.

27. *Sovetskaya muzika*, no. 1 (Jan. 1934), 3.

28. *Sovetskaya muzika* was the official replacement for all independent journals that had survived up to this point; it served as the organ of the Composers' Union, also created by the state in 1934, replacing the last independent music organizations.

29. I. Stalin, "Voprosi leninizma", first published in *Pravda*, no. 115, May 22, 1925, and can be found in I. Stalin, "The Political Tasks of the University of the Peoples of the East", *Works* (Moscow: Foreign Languages Publishing House, 1954), vol. 7, 140.

30. K. Marx and F. Engels, *Selected Works* (Moscow: Progress Publishers, 1969), vol. 1, 98–137. Engl. transl. by Samuel Moore. I have changed Moore's "substance" to "content", since the word used in the standard Russian version is the same.

31. The first, pre-war series of the *Dekadï natsional'nogo iskusstva* (10-day festivals of national art):
    1936 March 11–21 Ukraine; May 17–25 Kazakhstan
    1937 January 5–15 Georgia; May 21–30 Uzbekistan
    1938 April 5–15 Azerbaijan
    1939 May 26 – June 4, Kirgiziya [Kirghizstan]; October 20–29 Armenia
    1940 June 5–15 Belorussia; October 20–27 Buryat-Mongolia
    1941 April 12–20 Tajikistan

32. From Chelyapov's speech to the Moscow Union of Composers, *Sovetskaya muzïka*, no. 3 (March 1936), 19.

33. See Leonid Maksimenkov, *Sumbur vmesto muzïki: Stalinskaya kul'turnaya revolyutsiya, 1936–38* (Moscow: Yuridicheskaya kniga, 1997).

34. *Vlast' i khudozhestvennaya intelligentsiya: dokumentï TsK RKP(b) – VKP(b), VChK – OGPU – NKVD o kul'turnoy politike, 1917–1953* (Moscow: Mezhdunarodnïy fond "Demokratiya", 1999), 289.

35. Arkadiy Klimovitskiy, "Syuita na finskiye temï – neizvestnoye sochineniye Shostakovicha", *Shostakovich: Mezhdu mgnoveniyem i vechnost'yu*, ed. L. Kovnatskaya (St Petersburg: Kompozitor, 2000), 308–27.

36. Georgy Khubov, "Sovetskaya opera," *Sovetskaya muzïka*, no. 1 (Jan. 1938), 15.

37. Minutes of the meetings of the presidium of the Organizational Committee of the Composers' Union of 6 Feb. 1941, RGALI, fund 2077 (Soyuz Sovetskikh Kompozitorov), list 1, folder 36.

38. Transcript of a plenary session of the Stalin Prize Committee of 21 Feb. 1943, RGALI, Fond 2073 (Komitet po Stalinskim premiyam v oblasti iskusstva i literaturï), opis' 1, delo 7.

39. Ye. Romanovskaya, "Muzïka v Uzbekistane," *Sovetskaya muzïka*, no. 9 (Sept. 1934), 3–9.

40. Ibid.

41. Georgy Khubov, "Muzïkal'noye iskusstvo Uzbekistana," *Sovetskaya muzïka*, no. 3 (March 1937), 7–14.

42. "Keroglu" is also transliterated variously as "Ker-oglï" and "Kyor-Oglï"; the complications arise from the double layer of transliteration involved: first from Arabic to Cyrillic, then from the latter to Roman.

43. Georgiy Khubov, "Iskusstvo azerbaydzhanskogo naroda," *Sovetskaya muzïka*, no. 4 (April 1938), 5–22.

44. B. Zeydman, "Gliyer i azerbaydzhanskaya muzïkal'naya kul'tura," in *R.M. Gliyer: Stat'yi, vospominaniya, materialï*, ed. by V. M. Bogdanov-Berezovskiy, vol. 2 (Leningrad: Muzïka, 1966), 216–36.

45. Quoted in Z. Safarova, *Muzïkal'no-esteticheskiye vzglyady Uzeira Gadzhibekova* (Moscow: Sovetskiy kompozitor, 1973), 96.

46. I thank Martin Stokes for acquainting me with this material.

47. Incidentally, Stalin's own attention to *Almast* was attracted in September 1930 by his wife, as she wrote to him: "Saw the new opera Almas[t], where Maksakova danced the *lezghinka* (Armenian) absolutely extraordinarily, I haven't seen a dance being performed in such an artistic way for a long time. I think you will like the dance a lot, and the opera as well." Quoted in Leonid Maksimenkov, *Sumbur vmesto muzïki*, 14.

48. Interview for the newspaper *Kommunist* (Baku) 26 March 1925, no. 66. Repr. in *Spendiarov o muzïke* (Yerevan: Izdatel'stvo TsK KP Armenii, 1971), 53–7.

49. F. A. Abukova, *Turkmenskaya opera: puti formirovaniya, zhanrovaya tipologiya* (Ashkhabad: ïlïm, 1987). As it happens, many Muslim cultures did indeed owe some debt to Ancient Greek music theory and practice, which had been absorbed by Muslim Arabic culture, and then by other peoples via the Ottoman Empire. So it would not be *prima facie* absurd to investigate whether the music of the Muslim and Turkic-speaking Turkmen might have had some highly attenuated links with Ancient Greece. But Abukova's approach, including

her conflation of Greek scales with the very different mediaeval/Renaissance modes and the major/minor system, is much closer to the Kuchka's mythologizing than to any such historical and ethnomusicologial investigation.

50. Uzeir Gadzhibekov, *Osnovï azerbaidzhanskoy narodnoy muzïki* (Baku: Izdatel'stvo AN Azerbaydzhanskoy SSR, 1945), 32.

51. See P. A. Karasyov, "Besedï s Nikolayem Andreyevichem Rimskim-Korsakovïm", *Russkaya muzïkal'naya gazeta*, 15, no. 49 (7 Dec. 1908), cols 1119–20. The quotation in question was discussed at length in Chapter 4.

52. Vlasov and Fere tried to justify this melodic doubling on the grounds that the successive strings of the traditional accompanying instrument were tuned a fourth apart – on the same grounds, parallel fifths should dominate Western music because of the tuning of the violin family.

53. Edward W. Said, *Orientalism* (London: Routledge & Kegan Paul, 1978).

54. In 1944, at a plenary session of the Organizational Committee of the Union of Composers, Khachaturian, who was chairing, openly complained that "they are trying to keep me within the boundaries of national music". RGALI, Fund 2077 (Soyuz Kompozitorov SSSR), List 1, Folder 92.

55. Uzeir Hajibeyov, first publ. 1925, repr. in Safarova, *Muzïkal'no-esteticheskiye vzglyady Uzeira Gadzhibekova*, 45.

56. I. Rïzhkin, "Stilevïye chertï sovetskoy muzïki," *Sovetskaya muzïka*, no. 3 (March 1939), 47–52.

57. See Uzeir Gadzhibekov, *Osnovï azerbaidzhanskoy narodnoy muzïki*.

58. Uzeir Gadzhibekov, "Muzïkal'noe razvitie v Azerbaydzhane," first publ. in *Maarif ve medenijet* (1926), no. 8 (in Azerbaijani); quoted in Safarova, *Muzïkal'no-esteticheskiye vzglyady Uzeira Gadzhibekova*, 145.

59. Uzeir Gadzhibekov, "O narodnosti v muzïke"; first published in *Narodnoye tvorhestvo*, no. 4 (1939), repr. in his *O muzïkal'nom iskusstve Azerbaydzhana* (Baku: Azernashr, 1966), 85.

60. Gadzhibekov, "O narodnosti v muzïke," quoted in Safarova, 145.

61. V. Vinogradov, *Uzeir Gadzhibekov i azerbaydzhanskaya muzïka*, (Moscow, 1972), 13–14.

62. Even something seemingly so innocuous as octave-doubling proved to be problematic, since Azeri music employed modal systems that were not based on octave cycles; degrees an octave apart were accordingly assigned different functions. The introduction of octave doubling in the scoring of the new operas meant the erosion of this fundamental component of Azeri music.

63. Gadzhibekov, *Osnovï azerbaydzhanskoy narodnoy muzïki*, 32.

64. Uzeir Gadzhibekov, "O narodnosti v muzïke", 86.

65. Ibid., 85.

66. First published in 1931; quoted in Safarova, 161–2.

67. Safarova, 161.

68. For more on the achievements of his school see S. Khalfen, "Azerbaydzhanskaya shkola peniya," *Sovetskaya muzïka*, no. 3 (March 1940), 81–2.

69. Quoted in D. A. Arutyunov, *A. Khachaturyan i muzïka Sovetskogo Vostoka: yazïk, stil', traditsii* (Moscow: Muzïka, 1983), 15.

70. See David Brandenberger, *National Bolshevism: Stalinist Mass Culture and the Formation of Modern Russian National Identity, 1931–1956* (Harvard University Press, 2002), 43. The use of the phrase "first among equals" is, of course, a hypocrisy whenever one member has leadership status permanently, as of right.

71. Ibid., 97. It is most unlikely that Bukharin was attempting, however obliquely, to voice opposition to the shift in rhetoric; after a brief period of opposition in early 1929 (confined to the upper echelons of the Party), Bukharin had either endorsed Stalin's policies openly, or at best kept his head down from time to time. It was not until his show trial in 1938 that he once again showed any resistance. Cf. D. Gluckstein, *The Tragedy of Bukharin*, 237–52.

72. *Vlast' i khudozhestvennaya intelligentsiya*, 333.

73. Ibid., 337.

74. Ibid. The opera *Minin and Pozharsky* was written by Boris Asafyev to a libretto by Mikhail Bulgakov; even though it had been commissioned by the Bolshoi, the opera was never produced, most probably because it could not be allowed to rival the newfound prestige of Glinka's *Ivan Susanin* which covered the same historical events (albeit from a different angle).
75. Ibid.
76. Ibid.
77. Ibid., 344–6.
78. Eisenstein, "Alexander Nevsky and the Rout of the Germans", *Izvestiya*, 12 July 1938, repr. in *The Eisenstein Reader*, ed. Richard Taylor (London: British Film Institute, 1998), 140–4 (144).
79. I. Nest'yev, "Sergey Prokof'yev", *Sovetskaya muzïka*, no. 4 (April 1941), 59–70 (69).
80. A. Ostretsov, "4-ya ('Izhorskaya') simfoniya V. Shcherbachova", *Sovetskaya muzïka*, no. 5 (May 1938), 15–25.
81. Prokofiev's speech at the plenary session of the Organizational Committee of the USSR Composers' Union (March–April 1944), RGALI, fund 2077, list 1, folder 92.
82. Viktor Tsukkerman, "Neskol'ko mïsley o sovetskoy opere", *Sovetskaya muzïka*, no. 12 (1940), 66–78 (78).
83. Transcript of the Leningrad plenary session of the Organizational Committee of the Composers' Union, devoted to the problems of Soviet symphonism (6–15 May 1941), RGALI, fund 2077, list 1, folder 42.
84. Transcript of the plenary session of the Organizational Committee of the Composers' Union, 28–31 March 1944), RGALI, fund 2077, list 1, folder 92.
85. Ibid.
86. Ibid.
87. Ibid.
88. B. Shteynpress, in the transcript of a Session Devoted to the Discussion of B. S. Shteynpress's Work *Narodnost' i modernism*, 1 July 1949, RGALI, fund 2077, list 1, folder 370.
89. L. Mazel' "Ob obshchenarodnom russkom muzïkal'nom yazïke", *Sovetskaya muzïka*, no. 2 (1951), 37–9.
90. N. Bryusova, "Put' k narodnomu muzïkal'nomu yazïku", *Sovetskaya muzïka*, no. 2 (1951), 34–6.
91. "Ob opere 'Bogdan Khmel'nitskiy'", *Sovetskaya muzïka*, no. 7 (July 1951), 3–7, reprint of the article in *Pravda* of 20 July 1951.
92. D. Shepilov, P. Lebedev, "O nedostatkakh v razvitii sovetskoy muzïki", Letter to the Secretaries of the Central Committee of the Communist Party, quoted from V. Rubtsova, *Tak eto bïlo: Tikhon Khrennikov o vremeni i o sebe* (Moscow: Muzïka, 1994), 190.
93. "Vazhnïye zadachi sovetskoy muzïkal'noy kul'turï", *Sovetskaya muzïka*, no. 8 (August 1951), 3–9 (7).
94. Transcript of the Stalin Prize Committee meeting, 8 Jan. 1953, RGALI, fund 2073 (Komitet po Stalinskim premiyam), list 2, folder 10.
95. I thank Madeleine Reeves for providing me with first-hand material used in this section.

GLOSSARY OF NAMES

Aksakov brothers, Ivan Sergeyevich (1823–86) and Konstantin Sergeyevich (1817–60). Russian critics and writers, founders of the Slavophile movement.

Aleksandrov (Mormonenko), Grigoriy Vasilyevich (1903–83). Soviet film director and script writer.

Alexander I (1777–1825), Emperor of Russia (1801–25), King of Poland (1815–25). Introduced some liberal reforms in the earlier part of his rule but after a revolutionary conspiracy among army officers and a kidnap attempt (both 1818) he came under the sway of the conservative Metternich. The news of his death was immediately followed by the abortive Decembrist rising.

Alexander III (1845–94), Emperor of Russia (1881–94). Notorious for his reactionary policies, he presided over continued eastward expansion of the Empire, but avoided conflict with the major Western powers.

Annenkov, Pavel Vasilyevich (1814–87). Russian critic and historian, best known for his memoirs, *The Extraordinary Decade.*

Ariosto, Ludovico (1474–1533). Italian poet. Best known for his epic *Orlando furioso* (1516).

Arnold, Yuriy Karlovich (1811–98). Russian music theorist (author of essays on Russian folk and church singing), critic, composer.

Arnshtam, Lev Oskarovich (1905–79). Soviet film director best known for his films *Zoya* (1944, with Shostakovich's music), *Glinka* (1947), and the cinematic version of Prokofiev's *Romeo and Juliet* (1955).

Artôt-Padilla, Désirée (1835–1907). Belgian opera singer (mezzo-soprano) of European fame. In 1868 Tchaikovsky contemplated proposing to her, and was shocked to discover that she had decided to marry the Spanish baritone Padilla y Ramos.

Asafyev, Boris Vladimirovich (wrote under the pseudonym Igor Glebov, 1884–1949). Soviet musicologist and composer. Author of the pioneering theory of "intonation" and leading member of ASM in the 1920s, but under pressure from RAPM switched to composing pastiche ballets and operas. When he returned to writing, in the 1940s, his outlook had changed dramatically to conservative nationalism, in keeping with state policy.

ASM – Association for Contemporary Music (*Assotsiatsiya Sovremennoy Muzïki*). Soviet composers' organization. Founded in 1924, it promoted close links with progressive Western composers, ran concert series and published a journal containing critical and polemical articles. Officially disbanded by the state in 1932 (along with all other non-state cultural organizations), but effectively defunct from about 1930 due to pressure from RAPM.

Atatürk ("Father Turk", name bestowed on Mustafa Kemal, 1881–1938). Founder and first president of Republic of Turkey. On the collapse of the Ottoman Empire successfully led war of independence against occupying powers, and established a modern secular Turkish state. In the cultural field, Atatürk was a determined Westernizer, replacing the Arabic with the Roman alphabet and introducing Western artistic institutions, including opera.

Avraamov, Arseniy Mikhaylovich (1886–1944). Russian composer, music theorist and folk-song collector. In the 1920s and early '30s he experimented with tuning systems, invented a method of recording film sound tracks, and produced an avant-garde work *Simfoniya gudkov* (Symphony of Sirens, 1922).

Azeyev, Yevstafiy Stepanovich (1851–1918). Russian choirmaster and composer of church music.

Bakhmetev, Nikolay Ivanovich (1807–91). Russian composer of church music, 1861–63 Director of the Court Cappella in St Petersburg.

Balakirev, Miliy Alekseyevich (1837–1910). Russian composer. Better known for the teaching and leadership he gave to the Kuchka than for his own works, although the virtuosic *Islamey* remains prominent in the piano repertoire. Helped found the Free Music School of St Petersburg (1862), but the strain of running this institution drove him to a nervous breakdown in 1872. He suspended his musical career until the Imperial Court employed him as Kapellmeister and conductor of the Imperial Music Society in 1883.

Bartók, Béla (1881–1945). Hungarian composer, ethnomusicologist and pianist. Considered one of the pioneers of modern ethnomusicological methodology, scientific rather than nationalistic in motivation; his researches ranging over Hungarian, Romanian, Slav, Turkic and Arabic music. His one opera, *Bluebeard's Castle*, and many orchestral, chamber and piano works remain in the repertoire. Emigrated to the USA in 1940 because of Nazi pressure on Hungary.

Bedny, Demyan (pseudonym adopted by Yefim Alekseyevich Pridvorov, 1883–1945). Russian/Soviet poet, author of agitprop verses and satirical plays. Officially in good standing until the banning of *Bogatïri* (*The Warriors*) in 1936, after which he was expelled from the Communist Party and from the Union of Writers.

Belinsky, Vissarion Grigoryevich (1811–48). Russian literary critic, best known for his essays on Pushkin. Usually categorized as a Westernizer (*zapadnik*), in opposition to the Slavophiles.

Belïy, Viktor Arkadyevich (1904–83). Soviet composer, member of Prokoll and RAPM. Wrote several popular mass songs such as *Orlyonok* (*The Eaglet*, 1936).

Bellini, Vincenzo (1801–35). Italian opera composer. Best known for his 1830s works: *La sonnambula, Norma* and *I puritani*.

Belsky, Vladimir Ivanovich (1866–1946). Russian librettist, best known for his collaborations with Rimsky-Korsakov (*Tsar Saltan, Kitezh, The Golden Cockerel*).

Bely, Andrey (pseudonym adopted by Boris Nikolayevich Bugayev, 1880–1934). Russian novelist, poet, and literary critic, best known for his influential symbolist novel *Petersburg* (1913).

Belyayev, Viktor Mikhaylovich (1888–1968). Soviet musicologist, prominent member of ASM. Best known for his ethnomusicological work on the Caucasus and Central Asia.

Berdyayev, Nikolay Aleksandrovich (1874–1948). Russian religious and political philosopher. Exiled from Soviet Russia in 1922.

Berlioz, Hector (1803–69). French composer, conductor and writer.

Bernandt, Grigoriy Borisovich (1905–?). Soviet musicologist. Best known for his essays on Chopin, Wagner, and Odoyevsky.

Blanter, Matvey Isaakovich (1903–90). Soviet composer of popular music. Best known for his song *Katyusha* (1939).

Blok, Aleksandr Aleksandrovich (1880–1921). Russian poet. The most eminent figure of the Russian literary "Silver Age", associated with Symbolism. In his last years wrote revolutionary verses.

Blyma, Franz Xavier (1770–1812?). Russian Kapellmeister and composer of Czech extraction, best known for his comic opera *Starinnïye svyatki* (*Old Yuletide*, 1800).

Bodyansky, Osip Maksimovich (1808–77). Ukrainian/Russian scholar of Slavic history and languages. Best known for his commentary on the pseudo-medieval epic *The Lay of Igor's Campaign*, and among the first to cast doubt on its authenticity.

Borodin, Aleksandr Porfiryevich (1833–87). Russian composer and chemist. Member of Kuchka best known for the Polovtsian Dances from his unfinished opera, *Prince Igor*. As a chemist eminent internationally (one reaction still bears his name today).

Bortnyansky, Dmitro (Dmitriy) Stepanovich (1751–1825). Ukrainian composer, from 1796 Director of Russian Imperial Cappella Choir. Successful composer of operas in Italy during 1770s, and later of French *opéras comiques* after his return to Russia, but best known for his sacred music for the Orthodox Church.

Brown, David (1929–). British musicologist. Best known for his writings on Russian music, including works on Glinka and Tchaikovsky.

Brusilovsky, Yevgeniy Grigoryevich (1905–81). Soviet composer, composer of several Kazakh operas.

Bryusov, Valeriy Yakovlevich (1873–1924). Russian poet, novelist, playwright, translator and critic, one of the founders of the Russian Symbolist movement.

Bryusova, Nadezhda Yakovlevna (1881–1951). Soviet musicologist, sister of Valeriy Bryusov. In the 1920s she was a member of the Moscow Conservatoire's Red Professors Association and an active member of RAPM.

Bukharin, Nikolay Ivanovich (1888–1938). A leading Bolshevik, and from 1917 a senior member of the Soviet government. Demoted by Stalin in 1929 and executed in 1938 for alleged political crimes.

Cavos, Catterino (1775–1840). An Italian Kapellmeister and composer who spent most of his life in Russia. Best known for his opera *Ivan Susanin* (1815); conductor for the première of Glinka's *A Life for the Tsar* (based on the same plot) in 1836.

Chaadayev, Pyotr Yakovlevich (1794–1856). Russian political essayist. His "Philosophical Letters" (1829), written in French, painted a dismal picture of Russia, and argued that a Westernizing course had to be adopted urgently. Publication of the letters in Russian was halted by the authorities after the translation of the first letter, and they declared Chaadayev insane. He nevertheless came to be seen as a father figure by the next generation of Westernizers.

Chekhov, Anton Pavlovich (1860–1904). Russian short-story writer, dramatist and physician. Proto-modernist, pioneering stream-of-consciousness techniques and beginning and ending stories *in medias res*. After initial failure, his plays were taken up by the Stanislavsky theatre.

Chirkov, Boris Petrovich (1901–82). Soviet film actor; best known for his role as "Maxim" in the trilogy *The Youth of Maxim, The Return of Maxim, The Viborg Side* (1934–8).

Chopin, Frédéric (or Fryderyk, 1801–49). Franco-Polish composer and pianist. His piano works were innovative both compositionally and technically. The Mazurkas were highly influential as examples of musical nationalism.

Cui, Tsezar (César) Antonovich (1835–1918). Russian composer, music critic and army officer. Member of Kuchka.

Danilov, Kirsha (Cyril). Semi-mythical author of early Russian epic songs (*bïlina*). Although the words (and in some cases the music) of several epic songs were transcribed in the early and mid-eighteenth century, none were published until 1804, while the complete collection with melodies included, appeared in 1818, ascribing all the songs to Danilov.

Dankevich, Konstantin Fyodorovich (1905–84). Ukrainian Soviet composer, best remembered for his banned opera *Bogdan Khmelnitsky* (1951).

Dargomïzhsky, Aleksandr Sergeyevich (1813–69). Russian opera composer. His final work, the incomplete *Stone Guest*, was regarded as a model of Russian progressive composition by the Kuchka. The completion by Cui and Rimsky-Korsakov (1872) failed to stay in the repertoire, but strongly influenced the earlier version of Musorgsky's *Boris Godunov*.

Decembrists (1820s). Russian insurgents. One of the groups of military conspirators of the period, the Decembrists made their move in the confusion over the succession after the death of Alexander I (December 1825). Defeated when most of the St Petersburg garrison failed to join the insurgency. Five participants were executed, and the remainder exiled to the eastern fringes of the empire. This was the first open conflict between the state and liberal elements.

Dehn, Siegfried (1799–1858). German music theorist and teacher, author of textbooks on harmony and counterpoint. His most distinguished students included Glinka, brothers Anton and Nikolay Rubinstein, and Peter Cornelius.

Diaghilev, Sergey Pavlovich (or Serge, 1872–1929). Russian musical impresario and art critic. Played a crucial role in the shaping of Western perceptions of Russian culture. He first brought hitherto obscure Russian painting to Paris (1905), then music (1907) and ballet (1909), bringing renown to, among others, the painters of the *Mir Isskustva* group, Nijinsky, Rimsky-Korsakov, Musorgsky and the young Stravinsky.

Dobrolyubov, Nikolay Aleksandrovich (1836–61). Russian literary critic. His materialist outlook brought him close to Chernïshevsky, and his sharp social analyses were highly valued by several generations of Russian revolutionaries including Lenin.

Dostoyevsky, Fyodor Mikhaylovich (1821–81). Leading Russian novelist. Arrested for membership of a group of liberal intellectuals (1849); served four years imprisonment and five years military service in Siberia. His experience changed his ideas radically and he embraced Russian Orthodoxy and conservatism.

Dunayevsky, Isaak Osipovich (Iosifovich) (1900–55). Soviet composer of popular music. His songs, operettas and film scores met with unparalleled popular and official success in the Soviet Union. His 1934 film score *Vesyolïye rebyata* (The Merry Fellows), approved by Stalin, marked a relaxation of official attitudes to jazz, which had been hostile in the early years of Stalin's rule.

Dzerzhinsky, Ivan Ivanovich (1909–78). Soviet composer. At a very young age he became a celebrity owing to the Stalin's approval of his opera *Tikhiy Don* (Quiet Flows the Don). Lacking in compositional technique, he could never replicate this success.

Eisenstein, Sergey Mikhaylovich (1898–1948). Eminent Soviet film director. Famed alike for his earlier revolutionary and modernist works *Strike* (1924) and *Battleship Potemkin* (1925), and for his more conservative Stalin-era works *Alexander Nevsky* (1938) and *Ivan the Terrible* (1942–47). Prokofiev provided the scores for the later films.

Fedorovsky, Fyodor Fyodorovich (1883–1955). Russian/Soviet set designer. Before the Revolution, he worked for the Zimin Private Opera Company, the Bolshoi and for some Diaghilev productions in Paris. His post-Revolutionary work was mainly with the Bolshoi, creating classic examples of the monumental high Stalinist style in several productions of Russian operas. Among other projects, he designed the stars for the top of Kremlin towers.

Fere, Vladimir Georgiyevich (1902–71). Soviet composer. He wrote many Kirghiz operas and ballets, mainly in collaboration with V. Vlasov and A. Maldïbayev.

Fomin, Yevstigney Ipatovich (1761–1800). Russian opera composer. Best known for his opera *Yamshchiki na podstave* (Coachmen at the Station, 1787), based on melodies of Russian folksongs.

Gevaert, François-Auguste (1828–1908). Belgian composer and musicologist. The composer of several operas, but best known for his pedagogical and theoretical writings, including treatises on orchestration and harmony.

Gippius, Yevgeniy Vladimirovich (1903–85). Soviet musicologist, specialist in Russian and Belorussian folk music.

Glazunov, Aleksandr Konstantinovich (1865–1936). Russian composer. A pupil of Rimsky-Korsakov's and the most eminent of the second-generation Russian nationalists, although he also came under the influence of Wagner. Remained as director of St Petersburg Conservatoire after the Revolution, but left the Soviet Union in 1928, for musical tours in Europe and the USA.

Glière, Reingold (Reinhold) Moritsevich (1875–1956). Russian/Soviet composer. Before the Revolution, wrote in a late-nationalist/Wagnerian idiom, culminating in his Third Symphony "Ilya Muromets" (1911). During the Civil War period, worked for Proletkult, and wrote the Revolutionary ballet *The Red Poppy*, in a much simpler style. Invited to Azerbaijan to create a prototype Azeri opera, resulting in *Shakh-Senem* (1923). Sent to Uzbekistan in the late 1930s for the same purpose.

Glinka, Mikhail Ivanovich (1804–57). Russian composer. His *A Life for the Tsar* (1836) was the first all-sung Russian opera. Retrospectively regarded as the founding father of Russian music by the Kuchka and others.

Gnedich, Nikolay Ivanovich (1784–1833). Russian translator and poet. He made the first Russian verse translation of the *Iliad* (1829).

Goethe, Johann Wolfgang von (1749–1832). German poet, novelist, dramatist and politician.

Gogol, Nikolay Vasilyevich (1809–52). Russian novelist, dramatist and short-story writer. Best known for his novel *Dead Souls*. Both Musorgsky and Shostakovich based operas on Gogol stories.

Goncharov, Ivan Aleksandrovich (1812–91). Russian writer and critic. Best known for the novels *Obïknovennaya istoriya* (A Common Story, 1847) and *Oblomov* (1859), the later a wry and highly influential anti-Westernizing statement.

Gorbachev, Mikhail Sergeyevich (1931–). Soviet leader (1985–91). Initiated a reform process that ended in the removal of the Communist Party's political monopoly and the dissolution of the USSR.

Gorbunov, Kirill Antonovich (1822–93). Russian artist. Born a serf, he was freed in 1841. Best known for his portraits of Lermontov and Turgenev.

Gorky, Maxim (pseudonym adopted by Aleksey Maksimovich Peshkov, 1868–1936). Russian/Soviet writer. Born poor, he slowly won financial security through his work as a journalist, editor and dramatist. Closely associated with Lenin during 1905 Revolution. Went into exile to Capri in 1906. Worked with Bolsheviks during 1917, but became increasingly opposed to them after the October Revolution. Left for Capri in 1921 on health grounds, but finally returned to the Soviet Union in 1932, where he became a propagandist for Stalinism, and the figurehead of Socialist Realism.

Gorodetsky, Sergey Mitrofanovich (1884–1967). Russian/Soviet poet. Prominent before the Revolution as a Symbolist and later as an Acmeist. The Soviet part of his career was dominated by translations and opera librettos, including *Ivan Susanin*, the Soviet version of Glinka's *Life for the Tsar*.

Gorodinsky, Viktor Markovich (1902–59). Soviet musicologist. Rose through the administrative ranks to become head of the arts section of the Communist Party Central Committee (1935–7).

Grechaninov, Aleksandr Tikhonovich (1864–1956). Russian composer. Best known for his operas (the nationalist *Dobrïnya Nikitich*, 1901, and the symbolist *Sister Beatrice*, 1910), and for his church music.

Grigoryev, Apollon Aleksandrovich (1822–64). Russian literary critic and poet. Belonged to the second generation of the Slavophiles, the so-called *pochvenniki* (from *pochva*, soil), He placed more emphasis on the individual than the older Slavophiles (for whom the commune was central), and also questioned the fundamental opposition they had posited between the pre-Petrine and Petrine Russia.

Gurilyov, Alexander Lvovich (1803–58). Russian composer. Wrote many salon songs ("romances") and made arrangements of urban popular songs (some clearly influenced by the practices of gypsy choirs).

Hajibeyov, Uzeyir Abdulhuseyn oglu (1885–1948). Azerbaijani Soviet composer. Founder of Azerbaijani opera.

Hartmann (Gartman), Viktor Aleksandrovich (1834–73). Russian architect. Pioneer of the highly decorative "neo-Russian" style. His sketches inspired Musorgsky's *Pictures at an Exhibition* (1875).

Helmholtz, Hermann von (1821–94). German physician and physicist. Best known for his researches in ophthalmology and musical acoustics, publishing *On the Sensations of Tone as a Physiological Basis for the Theory of Music* in 1863.

Hermogen (St Hermogenus, ?–1612). Patriarch of Muscovy during the Time of Troubles (1606–12). Opposed the marriage of False Dmitri I to a Catholic bride. Later opposed Polish proposals to install Wladyslaw IV, again fearing a threat to Orthodoxy, and inspired an uprising against Polish control of Muscovy. Killed during imprisonment by Poles in 1612, but credited with the idea of electing the first Romanov to the throne, which occurred in 1613.

Herzen (Gertsen), Aleksandr Ivanovich (1812–70). Russian writer and political thinker. Left Russia permanently in 1846, supported revolutionary movements across Europe in 1848. Published many polemical essays and journals during his British exile (1852–64), all calling for political reform in Russia. His influence is widely believed to have contributed to the emancipation of the serfs (1861).

Hindemith, Paul (1895–1963). German composer. In the early 1920s came to prominence as an irreverent neo-classicist, and was invited to perform in the Soviet Union by ASM. Singled out for denunciation by Goebbels as a "degenerate" artist in 1934. On the invitation of the Turkish government, helped to re-shape Turkish music education and concert life. Emigrated to the USA in 1940.

Homer (8th or 7th century BC). Greek poet. The epics *The Iliad* and *The Odyssey* are attributed to him. Nineteenth-century nationalism led writers across Europe to search for (or fabricate) their own national Homeric epics.

Ilyin, Ivan Aleksandrovich (1883–1954). Russian religious philosopher. Left Soviet Russia in 1922, and wrote his most important works in exile.

Insarsky, Vasiliy Antonovich (1814–82). Russian writer, author of *Zapiski* (Memoirs) where he described his meetings with Glinka, Belinsky, Lermontov, and other important figures in Russian culture.

Irving, Washington (1783–1859). American writer. Best known for his short stories, *Rip van Winkle,* and *The Legend of Sleepy Hollow.* Much read in translation in Russia and the Soviet Union.

Jurgenson, Pyotr Ivanovich (1836–1903). Russian music publisher. Best known as Tchaikovsky's principal publisher, he was a close friend of the composer.

Kara-Murza, Christopher (Khachatur) (1853–1902). Armenian composer, choral conductor and folksong collector.

Karamzin, Nikolay Mikhaylovich (1766–1826). Russian writer. Best known for his twelve-volume *History of the Russian State* (incomplete), written under the patronage of Tsar Alexander I, and so favourable to the autocracy that it was dubbed "The Epic of Despotism" by its detractors.

Kastalsky, Aleksandr Dmitriyevich (1856–1926). Russian composer and music scholar. He worked predominantly in the field of church music. From 1910 he was director of the Synodal School, which in 1918 became the People's Choral Academy. He wrote influential studies of Russian "folk harmony".

Katkov, Mikhail Nikiforovich (1818–87). Russian essayist and publisher, who played a role in the establishment of "classical" education in Russia. Politically, he moved from mild liberalism to a reactionary and extreme nationalism by the time of the Polish uprising of 1863–4. He enjoyed the patronage of Alexander III.

Kern, Anna Petrovna (1800–79). Russian noblewoman. The wife of general Yermolai Kern, she was much admired by Pushkin and the subject of one of his most celebrated poems.

Kern, Yekaterina Yermolayevna (1818–1904). Daughter of Anna Kern. She had a lengthy affair with Glinka, and was the dedicatee of several of his works.

Kerzhentsev (Lebedev), Platon Mikhaylovich (1881–1940). Bolshevik and Soviet cultural administrator. Occupied a number of important government positions after 1917. Chairman of the Committee for Artistic Affairs (1936–8), in which capacity he presided over the anti-formalism campaign and consolidated the grip of the state over all the arts.

Khachaturian, Aram Ilyich (1903–78). Soviet Armenian composer. Best known for his ballet *Spartacus,* he also composed many symphonic and chamber works. Held posts in the Composers' Union and was widely regarded as the finest Soviet composer after Shostakovich and Prokofiev, but was denounced as a "formalist" in 1948.

Khodasevich, Vladislav Felitsianovich (1886–1939). Russian poet and literary scholar. Author of several studies of Pushkin's works. Emigrated to Paris after the Revolution.

Khomyakov, Alexey Stepanovich (1804–60). Russian poet and religious thinker. One of the founders of the Slavophile movement, his posthumously published writings influenced both Dostoyevsky and Pobedonostsev.

Khrushchev, Nikita Sergeyevich (1894–1971). Soviet politician. A loyal Stalinist until Stalin's death, he became First Secretary of the Communist Party (1953–64) in the ensuing power struggle, and now as an advocate of reform policies he denounced Stalin and the personality cult (1956), initiating the "Thaw period" that allowed much greater artistic freedom and openness to the West. At the same time supported the suppression of the Hungarian Revolution (1956) and encouraged the construction of the Berlin Wall (1961). Became state premier in 1958, but was removed from power by Party colleagues in 1964 worried about his erratic performance, whether over agricultural policies or the Cuban missile crisis.

Khubov, Georgiy Nikitich (1902–81). Soviet musicologist and music critic. Deputy editor-in-chief (1932–9), then editor-in-chief (1952–7) of *Sovetskaya muzïka*, organ of the Composers' Union.

Kireyevsky, Ivan Vasilyevich (1806–56). Russian journalist and literary critic. Together with his brother Pyotr Kireyevsky, he was one of the founders of the Slavophile movement.

Kireyevsky, Pyotr Vasilyevich (1808–56). Russian journalist and folksong collector. Together with his brother Ivan Kireyevsky, he was one of the founders of the Slavophile movement. His collection of folksong texts, when published posthumously, constituted an important source.

Klïchkov (Leshchenkov), Sergey Antonovich (1889–c.1940). Russian/Soviet writer. Wrote prose and poetry on peasant themes in the manner of Yesenin. Arrested in 1937, precise date of death unknown.

Komitas, Soghomon (1869–1935). Armenian priest, composer, choral director and musicologist. Considered the founder of Armenian "classical" music, but also preserved knowledge of traditional songs, dances and liturgical music through his ethnomusicological researches. In 1915 saved from the late Ottoman Armenian genocide through the intervention of Turkish writers and the US ambassador. From 1919 lived as an invalid in Paris.

Konyus (Conus), Georgiy Eduardovich (1862–1933). Russian/Soviet music theorist and composer. He devised a "metrotectonic" theory of music that addressed temporal aspects of musical structure.

Krasheninnikov, Nikolay Aleksandrovich (1878–1941). Russian writer. Well-known before the Revolution, he continued to publish his works during Soviet times, setting many of them in Bashkiria. He wrote a revised libretto, under the title *Minin*, for an early Soviet version of Glinka's *A Life for the Tsar* (staged in Baku, 1926).

Kremlyov, Yuliy Anatolyevich (1908–71). Soviet musicologist. His writings ranged widely over music and aesthetics.

Kruglikov, Semyon Nikolayevich (1851–1910). Russian music critic. Studied music theory with Rimsky-Korsakov, and became a close friend of the composer. Their voluminous correspondence is a valuable source of information on Rimsky-Korsakov's changing views in his later years.

Kuchka (late 1850s–70s). Russian nationalist school of composers consisting of Balakirev, Rimsky-Korsakov, Musorgsky, Borodin and Cui. Dubbed the "moguchaya kuchka" ("mighty little heap") in 1867 by the music critic Stasov, their artistic advisor; known also as "The Mighty Handful" and "The Five" in English-language writings. Under the leadership of Balakirev, created a "Russian" style that drew from Glinka and Dargomïzhsky, but also from Western composers such as Schumann and Liszt. The members drifted apart during the 1870s, when Balakirev withdrew from musical life.

Kukolnik, Nestor Vasilyevich (1809–68). Russian playwright, novelist and critic. Best known for his play *Ruka Vsevïshnego Otechestvo spasla* (The Hand of God Saved the Fatherland, staged 1834), based on the successful campaign to end Polish control of Muscovy, led by Minin in 1612. The play was praised by Nicholas I, but derided by progressive critics. Kukolnik was a close friend of Glinka, and assisted in compiling the libretto for *Ruslan and Lyudmila*.

Kuliyev, Mustafa (1893–1938). Azeri essayist, scholar of literature and theatre. First Minister of Culture of Soviet Azerbaijan (1922–28). Arrested and executed in 1938.

Laroche, Hermann (Larosh, German Avgustovich, 1845–1904). Russian music critic. A classmate of Tchaikovsky at the St Petersburg Conservatoire (1862–6), and a close friend in later years. Best known for his writings on Glinka and Tchaikovsky, his opinions on the Kuchka were generally negative, and they regarded him as an enemy.

Lenin (pseudonym adopted by Vladimir Ilyich Ulyanov, 1870–1924). Russian political thinker and revolutionary leader, first leader of Soviet Union. Founder of Bolshevik faction of Russian Social Democrats.

Lermontov, Mikhail Yuryevich (1814–41). Russian poet, novelist and dramatist. In 1837 his verses on the death of Pushkin implicated the Imperial Court, and he was sent to the Caucasus to fight as a dragoon officer. Wrote a highly innovative novel, *A Hero of our Time* (1839). Died in a duel (also possibly due to a Court conspiracy).

Leviyev, Minasai Betyanovich (1912–90), Soviet Uzbek composer. Produced a series of Uzbek national operas, ballets and symphonic suites.

Linyova, Yevgeniya Eduardovna (1853–1919). Russian folksong collector, singer, and choral conductor. She made pioneering phonograph recordings of folksongs which led to the first serious studies of their hetero/polyphonic textures.

Listopadov, Aleksandr Mikhaylovich (1873–1949). Russian folksong collector, best known for his transcriptions of Don Cossack songs.

Liszt, Franz (1811–86). Hungarian composer and pianist. His music was studied by the Kuchka, who espoused "progressive" musical values.

Lopatin, Nikolay Mikhaylovich (1854–97). Singer and folksong collector. While serving as a rural judge, he published two collections of folksongs (one in collaboration with V. P. Prokunin).

Lossky, Nikolay Onufriyevich (1870–1965). Russian idealist philosopher and religious thinker. His religious awakening after a near fatal accident lost him his professorship in Petrograd, and he left Soviet Russia in 1922. Worked in Prague with Russian ex-Marxists, but in 1947 took up a position in a Russian Orthodox seminary in New York.

Lunacharsky, Anatoliy Vasilyevich (1875–1933). Bolshevik, first Soviet minister of culture and education (1917–29). Presided over spread of mass music education and literacy. Demoted by Stalin to diplomatic positions.

Lvov, Aleksey Fyodorovich (1798–1870). Russian violinist, composer, and writer on music. Succeeded his father, Fyodor Lvov, as director of the Court Cappella (1837–61), overseeing the compilation and publication of the complete annual cycle of ancient *znamenniy* chant in four-part harmonization. Best known as the composer of the first Russian national anthem (1833).

Lvov, Fyodor Petrovich (1766–1836). Russian musician, father of Aleksey Lvov and nephew of Nikolay Lvov. Director of the Court Cappella (1826–36).

Lvov, Nikolay Aleksandrovich (1751–1804). Russian polymath writer. He published an early collection of Russian folksongs with arrangements by Ivan Prach (Pratsch) in 1790; this very influential collection was the first to classify songs by genre.

Lyadov, Anatoliy Konstantinovich (1855–1914). Russian composer. Wrote in a late nationalist manner, but also assimilated various contemporary Western influences. Best known for his symphonic poems *Baba-Yaga* (1905) and *The Enchanted Lake* (1909).

Lyapunov, Sergey Mikhaylovich (1859–1924). Russian composer and pianist. A pupil of Balakirev, he wrote in the style of the Kuchka. Best known for his Liszt-influenced set of twelve Transcendental Etudes.

Lysenko, Trofim Denisovitch (1898–1976). Soviet biologist. Through political manoeuvring, he won official backing to pursue a campaign against genetics and geneticists, and to implement his own theories in agricultural science. He won attention partly through the abuse of genetics by racists, including the Nazis, and partly through the dramatic results he promised. Many geneticists lost their jobs, were sent to labour camps or executed through his endeavours, but the survivors were rehabilitated after Stalin's death and resumed their criticism, finally bringing about official rejection of Lysenkoism in 1964.

Maldïbayev, Abdïlas (1906–78). Soviet composer and singer. Sang tenor roles in the first Kirghiz "music dramas" and operas while studying composition under Vladimir Fere. He subsequently collaborated with both Fere and V. Vlasov in the composition of further Kirghiz national operas.

Maliavine (Malyavin), Filipp Andreyevich (1869–1940). Russian painter. Studied both icon painting at a Greek monastery, and academic painting under Repin at the St Petersburg Academy of Arts. Left Russia in 1922.

Mamontov, Savva Ivanovich (1841–1918). Russian industrialist and patron of the arts. In 1870, created an artistic colony north of Moscow at Abramtsevo that united most of the finest Russian painters, sculptors and decorative artists of the time. In 1885 he began staging innovative opera productions at the colony, and a decade later he began staging operas in Moscow at the "Private Opera". He took charge of production himself, and conducted the orchestra. The sets at the Private Opera were created by Abramtsevo artists, and Mamontov employed Shaliapin and Rakhmaninov among other prominent musicians.

Marr, Nikolay Yakovlevich (1865–1934). Georgian/Soviet linguist and archaeologist. His initial scientific work in Armenia and Georgia gave way to increasingly ambitious speculative theories on the single origin and destiny of all languages. His theories acquired an official status in the Soviet Union during the 1930s and '40s until Stalin published a refutation in 1950.

Martïnov, Ivan Ivanovich (1908–?). Soviet musicologist. His writings ranged widely, and he was a consistent supporter of Shostakovich.

Marx, Karl (1818–83). German political thinker, historian, journalist, economist and revolutionary. All European social-democratic parties in the late nineteenth/early twentieth centuries acknowledged him as their major influence, but they split at the beginning of the First World War, with the Bolsheviks in the minority against the reformism and determinism that had resulted in majority support for the war. A distorted form of Marxism was employed as Soviet state ideology to justify Stalinist rule.

Mazel, Lev (Leo) Abramovich, 1907–2000). Soviet musicologist. He made an important contribution to the teaching of music analysis in the Soviet Union by writing a number of textbooks. He also consistently supported the music of Shostakovich by providing ingenious positive interpretations of his works in the climate of official suspicion towards the composer.

Melgunov, Nikolay Aleksandrovich (1804–67). Russian writer and music critic. A friend of Glinka, he attempted to promote the composer's work in Paris. His laudatory article on Glinka's opera *A Life for the Tsar*, published posthumously, was praised by Stasov and came to be regarded as a model for Glinka criticism.

Melgunov, Yuliy Nikolayevich (1846–93). Russian music theorist and folksong collector. He published a pioneering collection of songs (1879–85), attempting to reconstruct their hetero/polyphony from separately transcribed variants.

Mercy-Argenteau, Marie-Clothilde-Elisabeth, Comtesse de (1837–90). French musical patron and amateur pianist. Developed a keen interest in Russian culture in the early 1880s, and became a patron of the Kuchka, and particularly of Cui.

Metallov, Vasiliy Mikhaylovich (1862–1926). Russian scholar of church music and composer. His principal contribution to church music scholarship was his rebuttal of the long-standing theory that the eight-*glas* system (*os'moglasiye*) of Russian chant is based on eight modes. He was the first to demonstrate that *glas* is not a mode, but a stable collection of melodic formulae (*popevki*).

Meyerbeer, Giacomo (1791–1864). German composer of Italian and French-language operas. Best known for his French grand opéras, *Robert le diable*, *Les Huguenots* and *Le prophète*. Popular with Russian audiences in the mid/late nineteenth century, and as great an influence on Russian opera of the period as Glinka.

Minin, Kuzma Minich (?–1616). Russian merchant and leading figure in insurgency against Poles (1612). Supervised the financing of the insurgency and afterwards ennobled for his services to Michael, the first Romanov Tsar.

Mir Iskusstva (1890s–1920s). Group of Russian artists who founded a journal of the same name in 1899. Several of the artists had belonged to Mamontov's artistic colony at Abramtsevo, and they united symbolism and art nouveau influences from the West with a strong interest in the aesthetics of pre-Petrine Russian arts and crafts. Merged into the Union of Russian Artists in 1904, but the *Mir iskusstva* name was revived in 1910. Artists from the movement created the striking and innovative sets for Diaghilev's *Ballets russes.*

Mordvinov (Sheftel), Boris Arkadyevich (1899–1953). Soviet opera producer. A student of Stanislavsky and Nemirovich-Danchenko, he rose to the position of Chief Producer at the Bolshoi Theatre (1936–40). His arrest in 1940 led to a three-year spell in the labour camps, after which he was only able to work in provincial opera houses.

Mosolov, Aleksandr Vasilyevich (1900–73). Soviet composer. Worked for the post-October revolutionary government before fighting with Red Army during Civil War. A leading figure in ASM during the 1920s, he wrote uncompromisingly modernist music, drawing from expressionism, machine-age styles, and from Central Asian traditional music. His never recovered as an artist from the imposed conservatism of Socialist Realism.

Mozart, Wolfgang Amadeus (1756–91). Austrian composer. Pushkin famously contributed to the Mozart myth with his "little tragedy" *Mozart and Salieri.* Russian interest in Mozart, dormant during the mid-nineteenth century, reawakened in later decades, Mozart pastiches appearing in works such as Tchaikovsky's *Mozartiana* suite and *The Queen of Spades* and Rimsky-Korsakov's *Mozart and Salieri.*

Muradeli, Vano Ilyich (1908–70). Soviet Georgian composer. His 1947 opera *The Great Friendship* notoriously sparked off the condemnations of formalism at the Composers' Union in January 1948.

Musorgsky, Modest Petrovich (1839–81). Russian composer. The most experimental of the Kuchka, partly under the influence of Dargomïzhsky.

Napoleon (1769–1821). French military leader, Emperor of the French (1804–14). His invasion of Russia proceeded as far as Moscow, but much of the city was destroyed by the Russians before the entry of Napoleon's army; lacking supplies, and defeated in battle, Napoleon was forced to retreat, and his power was progressively eroded thereafter. On the Russian side, the conduct of the campaign did much to lay the foundations for subsequent Russian nationalism.

Narkompros (1917–46). Soviet Ministry of Arts, Sciences and Education. After 1946 subject to several phases of reorganization and changes of name.

Nestyev, Izrail Vladimirovich (1911–93). Soviet musicologist. His writings range widely, but he is best known for his monograph on Prokofiev, which has been translated into English.

Neverov, Yanuariy Mikhaylovich (1810–93). Russian essayist. Best known for a memoir on his friendship with Turgenev.

Nikolsky, Aleksandr Vasilyevich (1874–1943). Russian/Soviet choral conductor, composer, writer on music. Best known for his researches on Russian church music.

Odoyevsky, Vladimir Fyodorovich (1803–69). Russian writer. Known as "the Russian Hoffmann" for his short stories and music criticism.

Olenin, Aleksandr Alekseyevich (1865–1944). Russian/Soviet composer. A student of Lyadov and a close friend of Balakirev. Together with his sister, the renowned chamber singer Maria Olenina d'Alheim, he founded "The House of Song" (1908–18), where vocal cycles of Russian and Western composers were performed in their entirety.

Orlova, Lyubov Petrovna (1902–75). Soviet actor. From the mid-'30s onwards, the first screen actor to be given "star" status, in the Hollywood manner, with Stalin's approval.

Ossian (mythical). Narrator and alleged author of James MacPherson's *The Works of Ossian* (1761–65). "Ossian" soon won international renown as a Celtic equivalent to Homer, influencing contemporary poets, and inspiring others to search for their own "national epics".

Ossovsky, Aleksandr Vyacheslavovich (1871–1957). Russian/Soviet music critic and musicologist. A leading figure in Soviet musicology, he is best known for his writings on Glinka, Musorgsky, and Glazunov.

Ostrovsky, Aleksandr Nikolayevich (1823–86). Russian dramatist. His work inspired operas by, among others, Serov, Tchaikovsky, and Janáček.

Palchikov, Nikolay Yevgrafovich (1838–88). Russian folksong collector. He collected songs in a single village while working there as a magistrate; his pioneering collection was published posthumously.

Pan-Slavism (nineteenth century). Russian political doctrine. Although the idea of uniting all the Slav nations under Russian leadership can be traced back to the seventeenth century, it gained some momentum after Napoleon's invasion (1812), and became a strong current in Russian political thought after the Crimean War. Although Pan-Slavists claimed to be standing up for the rights of smaller Slav nations against Prussian expansionism or the Ottoman Empire, in practice they supported forced Imperial policies of Russianisation of Poles in the West, and of Turkic peoples in the East. The Slavophiles split over this issue.

Pavlenko, Pyotr Andreyevich (1899–1951). Soviet novelist, journalist and author of screenplays. Enjoyed the direct patronage of Stalin.

Peter the Great (1672–1725). Tsar of Russia (1682–1725). Fought campaigns with Black Sea and Baltic Sea rivals for trading purposes, resulting in expansion that created the Russian empire. Founded St Petersburg on land recaptured from Sweden, funded by a new direct tax on serfs. Introduced Westernizing measures to the court and church, and ended the oligarchical status of the boyars.

Pisarev, Dmitriy Ivanovich (1840–68). Political thinker. His radicalism influenced many on the Russian Left, including Lenin.

Pobedonostsev, Konstantin Petrovich (1827–1907). Russian statesman. Appointed Chief Procurator of the Holy Synod (1880) and, as a nationalist and religious conservative, exercised more influence over Alexander III than any other individual. Adhered to the most reactionary aspects of the Slavophiles' programmes. Enthusiastically promoted policies of forced Russification, among them the anti-Semitic pogroms.

Polotsky, Simeon (1629–80). Russian churchman, poet and political thinker. His major work was *The Rod of Government*. Promoted Western influences.

Popov, Gavriil Nikolayevich (1904–72). Soviet composer. His modernist Septet (1927) and Symphony No. 1 (1928–35) indicated a talent nearly equal to Shostakovich, and his music was widely known to Soviet audiences through his film score for *Chapayev* (1934).

Potulov, Nikolay Mikhaylovich (1810–73). Russian scholar of church music. Published his own harmonization of the Russian chant cycle, based on the principles of the "strict style" formulated by V. F. Odoyevsky.

Pozharsky, Dmitriy Mikhaylovich (1578–1642). Russian prince, military leader. During the "Time of Troubles" fought the Polish occupying forces, and placed himself at the service of the Romanov claimant to the throne, the future Michael I, who latter dubbed him "Saviour of the Nation". Awarded various administrative positions by the new Tsar, and helped to put down sporadic uprisings.

Prach, Ivan (Práč, Jan Bohumir or Pratsch, Johann Gottfried, ?–1818). Czech/Russian composer. Educated in Silesia, he worked in St Petersburg, where he published an influential folksong collection together with N. A. Lvov in 1790 (he was responsible for the arrangements of the folksong melodies).

Preobrazhensky, Antonin Viktorovich (1870–1929). Russian/Soviet musicologist. Eminent scholar of Russian church music.

Prokofiev, Sergey Sergeyevich (1891–1953). Russian/Soviet composer and pianist.

Prokoll (Production Collective, 1925–32). Soviet organization of composers. Founded at Moscow Conservatoire by composers engaged in writing pieces for the first anniversary of Lenin's death, and later including both Khachaturian and Kabalevsky among its members.

Prokunin, Vasiliy Pavlovich (1848–1910). Russian folksong collector and composer. Published two important folksong collections, one in 1872–3, the other, in collaboration with N. M. Lopatin, in 1889.

Pushkin, Aleksandr Sergeyevich (1799–1837). Russian poet. Regarded as the founder of modern Russian literature. His liberal ideas led to his temporary exile after the Decembrist uprising in 1825, and he wrote his greatest works under close police surveillance. Many composers based operas on his works, including Musorgsky, Rimsky-Korsakov and Tchaikovsky. Stalin created a literary cult around him for the centenary celebrations in 1937.

Rakhmaninov, Sergey Vasilyevich (1873–1943). Russian composer and pianist. One of the most influential pianists of the twentieth century, composer of many virtuosic piano pieces, alongside symphonic and operatic works. Left Russia permanently after the October Revolution, settling in the USA two years later. After an absence of a decade or more, his works returned to Soviet concert halls after he gave a charity recital for Soviet war relief.

Radishchev, Aleksandr Nikolayevich (1749–1802). Russian political thinker. An admirer of the American and French revolutions, and a critic of serfdom, his radicalism led Catherine the Great to exile him to Siberia.

RAPM – Russian Association of Proletarian Musicians (*Rossiyskaya Assotsiatsiya Proletarskikh Muzïkantov*). Soviet musicians' organization founded in 1923. Won increasing support from the state by the end of the 20s, enabling it to undermine ASM, its chief rival. Dissolved by the state in 1932 (together with all other non-state cultural organizations).

Razumovsky, Dmitriy Vasilyevich (1818–89). Russian music historian. An eminent scholar of Russian church music, he taught the first course on the subject at Moscow Conservatoire (1866–89); among his students was Sergey Taneyev.

Rechmensky, Nikolay Sergeyevich (1897–1963). Soviet composer and folksong collector. He wrote a number of works based on Chechen and Ingush folk themes.

Riemann, Hugo (1849–1919). German musicologist. His pedagogical works on music theory were widely studied at St Petersburg and Moscow conservatoires.

Rimsky-Korsakov, Nikolay Andreyevich (1844–1908). Russian composer. The most prolific and polished of the Kuchka, in his later years he became a professor at St Petersburg Conservatoire and distanced himself from the Kuchka's nationalism.

Rïleyev, Kondratiy Fyodorovich (1795–1826). Russian soldier and poet. Author of historical and civic verses. A participant in the abortive Decembrist uprising of 1825; tried and sentenced to death.

Rïzhkin, Iosif Yakovlevich (1907–?). Soviet musicologist, professor at Moscow Conservatoire from 1939.

Romanov dynasty (1613–1917). Tsars of Russia (from 1721 emperors). The establishment of the dynasty ended the "Time of Troubles", and the family ruled until Nicholas II's abdication following the February Revolution.

Roslavets, Nikolay Andreyevich (1881–1944). Russian/Soviet composer. As a post-Scriabin modernist, he was a leading composer and polemicist for ASM. He was an enthusiastic supporter of the Revolution and condemned RAPM for its "pseudo-proletarian" outlook. He abandoned his modernism in 1930, worked in Uzbekistan, and after his return to Moscow was given only menial teaching positions.

Rossini, Gioachino (1792–1868). Italian opera composer.

Rostopchin (Rastopchin), Fyodor Vasilyevich (1763–1826). Russian general. Commander of forces in Moscow in 1812, famed for his agitational recruitment drive in building an army capable of defeating Napoleon, and for his campaign to equip the army by donation.

Rozanov, Vasiliy Vasilyevich (1856–1919). Russian thinker who published a number of religious-philosophical essays.

Rubinstein, Anton Grigoryevich (1829–94). Russian pianist, composer and conductor. Founder of the St Petersburg Conservatoire and promoter of Russian music as a conductor.

Rupin (Rupini), Ivan Alekseyevich (1792–1850). Russian singer, composer and folksong collector. Best known for his arrangements of Russian folksongs published in the 1830s.

Said, Edward (1935–2003). Palestinian-American literary theorist. The leading theorist and critic of Orientalism, the pervasive cultural corollary of European conquest and colonialism in the East, whether in the news media, popular culture, the arts or scholarship. His theorizing has been influential within musicology.

Samarin, Yuriy Fyodorovich (1819–1876). Russian thinker and public figure. A leading Slavophile, he played an important role in the liberation of the serfs.

Samosud, Samuil Abramovich (1884–1964). Soviet conductor. 1918–36 chief conductor of the Maly Opera House (MaleGOT, Petrograd/Leningrad); 1936–43 chief conductor of the Bolshoi. An important influence on the production of many Soviet operas, including Shostakovich's *The Nose* (1930) and *Lady Macbeth of Mtsensk* (1934), Dzerzhinsky's *Quiet Flows the Don* (1935), and Prokofiev's *War and Peace* (Part I, 1946).

Sannikov, Grigoriy Aleksandrovich (1899–1969). Soviet poet. Joined the Bolsheviks in 1917, and produced many works on the subject of the Revolution.

Schumann, Robert (1810–1856). German composer. The Kuchka studied his works carefully and assimilated various harmonic and rhythmic ideas into their own music.

Scriabin, Aleksandr Nikolayevich (1872–1915). Russian composer. The most prominent musical figure to reject Russian nationalism in favour of a more cosmopolitan and innovatory approach to composition.

Serov, Aleksandr Nikolayevich (1820–71). Russian opera composer and music critic. His low estimation of Glinka earned him the hostility of Stasov and Cui (the two Kuchka music critics). Best known for his opera *Judith*.

Shaliapin, Feodor Ivanovich (1873–1938). Russian singer (operatic bass).

Shchedrin, Rodion Konstantinovich (b. 1932). Soviet composer. Moved from a folk-inflected Socialist Realism to an eclectic mix of avant-guardism, jazz, neoclassicism and pop from the 1960s onwards.

Shcherbachov, Vladimir Vladimirovich (1889–1952). Soviet composer. Head of music section of Culture Ministry (1918–23), then a professor at Leningrad Conservatoire, where the conductor Mravinsky and the composer Popov were among his pupils.

Shebalin, Vissarion Yakovlevich (1902–63). Soviet composer. A member of ASM in the '20s, he later became director of Moscow Conservatoire (1942–8), but was condemned for his "formalism" in 1948.

Shekhter, Boris Semyonovich (1900–61). Soviet composer. Studied under Myaskovsky. A member of RAPM and composer of many works based on revolutionary songs.

Shestov, Lev Isaakovich (1866–1938). Russian philosopher. His fragmentary writings offered a post-theistic "philosophy of despair". Emigrated from Russia in 1921. Influenced Berdyaev and Bulgakov.

Shishkov, Aleksandr Semyonovich (1754–1841). Russian admiral, statesman and essayist.

Shostakovich, Dmitriy Dmitriyevich (1906–75). Soviet composer.

Shteynberg, Maximilian Oseyevich (1883–1946). Soviet composer. Shostakovich's principal composition teacher.

Slavophiles (19th century). A Russian nationalist movement. Emerging in the wake of the abortive Decembrist uprising (1825) and in reaction to Chaadayev's Westernizing polemics, united more by their anti-Westernism than by any positive programme. Idealized Tsarist autocracy, Orthodox Christianity and other Russian institutions, looking back to a supposed golden age before Peter the Great's Westernizing reforms. There were, nevertheless, liberal elements favouring freedom of speech and of the press, and the emancipation of the serfs.

Smolensky, Stepan Vasilyevich (1848–1909). Russian music scholar and choral conductor. Published a number of crucial early sources of Russian church music; directed the Synodal School of church singing and the celebrated Synodal Choir in Moscow (1889–1901).

Sokalsky, Pyotr Petrovich (1832–87). Ukrainian composer, music critic and folksong collector. Principally known as a composer of Ukrainian operas, but also remembered for his research on Russian and Ukrainian folk music (*Russkaya narodnaya muzïka, velikorusskaya i malorusskaya*, 1888).

Sokolovsky, Mikhail Matveyevich (flourished late 18th century). Russian violinist, Kapellmeister and composer. Composer of one of the earliest Russian comic operas, *Mel'nik – koldun, obmanshchik i svat* (The Miller – a Sorcerer, a Cheat and a Matchmaker, 1779).

Solovyov, Sergey Mikhaylovich (1820–79). Eminent Russian historian, author of 29-volume *History of Russia*.

Solovyov, Vladimir Sergeyevich (1853–1900). Russian religious philosopher and poet, a significant influence on Russian Symbolists. Son of Sergey Solovyov.

Spendiarov (Spendiarian), Aleksandr Afanasyevich (1871–1928). Armenian/Soviet composer. A student of Rimsky-Korsakov. Best known for his opera *Almast* (1918).

Stakhovich, Mikhail Aleksandrovich (1819–58). Russian guitarist and folksong collector. Published a collection of forty Russian folksongs (1851–4).

Stalin (name adopted by Iosif Vissarionovich Dzhugashvili, 1878–1953). Bolshevik, leader of Soviet Union (*c.* 1928–53). Creating a power base in the Soviet bureaucracy, abandoned revolutionary internationalism to create a conservative nationalist regime that pursued industrialization ruthlessly. Promoted Russian cultural and political nationalism, while encouraging a purely cultural nationalism in the Caucasian and Central Asian republics.

Stanchinsky, Aleksey Vladimirovich (1888–1914). Russian composer. His unpublished proto-modernist works, largely for piano, circulated among musicians, Prokofiev being among those who acknowledged his influence.

Stasov, Vladimir Vasilyevich (1824–1906). Influential Russian music and art critic. Promoted and advised both the Kuchka and the Peredvizhniki movement in the visual arts. Did much to shape the Kuchka's nationalism and progressive aesthetics.

Stravinsky, Igor Fyodorovich (1882–1971). Russian composer. Rose to fame in the West through Diaghilev's *Ballets russes*. Opposed to the Revolution and chose to live in exile, first in Switzerland and France, then from 1939 in the USA.

Surin, Vladimir Nikolayevich (1906–?). Soviet cultural official. Served as a member of the Committee for Artistic Affairs in the 1940s, deputy minister of Culture (1954), and later appointed Director of Mosfilm Studio.

Susanin, Ivan (?–1613). Russian folk hero. Allegedly sacrificed his life in order to prevent a detachment of Polish troops reaching Michael, the first Romanov tsar. Instead of leading them to their target, he led them deep into forest land where they froze to death. Used for propaganda purposes both by nineteenth-century tsars and by Stalin.

Sviridov, Georgy Vasilyevich (1915–98). Soviet/Russian composer. A pupil of Shostakovich, he was best known for his vocal and choral music.

Szymanowski, Karol (1882–1937). Polish composer.

Tairov (Kornblit), Aleksandr Yakovlevich (1885–1950). Russian theatre director and actor. A disciple of both Stanislavsky and Meyerhold, he rejected the opposing paths taken by these two directors, attempting to create a third approach that emphasized actorly freedom. In the 1920s moved towards the Meyerhold camp, before submitting to the conservatism of Socialist Realism in the '30s.

Taneyev, Sergey Ivanovich (1856–1915). Russian composer and music theorist.

Taruskin, Richard (b. 1945), U.S. musicologist. Has published influential writings on Stravinsky and various aspects of Russian music from the Kuchka to Shostakovich; author of the six-volume *Oxford History of Western Music*.

Tchaikovsky, Pyotr Ilyich (1840–93). Russian composer. Although influenced by the Kuchka's nationalism earlier in his career, he employed their idiom only sporadically in his maturity, leading the Kuchka to question his Russianness.

Tertz, Abram (name adopted by Andrey Donatovich Sinyavsky, 1925–97). Soviet writer and literary scholar. Best known for his satirical essay "What is Socialist Realism?" (1959), he published much of his writing in the West without authorization. Arrested in 1965 when his identity was revealed to the authorities, primarily on the grounds of this illicit activity rather than the content of his work. Allowed to emigrate.

Tisse, Eduard Kazimirovich (1897–1961). Russian cinematographer. Eisenstein's most important collaborator, both in his agitational and modernist 1920s works, and in his more conservative historical films of the Socialist Realist period.

Titov, Aleksey Nikolayevich (1769–1827). Russian composer and violinist. Combined an officer's career with that of an opera composer. His style was influenced by Russian popular songs of the time. He is also remembered for creating one of the first operas on a Russian historical theme, *Muzhestvo kiyevlyanina, ili Vot kakovï russkiye* (The Courage of a Kievan, or This is What Russians Are Like, 1817).

Tolstoy, Feofil Matveyevich (pen-name Rostislav, 1810–81). Russian music critic and composer. A specialist in Italian and Russian opera, his writings won him the hostility of fellow critics Serov, Stasov and Cui. Musorgsky satirized him in his song *Rayok* (The Peepshow).

Tolstoy, Lev Nikolayevich (1828–1910). Russian novelist, and political and religious thinker.

Trauberg, Leonid Zakharovich (1902–90). Soviet film director. Best known for his trilogy of "Maxim" films which he co-directed with Grigoriy Kozintsev and which met with the approval of Stalin (the music was written by Shostakovich).

Tsukkerman, Viktor Abramovich (1903–88). Soviet musicologist. Author of several music-theoretical textbooks and of volumes analysing the styles of Beethoven, Glinka, Tchaikovsky.

Tsvetayeva, Marina Ivanovna (1892–1941). Russian poet. Having begun her career as a Symbolist, she developed a highly distinctive style of her own.

Turchaninov, Pyotr Ivanovich (1779–1856). Russian composer of church music.

Turgenev, Ivan Sergeyevich (1818–83). Russian novelist. Best known for his novel *Fathers and Sons*, his Westernising ideas led to conflict with both Dostoyevsky and Tolstoy.

Tyutchev, Fyodor Ivanovitch (1803–73). Russian poet. An extreme Slavophile, he was adopted posthumously by the Russian Symbolists as one of their own.

Uspensky, Nikolay Dmitriyevich (1900–87). Soviet musicologist. Leading scholar of Russian church music during the Soviet period.

Varlamov, Aleksandr Yegorovich (1801–48). Russian composer. An eminent writer of romances (Russian art songs) of Pushkin's generation.

Vasilenko, Sergey Nikiforovich (1872–1956). Russian composer and conductor. Influenced early in his career by folksong and Old Believers' chants, then by Symbolism at the turn of the century, and from 1910 by Eastern music, especially the music of Russian/Soviet Central Asia. Created the first Uzbek opera in 1938.

Vasilyev-Buglay, Dmitro (Dmitriy) Stepanovich (1888–1956). Soviet composer and choral conductor. Fought with Red Army during Civil War. Best known for his romances and popular songs on texts by Mayakovsky and Yesenin.

Verstovsky, Aleksey Nikolayevich (1799–1862). Russian composer. Initially popular for his popular opéra-vaudevilles and ballads, he later turned to full-scale opera and is best known for *Askold's Grave*, inspired by Weber's *Der Freischütz*. Dominated Russian opera in the mid-nineteenth century, but marginalized in favour of Glinka in nationalist music history.

Vilkovir, Yefim Borisovich (1888–1963). Russian music pedagogue and administrator. Worked for Narkompros (1924–6), then appointed as an editor at Muzgiz (State Music Publishers, 1925–33).

Vishnevsky, Vsevolod Vitalyevich (1900–51). Soviet dramatist. Fought in the Civil War, wrote a number of plays on war subjects that lay the foundation of Socialist Realist theatre.

Vlasov, Vladimir Aleksandrovich (1902–86). Soviet composer. In collaboration with fellow composers V. Fere and A. Maldïbayev, he produced a repertoire of Kirghiz operas.

VOSM. All-Russian Association for Contemporary Music, a later renaming of ASM.

Wagner, Richard (1813–83). German composer, conductor, music theorist and essayist. The Kuchka remained aloof from his influence until Rimsky-Korsakov attended the Russian première of *The Ring* in 1888–9.

Westphal, Rudolf Georg Hermann (1826–92). German philologist. Lectured at the Moscow Lyceum (1875–80), teaching his theories on metre and rhythm in both the poetry and the music of different peoples. Yuliy Melgunov became one of his followers.

Wilson, Edmund (1895–1972). American literary critic. Wrote prolifically on twentieth-century literature. Among his friends were Scott Fitzgerald and Vladimir Nabokov.

Yastrebtsev (Yastrebtsov), Vasiliy Vasilyevich (1866–1934). Russian writer of memoirs, biographer of Rimsky-Korsakov.

Yevseyev, Sergey Vasilyevich (1894–1956). Soviet composer and music theorist. A student of Taneyev, he became a Professor of the Moscow Conservatoire in 1935, where he created and taught the course "Foundations of Russian Harmony and Polyphony".

Yusupov, Usmon (Usman) Yusupovich (1901–66). Uzbek state official. A cotton factory worker who joined the Communists at the age of 25, he quickly rose through the ranks to become First Secretary of the Uzbek Communist Party (1937–50) and Minister of the Cotton Industry of the USSR (1950–53).

Zakharov, Vladimir (1901–1965). Soviet composer. He was a successful writer of mass songs and folk-style songs, and directed the Pyatnitsky Folk Choir from 1932.

Zhdanov, Andrey Aleksandrovich (1896–1948). Bolshevik, leading government member under Stalin. He joined the Party in 1915, and during Stalin's consolidation of power, rose to become Secretary of the Central Committee by 1934, and at the same time became the head of the Leningrad Party (1934–44) after the assassination of Kirov. He was close to Stalin and helped to organize the show trials and executions of the late '30s. In the sphere of artistic policy, he promulgated the doctrine of Socialist Realism in 1934, and in 1946–8 spearheaded a new campaign against "formalism" in the arts, afterwards linked to his name as the "zhdanovshchina".

Zhemchuzhnikov, Aleksey Mikhaylovich (1821–1908). Russian poet and satirist, member of the Senate (until his resignation in 1858). Together with his brother Vladimir and cousin Aleksey Tolstoy, he wrote satirical poetry under the name Kozma Prutkov.

Zhukovsky, Vasiliy Andreyevich (1783–1852). Russian poet. Considered the leading figure in the introduction of Romanticism to Russian literature. He translated Byron, Walter Scott, and wrote his own Romantic ballades. He was close to the court, being a reader to Empress Maria (from 1815) and tutor to the future Alexander II (1826–41). He used his influence at the court to promote and protect the careers of Pushkin, Lermontov and others.

INDEX

Biographical details of many of those listed in the index are to be found in the Glossary of names on pages 380–395 above

Aksakov, 12, 380
Aleksandrov, 70, 380
Alexander I, 2, 380, 382, 385
Alexander II, 385, 395
Alexander III, x, 250, 292, 390
Anderson, viii
Annenkov, 11, 380
Ariosto, 56, 360n8, 380
Armenia (Armenian), 239–40, 314, 320, 323, 325–6, 334, 337, 377n31, 377n47, 377n48, 385, 386, 388, 393
Arnold (Arnol'd), Yuri, 81, 252–5, 273–4, 368n37, 380
Arnshtam, Lev, 70, 380
Artôt-Padilla, 159, 380
Asafyev (Asaf'yev), 111, 116, 125, 133, 227, 262–4, 307, 349, 364n55, 365n64, 365n76, 366n81, 368n52, 376n24, 379n74, 380
ASM, 307–309, 376n23, 380, 381, 385, 389, 393, 395
Atatürk, 322, 380–1
Avraamov, 242–4, 309, 372n25, 372n26, 381
Azerbaijan (Azerbaijani, Azeri, Azerbaidzhan), 313, 315, 319–26, 330–38, 375n8, 377n31, 377n43, 377n44, 378n50, 378n57, 378n58, 378n59, 378n60, 378n61, 378n62, 378n63, 378n68, 383, 387
Azeyev, 278, 381

Bakhmetev, 266, 271, 381
Balakirev, xi, 37, 43, 46–7, 49, 108–9, 141, 143, 149–54, 156, 159–64, 170, 172, 174, 180–81, 188, 190, 194, 199–201, 203–5, 209, 211, 228–9, 236, 245, 256, 259–60,

271, 275–6, 279, 325, 327, 338, 345, 359n89, 361n23, 364n49, 365n62, 366n2, 367n14, 367n20, 367n25, 367n26, 367n28, 368n32, 368n37, 369n57, 370n77, 371n97, 373n50, 374n74, 374n79, 381, 386, 388, 390; Folksong collection, 37, 166, 228–9, 245, 256, 271, 325, 345, 371n97; *In Bohemia* (Czech Overture), 153, 367n19; Overture on Three Russian Themes, 47; Symphony No 1, 150, 152, 180–1, 200; *Tamara*, 49, 152, 154, 338, 367n29
Bartók, 315, 322, 338, 347, 381
Bedny, 339–40, 381
Beethoven, viii, 77, 92, 102–3, 108, 114, 187, 202, 209, 313, 360n8, 364n39, 394
Belinsky, 53, 55, 72, 116, 381, 385
Belïy, 310–11, 358n48, 376n25, 381
Bellini, 76, 82, 381
Belorussia (Belorussian), 172, 303, 314–5, 320, 377n31, 383
Belsky, 56, 214, 370n93, 381
Bely, 21, 50, 381
Belyayev, 345, 361n27, 381
Berdyayev, 15, 28–9, 39–40, 357n37, 358n62, 358n75, 359n76, 381, 392
Berlioz, 17, 46, 92, 132–3, 161, 209, 381
Bernandt, 347, 381
bïlina, 127, 152, 173, 237, 352, 365n79, 382
Blanter, 352, 381
Blok, 50, 57, 359n99, 381
Blyma, 74, 381
Bodyansky (Bodyanskiy), 42, 359n81, 381
Borodin, 42, 44, 46–9, 96, 104, 126, 141, 143, 154–6, 161–62, 169–72, 180–82, 186–7, 190, 192, 203, 215, 216, 220, 227, 229, 232, 264, 337, 339, 344,

367*n*30, 368*n*32, 382, 386; *Bogatïri (The Warriors)*, 220, 339, 381; *Prince Igor*, 42, 94, 140, 143, 154–7, 169, 171–2, 176, 181–2, 186–7, 216, 219, 222, 225, 232, 320, 337, 353, 382; Symphony No 1, 368*n*32; Symphony No 2, 44, 47, 156, 190, 192

Bortnyansky, 176, 266, 268–9, 279, 282, 366*n*90, 373*n*66, 382

Brown, D., 77, 113–14, 132, 363*n*16, 363*n*25, 364*n*34, 364*n*53, 365*n*61, 366*n*80, 382

Brown, M. H., 358*n*65, 363*n*18, 365*n*57, 369*n*54

Brusilovsky, 319, 326, 331, 382

Bryusov, 57, 382

Bryusova, 350–51, 379*n*90, 382

Bukharin, 303, 339, 375*n*7, 378*n*71, 382

Calendar songs, 43, 173, 251

Cappella (Court Cappella), 134, 265–6, 269, 271–2, 275–6, 278, 373*n*63, 381, 388

Cavos, 60, 75, 78, 80, 118, 382

Chaadayev, 8–10, 13, 357*n*18, 357*n*25, 382, 392

changing-background variations (also Glinka variations, ostinato variations), 42, 113–14, 129, 145–6, 151, 157, 172, 205, 223, 257

Chechens, 303, 305, 391

Chekhov, x, 1, 12, 26–8, 39, 358*n*59, 382

Chesnokov, 266, 281, 296–7

Chirkov, 72, 382

Chopin, 108, 111, 158, 202, 204, 210–12, 363*n*30, 366*n*2, 381, 382

Church music (Russian), x–xii, 108–9, 134–7, 174–182, 244, 253, 265–300, 366*n*84, 380, 381, 382, 384, 385, 389, 390, 391, 393, 394

Cui, 42, 45–7, 140, 147–8, 162, 180, 183, 194, 203, 208, 367*n*16, 382, 386, 388, 392, 394

Danilov, 2, 127, 360*n*8, 365*n*78, 382

Dargomïzhsky, 71, 96, 117, 140, 160, 185–6, 194, 206–7, 235, 366*n*2, 382, 386, 389

Decembrists, 6, 57–8, 69–71, 380, 383, 391, 392, 393

Dehn, 100, 134–5, 383

Diaghilev, viii, x, 1, 45–51, 92, 141, 329, 342, 383, 389, 393

Dobrolyubov, 23, 358*n*54, 383

Dostoyevsky, x, 1, 3, 12–13, 17, 20–1, 25, 39, 54, 125, 356*n*4, 357*n*34, 357*n*38, 358*n*46, 358*n*47, 358*n*49, 360*n*7, 365*n*74, 383, 386, 394

Dunayevsky, 352, 383

Duncan, 48

Dzerzhinsky, F. E., 303, 375*n*7

Dzerzhinsky, I. I., xiii, 383, 392

Eisenstein, 341, 345, 379*n*78, 383, 394

Engels, 68, 312, 377*n*30

epic opera, 42, 117, 119, 125, 214

Fedorovsky, 48, 383

Fere, 314, 325–8, 378*n*52, 383, 388, 395

Folksong

Russian folksong: as source of art music, vii, x, xi, xiii, 44, 72, 79, 82, 84, 86, 105, 109, 111,113, 129–30, 138, 151, 162, 163–73, 193, 208, 215, 217, 223–4, 226–8, 241, 251, 280, 307–8, 344–6, 349, 351–2, 368*n*37, 383; and national character, 11, 29–41; theory of, 108–9, 245–6, 248, 253–5, 272, 324, 349, 358*n*65; arrangement of, xi–xii, 109, 251–4, 256–60, 264, 307–8, 323–5, 350–1, 370*n*91, 371*n*9, 371*n*15, 391; negative attitude to, 308–9; relationship with chant, 281–4, 288, 293

Non–Russian folksongs, 42; of the Soviet republics, 313, 315, 344–5; Caucasian, 163; Finnish, 130, 365*n*79; Moravian, 153; Ukrainian, 247, 251, 259, 393; Uzbek, 315

Fomin, 34–5, 77–8, 89, 170, 383

Georgia (Georgian), 130, 152–4, 156, 239–40, 289, 303, 313–15, 320, 323, 326, 352, 375*n*5, 375*n*8, 377*n*31, 388, 389

Gevaert, 241, 289, 383

Gippius, 232, 250–1, 371*n*14, 383

Glarean, 245

Glazunov, 44–5, 47–8, 126, 141, 143, 156, 161, 201–2, 209, 211–12, 344, 383–4, 390

Glière (Gliyer), 201, 315, 319, 321–2, 326, 330–32, 334, 337–8, 377*n*44, 383

Glinka, vii–x, xiii, 1, 17, 41–7, 52–3, 56, 58–63, 65, 68–73, 74–139, 140, 143–50, 153–4, 161, 164–67, 169–70, 173, 175–6, 181, 185–8, 193–4, 202, 209, 211, 219–20, 222–3, 227, 240, 244, 257, 268,

Glinka (*cont.*)
  272, 275, 280, 288, 307, 320, 322–3, 326,
  329, 334, 338, 341, 357n24, 359n84,
  359n1, 360n2, 360n8, 361n20, 361n22,
  361n23, 361n24, 361n28, 361n37, 362n40,
  362n41, 362n42, 362n43, 362n45, 362n46,
  362n1, 362n3, 362n7, 363n9, 363n15,
  363n16, 363n20, 363n23, 363n24, 363n30,
  363n32, 364n33, 364n35, 364n38, 364n39,
  364n41, 364n42, 364n43, 364n48, 364n53,
  364n54, 364n56, 365n57, 365n59, 365n67,
  365n79, 366n80, 366n81, 366n82, 366n83,
  366n85, 366n86, 366n87, 366n88, 366n89,
  366n91, 367n16, 368n37, 368n51, 369n52,
  373n56, 374n73, 379n74, 380, 382, 383,
  384, 385, 386, 387, 388, 389, 390, 392,
  394, 395; *Ivan Susanin* (Soviet version of
  A Life for the Tsar), xiii, 61–70, 320, 341,
  353, 361n31, 379n74, 384; *Kamarinskaya*,
  42, 45, 47, 76, 113–4, 129, 133; *A Life for
  the Tsar*, x, 41–2, 45, 52, 59–62, 70,
  74–7, 81–106, 111, 115–7, 122, 125–6,
  128, 130–5, 138, 140, 147, 166–7, 175–6,
  179, 222, 264, 317, 320, 334, 341, 360n2,
  361n20, 361n21, 361n22, 361n23,
  361n30, 362n1, 362n2, 363n28, 363n32,
  364n36, 382, 384, 386, 389; *Ruslan and
  Lyudmila*, x, xiii, 42, 44–5, 47, 55–6, 61,
  73, 101–2, 104–7, 109–19, 121–39,
  144–49, 156, 181, 185–8, 219–20, 225,
  320, 338, 353, 360n8, 360n9, 363n32,
  364n42, 364n57, 365n59, 365n67,
  365n74, 366n80, 367n13, 367n15, 387;
  Valse-Fantasie, 71–2
Gnedich, 2, 55, 384
Gogol, 11, 21–3, 38–9, 41, 44, 53–4, 264,
  357n24, 357n32, 358n71, 358n72,
  358n74, 360n4, 384
Goncharov, 22–3, 384
Goncharova, Natalya, 49–50
Gorbachev, 58, 384
Gorbunov, 31, 383
Gorky, 52, 384
Gorodetsky (Gorodetskiy), 62–7, 361n31,
  361n34, 361n35, 361n36, 384
Gorodinsky (Gorodinskiy), Viktor, 62, 346,
  361n29, 384
Grechaninov, 218–19, 290, 295–6, 299, 307,
  370n94, 384
Greenfeld, 356n1, 357n33
Grigoryev, 22–3, 381, 384
Gurilyov, 32, 34–6, 82, 384
Guthrie, 249

Hajibeyov (Gadzhibekov), 320, 324–5,
  330–37, 377n42, 377n45, 378n50,
  378n55, 378n57, 378n58, 378n59,
  378n60, 378n61, 378n63, 378n64, 384
Hartmann (Gartman), 44, 384
Helmholtz, 241, 384
Hermogen, 265, 384
Herzen (Gertsen), 10, 19, 357n42, 385
hetero/polyphony, 33–4, 113, 166, 170,
  172, 229, 230–2, 235–238, 240, 245, 251,
  264, 282, 291, 351, 387, 389
Hindemith, 307, 322, 385
Homer, 2, 54, 214, 385, 390

Ilyin, 19–20, 385
Insarsky, 31, 385
Irving, 56, 385

Jurgenson, 137, 266, 272, 371n9, 385

Kalinnikov, 156, 280
Kara-Murza, 325, 385
Karamzin, 2, 360n8, 385
Kastalsky (Kastalskiy, Kastal'skiy), xii, 137,
  227, 236–41, 251–2, 257, 262, 264, 266,
  281, 283, 286–91, 299, 350–51, 371n1,
  371n3, 372n20, 372n21, 373n55, 374n81,
  374n91, 374n92, 375n94, 385
Katkov, 249–50, 385
Kazakhstan (Kazakh), 239–40, 303, 314,
  316, 319, 326, 354, 377n31, 382
Kern, A. P., 73, 385
Kern, Ye. Ye., 73, 385
Kerzhentsev, 65, 315, 385
Khachaturian, 73, 330, 337, 347, 378n54,
  385, 391
Khodasevich, 58–9, 385
Khomyakov, 12, 16, 60, 357n35, 357n38,
  361n24, 386
Khrushchev, 353, 386
Khubov, 319, 377n36, 377n41, 377n43, 386
Kipling, viii
Kireyevsky (Kireyevskiy), I. V., 12–17, 31,
  40, 53, 357n39, 357n41, 359n78, 360n3,
  386
Kireyevsky, P. V., 386
Kirghizstan (Kirghiz), 303, 305, 314, 316,
  325–7, 354–5, 377n31, 383, 388, 395
Klïchkov, 340, 386
Komitas, 325, 386
Konyus, 240, 386
Krasheninnikov, 61–3, 386
Kremlyov, 72, 362n49, 362n51, 386

Kruglikov, 47, 359n91, 370n75, 369n76, 370n78, 374n76, 386–7
Kuchka (kuchkist), vii, ix–xiii, 1, 42–8, 51, 61, 72, 92, 104, 108, 115, 117, 129–30, 139–143, 145, 148–9, 151–4, 156–7, 159–63, 166–7, 169–70, 172–4, 176–7, 179, 181–8, 190, 192–4, 199–206, 208, 210, 212, 214–5, 217–20, 222–9, 232, 236–8, 240, 244, 251, 255, 259–60, 264–5, 286–7, 291, 307–11, 313, 320–3, 323, 325–7, 330, 332, 338, 344–5, 348, 350, 352–3, 366n2, 369n61, 369n63, 369n65 369n68, 370n86, 377n49, 381, 382, 384, 386, 387, 388, 389, 392, 393, 394, 395
Kukolnik, 52, 69, 386
Kuliyev, 321–2, 329, 333, 387

Laroche (Larosh), 52, 104–5, 109, 111, 115–17, 126, 132, 147–8, 229, 270, 364n43, 364n45, 364n51, 364n55, 365n63, 365n66, 365n67, 365n77, 367n16, 387
Lasso, 135
Lenin, 52, 57–8, 68, 71, 301–3, 320, 329, 332, 349, 352, 375n4, 375n6, 376n9, 383, 387, 390
Lermontov, 57, 115, 152, 341, 384, 385, 387, 395
Leviyev, 301, 387
Linyova, 32–3, 81–2, 224, 235–7, 250–51, 255, 257, 371n17, 372n18, 372n19, 372n23, 372n35, 387
Listopadov, 242, 372n18, 372n24, 387
Liszt, vii, 46, 108, 139, 161, 178, 183, 187–93, 204–5, 210, 215, 217–8, 323, 363n30, 367n29, 369n68, 386, 388
Lopatin, 257–8, 373n47, 387, 391
Lossky, 28–9, 387
Lunacharsky, 48, 387
Lvov, A. F., 136, 271–2, 275, 294, 373n64, 373n66, 374n66, 373n68, 375n97, 387
Lvov, F. P., 269–70, 366n90, 373n63, 373n62, 387
Lvov, N. A., 30, 77, 172, 252–3, 325, 358n65, 363n18, 368n47, 373n63, 388, 390
Lyadov, 48, 236, 259, 264, 347, 371n97, 373n49, 387, 390
Lyapunov, 48, 156, 201, 36n32, 387
Lysenko, 349, 387

magic opera (*volshebnaya opera*), 117–19, 126
Maldïbayev, 314, 325–8, 383, 388, 395

Maliavine, 342, 388
Mamontov, 370n89, 388, 389
Marr, 348–9, 388
Martïnov, 346, 388
Marx, A. B., 109
Marx, K., 58, 68, 243, 310, 312, 377n30, 388
Marxist, 243, 303, 308, 348, 387
Mazel, 347–50, 379n89, 388
Melgunov (Mel'gunov), N. A., 75–6, 86, 362n7, 363n9, 363n24, 371n2, 388
Melgunov (Mel'gunov), Yu. N., 167, 170–72, 208, 227, 229–235, 237–8, 241–2, 245–7, 249–50, 252, 257, 282, 287, 371n97, 371n9, 371n10, 371n11, 371n12, 372n22, 372n29, 372n30, 388, 395
Mendelssohn, 17, 204
Mercy-Argenteau, 46, 388
Metallov, 267, 269, 281, 284, 296–7, 373n59, 373n65, 374n78, 374n85, 388
Meyerbeer, 76, 388
Minin, 5, 61–4, 68, 340, 357n17, 361n32, 379n74, 386, 389
Mir iskusstva, 56, 342, 389
Mironov, 318
Mordvinov, 62–3, 361n31, 389
Mosolov, 225, 315, 389
Mozart, 42, 73, 205–7, 211, 243, 256, 360n8, 389
mugam opera, 389
Muradeli, 352, 389
Musorgsky (Musorgskiy) viii, 43–4, 46–8, 94, 96, 104–5, 141, 162, 169, 172–3, 177, 179–181, 191, 193, 203–4, 215–16, 220–21, 229, 232–3, 235–6, 245, 259, 264, 307, 309, 312, 358n66, 359n85, 359n90, 364n44, 364n53, 368n37, 368n48, 368n53, 369n54, 369n59, 370n96, 372n28, 382, 383, 384, 386, 389, 390, 391, 394; *Boris Godunov*, 44, 47, 49, 62, 93, 140, 161–2, 169, 173, 177–9, 181–2, 184, 188, 190–1, 193, 204, 215, 217, 220–1, 225, 259, 359n96, 359n97, 382; *Khovanshchina*, 44, 48, 140, 169, 172–3, 179, 182; *The Marriage*, 162; *Night on the Bare Mountain*, 47, 140, 182; *Rayok* (*The Peepshow*), 220, 394; *Songs and Dances of Death*, 215–6

Napoleon, 3–4, 14, 23–5, 70, 389–90, 392
Narkompros (Culture Ministry), 389, 392, 395
narodnost' (nationality), 9, 53, 105, 346–351, 353, 379n88

Nestyev (Nest'yev), 342–3, 378n79, 389
Neverov, 75–6, 85, 92, 361n20, 361n22,
   362n2, 362n7, 362n8, 363n12, 363n27,
   363n31, 389
New Folklore Wave, 244
New Trend, xii, 137, 265, 280–81, 283–5,
   290–292, 295–297, 299–300
Nikolsky (Nikolskiy), 257, 283, 374n83,
   374n84, 389

O***, 120, 122–23, 126–8, 364n42, 365n71
Obikhod, 276, 287, 294, 373n64
Odoyevsky (Odoyevskiy), vii, 16, 41, 46, 52,
   75–6, 85, 87–90, 105, 109, 138, 163–166,
   170, 179, 208, 244, 252–4, 272–4, 281,
   283, 325, 359n89, 360n2, 361n21, 362n1,
   362n7, 363n10, 363n11, 363n26, 364n46,
   365n70, 366n92, 368n39, 369n55,
   370n85, 372n39, 374n70, 374n71, 381,
   389, 390
Olenin, 260–61, 327, 389
Orientalism/Oriental style, xi, xiii, 42,
   47–9, 92, 105, 108, 118, 122, 130–1,
   143–160, 163, 203, 214, 219–20, 230,
   243, 310–1, 327–38, 352, 366n4, 366n12,
   367n13, 367n15, 367n19, 367n24,
   367n29, 378n53, 392
Orlova, 71, 389
os'moglasiye, 253, 285, 293, 374n85, 389
Ossian, 2, 390
Ossovsky (Ossovskiy), 69, 359n1, 361n24,
   362n43, 390
Ostrovsky, 46, 244, 390

Palchikov, 233–5, 237, 246, 390
Palestrina, x, 135, 138, 272, 280, 283
Pan-Slavism, 12, 50, 153, 344, 366n2, 390
Pavlenko, 71, 390
Peter the Great, 1, 8–9, 12–13, 267, 293,
   295, 341, 390, 393
Pisarev, 57–8, 360n12, 390
Pobedonostsev, 265, 275, 292–5, 299–300,
   375n97, 375n98, 375n99, 375n101, 386,
   390
podgoloski, 170–1, 229–37, 239, 241, 243,
   257–9, 262, 283, 288, 371n14, 372n18
Polotsky, 267, 390
popevki, 284, 374n85, 389
Popov, 344, 351–2, 391, 392
Potulov, 273, 276, 279, 286, 390
Pozharsky, 5, 68, 340, 357n17, 361n32,
   379n74, 390

Prach, 77, 164, 172, 252–4, 325, 358n65,
   363n18, 368n47, 387, 390
Preobrazhensky (Preobrazhenskiy), 267,
   277, 281, 284, 288, 373n58, 373n62,
   374n67, 374n77, 374n87, 374n92,
   375n94, 390
Prokofiev, 343–5, 347, 352–3, 379n82, 380,
   383, 386, 390, 391, 392, 393; Russian
   Overture, 341–4
Prokoll, 381, 391
Prokunin, 232, 256–8, 371n9, 371n16,
   373n47, 387, 391
protyazhnaya, 30–43, 78–81, 86, 119, 126,
   129, 135, 166–70, 173, 179, 250–51, 264,
   347, 358n65, 358n66
Pushkin, ix–x, xiii, 2, 5, 22, 38–40, 42,
   45–6, 52–8, 61–2, 69–73, 115–19, 126,
   132–3, 153, 207, 340–41, 347, 357n17,
   357n39, 358n70, 360n78, 360n7, 360n9,
   360n10, 360n12, 360n13, 360n16,
   365n68, 365n69, 370n93, 381, 385, 386,
   387, 389, 391, 394, 395; *Ruslan and
   Lyudmila*, 42, 55–6, 116, 118–19, 125,
   153, 360n8

Radishchev, 40, 359n77, 360n8, 391
Rakhmaninov, xii, 48, 137, 142, 156–7,
   182, 266, 297–9, 347, 373n56, 374n73,
   388, 391; All-Night Vigil, 297–9
RAPM, 307–11, 315, 350, 352, 376n19,
   376n23, 380, 381, 382, 391, 392, 393
Razumovsky (Razumovskiy), 272, 276,
   278, 374n72, 391
Rebikov, 291
Rechmensky, 317, 391
Riemann, 45–6, 241, 359n88, 372n29, 391
Rïleyev, 70–1, 392
Rimsky-Korsakov, x–xi, 42–3, 47–9, 56,
   96, 127, 129–30, 132, 140–1, 149–52,
   154–5, 160–3, 166–172, 178–224, 228,
   232, 237, 239, 241, 245, 259, 276–9, 307,
   315, 318, 323, 326, 345, 367n27, 367n29,
   368n37, 368n46, 368n49, 369n70,
   369n71, 370n74, 370n75, 370n78,
   370n81, 370n86, 370n87, 370n89,
   370n92, 370n93, 370n94, 371n97,
   371n13, 372n27, 374n76, 381, 382, 383,
   386, 389, 391, 393, 395; Folksong
   collection, 151, 173, 224, 228, 244–5,
   345; *Christmas Eve*, 132, 173; Easter
   Overture, 47, 182; *The Golden Cockerel*,
   xi, 48–9, 56, 141, 218–25, 370n93, 381;
   Iz Gomera (From Homer), 214,

Kashchei the Immortal, 141, 218–9, 369*n*65; *The Legend of the Invisible City of Kitezh*, 94, 214–9, 225, 370*n*92, 381; *The Maid of Pskov*, xi, 129–30, 141, 151, 160–2, 166–8, 173, 180–200, 204; *May Night*, 43, 170–3, 194, 221, 370*n*89; *Mlada*, 154, 202–3, 211; *Mozart and Salieri*, 206–7, 389; *Pan Voyevoda*, xi, 94, 211–5, 370*n*92; *Sadko* (orch. fantasy), 187–9, 190, 367*n*29; *Sadko* (opera), 43, 127, 162, 173, 204, 215, 367*n*29, 370*n*89, 370*n*93; *Servilia*, xi, 209–11, 214–5, 370*n*86; *Sheherezade*, 49, 141, 143, 154; *Snowmaiden*, 43, 47, 203, 211, 225, 370*n*89; Spanish Capriccio, 47, 141; Symphony No1, 187, 369*n*71; *The Tsar's Bride*, 204–8, 215, 370*n*86, 370*n*92; *The Tale of Tsar Saltan*, 218–9, 370*n*93, 381

Rïzhkin, 331–2, 378*n*56, 391

Romance (*romans*), Russian romance, romance style, 34, 38, 41–3, 45, 59, 83–5, 92–3, 95, 97, 99, 105, 116, 119, 121, 126–7, 132, 144–5, 147–9, 151, 154, 179, 204, 308, 347, 384, 395

Roslavets, 225, 308, 315, 318, 376*n*20, 391

Rossini, 83, 109–10, 360*n*8, 364*n*33, 391

Rostopchin, 3–5, 356*n*5, 356*n*6, 391

Rozanov, 27, 392

Rubinstein, Anton, 46–7, 61, 86, 149, 154, 383, 392

Rupin, Ivan, 32–3, 81, 392

Said, 329, 378*n*53, 392

Saisons Russes, 48–9, 51, 92

Samarin, 12, 392

Samosud, 62, 392

Sannikov, 340, 392

Schumann, 46, 11, 139, 156, 161, 187, 201, 204, 250, 280, 323, 369*n*61, 369*n*63, 386, 392

Scriabin, xii, 48, 61, 160, 214, 225, 307, 323, 347, 391

Serov, 45–6, 61, 81, 102, 122, 140, 174, 181, 220, 364*n*38, 365*n*72, 366*n*2, 390, 392, 394; *Power of the Fiend*, 45–6; *Rogneda*, 173, 181

Shaliapin, 47, 49, 359*n*97, 392

Shchedrin, 353, 392

Shcherbachov, 344, 379*n*80, 392

Shebalin, 344–5, 350, 392

Shekhter, 331, 392

Shestov, 19, 358*n*44, 392

Shishkov, 2, 356*n*2, 392

Shostakovich, viii, xiii, 262, 313, 315–6, 345–7, 349–51, 353, 377*n*35, 380, 384, 386, 388, 390, 392, 393, 394

Shteynberg, 317–18, 392

Slavophiles (Slavophilism), xi, 2, 8–10, 12–19, 22–3, 25, 29, 44, 51, 54, 60, 76, 266, 280, 292, 317, 380, 381, 384, 386, 390, 392, 393, 394

Smolensky (Smolenskiy), 266, 268, 271, 280–87, 292, 294, 373*n*57, 373*n*61, 373*n*68, 374*n*82, 374*n*83, 393

Sokalsky, 227–9, 247–50, 259–60, 393

Sokolovsky, 74, 393

Solovyov, S. M., 17, 394

Solovyov, V. S., 22, 50, 357*n*38, 358*n*49

Spendiarov, 320, 323, 325–6, 377*n*48, 393

Spohr, vii, 360*n*18

Stakhovich, 230–1, 371*n*8, 393

Stalin, xii–xiii, 52, 58, 62, 65, 68–9, 71, 73, 76, 244, 262, 264, 301, 303–6, 311–3, 315, 319–21, 323, 327, 329, 331–2, 339, 341, 347–9, 351, 353, 355, 361*n*38, 362*n*47, 375*n*1, 376*n*9, 376*n*12, 376*n*14, 376*n*29, 377*n*47, 378*n*71, 382, 383, 384, 385, 387, 388, 389, 391, 393, 394, 395

Stalin Prize, 71, 317, 344, 353, 377*n*38

Stalinism/–ist, 57, 63–4, 68, 240–1, 262, 304, 354–5, 378*n*70

Stanchinsky, 225, 393

Stasov, 42–6, 60, 71, 76, 86, 101, 108–11, 114, 125, 147, 152–3, 160–162, 169, 174–5, 184, 194, 199–200, 203–4, 206–9, 211, 216, 227, 235–6, 242, 265, 320, 359*n*86, 359*n*87, 359*n*89, 359*n*90, 361*n*23, 363*n*9, 363*n*25, 364*n*44, 364*n*47, 364*n*48, 364*n*49, 365*n*62, 366*n*87, 366*n*2, 367*n*14, 367*n*20, 367*n*21, 367*n*26, 368*n*52, 370*n*83, 372*n*19, 386, 388, 392–3

Stravinsky, viii, xii–xiii, 43, 48–9, 61, 130, 141, 225, 338, 341–3, 347, 353, 369*n*65, 371*n*98, 373*n*53, 383, 393; *Firebird*, 43, 49, 141, 343; *Les Noces*, 225, 353; *Petrushka*, 225, 341–4, 353; *Rite of Spring*, 48, 51, 225

Surin, 346, 393

Sviridov, 353, 393

Synodal Choir, 280–1, 283, 285–6, 292, 385

Szymanowski, 348, 393

Tairov, 339–40, 393

Tajikistan (Tajik), 303, 305, 315, 354, 377*n*31

Taneyev, 279–80, 371n4, 373n40, 373n41, 373n42, 372n44, 374n80, 391, 393
Taruskin, Richard, viii, xii, xiii, xiv, 43, 77, 143–4, 146–7, 149, 155–60, 181, 221, 358n66, 359n84, 359n85, 361n23, 363n17, 363n25, 363n29, 366n4, 366n5, 366n6, 366n9, 366n12, 367n13, 367n24, 368n40, 369n59, 369n65, 370n95, 370n96, 371n98, 393
Tatarinova, 243
Tatars, 4, 214, 305, 341
Tchaikovsky, 1, 5, 45–7, 61, 113, 116, 142–3, 156–160, 174, 204, 208, 211, 228–9, 244, 255–6, 266, 278–80, 341, 361n30, 364n53, 365n61, 367n28, 370n77, 371n9, 371n16, 372n27, 373n41, 373n42, 374n79, 374n80, 380, 382, 385, 387, 389, 390, 391, 394; *Eugene Onegin,* 45–6, 116, 205, 264; *Opricnhik,* 244; *Romeo and Juliet,* 143, 157–9, 204; Symphony No 1, 156; Symphony No 4, 5; *Voyevoda,* 244
Tertz, 58, 394
Tisse, 71, 394
Titov, A. N., 77–8, 267, 394
Tolstoy, F. M., 75, 81, 394
Tolstoy, L. N., 1, 3, 12, 24–5, 39, 356n5, 358n57, 394
Trauberg, 339, 394
Trotsky, 300, 375n102, 376n19
Tsukkerman, 344–5, 352, 379n82, 394
Tsvetayeva, 57, 394
Turchaninov, 269–71, 275, 279, 294, 373n66, 374n66, 374n68, 375n97, 394
Turgenev, 10, 22, 30–3, 38, 357n30, 358n65, 358n68, 384, 390, 394
Turkmenistan (Turkmenian, Turkmen), 239–40, 303, 314–5, 324, 354, 377n49
Tyutchev, 18, 357n24, 394

Ukraine (Ukrainian), 132, 174, 247, 251, 259, 267–8, 303–4, 314–15, 320, 351, 368n53, 372n35, 375n5, 375n8, 376n31, 382, 393

Uspensky (Uspenskiy), 138, 319, 366n92, 366n93, 394
Uzbekistan, 303, 315, 317–19, 326, 334, 377n31, 377n39, 377n41, 383, 387, 391, 395

Varlamov, 163, 394
Vasilenko, 331, 394
Vasilyev-Buglay, 352, 394
Verstovsky, 75, 82–4, 93–4, 118–21, 220, 394
Vilkovir, 62, 361n28, 394
Vishnevsky, 340, 395
Vlasov, 314, 325–8, 378n52, 383, 388, 395
VOSM, 309, 395

Wagner (Wagnerian), 102, 104, 126, 193, 209–10, 212–15, 217–18, 290, 321, 330, 370n89, 370n92, 381, 383, 395
Weber, 360n8, 360n18, 394
Westernizers (*zapadniki*), 8–10, 19, 317, 380, 381, 382
Westphal, 241, 249–50, 372n29, 395
Wilson, 1, 395

Yastrebtsev, xi, 141, 149, 154, 162, 182, 187–8, 205–6, 208, 211, 367n18, 367n27, 368n33, 368n35, 368n36, 368n43, 368n44, 368n45, 369n56, 369n60, 369n64, 369n66, 369n67, 369n69, 370n73, 370n79, 370n82, 370n90, 371n97, 395
Yevseyev, 241, 259, 373n49, 395
Yusupov, 317, 395

Zakharov, 352, 395
Zarlino, 245, 254
Zhdanov, 301, 375n2, 395
Zhemchuzhnikov, 32, 395
Zhukovsky, 69, 119, 360n8, 395
znamenniy chant, 134, 179–80, 267–8, 275–6, 280, 288, 292, 294, 297, 366n84, 373n61, 374n73, 375n97, 387